Parallel Civilisations

Parallel Civilisations

Greece - India

Translation from Spanish by

Sydna Younson

Original title in Spanish:
Civilizaciones Paralelas Grecia - India

Julio Ozán Lavoisier

Motilal Banarsidass Publications

MOTILAL BANARSIDASS
PUBLICATIONS

4741/23, Ansari Road, Daryaganj, New Delhi - 110002 (India)
Email: publications@mlbd.com | sales@mlbd.com | exports@mlbd.com
Indian Website: www.mlbdonline.com | Foreign Website: www.mlbd.com

Parallel Civilisations
by
Julio Ozán Lavoisier

First Edition Published in 2025

Published in India by Motilal Banarsidass Publications

ISBN : 978-81-97087-08-0 (PB)

Printed and bound in India

I have the pleasure and the duty of dedicating this work
to my wife, Susana Beatriz Poquet

Contents

Part 1: The Origin

Prologue 3

The Purpose of this Book....5

Synthesis from the First Principles 9

- On Understanding 11
- The Meaning of Myths 13
- The Myth in Plato 17
- Why Mircea Eliade?....21
- On Mircea Eliade 23
- The Origin of Time....25
- Time and Divinity 28
- Beyond Eliade....31
- Myths and Universal Consciousness....35
- My View of the Subject 38
- Vital Plane and Evolution....40
- Myths in the Present 42
- On Initiations....45
- Mythology and Philosophy....48
- Mythical and Unitive Mentality....51
- Schelling's Philosophy of Mythology 55
- Epistemological Clarification 62
- Conclusion....63

Part 2: Greece and India

Greece....77

The Myth of Ariel....77

Greek Spirit and Religion....83

The Greek Gods....90

Greek Art....94

Virtues of Polytheism....96

Religion and Nature....98

Circular and Linear Vision....100

The Cyclical Vision of Time....106

The Greek Virtues....111

Heroism and Temperance....116

On Life and Death....118

The Social Being....122

The Universal Being....124

Pericles....126

The Greek Miracle....128

Hadrian....131

Conclusion....132

On the Greeks and Hindus....135

On Greek and Hindu Myths....135

Genesis in India....138

Parallels in the Epic and Myths....140

Dark and Luminous Gods....143

Dionysus and Apollo....147

The Heroic Sense of Life in Greece....153

The Heroic Sense of Life in India....156

The Greek Tragedy....160
Pilgrimages and Festivals in Greece....162
Pilgrimages and Festivals in India....168
Similitudes in Religious Architecture....170
Other Similitudes....173
Philosophical Conclusions....176
Plotinus and the Indian Doctrines....176
On Life and Happiness....182
On Beauty....190
The Search for Unity....192

Part 3: The Indic Civilisation

Preliminary Ideas....197
The Medieval Era in Europe and in India....197
Christianity and Civilisation....202
The Latent Force of Unity....206
Neoplatonism and Christianity....207
Indic Thought and my Philosophy....209
On Monotheism and Polytheism....214
On Monism and Dualism....222
The Philosophical Bases....229
On Psychology....231
On the Evolution of Consciousness....235
On Philosophy of History....239
On Ideas, Knowledge and Life....240
A Sketch of the Universus....244
Synthesis of my Proposal....249

Buddhism and Hinduism 254
The Unity of Dhamma and Dharma 254
On understanding Dhamma and Dharma 261
On Buddhism and Hinduism 263
Buddhism in the History of the Indic Civilisation 265
Buddhist Culture in the Indic Civilisation 270
Perspectives in the East and West 272
The Evolution of the Spirit in Hinduism 276
The Evolution of the Spirit in Buddhism 284

Part 4: Hinduism

The *Vedas* 291
The Heritage of the *Vedas* 295
The Decline of the *Vedas* 298
A Crucial Time 301
After the *Vedas* 303
Samkhya in Hinduism 308
The Gunas in Facts 312
The Gunas in History 317
Yoga, an Introduction 321
On Knowledge in Patanjali 323
Patanjali's God 328
Patanjali and My Vision 332
Introduction to the *Upanishads* 336
The *Aitareya Upanishad* 343
The *Prasna Upanishad* 345
The *Mandukya Upanishad* 347

The *Kena Upanishad* 350
The *Isha Upanishad* 352
The *Mundaka Upanishad* 354
The *Bhagavad Gita*, an Introduction 358
The *Bhagavat Gita* 361
The Karma Yoga of the *Gita* 367
The Wisdom of the *Gita* 371
On the Danger of Sentiments 374
Intuitionists, Intellectuals, Devotes and Animals 376
The *Brahma Sutras* 379
Shankara 382
Shankara and the *Taittiriya Upanishad* 386
The *Vivekacudamani* 391
Ramanuja 398
Ramanuja and the *Brahma-Sutras* 405
Aurbindo and the *Isha Upanishad* 409
General Commentary 414
On Spirit and Matter 414
On the Observer 419
On the Atman 421
On Revelation 424
On Spiritual Techniques 426
On the Mind and the Yoga's 431
On the Powers 436
On Reincarnation and Karma 439
On the Internal Plane 441

On Maya....................444
On the Limits of Transcendental Knowledge....................453
Vital Idealism....................461
Conclusion....................463
Epilogue....................466

Part 1
The Origin

Prologue

Although it had been on my mind for many years, the all-consuming idea that gave rise to this book took shape after a lecture I gave at Nalanda University in Bihar, India. There were participants from every Buddhist country at this Conference, from the entire Far East, and though there were only three participants from the West, the importance of the gathering cannot be underestimated.

This University, Buddhist in his origin, has a long history. It was already famous in the fifth century when people not only from India but from all of Asia, including China, went to study there. It was liberal in character and the relevant doctrines of the time such as a resurgent Hinduism were also taught there. Later it was abandoned, having been destroyed by Muslims, who held sway in the valley of the Ganges for a thousand years.

The University reopened only in the XXI century with the laudable objective of reinstating Buddhist teaching in India, including Hinduism, with the same openness as in the days of old. The main theme of the Congress in which I participated was the similarity and compatibility of the Buddhist tradition (Dhamma, in Pali, the language of the Buddha) and the Hindu tradition (Dharma in Sanskrit). I was elated by the discovery that such a prestigious institution was involved in the same project as mine: the study of these disciplines to highlight their kinship.

The Indian civilisation is fundamentally the result of the succession and interaction of these two traditions; this is one of the civilisations that I will be dealing with in this book. The other civilisation of interest to me is the Hellenic. I think that the parallel drawn between them summarises the essence of the Indo-European spirit. And I am convinced that in that spirit, expressed in Eastern and Western idealism, which I try to converge and complete in my philosophy, the most decisive answers for the universal culture beginning with the new millennium can be found.

Herein lie the points by which we can establish a parallel between the spirit and the ideals, that is, in what is essential and decisive, between the Greeks and the Indians, and which have ultimately determined their civilisations: Principally, the idealist sense of life from which spring the ideas and actions that I will summarise as follows: The search for Unity; philosophical-religious monism; convergent polytheism or inclusive monism; monistic pantheism; the sense of perfection; an elevated and paradigmatic morality; the heroic meaning of life; the cyclical vision of time; integration with Nature; the aesthetic meaning of life; the sacredness of Life and Nature; religious festivals in which this sacredness is joyfully celebrated. These and other points in common will be explained and exemplified in the course of this work.

The reader should bear in mind that this book is preceded by eight treatises articulated in a philosophical system that sustains them, which would be difficult to summarise here. Thus, if the reader finds any assertion which seems to be unfounded, he would do well to consult those treatises.

The Purpose of this Book

The content of this book can be easily summarised, it is about the reencounter of the human being with himself; this reencounter, however, is not so simple. Since the birth of our species man has tended to be alienated from himself, although not expressly so, being occupied in trying to resolve immediate problems on which his survival depended, he has taken other paths and has become accustomed to traversing them to the point of believing that he is on the right track. Inexorable scientific and technological progress has helped him to believe this and, although it might have brought him many advantages and facilities, this direction does not lead him towards meeting his own being.

Fortunately this derailment has been observed by some philosophers, religious men and artists, but even amongst them there are differences about the correct path to be taken. In my earlier works, I have elaborated various guiding principles. In idealism, I have found the most serious and fruitful insights for this project. For this reason I have written commentaries on Buddhism in *The Evolution of the Spirit*; I have followed in the footsteps of the most inspired Western idealists in *The Search for Universal Consciousness*, and in the present work I will discuss Hinduism. These are the three great currents of *Universal Idealism*, a key concept of my philosophy, which seeks to assimilate them. These works belong to isolated thinkers who have not been able to change the direction of the majority, particularly in the West; Western civilisation has been going astray for some 1700 years. If we understand that this derailment implies alienation, we will understand the need to escape from this state. It is true that if absolute alienation reigned, no civilisation would have been possible as chaos would have been the norm, but history is full of individual and collective alienation. We have seen civilisations fall and horrendous wars, wherein general alienation has played a major role.

The fact is that the human being finds himself in an intermediate state between mental health and ill health; and most psychologists agree on this. What is surprising is that with rare exceptions, men accept this state with the greatest naturalness, and conform to it with a bit of happiness and sadness, with satisfaction and dissatisfaction, with sense and madness, so that there is no real intrinsic evolution, and if there is progress, it is extremely slow.

In the work just cited, *The Search*, I have tried to summarise the development of idealism; I would like to clarify this. Firstly, I do not believe that there has been an evolution in this field as happens in the natural sciences and other manifestations of the spirit. As religions are cultivated in this field, I do not think that this evolution exists here either. Every idealist philosophy, as well as every mystic, has a complete vision of the matter, and expresses it in his own way; so that it germinates in certain spirits and in certain epochs better than in others, but in some it does not take root. We have, thus, different reasons that motivate the philosopher to revisit this subject, to sow again. Firstly because, naturally, he has seen something that has amazed him and that contains the essence of his soul and the soul of all beings; this compels him to share his experience; secondly, because this precious and nutritious fruit has withered in today's world; thirdly, because he believes that what has been sown (explained) must take root again in another way. The current philosopher then, at least in my case, does not try to be more accurate than the previous ones, only he has in his favour the experience of the errors committed by his predecessors, and only in this sense can he claim an *improvement*.

I believe that religion and philosophy have the same objective. As is well known, the two great conceptions of the East, Hinduism and Buddhism, never saw the need to separate the disciplines, they are religion-philosophies, and both partake of the same experience of the Transcendent and the Sacred, although numerous branches, especially on the religious side, have grown from these common roots. The advantage offered by religion is that the roots can be accessed from diverse branches; this means that various paths can be provided for the human being's, different ways of being and believing. The advantage that philosophy provides is that its objective is the essence of all things, and it can thus directly go towards its objective, and try, at least, not to get entangled in the branches, although this, as I said, can be expeditious for others.

Especially during times of spiritual perigee, the human being tends to divert the flow of his intelligence towards external objectives, and he thus deviates his path away from his consciousness; this makes him retreat to the *state of survival*, an elementary animal stage where the law of the jungle prevails. He might impose himself with clubs or with missiles, on a horse or with an airplane, there is no substantial change; he just does more damage. During times of apogee he brings the spirit closer to the centre of consciousness, and this takes him to the *stage of creative contemplation*. For the basis of these premises, the reader can consult *The Spirit in History*.

It follows from what has been said, and from the empirical evidence, that there is a great abyss between the advanced technological stage and the incipient human condition, and everything seems to indicate that man is closer to his destruction than to his realisation, and this makes a radical transformation necessary, in turn involving an awareness; hence the need to delve into matters of the spirit.

We need to begin from a tabula rasa, which is a prerequisite to understanding and interest (as interest and understanding go hand in hand) in these subjects connected to the concept of "religion". The reader should put aside and, if possible, forget any pre-conceptions that have been inculcated in him through centuries old systematic indoctrination. I agree that this is not easy, but it is necessary. For our part, we should redefine the concepts of *Spirit, God, Divinity, the sacred,* etc., But before this I consider it necessary to begin from the Origin, from the *myths*, which will be the subject of the first part of this work.

As can be surmised, we are dealing with impalpable realities only accessible to subtle spirits desirous of understanding them. Rationalist or theological prejudices are obstacles which, if not overcome, nullify all explanations; lamentably this duality of believers in reason and believers in faith has created irreconcilable positions for centuries and, to the extent that they remain enclosed in their dogmas, their understanding of this text will also be foreclosed. A little less than two centuries ago the *believers in matter came* also to be a part of this current, as they are equally unable to understand matters of the spirit. And not too long ago there appeared (in the words of M. Eliade) "that odious spiritual hybridity inaugurated by Mme.

Blavatsky in the Theosophical Society, continued and aggravated by the numerous contemporary pseudo-morphoses", and its intrusion into the field of comparative religions has led to an unseemly and undesirable confusion, adding to the general bewilderment. So we are left with a reduced audience of *clear and open minds*, an essential condition if one is to be nurtured by the immaterial substance that underlies this work and idealism in general.

Toynbee's most interesting and fruitful idea or observation is that of *mimesis*, which is a fact of great importance that occurs in the history of civilisations. In a few words it consists of this: Peoples who stand out for their spiritual and cultural superiority generally generate in neighbouring peoples the desire to imitate, to be like them. Since all peoples are neighbours nowadays, as we have access to the most distant cultures, which is a new fact in history, the matter acquires an inestimable magnitude. *Mimesis* is a natural resource in man that I fundamentally attribute to the human being's latent intuition of the Idea of perfection; of the Good, Plato would say. It will be understood that my intention is to present as models two cultures that I hold to be paradigmatic, the Hellenic and the Indic, so that we can nourish ourselves from them through this uplifting process of *mimesis*. It is not my interest to make an account of these cultures, but to highlight, and if possible to awaken, the spirit that underlies these exemplary civilisations.

Synthesis from the First Principles

For Aristotle "all men together affirm that the science that we call philosophy or wisdom deals with first causes and the first principles of things". (*Met. I,1*) Man has been progressively straying from this philosophical aspiration, to the point that he has eventually created new disciplines alien to religion and philosophy. The word *alien* is key to understanding the problem that implies alienation with respect to the *first principles*. Indeed, the human spirit, alienated from its essence and its centre of consciousness and from an external perspective, seeks solutions for human needs, and new disciplines emerge or ancient sciences that adequately respond to material exigencies are recovered; but we have to remember that they are alien to the *first principles*, that is, to philosophy as such.

From the aforesaid and due to the diversity and multiplicity of the modern world, man has been progressively specialising, and this has become a necessity and even seems to us to be the most natural thing in the world. But if we see this from the philosophical point of view we will note the seriousness of the matter. Thus Ortega y Gasset does not hesitate to equate specialisation with barbarism. (*The Reb.*) Why this tremendous statement? I will try to explain it from my perspective. Naturally the problem is not that the craftsman applies himself to his task, but when the whole society is made up of specialists, it disintegrates without a unifying factor, there is no participation in a fundamental order, there are no moral, aesthetic, religious or philosophical, or spiritual general principles; and this is effectively barbarism.

The matter becomes serious on another plane: the new disciplines have not been limited to resolving material needs, those that seek to resolve matters of the spirit have also appeared, but from a perspective external to them. Thus modern psychology tries to make inroads into the field of religion and concludes that "it is the product of a collective neurosis", (Freud) or a creation of the unconscious (Jung); a subject I have dealt with in my *Psychosophy and Psychology*

2nd part. Scientific anthropology that tries to explain human affairs through biology also appears. Additionally, an anthropology of religion that seeks to explain this discipline through the customs and behaviour of the faithful. Even philosophical anthropology that seeks to explain the essence of man, does this through a very human perspective. I have nothing against these investigations, I only point out the narrowness of this vision.

And there has been no lack, as we have seen, of a philosophy of alienation that, denying all spirituality, seeks to explain human history through material, especially economic, relations. Since the ideologue of this barbarism (Marx) constructs his philosophy through these "principles" he projects his vision onto all philosophies, religions and arts which he sees as a product of the so called worldly relations. Does he notice the inversion? From an alienated and externalised mind he tries to explain and replace the *first principles*. This is more than barbarism, it is complete alienation and disintegration, and with total consternation he tries to order society from these external principles.

What can be deduced from the aforesaid is that what these new disciplines or visions have in common is that the effects seek to explain the causes. That morality, the arts, religion and philosophy, which are the specific sciences of the spirit, are in crisis, is unsurprising given the general alienation.

Considering this situation it is natural that my work proclaims from the beginning a *Return to the Sources*, that is, to the *first principles*. There I explain how the self, located in the external faculties, tries to explain the facts of consciousness instead of doing so from consciousness itself.

The most notable result of this process is that it has led modern man to search for happiness through external paths, especially through the acquisition of material goods, whereas Plato, Aristotle, Buddhism and Hinduism, focused on first principles, agree that happiness is achieved through virtues. I have to insist on this point until I shatter the hard carapace in which the self of modern man has enclosed itself, because it is the very design of all living beings to attain an eternal Happiness.

On Understanding

We believe, as a consequence of an artificial mechanism, but one that has become natural, that the misunderstanding between men is always arrived at because of someone else, when in reality it comes from each one's lack of understanding of himself, since each one has his particular or even general interests that he looks at from his *individual perspective*. The Greeks already had the solution and it was engraved in marble on the portal of the famous oracle of Delphi dedicated to Apollo, the god of light and wisdom: "Know Thyself."

But while we can admit that Apollo knows himself, for mortals the matter is complex because our mind is far from divine. I believe with conviction that *knowledge of the spiritual faculties and mental mechanisms* of the psyche in general is essential to solve this problem of misunderstanding regarding ourselves and others. These faculties and mechanisms are an inseparable part of my theory of knowledge, which is why I will make use of them throughout this treatise, but since I have already explained them in previous works, particularly in my *Psychosophy*, I will make only a brief allusion here; the interested reader will do well to consult said text. In the same way I will refer to morality and aesthetics as ways of transcendental knowledge whose foundation has been exposed in *The Roots of Morality* and *The Roots of Art*.

When Aristotle defines man as a rational being, he does so only to differentiate him from the rest of the animals, but this does not mean that we are rational in a finished or absolute way to the point that we can solve everything with reason; this is what he believed in, too optimistically, rationalism. But human reason, besides being very relative, is insufficient, and it is only one aspect, one part of the complex mechanism of the mind. Reason has shown itself to be very efficient when dealing with external objects and in its capacity for abstraction with respect to them, that is, when it can be objective. But as soon as any knowledge involves the human being, the matter becomes more complicated because other faculties intervene, such as feelings, emotions, passions, personal tendencies, character, fears, desires, bodily needs, and the identification of the mind with the body, which make up the subjective faculties.

From the complex interaction of all the faculties and tendencies memory is nourished, a faculty closely linked to reason that makes use of it every time it thinks; hence the enormous amount of obtuse reasons that man generates.

Other faculties of enormous importance are the *intuitions of the spiritual faculties*, which I have called *unitive*, which are neither subjective nor objective. These faculties have an upward direction opposite to the subjective faculties, for which reason they tend to transcend the subject and man as an animal; we could call them divine because they are the ones that have imagined all the divinities that man has as paradigms.

To the extent that reason is nourished by these intuitions and makes use of these unitive faculties, it purifies and elevates itself, the same happens with the feelings that must go in harmony with them. When these faculties go hand in hand and are nourished in unison by *transcendental intuitions*, what are called *unitive experiences* occur, which generate awareness and changes in the *level of consciousness*. Generating this transformation of consciousness is, in my opinion, the specific task of philosophy; rather than filling reality with reasons.

To be sure, a philosophy must present an integral vision of reality, a system that encompasses all the disciplines of the spirit projected into the inner and outer world, the *Universus*. The philosopher must have gone through the aforementioned *unitive experiences*, and *have a level of consciousness* that allows him to look from a perspective that includes partial perspectives; it is from this *essential perspective* that he must look at the World. The philosopher, moreover, has had time to meditate and reflect on the *displacements of the spirit* within said mechanisms of showing the right paths and the wrong ones; otherwise he will only be expressing personal opinions.

But his practical task is to show the way, paving it as far as possible so that the reader or aspirant can also reach that knowledge, because if he is only presented with the result, he would be left with a system of thought external to him, which he can accept as a belief and not live as an experience. Thus, there will be no transformation in it, but rather an accommodation on the rational plane which, as we have seen, is nothing more than an external part of the mind and knowledge.

I am speaking of an integral philosophy, a universal vision that provides a path with an *origin and a destination* (this time I refer the reader to my work *Origin and Destiny of Man*). There are, as we will see, other paths, whose differences I will try to point out, not to separate them but to clarify them, since they lead to the same Destiny.

The Meaning of Myths

To speak of myths in this age and culture has all the appearance of being absurd. It seems absurd because the interests of contemporary man depend on the values in fashion, which are a consequence, in turn, of the prevailing perspective. The reader will find this theme of perspectives, which is fundamental in my thinking and for the understanding of the human being, throughout my work.

The tangible world seems more real to contemporary man, not because it is more real, but because he views it from a fixed perspective that presents itself to him in this way. And this is so because the faculties he uses to see and judge the world are the most external of his psyche. In short, as contemporary man is externalised, the outside world seems more real to him.

Since the meanders of his internal world are such, he imagines them as unreal and consequently without importance. And myths lie in the least illuminated corners of his psyche. And so myths are nothing but a curiosity for contemporary man. I would like to highlight the value of this curiosity.

The conquest of the outside world does not always satisfies the human being, for the simple reason that the world continues to be external. This conquest does not integrate him into the world, rather, it seems to disintegrate him. Nevertheless, he continues to hope that the answers come from outside and that science and technology will resolve his life. But science and technology have a problem, and that is that they cannot resolve the fundamental problem of our existence; hence the current phenomenon of the satiated who are still dissatisfied, in the words of Aurobindo. But this dissatisfaction can awaken the curiosity through other ways and means of relating to the world, the desire to overcome this situation and reintegrate into reality and, in this way, begin to traverse the paths of the spirit.

The traditional means for this purpose are religion and the arts. In my opinion *myths are the artistic expression of religion*. We see that the poets constantly use relations that entirely escape logical schemata, but in the name of art we accept what they say. However, with myths we are not so indulgent and we evaluate them with cold reason that eventually discards them as absurd; when the absurdity lies in applying reason to them. It is absurd because as soon as we declare them absurd, we denigrate them and leave them ineffectual, when the entire purpose of the myth was to awaken us to *other ways of knowing*.

This is the attitude of the unbeliever in general, who negates everything that does not fit his logic. As all religions are suffused with myths that apparently have little or nothing that is "logical", he ultimately discards the whole religious phenomenon. This would be understandable if, by way of logic, he could resolve his petty emotions like jealousies, envies, loves and hates, fears and desires but nothing tells him about these passions. His logic also fails him in explaining his existence and all that is beyond time, space and his own life and death.

Then we have the believers in one religion who accept the myths of their religion as historical fact and reject the myths of other religions. This attitude is as absurd as affirming that only Spanish poets utter truths and the Persians, Chinese and Hindus speak falsehoods. This stubbornness against appreciating other religions is one of the great flaws of current Western culture (not the Hellenic). Unfortunately, since religious reality has disappeared from the contemporary horizon, our artists, with rare exceptions, do not express this reality either (for an explanation of this see *The Roots of Art*).

I am not proposing, nor have I proposed anywhere in my work, the adoption of any faith, but rather the opening of the spirit to other ways of seeing and feeling, which would help us to get out of the torpor of this mechanised barbarism in which we are immersed. In my opinion, the most appropriate attitude is to let these myths flow freely within us to see what triggers they unleash and what profound feelings they awaken in us.

In religions based on dogma, like Christianity and Islam, too sharp a distinction is made between belief and disbelief, and this makes us accept certain myths as historical or objective reality, or even reject the doctrine outright when these myths are not compatible with our reason. This has needlessly created countless unbelievers, since I do not see the need for distinctions and interpretations to be rigid when dealing with myths. Nor do I see the need for unconditional belief. We do not say that we believe in Rubén Darío or in García Lorca, but that we let their poetry resonate in our souls and in this way we are nourished by it. So we should do with myths, which are, as I said, the artistic expressions of religions.

But by this I do not mean to say that myths are pure rhetoric, like poetry they express profound realities that cannot be expressed in any other way. Moreover, when we observe them through a scientific filter we never really see their true substance and we roundly reject them as illusory; a very grave error that presumes that the affairs of the soul can be reflected as concrete things.

The research of psychologists such as Paul Diel, Jung and their followers has shed new light on how myths can be reassessed and has brought them out from the prolonged two thousand years of darkness. Unfortunately, as I pointed out in my *Psychosophy,* a psychological vision of the religious phenomenon ultimately distorts it. The work of some mythologists is more revealing because they try to see the myths from the same perspective by which they were created. I will cite two examples.

In *The Myth in Primitive Psychology* B. Malinowski says: "The myth (...) is not merely a story told but a reality lived. It is not of the nature of fiction, such as we read today in a novel, but it is a living reality, believed to have once happened in primeval times, and continuing ever since to influence the world and human destinies." "Studied alive," (which is what Malinowski did for many years with natives of ancient cultures) "myth, as we shall see, is not symbolic, but a direct expression of its subject matter; it is not an explanation in satisfaction of a scientific interest, but a narrative resurrection of a primeval reality, told in satisfaction of deep religious needs, moral cravings, social submissions, assertions, even practical requirements." "Myth is thus a vital ingredient of human civilization, it is not an idle tale, but a hard worked active force; it is not an intellectual explanation or an artistic imagery, but a pragmatic charter of primitive faith and moral wisdom."

In *Dionysus: Myth and Cult*, Walter Otto says: "No progress is possible if we have an attitude of superiority and think only about convincing the founders of venerable institutions about their errors and superstitions. They knew more about life than we do. During great moments of change (births and religious celebrations in general) they looked death in the face." "And, in truth, have we learnt anything more than our ancestors about life and death? In the best of cases, we are mostly in the same dilemma; there are no real reasons for us to feel superior and to judge them as primitive, especially if our reasons are born of the wonder we feel over rituals that we do not understand." "In any case scholars seem to agree that the initial practices of the cult could only have had the objective of getting useful results for man. But utility comes in between", Otto rightly clarifies: "when the cult degenerates and loses its creative and spontaneous aspect." "When the creative spirit is eclipsed, the more prominent is interest and utility." "The natural process has been inverted by academicians who have confused the final static product with the principle of life."

Mythology creates an unreal or semi-real irrational world, whose objective is to overcome the everyday and utilitarian mechanisms and faculties in order to put us in contact with, or at least bring us as close as possible, to the great truths as they are, which I have called the *primary manifestations of the Essence of the World*: Order itself, as ordering energy; the Good in itself, as an aspiration towards the perfection of the action; Love as integrating energy; Life in itself, which is the energy of life; the Beautiful in itself, which is an aspiration towards the perfection of forms; and intuition-instinct as an intelligent manifestation of universal Consciousness. These are the guiding principles of everything that exists, and all of them emanate from Unity and make Creation possible and ensure that it maintains itself and tends, to the extent of its possibilities, towards Unity, which is perfect, Order, Beauty, etc., absolutes. (For further explanations see *The Primal Manifestations* in *The Search for Universal Consciousness*)

Of course, the creator of myths does not know of these philosophical concepts, but he intuits the manifestations of the Transcendent, he knows that he must transcend this reality, scientific if you will, and project the spirit upwards. Naturally it will not be done with reason, this would anchor him in the material world, but with subtler, more artistic and intuitive means. These means not only serve to bring the spirits closer to artistic truths but also to conserve myths. A fantastic world guarantees that it remains isolated, and this makes it participate in the Eternal. And it is precisely these ideas in Themselves, the expressions of the Eternal, that are eternal truths.

Myths are fundamentally inspired by these, and by the obstacles they face with human passions or with the force of nature. Myths want to and must be exemplary, hence their need to remain in "another" reality. Concrete reality tries to tangentially touch that in the highest and most sublime acts, such as heroism, total dedication, love, sacrifice for great ideals, which respond equally well to the same inspiration and aspiration.

In my opinion, myth's powerful, albeit secret, force resides in the fact that it dispenses with time and space, and it participates, in its own way, in the Transcendent. Although intuition or its interpretation might not entirely correspond to transcendent reality, it maintains an attraction or "magic" through this participation. For this reason the task of the interpreter of the myth is not to reason but to participate.

The Myth in Plato

Plato was well aware that he had to create myths in order to explain truths in themselves. However, myths lose value when they respond too much to reason and to the aspirations of desires. This made him reduce the "magic" the "delight", the "grace" of the irrational in his myths. Plato saw far ahead of his times, but as a philosopher, not as an artist. Hence, he did not fully understand artists, who he wanted to dispense with in his Republic. He wanted perfect gods, who might have been interesting for philosophers, but the rest, who know or sense that these ideas are too abstract to live with, prefer more human even if imperfect gods. They want to learn how they can also be victims of their passions, and know what they can do to remedy themselves, they want the gods to resemble their spirit, but to be superior in order to be inspired by them; they do not want perfect but exemplary gods; hence their admiration for heroes, who are demi gods.

Myths are composed of the vague intuitions of the people, the folklore, the medicine men, the priests and the artists who shape them into a ritual or art. When they fall into the hands of genius, as for example the hands of the Greek tragedians or the authors of the Hindu epics, they take on a transcendent dimension that tends to escape the understanding of the common man. Genius has its reasons and knows how to extricate its most substantial experiences; Plato is a clear example.

When the Good, the Beautiful and Love are objects of a full apperception, they are not only ideas, but living experiences that exist a priori to every idea and every feeling that has taken shape. They are realities that have to be experienced in their Origin and in *statu nascendi*. In my conception, they are manifestations of the universal Consciousness that flows over all that is created and, certainly, over the human spirit that illuminates and inspires it. Genius has the capacity to make them conscious.

In the case of Plato these ideas are the result of *unitive intuitions*, as everything seems to indicate that the contact that he had with the Being itself was not stable, as would correspond to a total unitive experience. Proof of this is also the fact that the link he established between these primary realities and the phenomenic world was indirect. This mode of perception often leads him to resort to his theory of reminiscence: "According to that argument, Socrates, which you seem to repeat so often, that learning is nothing but remembering." (*Phaedo 73*)

Although I cannot be very precise, by the very nature of the matter, I would like to throw some light on this, not only because of this particular theory, but because I believe that by doing so, other concomitant points of significant importance must also be clarified.

When Essence is indirectly perceived, the link that the spirit establishes between it and things is a consequence of a particular contemplative state, thanks to which, even if time is not decisively transcended, it recedes and grows distant in the horizon, to the point that the reality contemplated seems joined to a distant time, to which the spirit is transported. This means that there is an impression that it is being remembered. But this distance, in reality, is not due to a past time but to an atemporal Eternal past time, only perceptible in itself in the absolute present (unified consciousness) for unified consciousness, absolutely integrated, from the essential perspective, which is that of universal Consciousness..

Plato observed that his perception was not a result of reflection, on the contrary, that thought must stop to give rise to images, which seemed to him to come from a remote space and time. It is this type of understanding that allowed him to visualise permanent immutable reality that illuminated his soul as well as the objects of his senses. Hence his obsession in explaining the link between the two; but when he tried to rationalise it, he saw his spirit transported to a time in the past and an unnamed place that decidedly transcended concrete reality. The framework within which he found himself then was that of the myth, and he readily took recourse to it as it gave him a greater freedom of expression and allowed him to imagine an ideal situation for his Ideas, and, moreover, to speak by approximation, as if it were so.

The theory of reminiscence is Plato's strongest support for proving the pre-existence of the soul and, thus, its immortality, and so by questioning this theory (and also his world of Forms), I remove this support. But it is not only for this reason that I delegitimise the thesis of the immortality of the soul. On the contrary, I believe that I have found a much more solid premise for it, and it is the active presence of the soul's participation in the Eternal. By being present, this experience does not need to resort to an uncertain time in the past, nor does it have to cling to the belief of life after death, nor wait, of course, to confirm it. It would seem logical to look for an explanation of the soul in the past and in the future, hence all the trials have taken recourse to this; but logic has the limits of space and time, which is only transcended by the experience of the present Eternal.

Plato's message is not entirely clear but it has a purpose and in some way corresponds to a transcendent Reality. The complex personality of this philosopher can confuse one because he is also a religious thinker. But, for me, this is not his obscure side but rather his way of being religious, of being both a mystic and mythical; two colours of the spirit that escape the visible spectrum of modern man.

I will now try to establish the difference between these two visions of the religious subject. I will do so, however, in broad brush strokes only to emphasise a few points that seem to me to be of crucial importance. But I no longer have to refer to Plato, I will express myself directly in my own language. We know, thanks to the works of Mircea Eliade, that the myth always refers to a particularly significant primordial time, which the religious man seeks, through the periodic repetition of the ritual, to update or revive; I would say re-experience it. The relation between the myth and the Eternal is evident. Through these acts, man tries to make of the present time a time like that of the original, which is either eternal or participates in Reality. The ritual seeks to eternalise this a temporal Reality by cyclically repeating the original actions laid down by the gods themselves or by their chosen intermediaries. In order to come into contact with the primordial, in order to approach it and to have a certain experience of Divinity and the Eternal, mythical man needs the rituals transmitted to him through tradition, that is, which he inherits. He finds his source of inspiration in the past and although he is conscious that he lives in a successive time, it makes sense if it is re-joined with the primordial time that makes it sacred and eternal.

The ritual reproduces the universal Creation or the creation of certain acts that are carried out by the gods or heroes significant for the culture that puts them into practice. Mystical experience (in order to better highlight the contrasts, I will refer here to the highest religious experience, the *total unitive experience*), includes the mythical experience, as it provides a knowledge of the origins, not from this or that concrete task, but the permanent creation that takes place in each present. While the ritual tries to integrate mythical time, the mystical experience produces this effect by integrating the eternal present, making everything ipso facto sacred, so that profane time becomes sacred time. The ritual of evoking mythical time then becomes unnecessary as this time becomes present. A religious experience happens when the evocation of the myth takes place and, in my opinion, this achieves its greatest expression in the mystical experience. M. Eliade tells us, in *Aspects du Mythe*, that "The traces of mythical behaviour are also found in the desire to find the intensity with which one has lived or known something for the first time." The mystical experience updates this desire, and makes it seem as if everything were seen as if for the first time, with other eyes and with another spirit. The mythical search is nothing but the search for mystical experience. While the myth tries to "recover a remote past, the beatific age of the beginnings", (*Op. cit*) the mystical experience updates the beatific age of the Origin. The mystic discovers the Sources on his own and thus he has the *direct experience of the Creative*.

Eliade ends the cited work by saying: "...it is always the same struggle against Time, the same expectation of freeing oneself from the weight of dead time, of Time that annihilates and destroys". I completely agree with him but we still have to address the decisive question: Can this hope become reality? The body is obviously connected to time and space, not the spirit, if the latter is identified with the former, it remains connected to the same coordinates ensuring that fear and desire opportunely appear, assuring the ties, however, if there is an identification with the Eternal, the path to liberation has begun. There is, thus, a time that gives life and that takes it away, and there is another that is eternal Life; knowledge of the latter liberates the spirit from the former. This, in short is the religious problematic. But one has to keep in mind that this is not only a matter for those who specialise in religion. Every human being is confronted with the alternative that he puts forth. *Herein lies man's great choice!* And as we will see this is the fundamental theme around which the sacred texts of Hinduism revolve.

Why Mircea Eliade?

I would firstly like to acknowledge my debt to M. Eliade in my studies on comparative religions, especially as concerns myths. Besides a searching personal vision, Eliade has consulted and commented on every writer on this subject within his reach over his long life. This "Toynbee of religion" is objective and even-tempered in his comments and one notes, above all, without being a philosopher, a genuine desire for knowledge and an urge to get to the roots of the subject. I know of no other writer better prepared than him in the field of comparative religions.

Looking back retrospectively on the essence of his work, Eliade recounts to us in a Prologue to the French edition of *The Myth of the Eternal Return*, "Had we not feared to appear overambitious, we should have given this book a subtitle: *Introduction to a Philosophy of History.*" He later adds: "In studying traditional societies, one characteristic has especially struck us: it is their revolt against concrete, historical time, their nostalgia for a periodical return to the mythical time of the beginning of things, to the 'Great Time'." "In our opinion, it is justifiable to read in this depreciation of history (...), and in this rejection of profane, continuous time, a certain metaphysical 'valorisation' of human existence." As we can see, Eliade is referring, albeit with undoubted shyness, to a "philosophy of history" and to a "certain metaphysical valorisation," fields in which he does not venture to penetrate as they transcend his profession. In several of his works we also find a clear invitation to philosophers that they engage in these matters with the undoubted interest of giving them a philosophical dimension and structure. Well, we have proposed to give fruition to this desire. Not only, of course, to fulfil his aspiration, but because it is a legitimate one, because we are certain that he is essentially speaking of the central crux of philosophy; which is what he himself anticipated.

Apparently we have to use very little of his extensive work, but, if we look at it carefully, we will see that the numerous symbols, rituals, myths, sacrifices and other things that he comments on are inspired by this essence and refer to it; and this is the end of the thread that we have to follow to express its transcendent and philosophical dimension. We can anticipate that we should not try to comment on these myths and rituals or symbols, but on what they express, which is not really a phenomenon but a way of seeing that obeys a mentality, a spirit that it creates. It is this spirit and its central idea that interests us.

Eliade says in the same *Prologue*: "With us, it is an old conviction that Western philosophy is dangerously close to "provincializing" itself (..): first by jealously isolating itself in its own tradition and ignoring, for example, the problems and solutions of Oriental thought; second by its obstinate refusal to recognise any "situations" except those of the man of the historical civilisations, in defiance of the experience of "primitive" man, of man as a member of the traditional societies." I fully agree with this even if it gives rise to a wrong interpretation. Let me explain: Eliade connects "Oriental thought" with "the experience of "primitive" man." It is not that there is no connection, but it obviously inclines not only those zealous of Western tradition, but also those lacking in correct information, to think that Oriental thought is, without further ado, "primitive," and this is false as we will see. During my long life I have not found anything more evolved than Buddhism and Hinduism. On the other hand, he leads one to think that this spirit and thinking is exclusive to the Orient. I have devoted an entire treatise to expounding that in the West not only have been alive, but that the highest thinkers share the same spirit and even the same ideology: I am speaking of the *universal idealism*. (I refer the reader to *The Search for Universal Consciousness*.)

In a later book (*The Quest 98*), Eliade observes (and this is in keeping with what I have expressed in *The Spirit in History*): "Today history is becoming truly universal for the first time, and so culture is in the process of becoming planetary." And since the "historian of religions recognises a spiritual unity subjacent to the history of humanity," "the history of religions can play an essential role in this effort towards the planetarization of culture; it can contribute to the elaboration of a universal type of culture." My effort, expressed in my work, to converge the spirit of the East with that of the West in a philosophy that understands and explains them, has that purpose.

On Mircea Eliade

I consider that the study of Eliade's work is more than useful, it is indispensable, to understand the universality of the religious phenomenon, that is, to bring us out of the unilateralism of particular religious doctrines. We have to recognise the debt that he himself owes to a multitude of scholars whom he cites so opportunely; it is in the task of gathering together each of the branches that he has found that he presents the great tree of religions, according to a personal but universal vision; herein lies his value. This task is not just that of an erudite scholar, there is a unifying factor that has allowed him to encompass such varied studies. Eliade is more than an anthropologist, he is not content with verifying the similarity of the events and the attitude of men, behind them he also notices something that transcends and encloses them. I believe we could say that he uses an a priori factor that allows him to give uniformity and coherence to the varied religious manifestations, and this is the sacred, with its different modalities, its hierophanies, as he calls them. Eliade knows how to maintain his boundaries, and this gives his work validity as scientific as is possible in the spiritual realm; with a wise prudence he keeps himself apart from any beliefs and philosophical systems, and even from any established morality.

Another of Eliade's immense contributions is that he discovers amongst the ashes left by Christianity and Islam a great number of documents of diverse religions which makes us recognise their value and see them as they were – the monotheist religions from another angle – as one more vision and not the only one; he brings us out of the dogma and monopoly established by them. Another aspect of great value in his work is that he gives us many examples of religious experiences. Since my work is directed towards the same experience, the final destination is the same. What Eliade abundantly provides are proofs of the existence of a reality that is in the world and, no doubt, as I prefer to see it, in the human psyche.

I believe that beyond its limits lies the philosophy that, besides complementing his work, can give it a meaning and an explanation, a reason for these religious events. In my opinion, the greatest benefit that we can derive from Eliade's rich documentation is the knowledge that all religious manifestations, from the least elaborate of archaic cultures, to the most complex and developed, always have common roots although their expressions might be different. With Eliade we see an end to the theory of true and false doctrines, as they all answer to the same fundamental reality. With him we learn to respect all religions, all the manifestations of the sacred. His work opens the doors to a whole new spiritual world that materialist and theological dogmas had shut away. In his proposal there is a general reconsideration and revaluation of religions in general, which are presented on equal terms, without being subjected to value judgments in a way that leaves us free to choose and armed with rich documentation.

All these religious manifestations emanate from a religious experience that Eliade naturally cannot provide. It is here where our philosophy has to be inserted and offers us a path to this experience, and which ratifies the reality that underlies a multitude of manifestations. I also offer a continuation of the same proposal that will take us beyond the rituals or concrete religious events, and allow us to fully enter into spiritual reality. As I do not see any contradiction between my philosophy and Eliade's work, following the same path is not a hindrance. Besides, Eliade himself has made forays in this direction with certain specific works that greatly transcend the anthropological vision, such as those dedicated to Hinduism, especially to its techniques directed towards the religious experience, that is, the yogas (*Yoga, Immortality and Liberation*, and the commentaries on the *Yoga Sutras of Patanjali*).

What has been called idolatry, persecuted, condemned and destroyed by Semitic monotheisms finally ends with Eliade. He categorically affirms this: "The adoration of a cosmic or telluric object in itself is never found in the history of religions." "A sacred thing, whatever its forms and substance, is sacred because it reveals or shares in ultimate reality." "All symbols, hierophanies, myths, rituals, etc. (...) are linked by correspondences, analogies, participations, like a cosmic network, an immense fabric in which everything is united." (*History of Religious Ideas, 48*) "This totality cannot obviously be accessed by a spirit that is accustomed to working through analysis." (*Op. cit.*) "Besides", continues Eliade, "the intuition that modern man is capable of cannot comprehend the richness of nuances and correspondence that any cosmic reality (i.e.: sacredness) implies in the consciousness of archaic man." (*Op. cit.*) Eliade emphasises the synthetic character that every archaic religious act has, intuitively perceived as a whole, and that therefore, should be understood in a similar manner. The sacred, finally, has a correspondence with the absolute.

It will be understood, given the importance that I have given to intuition and unitive knowledge throughout my work, how my philosophy is inserted in Eliade's research, and can strive to give it a meaningful and philosophical support. In principle, the conclusion is simple: however incipient the universal vision of the archaic religions may have been, and this is just a way of referring to it as we do not know its dimension and reach, it expressed a connection or participation with what I understand by universal Consciousness; and my entire philosophical system points to this.

The fundamental link between Eliade's work and mine is the Great Link, the Unity. We see that the search in history has been the same, from the adoration of the telluric gods, of the Earth (Gaia), to Plotinus, Schelling and my own vision. The Basis is the same, and what is more important is not these philosophies, no matter how well formulated, but the experience of the Unity, which might have been more real in an ancient priest or in a sun worshipper than in a contemporary thinker.

The Origin of Time

In ancient times, Eliade remind us, "the earth means everything that surrounds man, the entire place with its mountains, its seas and its vegetation". "Men are joined to the cosmic environment that surrounds them in an infinitely closer way than that which can be conceived by a modern, profane mentality. In a certain sense, it could even be said that man was not yet born." "In that stage his life could be considered as a prenatal phase: man immediately continued to participate in a maternal cosmic life." (*Treat. Hist. Relig. 225*) Curiously, one of the classic questions used by Zen masters to awaken the disciple reads so: Who were you before you were born?

In *Origin and Destiny of Man*, a book entirely conceived outside the thinking and work of Eliade some fifteen years ago, I have elaborated on this theme. On seeing the connection, I am tempted to interpolate various chapters of that book into this one, but as that would be inappropriate, I will limit myself to inviting the reader to read it. In the first pages one can find my theory of the original Unity of all beings including, of course, the human being, who originally lived as integrated in the World. However, this integration was relative and variable, as it is at present in other animals; his rudimentary mind did not allow him to understand the Absolute (and even today he seems to suffer from this incapacity), but he felt and lived it at certain times as he had the unitive faculties that lay (and still lie) latent in him. I talk about these in the chapter *The Origin of the Unitive Faculties*. I will extract a passage from the chapter *The origin of the Homo Sapiens*:

"...In each case the fundamental change happens when man creates his first abstraction, the self, on which will accumulate the other abstractions that will constitute the world, *the* (psychic) *reality* of contemporary man. The self would be the first differentiation established by discernment and its origin; then reality will be filled with dualities and differentiated individuals."

"With this change, the human being will lose his unity with the environment, he will become another, so that the environment will become progressively stranger, and he will be obliged to relate to it, live and know it in a certain way. When he was part of the environment he could spontaneously perceive the totality of his circumstances; his perception was sharper, small details revealed his immediate situation and his reaction was natural and instinctive. He will lose these faculties as he separates himself from the environment. In compensation, he will gradually acquire the capacity to resolve the situation, thanks to his power of abstraction: the *ability to* anticipate it, to *foresee*. Before leaving his lair to find sustenance or before even taking a walk, he will think about the possible danger and will decide to take with him his stone or club, and from the point of view of survival this is clearly an improvement, but we cannot help thinking that this attitude implies a prior relationship with his insecurity and fear. Thus, internal and external reality divided by the foreseeing begins to be divided in time: the *concept of time* will gradually take shape."

"After a while, our ancestors would feel the desire (that they earlier lacked) to improve their instruments in quality and quantity, from which new advantages will be derived, which we all know, and new disadvantages, which we generally ignore, because from the original change we have been acquiring a perspective that stops us from seeing certain aspects of reality. Amongst these, naturalists (Darwin the first) have pointed out the intrinsic lack of adaptability to the environment that creates man's growing dependence on the instruments he uses; a matter of great importance that only seems to preoccupy anthropologists and philosophers, aware of the internal degradation that this implies."

"It is worth pointing out that all desire is a projection into the future, that is, an *alienation from the present*. The human spirit will, thus, distance itself from its unity and its present. Since man is increasingly more preoccupied with his instruments or means, it will be ever more difficult for him to live in unison with this reality. It will progressively become "external" to man, who will, thus, perceive a distance between him and things which, in turn, will remain separated on being discerned. In this way the *concept of space* is formed. The concepts of time and space will come to constitute the foundations of all *cumulative knowledge*, and they will become so indispensable so as to become the *a priori* categories of knowledge of the tangible world, in the way Kant had established with penetration and assurance. These categories form the basis of what has been called *Homo sapiens*. It is unnecessary to highlight how beneficial this knowledge has been for man, but we should remember that it has involved the distancing of other faculties and, as a result, the ignorance of other realities, both internal and external." "Let us remember that survival after a genetic change implies an adaptation. This means that man not only shifted his perspective towards his individuality out of fear, but dragged the latter along with the former. Of course it is true that he adapted to this shift or mutation for the advantages that accrued, but also out of constant fear. In this separation in time and space, in this distancing and differentiation from the environment that earlier was its unity, we cannot fail to see the germ of an *alienation*." Maybe this extract from *the genesis* of *Homo sapiens* will help us to understand why man insists on returning to his Origin.

Eliade reminds us that archaic man in his ritual tried to involve the community in a common past, in a shared experience of coherence and universality. Although the experience of the priest or medicine man might be personal, his interest lies in integrating the community in *the original Unity* that he intuits. “On the occasion of the re-enactment of the myths, the entire community is renewed and it rediscovers its roots, it relives its origins.” (*Aspects du Mithe 52*) “The solidarity that exists between the telluric on the one hand, and the vegetable, the animal, and the human on the other is due to life which is the same everywhere. Its unity is of a biological nature. When any of these ways of life is tarnished or made sterile due to a crime against life, all the others are also affected, by virtue of their organic solidarity.” (*Trat. Hist. Relig. 234*) I cannot fail to see here an intuition of the universal moral Order (to which I will return later), that is, an active unitive consciousness. (I have elaborated on these themes in *The Roots of Morality*)

“We can never emphasise enough -add Eliade- the tendency to restore that time, mythical time, the mythic time of great time. This restoration is the result of every ritual and every significant gesture without distinction; a rite of the repetition of a fragment of original time. And original time serves as a model for all times. What happens on one day ceaselessly repeats itself. It is enough to know the myth to understand life.” (*Op. cit. 353*) “However paradoxical it might appear, what we might call the history of primitive societies is reduced exclusively to mythical events that took place in *illo tempore* and that have not stopped repeating themselves from then until our time. Everything that to the eyes of a modern man is truly historical, unique and irreversible, is considered by the primitive as something unimportant as it lacks any mythical historical precedent.” (*Op. cit. 354*) In this way “all times are susceptible of becoming sacred time, the duration can become eternity at any moment.” (*Op. cit. 355*)

Time and Divinity

Another important observation that could not escape Eliade’s penetrating gaze is that of the *Deus otiosus*. This is the supreme God to whom the creation of man and the World is attributed, but after this work he withdraws to the skies or even beyond the firmament and man knows nothing more about Him, as He apparently has not done any work after his original intervention. At times, in some traditions, he does not even finish his creation himself, delegating this task to his son, wife or some other divinity. Usually all powers are attributed to him, he is omniscient, eternal, etc., but he no longer concerns himself with human affairs; he is entirely transcendent. Men rarely approach him due to his remoteness and indifference, only in cases of great catastrophes or in which the minor gods have shown themselves to be insufficient. "The Supreme Being seems to have lost all religious presence; he is absent from worship and the myths show that he has withdrawn far from humans; he has become a *Deus otiosus*." (*Aspects du Mithe 123*) Eliade provides numerous examples including all kinds of religions, even the most elaborate; we do not need to bring them up here. Even in Christianity it is clear that the Creator God has been eclipsed by his son and mother, just as in Hinduism we can observe that out of thousands of temples devoted to the gods only one is dedicated to Brahman, the Creator God. He is relatively forgotten and has been replaced by gods who are more accessible to the human being. Eliade gives us no explanation of this phenomenon, he just states the facts. I believe that my vision can contribute to the explanation of this matter without fundamentally contradicting his research.

Fundamentally I think that it is not God who is eclipsed but rather that man becomes alienated from him. The concept of God, as the reader will have already observed, is not to my liking as it expresses preconceived ideas that have little or nothing to do with what I understand of this reality. In my way of seeing, man alienates himself from his own consciousness, distances himself from his centre and loses his universal vision by approaching his individual point of view. Obviously from the latter, a universal absolute, a unity of consciousness becomes an abstraction, it stops being an experience, a reality. The fact is that there has been a shift from the centre of consciousness towards the *external faculties*, towards discernment, which only knows of material things and has a duality because of its nature. He has distanced himself from his *original consciousness* that sees *unitively*, and only sees the separate multiple, in such a way that his spirit has been placed in a kind of perigee and his *unitive or original consciousness* remains beyond his horizon. But a trace of it remains, since it is truly his own consciousness, and a memory of it remains even though it is a memory out of the ordinary. This *unitive memory* preserves the *unitive memories*, those that have been unitively perceived by the spirit and this is the spiritual reality that underlies material reality (see *Unitive Memory* in my *Psychosophy*). Being alienated from that consciousness and that memory, the necessarily vague idea that he has of the memory, of said Unity, the intuition that he has of the perfection that the Unity implies, is what he calls God; to whom he attributes the said perfection, the creation of the world in which he lives and of himself.

Of course this God transcends his individual consciousness, strictly speaking he is eclipsed by it, so by adapting it to his vision he materialises, anthropomorphises and denatures it and finally replaces it with another god within his reach, a son or a goddess involved with the matters of this world and human affairs; a more human god or goddess.

Nevertheless, this is not what happens with those who have been able to shift their spirit towards their *universal Consciousness*. In the treatise *The Search for Consciousness* I have given many examples of philosophers or mystics who have sufficiently transcended their individual consciousness in order to perceive the reality of the absolute One. They can create religions precisely because they speak for and from the same Sources, but since the great majority of mortals do not reach this stage, instead of elevating their level of consciousness, they opt to lower the level of the absolute God. This has led them, as we can see throughout history, to make some mystical sons of God and even God himself; but in this case, as the Zen masters say, we are confusing the finger that points to the moon with the moon itself.

The assassination of God the creator, referred to by Eliade, can also be explained by man's alienation from his original or unitive consciousness. The guilt that he feels on account of this and the rituals that he performs to rediscover this origin, which is a rediscovery of himself, confirm my theory.

We see that with the ritual of an ancient religious man we are transported to "the absolute beginning of the Creation of the World". This return is translated as "the recovery of original sacred time" (*Aspect du Mythe 54*). Therefore, the absolute in which time is transcended is sought to be achieved. Eliade never tires of reiterating that the ritual proposes the "abolition of time." In all the myths collected by Eliade "the need felt by man to periodically annul a differentiated and fixed condition in order to rediscover the primordial totality" is repeated. Its essential signification consists of the "the paradisiacal reintegration of primordial man."

I cannot fail to see here *the search for the consciousness* of his Origin, of the man himself. Eliade adds elsewhere, "We have the right to say (*Trat. Hist. Relig. 383*) that the myths of the search and the initiatory trials reveal, in a classic and dramatic form, the very act through which the spirit transcends a conditioned, polar and fragmentary cosmos, to recover the fundamental unity of before creation." This ratifies my theory that it is the spirit that, consciously or unconsciously, seeks its *unity and integration*; although in the myth one hearkens to a past, this is timeless and this timelessness is the *absolute present* that, as it is indiscernible, seeks it in a past that it can discern. This auroral, paradisiacal time that transcends profane time "constitutes", in Eliade's words, "that *eternal present* of mythical time." Besides, "the ancient spirituality survives, in its own way, not as a possibility of real fulfilment by man, but as a creative *nostalgia* for autonomous values: art, sciences, social mysticism, etc." I attribute this survival and nostalgia to the fact that it is alive and present in the human spirit, not to "archaic mentality" but to the *unitive consciousness* that feeds on the eternal, from which modern man has become alienated.

Beyond Eliade

Not only does the history of religions change with Eliade, he also throws light on the very history of man, especially on his origins. The meaning that he retrieves from ancient societies serve us to question current values and beliefs and program our future. As he confesses to us in *Aspects du Mythe* "What is interesting for our research is historiography: the effort of preserving the memory of contemporary events and the desire to know humanity's past as precisely as possible." However, what is particularly interesting for our purposes is the present and the future of humanity and the planet that we inhabit, making use of this historiography in the light of our philosophy.

I have said that the unitive consciousness is the source of morality, aesthetics, philosophy and religion. Eliade has devoted his life to the study of the latter, and he has done so with so much sagacity as to not enrol in any doctrine; even though he might observe the inciting path that Hinduism offers towards liberation (*Yoga, Immortality and Freedom*). But, as a good Westerner, he has only followed this path with his reason, and thus he does not speak to us from within, from his experience, but from his research. This means that he has not penetrated the *unitive consciousness* to be able to see the interrelation between the aforementioned disciplines, and this leads him not to judge religions from the moral point of view, and to isolate even religious art from religion itself and, of course, not to integrate their knowledge within a philosophical system. This book that the reader has in his hands tries to remedy these limitations, fill these gaps, and integrate these disciplines.

In his vast work Eliade does not speak of the Inquisition, and this is without doubt the greatest aberration that can be found in the history of religions. In a brief commentary that includes a moral appreciation in passing, he notes the progress in Iran made by Zarathustra who ended human sacrifices. But as A. Huxley points out: "the Inquisition shed much more blood than was shed on all the altars of archaic societies put together," and for "reasons" no less archaic, to purify the souls of sinners, for their salvation or to condemn them in life. Not without horror we look at the sporadic human sacrifices practiced by the Aztecs, but we have soon forgotten the countless ones carried out in our civilisation. The explanation is simple: the mote in another's eye and not the beam in one's own. But Eliade did not deal with these negative aspects of religion, no doubt he wanted to avoid them. I think that when making a critique of religions it is necessary to highlight these aspects, because if we are willing to point out the small errors we must also be willing to point out the large ones.

I see that Eliade insistently returns to his original discovery *The Myth of the Eternal Return*, which is not an erroneous premise, on the contrary, the path and objective are correct, but they are not enough, there is something behind and beyond them. For example, in *The Quest*, where he extracts the history of the research that has been done into religion, he believes he has found a synchrony amongst materialist ideologies and the growing interest in archaic and oriental forms of religion. Both respond to "yearnings and impulses that manifest a kind of nostalgia for the primordial and original, for the universal *matrix*". With which I completely agree, but this is not all, the *reason* is still missing, which inevitably brings us back to philosophy.

In fact, my vision of religions, better said of religion, has little to do with the history of religions, because in its essence it is outside of history, it is a present experience; that this has occurred at different times and its interpretation has been influenced by culture, is a secondary matter. The experience is the same although the analysis might be different; we notice the difference when we compare it with primitive peoples who are incapable of processing the phenomenon well, but Buddhism and Hinduism spoke of this same experience 2600 years ago.

It is probably on this point that I differ the most with Eliade. He notes that the study of religions should not limit itself to their history, but he continues to be a historian of them, it is his profession and his passion. While Eliade systematically goes back to the origin in the past to find meaning in the myth and symbol, where he believes the key to the matter lies, my search is through the knowledge of the mind and its mechanisms and it tries to find the solution in the present. But what is important is that we are speaking of the same mind and of the same consciousness, whose manifestations Eliade has found in diverse cultures from prehistory to the present. This consciousness, that I have called unitive, has existed and prevails because it is the nucleus of our mind, it is the centre of its equilibrium from which man has the doors open to his universality, and it is around this cosmic consciousness that Eliade revolves.

In the extensive compilation that Eliade makes in *From Primitives to Zen*, a reference book in which he deals with prophets, myths of creation, death, the sacred etc., he does not speak to us of Judaism and Christianity, although he comments on religions before and after them. The author admits that it is a grave omission for which he excuses himself by alleging that the Bible is a well-known text. But this can lead us to think that the texts are radically different and therefore should be kept apart and treated as such. This would be in keeping with the dogma held by the faithful of these religions, since in an objective view, such as the one he proposes, their myths, prophets cosmogony and everything else should be exposed in the same way. Eliade promises to deal with these two monotheistic religions at another time, but, apart from sporadic and brief references, to my knowledge he never kept his promise. Filling this lacunae seems essential to me, but, of course, we will not do so the way he would as this is not a treatise on the history of religions, but rather on philosophy, where a critique of the errors and successes is necessary in order to smooth the path towards knowledge.

Eliade insists on the dualism between the sacred and the profane, although he does not fail to see their interconnections. In my experience there is nothing in nature that is profane, what is profane is that which is against the sacred, that is, Nature, as well as against the project of awareness that everything is sacred. The lack of tolerance that inveighs against the freedom of ideas and beliefs is profanation.

It is clear then that I do not differ from Eliade, but that I want to go beyond him. Eliade constantly revolves around the *Myth of Eternal Return*, and he has his reasons: "The cosmogonic myth provides the model of all other myths of the origin." "This beginning is always implicit in the sequence of myths that relate fabulous events that took place after creation, specifically, the myths on the origins of plants, animals, the human being or on the origin of marriage, the family, death ... (*The Quest 106*) "Sacred, primordial history, formed by the totality of significant myths is fundamental because it explains and justifies the existence of the world, the human being and society." (*Op. cit. 107*) This is what is called the *paradigmatic function of the myth*. This obviously explains not only the structure of a society but also the mind of these peoples, which is what shapes their history. But these evolve, and not always in a positive manner; in any case there is no absolute evolution. My interest is focused not on these paradigmatic myths but on their *positive evolution*, and not actually on the myth but on the cosmic mentality of the human being, that is, the *paradigmatic unitive consciousness*, as an example, and in the Unity of consciousness as experience.

I believe that my recognition of the work of Mircea Eliade has been sufficiently expressed. Perhaps the most valuable thing about his work is his insistence on removing the Western scholar from the closed schemes that prevent him from opening up to the alternative ways of seeing, thinking and feeling that this researcher finds in other past and present cultures. However, despite the openness, we cannot fail to observe that he follows a deeply rooted Western custom of studying the other; I mean to say, from the outside, and not from within. That is why he does not enter the plane of philosophy proper, in the personal search for the *first principles*. As these, as we shall see when commenting on the *Upanishads*, "cannot be reached by prolonged study"; we, however, will see how they can be achieved.

The differences between my thinking and Eliade's will be exposed in the course of this work. I find no opposition between them, rather I see them as complementary. Eliade seems to have adhered to mythical thought, to the cyclical vision of history, to the need for a return that implies a meta-historical conception. The imponderable virtue of cyclical time is that it always refers us to the origin and that it does not allow us to forget it, that it keeps us connected with the Universus; let us not forget this. I have nothing to object to regarding this student of religions, only that I see in his vision a means and not an end, since even in cyclical time, however infinite it may be, as in the case of the Hindu kalpas, we are still, even if in a different way, subject to time.

My proposal for a *Return to the Sources*, to *the Origin of Man*, includes that path, but once travelled, it is projected towards the Transcendent. The return to a primordial time is necessary, but the Origin itself is beyond, where time stops in the Immutable. My proposal is not only meta-historical, it is meta-temporal and meta-physical.

Myths and Universal Consciousness

When I look at Eliade's studies in light of my theory of universal Consciousness, I cannot fail to see a parallel. They speak insistently of a *centre*, of a navel of the world, a cosmic axis, the post that marks this point, etc. This *centre* is beyond time and space, separated from the profane, it is sacred space and it is also from where the world was created, it is the origin. In the *Rig Veda* (*X 149*) it is conceived that the universe takes its extension from a central point. "By reaching the cosmic summit Buddha becomes contemporary with the beginning of the world. For the very fact of placing himself in the centre from where the whole world was born, Buddha has abolished time and creation and finds himself in the timeless instant before cosmogony." (*Trat. Hist. Relig. 338*); similar examples endlessly follow, but what has been said is enough.

A study of my work will reveal that all these central and sacred places of so many religions and places are also explained as a *Search for Consciousness* (refer to my work), for its origin, for its centre which is also the Creative, sacred par excellence, transcendent in time and space and residing in Unity. In other words, what is sought in so many specific places would be nothing but a common spiritual place in the human consciousness, even if it transcends it as an individual. These are external expressions of an internal psychic reality, although not subjective but *unitive*; for this reason in so many cultures these are the *manifestations of the universal Consciousness*. Besides, these places as symbols situated in a centre imply a series of obstacles and "reaching them is equivalent to an initiation, a heroic or mystical conquest of immortality" (*Op. cit. 340*). The labyrinth that precedes this centre also alludes to the difficulties of the inner path of liberation. "The way is arduous and full of dangers because it is actually a rite of passage from the profane to the sacred, from the ephemeral and illusory to reality and eternity, from death to life, from man to divinity." (*Op. cit.*). As I said, Eliade does not allude to a superior mind or consciousness, but refers to certain complicated circumambulations of temples like Borubudur, and to the effort that the pilgrim has to make on his upward journey, and to the long and weary pilgrimages to the holy places, "the tribulations of the ascetic always in search of the path towards himself, towards the *centre* of his being". This means that the external search of the holy place corresponds to an internal search, to a *Search for Consciousness*.

"It is not the first time that we have to state that in the eyes of archaic spirituality (*Trat. Hist. Relig.*), all objects come together and all planes correspond to each other." I can see here the intuitions of a *unity of consciousness*. As I have pointed out in *Origin and Destiny of Man*, archaic man was more *centred* in his unitive consciousness, albeit at a very basic level. In the same text I point out the relation between modern man and reason, which implies the intervention of time and space and in unison the loss of original Unity, an alienation from it. This connects us to another point on which Eliade insists: "All rituals have the quality of happening now at this instant. Each time a significant act is repeated in the rite, the archetypal gesture of the god or of an ancestor is imitated, the gesture took place at the origin of time, that is, in a mythical time." Here as well we see the transcendence of time, but also the realisation in the present of the paradigmatic fact. It does not seem to me to be a simple coincidence that the realisation of unity occurs in the present, and that all rituals seek a unity. In my opinion, the unity of consciousness underlies and inspires these rituals, which in turn tend towards the same consciousness.

I am not trying to reduce the art and rich meaning of particular myths to a universal Consciousness, but to point out the close and indissoluble link between them; everything that leans towards the eternal has its origin and destiny in this Consciousness and these rituals are considered to be as if they existed in eternity. (*Op. cit. 353*) Eliade has laid most emphasis on the myth in *The Myth of Eternal Return*, precisely where I most clearly see the relationship with my idea-reality of the universal Consciousness. In my first work, not coincidentally called *The Return to the Sources*, I have already spoken of *the nostalgia of the eternal*. Moreover, the interpretation of the Platonic theory of re-memorisation was explained as the innate desire of the human being to rediscover his consciousness. Eliade says in this respect: "What we could call the nostalgia for eternity is testimony to the fact that man aspires to a concrete paradise and he believes that the conquest of this paradise is feasible, here and now, on earth and in the present time." (*Op. cit. 364*)

This aspiration can only be achieved in Consciousness, since claiming its realisation through the transformation of nature is an illusory project. "In this sense", Eliade continues, "the ancient myths and rites linked to sacred space and time are reduced to other nostalgic memories of a terrestrial paradise and a kind of experimental eternity, to which man thinks he can still aspire." I therefore insist that these myths revolve around *states of mind*, and the importance of this interpretation resides in the fact that they can be realized, and I believe that they can only be so by these means. One is not talking about going back to the past but in making the paradigmatic event present, not repeating the inaugural act, which is a ritual, and without denying its approximative value, but discovering the present itself, which is *the experience of the Unity that stops time*. The value of this is not that it happened in the past but that it can become the present, that is, that it is eternal; and this responds to a unitive vision. The fact that these myths have a universal character that is typical of universal Consciousness also confirms my theory.

The reader will see how what has been said can be placed within Hinduism and Buddhism that tend towards the realisation of this Consciousness, albeit that "they give it other names".

My View of the Subject

The entire path covered by M. Eliade leads me to conclude that the archaic religious man intuits the Absolute, the Origin, the Beginning, which he projects into the past because he feels nostalgia for a reality that he lost at some undefinable time and that he tries to rediscover and revive. That loss effectively happens in the past, when man discovers his self and separates and alienates himself from his original Unity and enters time and space, that is, his reason, as I have explained in *Origin and Destiny of Man*. But that reality continues to be relevant in the meanders of his consciousness because it is always current, it is present; it is in his *unitive consciousness*. My proposal is certainly not to return to an archaic mentality, but to a *unitive mentality*, to the *unitive plane of consciousness*, which is present, albeit in a rudimentary form, in archaic man. This implies a *shift of the nucleus of consciousness* towards its centre from which man deviated in *illo tempore*, to rediscover himself with his Origin, the Creative, in short, with himself, with his *universal Consciousness*.

In line with this, Eliade recognises that "the majority of recoveries of the sacred lead to a kind of *cosmic religion that disappeared after the triumph of Christianity* and that survived amongst the European peasants". Naturally (for the enlightened) "the discovery of the sacred character of Life and Nature does not necessarily involve a return to paganism or to idolatry". (*The Quest*)

I have spoken sufficiently of the process of individuation, externalisation and alienation in previous works; I will only add here that it is in this process that the human being has distanced himself from his unitive consciousness. But, as I believe I have proven, the best minds of the West have intuited a Unity towards which they have directed their thoughts, from the Pre-Socratics until today; I have devoted an entire treatise to demonstrate this (*The Search for Universal Consciousness*). Unfortunately, idealist thinkers are an exception, not amongst philosophers, but amongst men.

This bears repeating: one is not returning to an archaic mentality, but to the *unitive consciousness* from which man has been alienated, something intuited by the most enlightened minds of the West and the East in order to reach the highest summits of human thought and sentiment; my work is directed towards these heights.

In *The Quest*, Eliade manifests the desire that his work contribute to the production of "a new humanism on a world scale." I also have this objective, although I believe that the concept of humanism should be used with caution, since Renaissance humanism effectively had a universal dimension, but later, by the same process that I have spoken about, it has tended to fall into a homocentric perspective; for this reason I prefer to use the Renaissance of universal or unitive consciousness.

In the present work I would like to direct the Western spirit to its origins, to the Hellenic spirit, in order to generate a *New Renaissance*, but this time incorporating the rich contributions from India, whose spirit has been kept alive. One is not, naturally, trying to incorporate or import beliefs from other traditions, but to acquire the experience of the spirit that underlies all these beliefs. In possession of this spirit each one will know how to express it in their own way according to their character and idiosyncrasies, as happened during the Italian Renaissance that extended throughout Europe, acquiring nuances from each tradition.

In short: what Eliade finds in common between the primitive rites and the Indo-Chinese mystical techniques is *the return to the origin*. I take this to be true, but despite having occasionally referred to the *eternal present*, he tends to see this origin in a timeless, vague past. In my opinion, the difference lies precisely in the fact that *the mystic experience proper happens here and now and finds its origin in the present*. In the case of Buddhism and Hinduism it is no longer just a ritual but precise spiritual techniques directed to that experience that transcends time and space; that original time and space, to which I referred when I spoke of the origin of self-awareness and reason (*Origin and Destiny of Man*). As I said then, what is transcendent is so because of reason, but once attained, it is here in the present. There is effectively a return to the origin, but when time and space are transcended there is no past, only the original unity remains, which is the Unity of the universal Consciousness.

The difference between the *archaic unitive consciousness* and the *evolved unitive consciousness*, capable not only of ritually repeating the origin but also of realising it, is then clear. In this my philosophy converges with Hinduism and Buddhism; even if they obey particular traditions (*Dharma, Dhamma*), while what I propose is the philosophical path of knowledge that we could assimilate to the *gnana yoga;* if we do not commit it to that tradition.

Vital Plane and Evolution

I have affirmed that the vital plane is the correct plane of the human being as well as the vision or *unitive perspective* that derives from it; it was on this plane that the archaic religious man had settled his spirit, even if it was in an elementary stage. This does not in any way mean that it is a stage that has been surpassed, as what man has subsequently done is to leave on a divergent path and become alienated from this plane, for the benefit of the individual and dual vision, so characteristic of discernment, when the correct thing would have been to have evolved within the vital plane. It is from this centre that Western man has become alienated from his centre of consciousness, and he has become disconnected from his neighbour, from other living beings and from the planet in general, that is, from everything.

Any connoisseur of Greek thinking cannot have failed to observe the reaction against mythical thinking amongst its philosophers, Eliade himself reminds us that Xenophanes "had criticised and rejected the mythological expressions of divinity used by Homer and Hesiod" (*Aspects of the Myth*). Even better known is Plato's rejection, who expands on the matter in his *Republic*, where he is shown to be very stern with these poets. I have explained myself sufficiently on this point in *The Roots of Art*. Suffice it to say here that the philosophers undoubtedly had their "reasons" but these are far from exhausting the Greek spirit. During the same period (between Xenophanes and Plato) poets such as Pindar and the tragedians as well as plastic artists took myths to their greatest religious, moral and artistic expression, and their works are and will always be paradigmatic; and these wise men certainly were not lacking in reason. Fortunately, poets and artists in general have not abandoned this mentality; nobody with any discernment would call Sophocles or poets in general "primitive". (I have spoken of the cosmic and even mythical vision of Hölderling and Rubén Darío in *in the said work*.)

In modern poets the myth may well have been lost, but there is a similar mentality, as if it were an extension of the archaic one; reason is present but at the service of another way of seeing and thinking that essentially dispenses with logic. And it is not as if they do not know it, it is just not the instrument or medium that they need; in them it is more a seeing and discovering than a construction. The beginning, the middle and the end are different from the logical mentality. This had been discovered by Aristotle, already in the twilight of Greek thinking, and it is only a branch of the leafy tree of his philosophy. And the "scientific" side of this multifaceted philosopher does not in any way mean a bypassing of his humanistic side, as the experts of this kind of knowledge have claimed. The Renaissance humanists reacted against this cold rationalism, and it took them more than a century to finally accept the humanist side of Aristotle in order to put him alongside his master, the *divine* Plato. (See *The Renaissance* in *The Roots of Art*)

The key lies in the equilibrium between these perspectives, in the tolerance and comprehension of both mentalities without sacrificing one for the benefit of the other, complementing them, and this is what happened in Greece in general. But we should not limit our vision to these two mentalities, what is decisive here is the universal perception underlying both. The danger lies in the *individual perspective*; and rational man as well as the artist can fall into this trap, as has happened in the present.

However, I can verify that both the Buddhist and the Hindu have managed to preserve this *unitive vision*, which has effectively evolved without abandoning this plane of understanding, that is, they have kept their spirits *centred*. Not all Hindus and Buddhists, of course, but the plethora of enlightened ones that they have generated is proof, together with fact that they are the object of such acceptance, respect and veneration, that people sense that this is the correct path to follow. The similarity between Buddhism and Hinduism should be seen from this essential point. Hinduism and Buddhism, fully aware of the ultimate goal of spiritual sciences, tend to integrate the individual consciousness in Brahman or in the Consciousness of the Buddha.

Although in Hinduism this has not been raised in the way that I am exposing it, undoubtedly there is a sense of the relationship between these mentalities, thus it preserves its myths in its epics and in its art, which continue to be effective ways to bring the human spirit closer to its ultimate design. What is more, I am fully aware that in my eagerness to clarify these mental mechanisms with a philosophical language, to a certain extent I am denaturalising man's psychic reality, because, as I have already expressed, art is a unitive means of perception and expression so it develops essentially on the margins of time and space, it is timeless, and even the most ancient art can awaken unexpected intuitions of the Transcendent in the most modern spirit; and it continues to do so in the Hindu spirit. Conscious of this, the Hindu philosophers have not renounced their mythical past, on the contrary, they follow ancient rites and recite the *Mahabarata* and the *Ramayana*, whose origins are lost in the remote past. This still has a great impact on children's education whose minds are not ready to understand the Absolute or Brahman, but these stories awaken and maintain his *unitive consciousness*. It is in this consciousness that the essence of the matter lies, not in the concepts that claim to be philosophical truths. *The truths are contained in the experience of Consciousness*, it is to it that Hinduism, Buddhism and my philosophy ultimately incline.

Myths in the Present

Eliade concludes his *Treatise on the History of Religious Ideas* by observing that there is a dialectic of hierophanies that allows for the "spontaneous and integral rediscovery of all religious values," which occur circumstantially in history, and for this reason "in the final analysis the history of religions is reduced to the drama provoked by the loss and rediscovery of these values, a loss and rediscovery that can never be definitive."

Eliade deciphers in the hierophanies "the desire to unify creation and abolish multiplicity". "In them we are faced with a way of life that inclines towards repose, equilibrium and unity, it imitates the spirit in its impulse towards unification and stability", (*Op. cit. 407*) it speaks of "that need that man constantly experiences to realise archetypes", of "a nostalgia for transcendent forms". In any case, although he might insinuate it, as we will see, a relationship with a higher consciousness is not clear in his exposition. There is talk of *sacred places*, of a *pure land*, but never of a *pure consciousness*, a sacred centre is mentioned but not a *centre of the mind*, a *Universus* is not spoken of, but places and times that make it up, not of a mental integration, to where my philosophy points.

"What we could call *symbolic thought* gives man the possibility of free movement through all levels of reality." "The magical religious experience allows the transformation of man himself into a symbol. All anthropo-cosmic systems and experiences are possible to the extent that man himself becomes a symbol." "The macrocosmic experiences are no longer external to him nor, after all, strange and objective; they do not alienate him from himself, but on the contrary, lead him towards himself, they reveal to him his very existence and his own destiny." (*Op. cit. 407*) This symbolic thought, in my opinion, is the unitive, it is man's awareness of his universality.

"For archaic man, all levels of reality have a porousness as perfect as the emotion experienced in the presence of a starry night, for example, it is the same as the most "intimate" personal experience of a modern man; and this because, thanks above all to the symbol, the authentic existence of ancient man is not reduced to the fragmentary and alienated existence of the civilised man of our time." I have explained this point as the loss of the unitive consciousness and the adoption of an individual perspective.

As Eliade has observed, the modern world has been desacralised and is composed of individuals leading a desacralised existence. This consequence is not unconnected to Christianity, since having monopolised the sacred, it does not know how to maintain this sentiment. In my opinion, this relates not only to ecclesiastical politics but also to dualist doctrine directed at belief and not religious experience. These affirmations will become clearer below.

Eliade observes that certain psychologists, surely referring to Jung and his followers, insist that the "unconscious is religious,". He says this because "for men in desacralised societies, religion has become unconscious; it lies buried in the deep layers of his being; but this does not mean that it does not continue to fulfil an essential function in the economy of the psyche". (*Init., rites, soci., secrètes, 270*) "The initiatory scenarios no longer feed the imagination, but the life of the imagination, like oneiric life, is as important for the psychic totality of the human being as daytime life." But Eliade, always faithful to his field avers: "We are alighting here on a problem that surpasses the competence of the historian of religions and which is the heritage of psychologists." (*Op. cit. 266*)

I have dwelt at sufficient length on this subject in my *Psychosophy*, where I give a critique of Jung's religious vision, so I will not repeat myself here. I will say only the following: I agree that in desacralised societies (in the West) religion has become unconscious. But in no way does this mean that the unconscious has become the domain of religion. This and philosophy, in their roots, are found on a higher plane than that of the conscious. I referred in the earlier chapter to this level of understanding, and have termed it vital, of direct or unitive perception. This level of understanding effectively lies unconscious in contemporary man, including in the psychologist, but it is on the margins of the subconscious, and its nature is so distinct that it can be awakened to the point of transcending and illuminating the conscious; strictly speaking, it is man's true consciousness. When we return to this plane we will understand that it is the heritage of philosophers and mystics with psychological perception. Only they can understand that man is a religious being because his essence is the sacred itself.

Intuiting this, Eliade says: "Will we continue to have the right to speak exclusively of a subconscious? Would it not be better to also presuppose the existence of a trans-conscious? Do we have any basis to affirm that the creations of the subconscious offer another structure than the creations of the conscious? But both problems should be discussed in their own perspective, which is that of philosophy." (*Op. cit. 406*) This time he trusts that the philosophers will be able to resolve the matter; we will try not to disappoint him.

As is usual in my philosophy of history, my proposal is to place our vision as far as possible in the circumstances of the time and place that we want to understand. If we put ourselves in the circumstances of the archaic man we will see that he is surrounded by the same universe as the contemporary man, but that his immediate reality is simple and made up of a few things, and thus Nature has a greater role to play, the rain, storms, seasons, fertility and life in general are more present, so the *universal context* forms part of daily life, the *universal vision* is more accessible and natural.

The complexity that surrounds contemporary man has been filled by countless things and tasks that constantly occupy his mind, in such a way that his psychic and material reality is replete with this multiplicity, and he concludes that reality is indeed what he is living through. All this that seems so natural, even seemingly a platitude, has great and decisive consequences from a philosophical, psychological and vital point of view. Man's basic, primeval and primordial reference is the *infinite universe*, it is from here that he has to think and act in order to be connected with everything, in order to participate in the universal reality that gives plenitude to life. The universal circumstances of archaic man are, as I said, the same as those of contemporary man, but due to the complexity of life, he has focused his life and mind on his *immediate circumstances* to the point of *alienating himself from his universality*, from his *essential references*. These references are not another point of view, they are the very essence of him, they are the centre of balance of his mind or spirit; hence the gravity of the matter, so that the alienation that he suffers comes from himself.

Of course, the complexity of today's world is the product of an indisputable material progress that has even led us to better understand the universe itself, yet it continues to be infinite, unfathomable, and thus it remains a mediate, distant and even alien circumstance, since it is studied as de-spiritualised matter and only by certain specialists, in the way that others apply themselves to microorganisms.

And here we find another problem that is a consequence of the same process: specialisation that is precisely the opposite of universalisation. This world of specialists has produced a general alienation; nobody is concerned with the totality and essential reference. Human reality is closeted within itself, busy with the quotidian, domestic, banal chores of *the great human anthill*.

On Initiations

Eliade has sufficiently demonstrated that the human mind has an intimate need to go back and repeat the initiation ritual that has manifested itself since antiquity, from societies with basic cultures up to the most spiritually evolved societies, and even in the modern world, already desacralised, by means of stories and various forms of literature. In his words: "The initiatory schemes are the expression of a psychodrama that responds to a profound need of the human being." (*Death and Mystic Initiations 190*). We do not need to repeat the initiatory schemes that Eliade has insisted on, it is sufficient to note what they have in common: in them all there is a sacrifice, symbolised by a physical death and a resurrection. This implies a radical change, a spiritual rebirth by which natural man becomes a supernatural being and is assimilated to the gods. These practices evidently refer us to the field of religion; the rituals that are practiced for this purpose are religious and are carried out by priests, Brahmans, medicine-men, shamans, etc., that is, by trained initiates.

It is obvious that the Christian rituals of baptism and the sacraments respond to the initiatory scheme. Thanks to this, the faithful left the profane world and "became integrated into the world of the chosen" (*Op. cit*). The death and resurrection of Jesus also responds to the same scheme, but with an important variation: while the other myths refer to a timeless past that the rite periodically repeated, "the resurrection (of Jesus) was an irreversible event that was not repeated every year such as, for example, the resurrection of Adonis. He was not an exponent of the sacredness of cosmic life, as was the case with the gods of vegetation or of initiatory rites as in the Mysteries." (*Op. cit.181*). Jesus was a historical fact, the Christian god becomes incorporated in time, he does not incite us, as in cosmic myths, to transcend time but, on the contrary, to remain within time. From a philosophical point of view what matters is knowledge, to make it intelligible as far as possible, to make comprehensible the spiritual reality to which these myths incline and try to realise the rituals, better yet, make of these mysteries an indubitable experience, to make the transformation, not of the gods or the heroes of the past, but of contemporary man, become a reality.

It is thus pertinent that we have the greatest respect for these rituals that spiritualise the human being and bring him closer to the deities, and make him a member of the Cosmos, as this is also an aspiration of philosophy, at least as I understand it. However, I observe that what these rituals have in common is that the means they use to generate the desired transformation are definitely magical. Indeed, the ritual is supposed to be sufficient to produce the change, so there is no doubt something miraculous about it, and it requires belief; and belief, especially in miracles, is not a valid resource for philosophy. However, we cannot fail to take into account the disposition and, above all, the preparation of the aspirant that precedes the ritual; and these have nothing magical about them. I know from experience and I have seen it in others' experiences, that asceticism, a retiring life, meditation and contemplation are highly conducive to producing a real and internal change. This means that if the aspirant is *prepared*, the ritual, which also involves the entrusting of the subject, of the self, to the master or guru, and through him to the divinity, would be like a necessary springboard to make a leap beyond oneself. Unfortunately, we have scarce information about the mystery of the Mysteries practiced in ancient times, despite this, later we will try to salvage what has remained from the rubble.

Considering the heights and perfection attained by the Greek civilisation in all the fundamental spheres of knowledge it is logical to suppose that these rituals were at the level of these demanding people; and with greater reason if we remember the relevance and importance that they gave to them. In the mass rituals, which were actually festivals similar to those practiced today in India, we have to accept that the multitude of participants, even if they were not intrinsically transformed, were connected in some way to the Cosmos.

I believe that the strong attraction that India exerts over so many Westerners is because they intuit that this tradition takes them back to their origins. There are many customs that in our culture have been distorted and eradicated by Christianity, but which India still preserves. We find in Greece and Rome the theory of reincarnation, for example, which is accepted throughout Asia. "The Indian who accepted existence and loved life did not want to preserve it indefinitely, he preferred to enjoy a long youth. On the other hand, immortality was not of such a nature as to tempt the sage or mystic — who aspired to liberation and not a continual prolongation of existence; a definitive detachment from the cosmos and the acquisition of absolute spiritual autonomy and not of a duration in time, even if were infinite. We find the same ideas amongst the Greeks: they did not aspire to immortality but to youth and long life." (*Trat. Hist. Relig. 269*) "Orphism seeks firstly the exit from the cycle of infinite reincarnations, or the abolition of the periodic return of existence." (*Op. Cit. 371*) The cult of the Mother goddess that expresses life on the entire planet can be found in all of Pre-Christian Europe and also among the Aztecs, Mayas and Incas. Eliade clarifies that "these are non-existent religions today, *with the exception of India*, and we are not always sure of understanding the rare documents that we have". However, I aver that this sacredness and consequent respect for Nature, which implies integration with the World, is today a necessity more than a convenient belief.

Eliade could not ignore the fact that many archaic or prehistoric rites, especially those of initiation, are transmitted to highly evolved societies like the Greek and Indian. The initiations in these evolved societies "are infinitely more complex than in those of primitive religions." (*Init., rites, socié. secrètes 224*) "The shaman is a man who *knows and remembers himself*, that is to say that he understands the mysteries of life and death, who shares the state of the spirit. He is not only an ecstatic but also a contemplator and a thinker. In subsequent civilisations, *philosophers* will enlist from amongst these people who are passionate about the mysteries of existence, inclined by vocation to an experimental knowledge of inner life." We will see what the philosopher can do with these elements.

Mythology and Philosophy

I would like to underline the differences of my vision from that of Eliade: for him "(religious) man is what he is today because a series of events took place ab origine". "For the homo religiosus real, authentic existence begins at the moment when this primordial history is communicated to him and he accepts the consequences." (*Myth and Reality, VI*) That is to say that for him spiritual, religious knowledge comes from an uncertain past (*in illo tempore*), which is transmitted by the medicine man; it comes, as he affirms, from the past.

In my opinion this is valid for archaic societies in which myths play a decisive role, but in today's society the situation is different. I am not referring to the human being entirely alienated from myths and religion, it is certainly not this type of man who interests us, but the religious man of today who has not abandoned that past in his mind; I am referring to he who has preserved his *unitive vision*, capable of penetrating spiritual reality.

Eliade himself, when he talks about the experiences of light in *Mephistopheles and Androgynus*, tells us about cases of religious experiences that have no historical connection. Strictly speaking, in my view, all transcendental experiences are not only present, but also experiences of the present, of the absolute present, they are a-temporal, a-historical and thus valid for all times. They do not, thus, depend on a historical situation but on *the position of the spirit in the mind*, on its closeness to the centre of human consciousness, where the realities of the spirit take place, where they are constantly updated, in any age and place; they are eternal truths that can be experienced until the end of time. Even more, I affirm that this is man's objective on an individual and social plane and that in it lies the future of humanity.

What has been said has to be interpreted well: from now on, I do not in any way mean that we have to dispense with the mythical past, on the contrary, because if, as I said, this consciousness or mentality has existed at all times, here we can find antecedents, in the form of myths and stories and literary forms like the epic in which the same experience is recounted in different ways. The Greek genius knew how to rescue in a particular way the exemplary myths that are relevant even today, and in India the epic has been recited for millennia with the same objective of awakening the spirit, always tempted to forget its true identity.

In relation to my commentary on the rememorisation of Plato, even Eliade collects some passages from Samkhya, Yoga and Buddhism that resemble my theory in this fundamental aspect: "The I (*Purusha*) is only apparently enslaved and liberation (*mukti*) is nothing but an awareness of its eternal freedom." At the time of awakening he comprehends that the spirit "impassively contemplated the drama of the personality".

It is not surprising that Eliade also finds a parallel with the Hellenic tradition: Plotinus wrote that "memory is for those who have forgotten." (*Aeneid 4,6,7*) and from Plato he takes a passage in which he rectifies a point, or makes an exception to his theory of rememorisation, with which his vision coincides with the aforesaid Indic doctrines: "For those who have forgotten, rememorisation is a virtue; but the perfect do not lose sight of the truth and have no need to remember it." (*Phaedo 249*) This means that the ascendant path, which involves an asceticism, a strict morality, a practice of spiritual techniques or a philosophical search, is necessary only for those who have forgotten its essence; in my language I would say those who have become alienated from its Essence.

Eliade recognises that in India as in Greece "there is a continuity between popular beliefs and philosophical speculations". This continuity and the philosophical speculations that derive from it are the main reasons that have led me to write this treatise.

Here it would be repetitive to follow Eliade in his *Mythologies of Memory and Forgetting*, an undoubtedly revelatory chapter in his work. What I draw from it is that in general the myths on this subject take us to a past, *ab origine*, this is what they want to remind us of and they do not speak of a continuous and eternal present as I express in my philosophy. But it should be understood that myth is not philosophy, it is not directly and rationally expressed, it is allegorical, it uses other resources for other mental faculties and, I must admit, it has shown itself to be more effective than philosophy; which makes us doubt, once again, man's rationality. The chords struck by the myth undoubtedly please the soul more than those struck by philosophy. It would be too simple to conclude that philosophical thinking is not within the reach of the masses. I am inclined to believe that magical thinking incites the spirit more, it is like a stronger and more effective drug, but I think its secret lies in the fact that it does not say it all; processed food does not nourish, but when each one carries out the process, it gently feeds the spirit. Given the heterogeneity of man, the myth provides food that is nourishing for the majority. Since it lends itself to individual interpretation, it is paradigmatic for all; herein lies the key to its success, it speaks a language that is never fully understood, but which everyone can understand in some way. And it is not as though it does not speak truths, these certainly are there, but hidden like the treasures that incite their discovery. What is certain is that the open and exposed coffer of philosophy does not seem to enthuse more than a few.

In any case what is interesting is the connection between certain paradigmatic myths and my philosophy. Eliade has complete faith in myths, in their power to awaken the sleeping man, to attract those distracted by worldly life. In this way he concludes his article on *Mythologies of Memory and Forgetting*: "Only the primordial myth is important. Only the events that occurred in the past of fable are worth knowing; for, by learning them, one becomes conscious of one's true nature - and awakens." Historical events (like Caesar's assassination) have no significance, as they "carry no soteriological message". In my opinion, what is important is the relation between the primordial myth and philosophy when both are directed to the transcendence of the human being.

Eliade insists that the myth invariably tends to bypass historical time, but this is conventional time, the time created by man, and this is also the objective of philosophy: to transcend time. Myth, in fact, tends to refer to the moment of creation when time did not exist and, in my opinion, this is so because the *unitive mind* intuits that the Origin is before time. In other words, like the philosopher, the mythical man wants to transcend time, and imagines that the way to do so is to regress to the moment when nothing existed, as time and nature go together. But the evolving mythical man discovers techniques to overcome time in the present. Herein lies the connection, in my view, between mythical and unitive man, both have a *unitive mentality*, they only differ in degrees of spiritual evolution.

It should be clear that this evolution has nothing to do with man's material or external progress, but with an elevation of the level of consciousness and with a refinement of intelligence, which has not occurred in the human in general, but rather in certain individuals who, having reached this level, are closer to the Origin. The rest, as concerns organised societies or civilisations, do not seem to have improved in the last 5000 years. Suffice to note that the *Upanishads* and Plato are still not understood.

Mythical and Unitive Mentality

Archaic man intuited the existence of the Transcendent, but I infer that he did not have direct experience of it, so he referred to a primordial past, to his ancestors who he believed had had that direct contact; the way to actualise and keep that contact alive, to make it happen, was through ritual. The literally superhuman power of religion consists of this vague intuition that there is a paradigmatic, perfect, absolute reality that transcends everyday reality that is mutating and perishable, and that, therefore, is unsatisfying, as it is never shown to be true or real.

This, in a nutshell, is my interpretation of Eliade's findings. But there is something fundamental I would like to add, which is that this transcendent reality is not in the heavens or in the past, but in our minds, since it is part of our mental structure. And not only this, it is the very core of our psyche from which modern man has become so alienated or estranged that he believes it to be external, remote and even non-existent. Even the religious man, as in the dualist doctrines of Semitic origin, believes it to be distant and external, but the reality is in the very centre of human consciousness. This is the *unitive experience* that grants a cosmic and integrated vision to total Reality. The Essence of the world, which is everywhere, is also in our mind. The final task, the ultimate objective of the spiritual sciences is to make it conscious. If the Essence of the world seems alien to man it is because he is alienated from himself.

Through religion, the human being tries, consciously or unconsciously, to integrate reality and to become integrated in it, but he is trying to integrate his mind in unison. When he does this he integrates the World; this is the unified Consciousness, the cosmic Consciousness. This is the monistic vision, the monistic pantheism that I propose.

All religions are approximations to this final unity of the spirit and nature, and for this reason all deserve to be taken into account, both ancient and modern. But inclining towards excesses is part of the human condition. The rituals that led the Aztecs and Incas to human sacrifice were unnecessary excesses that we do not need to justify. Much less the tortures and killings of heretics and infidels by Christianity, which were not even rituals, but executions to eliminate all opposition and achieve political and economic power. In actual fact this has nothing to do with religion, although the victims were judged in the name of a religious doctrine.

I must confess that in reading M. Eliade I realise that the search that concerns philosophers had already began in archaic societies, although in another way, with other means and a different mentality. And if we judge these seekers by their closeness to primordial reality, by the level of the unification of Nature and Spirit, I could not say that philosophers have been more veracious than their predecessors, that a rational mentality has been more effective than a mythical mentality, that logic has brought them closer than ritual.

Because, in keeping with my vision, *what is crucial is the closeness of the spirit to its centre of consciousness*, as this grants it the *essential perspective* from which Unity becomes reality. But I do think that mythical mentality, though rudimentary in its thinking, was not alienated from unitive consciousness, while the philosophers, by virtue of being so, have had to make such an effort to find the primordial Unity. Besides, my project is to revisit the lost unitive consciousness, to which the mythical consciousness was closer, applying to it an evolved reason, a reason at the service of unitive consciousness.

One only has to see the title of my works to see that they follow the eternal myth of the Return to the Sources, to the Origin, to the Roots, although they do not refer to a return to the time of our ancestors, but to our lost consciousness, which is not a return to the past, but an encounter with our present, with ourselves.

For Eliade this disconnect with the mythical mentality occurs in the principles of Greek philosophical thought; but this has to be correctly defined as it is true only in a partial and particular way. Strictly speaking, mythical thought is effectively questioned by some philosophers but not by Parmenides, Heraclitus, Pythagoras and, only in certain aspects, by Plato. I have concentrated on them sufficiently elsewhere and I will not repeat myself here. Moreover, we should avoid the usual mistake of reducing Greek thought to the philosophers, as the literati and artists had a far wider audience and influence in that singular people, who expressed the myths in the most elevated and significant way possible. No philosopher was rewarded or recognised by the State or by the public, all the tragedians, on the contrary, were on repeated occasions. The myths were alive not until the fall of Hellas, but of Rome, they lasted around 2000 years.

The myths in a strict sense, as I said, were criticised by certain philosophers, but what specifically interests us is the connection between mythical and unitive consciousness, and this has remained alert and active in idealist thinkers until today; even if we must acknowledge that there have been exceptional men who never reached the wider public. The Church cooperated in this and persecuted and condemned them when it could. We know of numerous works that were burnt, but we will never know how many went to the stake with their creators, geniuses, perhaps, of whose talents we will never know.

The Greeks did not only live through the myths of their heroic ancestors, these paradigmatic men served as a point of reference for living intensely in the present; and perhaps this is their most remarkable trait. But these people's concerns did not end there, their famous oracles testify to their passion to know the future, some as old as their race, who were consulted by notable men until the time of the fall of Rome. These oracles, who foretold the future, were part of their history and mythology, as we can verify in the tragedy.

There was thus a growing shift of the spirit in the age of the classical Greeks, and this gave way to systematic thought and to philosophy; the invaluable tool of the spirit in order to know with certitude where it is roaming and to realise its search for the first principles.

Idealism has been the result of this process which I have followed in my work with a double intention: firstly, to remind the reader that in the West not only has the essence of the world not been forgotten, but that amongst its most enlightened thinkers there has been a systematic search for Unity. Secondly: to rectify the digressions of these thinkers to channel them towards their final Destiny, the Unity of consciousness and, as a consequence, the unity of the Spirit and Nature.

As we shall see in due course, Hinduism and Buddhism have followed a *natural process*, and thus there has been no rejection of their past in the name of a modern vision; they are inclusive disciplines and not exclusive or that exclude, hence also the natural fusion between these two traditions. For this reason, the ancient Vedic gods have not been rejected, they have simply been receding on the horizon of time as ideas modified and Hinduism evolved. In this way evolution must be understood as an adjustment or a fine-tuning of ideas, as there is no opposition but renovation.

At the very core of Hinduism, in the *Upanishads*, we will see the convergence of archaic unitive consciousness and evolved unitive consciousness, the need to go back to the Origins of time, which is found in Brahma, to project itself in the Destiny (of the soul), beyond time in the Absolute Brahman.

In short, as I have already advanced, if we want to find a continuation of this mythical tradition, of that cosmic mentality, of that *unitive consciousness* in a modern and evolved society, in which spiritual practices are directed towards a real experience, we have to move to India; this is what we will do.

Schelling's Philosophy of Mythology

We have seen that M. Eliade, despite his acute perception and his incursions into the field of religion, very prudently remains on the fringes of philosophy and even expects philosophers to complement his specialised work on mythology. Curious to know if philosophers have contributed anything to this subject, I turned to the work of Ernst Cassirer, who dedicates the second volume of his *The Philosophy of Symbolic Forms* to *Mythical Thinking*. As he begins by quoting Schelling, the work promised to go beyond that of the romantic philosopher, but being a successor to Kant he could hardly achieve this goal and, indeed, could not develop a *Philosophy of mythology* for the reasons that I will give below.

The world of mythology is akin to the World of Ideas in the sense that it can only be accessed by transcending the limits imposed by reason. From this what results from the attempt is a study or a commentary that resembles anthropology because the effects are observed more than the causes; and philosophy deals with these. Kant's work, which I have commented on in previous works, was indispensable, since by establishing the limits of reason he put an end to all the errors or excesses that were committed in his name. His *The Critique of Pure Reason* marks a before and after in the history of Western thought, but his subsequent attempts to reach the noumenal were unsuccessful, precisely because he could not transcend the very limits that his reason imposed on him.

Fichte and Schelling access the Transcendent through *intellectual intuitions* which are the indispensable tools for it and those that idealism has always used. Lacking them, Cassirer, who adopts a Kantian perspective, was unable to see the world of mythology from within. His criticism is valid, his appreciations are accurate but his vision is external; for this reason I consider it unnecessary to comment on his work. I am not affirming that in order to deal with mythology one must have an intellectual intuition of the absolute, but rather enough vision to look at it from another perspective than that offered by reason.

For my part, I can clarify that it is not my interest to develop a philosophy of mythology, I consider it unnecessary for my purpose, which is to expose and apply my philosophy to these branches of the spirit; it is in light of this that I would like to make some observations that seem to me essential to understand the issue from within. For this I will take advantage of Schelling's *Philosophy of Mythology*, probably the only one that has been written, because we have a base in common and, in my opinion, it only needs some rectifications that I will expose when commenting on it.

To my understanding, mythology is the artistic expression of religion. For Schelling "it is a product of poetic imagination" (the quotes below are from the French version of *La philosophie de la mithologie*), with which I would agree if artistic imagination in general is understood as an expression of mythical consciousness that would be equivalent to archaic or original artistic consciousness. Schelling astutely observes that as soon as we want to grasp the mythical expression it escapes us: "How many who have attempted to capture the fleeting appearance of mythology, have not, like Ixion in the fable, embraced the cloud instead of Juno!" For Schelling, poetry would be "the natural condition, and even the necessary and direct product of mythology," "the regular development of a poetic people par excellence like the Greek." He does not fail to observe that the Hindus (as Indians) "are the only people who have in common with the Greeks a free art of poetry that is developed in all forms and likewise arose from mythology."

A conception that Schelling gathers to explain the phenomenon of mythology would be based on the principle of personification: "What are personified are the moral principles or natural phenomena." "The gods would be moral beings each endowed with a moral property." Schelling deviates from this theme and does not return to it, but this conception seems to me of the greatest importance, as long as we discover its origin, which we find in my philosophy as a prolongation of universal Consciousness, which emanates, in effect, the Good from which moral principles are derived in our individual consciousness. A poetic-religious consciousness will easily personify these virtues that it intuits as gods that possess them. Another question that Schelling asks himself is why similar mythologies are found in different peoples. This also finds its explanation in my conception that observes these moral incentives in the very nucleus of the mind. We will return to this topic in the next chapter.

It is interesting to highlight the conclusions that Schelling reached after commenting on various authors and a lengthy analysis that seem to me mostly unnecessary, and that few readers will be willing to follow in this already quite unknown work: "Mythology should be understood in its proper sense." "It is not allegorical", "for it the gods are beings that really exist, that do not signify anything other than what they are." "Mythology is the product of a necessary process, in relation to consciousness." Because "mythological representations have not been invented, they are not an independent product of thought and will, but are an incontestable and irrefutable reality for consciousness." Mythology "is a natural consequence of consciousness." Mythical representations "come from the backgrounds of the consciousness to which they impose themselves as a necessity and which leave no doubt as to their truth." Therefore, "we must understand them as they are expressed."

"The process that has engendered mythology had its raison d'être and its beginning in the first actual consciousness of humanity." That is to say that "the first actual consciousness was... already a mythological one". Therefore, "It is, we can say *historically* proven that there could not be another polytheism prior to the mythological one - that is, that one that is posited with the process proven by us, thus none in which there would not have been actual gods, that is, in which *God* would not have been the ultimate content." "The final content of the history of the gods is the production of an actual becoming *of God* in consciousness, to which *the gods* are related only as the individual, productive moments." The process is a theogonic process that is, "a process that has its source in an essential relationship of the human consciousness to God." It would be a consciousness that would engender God as a consequence of a theogonic consciousness. So that "human consciousness must be considered as the true seat and generating principle of mythological representations." It would be, then, a kind of artistic instinct; which would agree with my vision.

Schelling's aim is "to give mythological representations an objective basis." I think his attempt is legitimate and his results worth considering. However, I think that our viewpoint would adjust, to understand this matter and even his vision, if instead of looking for an objective knowledge we observed it from a unitive consciousness, since, in effect, in my conception, *mythical consciousness is a way of being and an expression of unitive consciousness*, and in this lies the importance of its understanding.

It will be clear that Schelling's initial proposition that mythology is the product of the imagination of poets is left modified or clarified: "Mythology is the product of human consciousness and not a creation of inventors and poets." The process is of a "theogonic character in which human consciousness would find itself compromised."

The duality of subjective-objective knowledge leads Schelling (and many others!) to fall into contradictions that he naturally tries to resolve with reason. So that said theogonic process begins by being subjective and ends by being objective. In my opinion, the entire *mythical phenomenon is unitive*, and it is precisely when the subject-object reality is prioritised that the mythical or unitive consciousness is disarticulated.

Schelling does not speak of the state of man's current consciousness, which is the one that interests us particularly. But he speaks of two previous stages and also of an original unity that he explains in his own way: "Man is created in the centre of the Godhead, and it is essential to him to be in the centre." "As long as he is in it, he sees things as they are in God, not by an external view that makes them appear devoid of spirituality and unity" (which would be what is I have called the individual perspective), but in a progressive "fusion realised in man, which ends in his absorption in God." "But since he comes out of his immobility", (that is what he calls this first stage, with which I would agree if referring to the immutability of the unity, although I do not think that human consciousness was at such a high level, which would require a supra-consciousness, which it has not yet achieved as a species, but unconsciously, as I believe happens to all living beings), "it must engage in struggles in order to maintain" (I would say to recover) "the primitive or divine unity that is already disordered and dissociated." From these struggles, for Schelling, "that intermediate world that we call the world of the gods" would be born, that is, the mythological world. At this stage, man would already have become aware of himself. "Having become aware of himself he strives to find the extra-divine world."

Schelling clarifies that "it is not with things that man has to deal in the mythological process, but with powers that show themselves within consciousness and with impulses of which he obeys." It is not then with the powers of an external nature, to which the origin of myths has been attributed so many times, but with our internal, mental nature.

"We can say that the false in mythology does not exist except for those who misunderstand it, who observe it for its isolated elements, who do not take into account more than its external side and not its essence," which is in the process. "That is why we do not look at mythology in its isolated moments, for us it represents a whole, an everything in which all the indissolubly united elements participate." "It is in the whole that its truth resides." "This truth is religious." And it is a truth that "does not exclude anything, it is a universal truth." "Its objective birth, independent of opinions, of thought and human will, gives mythology an objective content and an objective truth."

Schelling strives to find not only an objective value for mythology but also an "objective truth" as opposed to the false one that he believes he finds in the integrity of the mythological process that he considers necessary. He is prone to dualities which inadvertently incite him and even determine his judgment, when he falls into them he is forced to overcome them or to find their positive side. We have seen that "the theogonic process begins as subjective," but later he affirms that, seen as a whole, it is objective, which does not cease to be contradictory. Unitive consciousness, which is what must be applied to this knowledge, entirely dispenses with these dualities and does not assign more value to objective knowledge, but rather to spiritual experience, which is what grants knowledge in this realm, which is precisely transcendent to reason. What is decisive in unitive knowledge is the approach of the spirit to the Spirit, to universal Consciousness. If we need a truth, this is the Truth and partial truths are derived from it.

Schelling's ultimate purpose is to demonstrate the relationship between philosophy and mythology: "Philosophy only began to look at mythology in depth from the day it became aware of itself as a process, when it revealed itself as being the history of self-consciousness." "If one understands history in the broad sense of the word, the philosophy of mythology is but the first, the most necessary, and indispensable part of a philosophy of history." And since in his philosophy art occupies a pre-eminent place, he does not fail to link art with mythology: "every philosophy of art, to be complete, must give an important place to the exhibition of nature, as well as to the birth of mythology, which is what I did 50 years ago in my lessons on the philosophy of art." (See my comment on his *Philosophy of Art* in *The Roots of Art*) “It must postulate the existence of an original poetry, preceding plastic art and poetic creations.” “And the original source can only be mythology.” “It is the original poetry, the source of creations” (later).

In the process followed by mythical art, Schelling observes that “its progression is not made from the small to the great, but rather, it is always the great, the gigantic that constitutes the beginning.” “Homer is of such greatness that no subsequent age has been capable of producing works equal to his.” In the same way he points out that this happens with the Egyptian and Hindu temples. When referring to these, he acutely observes that they were not formed over time, but that “the force, that in mythological representations has led human consciousness beyond the limits of reality, has equally been the first to teach it the great, the significant in art; it is what has made humanity leap beyond, as if guided by a divine hand, all the previous stages and has conferred on the creations of antiquity an unequalled grandeur.”

When the deep meaning of myth is penetrated, that is, when mythical mentality is understood, as in the case of Schelling, it is not surprising that Homer is said not to have been superseded. But is this because subsequent authors have had less genius than the great Greek poet? This is not the reason, but rather because, to be precise, they have lost this mentality. And that is why when they have returned to the inexhaustible theme of Ulysses, they have demystified it in the double sense of the term. They have denatured both Ulysses and the mythical meaning of the poem, which is what Homer is inspired by, whom they cannot imitate but only parody because they lack such inspiration. They lack the Muse that Homer evokes before writing his Odyssey. (On the gradual distancing of the literati from the Muses and the consequent abandonment of the Invocation, see *The Roots of Art*). “Begin”, Homer tells the Muse, “to sing wherever you want, oh goddess born of Zeus!” It is the Muse who decides and narrates, not the poet. Homer’s grandeur lies in his universality; modern authors and their Ulysses have too much individuality (not to mention Joyce’s Ulysses, which has much of the vulgarity and nothing of the heroic).

Mythological religion, he rightly says, is “unquestionably the first form that religion in general has taken, and has been for a long time the universal religion of mankind." It is also the only "*religion that has been engendered naturally*," that is, regardless of reason and philosophy, it is "born from an actual relationship between the human essence and God." As I will not cease to emphasise later, Hinduism and Buddhism have continued to be a natural process.

I will leave to one side his assessment of the supposed "revealed" religion, which is nothing more than the dogmatic acceptance of a belief that Schelling adopted in his old age and that unfortunately comes to contradict the highest expressions of his idealist philosophy and art, in which there was no place for a personal God or for miracles or other magical solutions, nor for theologies charged with justifying them. From reading Part 1 of his *Lectures on the Philosophy of Mythology*, it can be seen that it was written at two very different moments in his thinking. We have dispensed with Part 2 because it is already very far from his original intuitions.

Regarding the two stages to which Schelling refers, he sees as "an alteration of consciousness" that passes from an "absolute one" God to a "relative one that subsists". It would be a step from primitive monotheism to polytheism, but since they are not clearly determined in mythical consciousness, he prefers not to clearly separate them; I think he is confused by his indefatigable reason. For example, he calls conscious monotheism "proper monotheism", that is, that determined by a belief justified by reason, since, as experience dictates, *the presence of divinity is always transcendent to reason*. The various forms of divinity, charged with feelings that are also alien to reason, are the product of *latent intuitions of the Transcendent*. For the rest, the subsequent or "conscious" or "revealed" monotheism, which is only "conscious" as a rational acceptance of a dogma, has not solved the problem of religion or of human consciousness.

Whoever *believes* in monotheism and does not have a direct experience of it, practically all, except for very rare exceptions, are not in a position to *believe* that their knowledge is greater or better than those who *believe* in polytheism, who may have greater religious experience, that is, greater actual knowledge than that. We are not even speaking of those who want to impose their *belief* on others; which, in addition to ignorance, is a brutality that, despite being a widely used resource, has nothing to do with religion.

The two stages that we are interested in highlighting, as we will see below, have nothing to do with polytheism and monotheism, which have coexisted to this day, with greater or lesser doses of one or the other under different names, but rather with those determined by the individual perspective and the universal perspective; in them lies the core of the problem.

Epistemological Clarification

To some extent we could equate the *intellectual intuition* to which Schelling appeals with the concept of Prajna used by Buddhism that I have translated as *transcendental intuition*, but the difference between the two indicates the abyss that separates the West from the East that has determined the history of his ideas and beliefs, and that, for the same reason, must be understood to the extent that it is possible for understanding, and that, to my knowledge, has not been indicated with the clarity that this great matter requires. And it is thus that the westerner, although he has had an intuition of the Transcendent, does not ultimately abandon his individual perspective. That is to say that although he intuits a Unity that leads him to transcend the subject-object duality, he does not manage to identify his spirit with it, he does not succeed in transforming his consciousness, as if failing to notice that he has discovered an *other* consciousness, so that it is as if the subject has discovered a Unity that transcends him; so the duality continues; he has not undergone an *ontological transformation*. Whereas the Hindu, and the Buddhist, no doubt due to a more acute insight, does not hesitate to accept it as his *true consciousness*, in which he tries to remain because he recognises it as the true home of his spirit; his doctrine, established by great visionaries, reminds him of it.

Probably my philosophy is speaking for the first time in the West of this *other consciousness*, which in my conception would be universal Consciousness; and I emphatically support the vital need for the absolute integration of the spirit with this Consciousness and thus with the *Universus*; All my philosophy, with all its branches, metaphysics, aesthetics, morality, the philosophy of history, and like this very epistemology, point to this integration. The difference, as I have not ceased to insist, is established by the experience of the spirit: intuition is not enough because it is still established by the subject, for this reason I have preferred the concept of *vital experiences*, in which not only the intellect intervenes, but also the sentiments and all the faculties in unison and integrated. Intuitions, without denying their importance whatsoever, can then show us the Transcendent, but because they are products of the intellect, in its highest function, to be precise, they do not leave us more than a *sample* of the Transcendent.

I would like to clarify that at no time have I tried to speak on behalf of Hinduism or Buddhism, nor from a personal experience, but from the *essential perspective* that derives from universal Consciousness, a product of the vital experience of the spirit.

Conclusion

In my view, mythical man does not use transcendental intuitions, his consciousness is inserted in the Transcendent, and this is what radically differentiates him from contemporary man, who does need them to overcome his individual consciousness. But of course, just as in the latter there are countless degrees of intelligence and perception, perhaps as many as human beings, in the former, mythical man, the same thing occurs, although from the Transcendent, the difference is in the position of the spirit, in its perspective. In both cases it is an incipient perception; just as I have spoken of an incipient reason in contemporary man, we can speak of an incipient perception of his world in mythical man.

The human being in general is in an intermediate state of transition, in the process of evolution, but this evolution, understand this well, has not been linear and ascending (see *The Spirit in History*), rather there have been ups and downs, periods of apogee and perigee. And here is the key to the matter that we have been dealing with: I have called them perigee because *the spirit moves away from the light of Consciousness*, and to the extent that it does so, it is *alienated* from itself and from the world that surrounds it, from its *universal circumstances*. And this is what differentiates contemporary man from mythical man, he was not alienated but integrated into the *Universus*, he needed to evolve, assuredly, but it was not necessary for him to sacrifice his initial, unitive perspective. Certainly, he had not reached the Essence, the Unity, the Absolute, but he made use of his light, with it he illuminated his reality, from it he understood it and towards it he was heading. But in a moment, which may have been prolonged in his evolution, he discovers his reason, which leads him to take another path that progressively distances him from his initial consciousness, from his universal vision. This occurs because reason conforms to and depends on the forms of time, space, and causation, as Kant acutely discovers. And, here is the drawback, these forms have the self as a reference, which implies a change of perspective, the adoption of *individual consciousness*, which necessarily leads him to alienate himself from his original consciousness, and thus to move away from his mythical consciousness. And he has done so to such an extent that, although he preserves it and applies it in his beliefs, emotions and actions, he does so unconsciously; he no longer knows or understands it. Hence, he now needs intuitions (reminiscences, Plato would say), and before them a rigorous asceticism and various spiritual techniques, to recover and *reintegrate into his Origin*.

If his reintegration into his Origin is his destiny (as I maintain in *Origin and Destiny of Man*), the importance and necessity of recovering mythical consciousness will be understood. That is to say that idealist philosophies, universal idealism, and my philosophy in particular, try to return to later surpass said mythical consciousness to rediscover the original and universal Unity. And for this they use the disciplines of the spirit, morality, art and, certainly, religion, which are the paths of transcendental knowledge essential to the philosopher for the realisation of his unconditional Freedom and Happiness.

The best expression of mythical consciousness is the unitive consciousness on which I have insisted in all my work, but this is not only mythical consciousness because it can incorporate the other faculties without falling into the individual perspective, such is the case of idealist philosophies. This I can assure you with certainty because all my thinking, all my feelings, all my mind works in this way. The state of absolute contemplation is nothing but the crystallisation and fullness of the mythical consciousness.

When speaking of mythical consciousness, I have said that morality, art and religion are nourished by it, but it is worth clarifying that there may be mistakes, deviations and atrophies in these disciplines, although not always intentional. Some examples that I have already pointed out elsewhere will suffice here: The Kantian morality of duty is irreproachable from the individual perspective (to which reason has unconsciously induced it) because it tends towards good conduct, towards the good, but if the spirit were not alienated from the Good itself, one would have, as Aristotle says, "the joy of doing good" and not the effort and even the pain that the obligation to apply it implies. From Aristotle's position we see unitive consciousness in action, in which the good emanates spontaneously, while from Kant's individual consciousness we observe an alienation with respect to the Good, hence the necessity, and even the imposition of a moral imperative, and the forced leap that the spirit needs to establish it. (See *The Roots of Morality*) In the case of modern art we find a genuine search for other forms of artistic expression, but we observe a notable individualisation, to the dehumanisation, de-universalisation and detriment of the artist. (See *The Roots of Art*) Art separated from mythical consciousness is an abstraction to which reason has led, thus moving it away from its Roots where the Creative itself is found. It should be recognised that poets, in their particular way, have been able to preserve their mythical heritage in the aforementioned sense of universal integration. Moreover, we can say that it is mythical consciousness that makes them poets.

In addition, in religion we certainly find numerous deviations, the most serious of them generated, precisely, by the adoption of the individual perspective. All mystics start out from an essential perspective or universal vision; it is their followers who, from an individual perspective, distort the original message. In the case of Christianity, what is expressed is evidenced, for this reason I have separated the doctrine of Jesus from the Pauline one, which is the one adopted by the Church to establish the doctrine they call "Christian"; hence the deviations and excesses of the Church, which have nothing to do with the gospels. The unconscious adoption of the individual perspective has led to the incorporation of the supposed God in conventional time, which is an aberration for the mythical or unitive consciousness that is inspired by timeless time, particularly in reference to its deities. This incorporation, which is considered to be an achievement of Christianity, is an error of perspective that distances the believer from his religious consciousness, intimately linked to mythical consciousness.

The mythical man has a unitive perspective in the sense that he takes primordial Unity for granted, he is immersed and integrated into the Whole from which he observes the multiple world. We assume that in most cases he has not reached an *essential perspective*, that is, the consciousness of absolute Unity, he has not yet evolved towards it, his knowledge is incipient, just as I have spoken of the *incipient reason* of contemporary man. The first cases in which we have records of having reached absolute Unity occur in history only around the 6th century B.C. Incipient reason does not mean that more reason is needed, but rather the harmonious incorporation of all the faculties; the plenitude of the human being depends on it. Incipient reason is naked reason, that is to say, without the necessary complement of the unitive faculties. The current triumph of naked reason implies the failure of morality and religion and explains the triumph of the functional over the aesthetic.

I believe that all the reason that the speculative faculties can give concerning myth and even more so concerning mythical consciousness will be fruitless since it is dealing with a reality that is fundamentally *alien* to said faculties. The myth in what is decisive is the product of the unitive faculties that dispense with the forms of time and space and that establish a direct relationship between consciousness and the object, which is not seen as such and which it incorporates into a spiritual and corporeal whole, into a Universe; hence the strength or power of the myth, since it is linked to the Transcendent, hence its sacred or religious character.

The link between myths and dreams has not ceased to be observed, but we know that not all dreams have a mythical value. There are certain types of dreams that are revealing. Jung speaks of "numinous dreams" that I prefer to call *unitive* because of their integrating function. There is, indeed, a relationship between myths and the *internal* or subconscious *plane*. This plane also dispenses with the forms of time and space, but said dreams only happen when there has been a transcendental intuition, generally unconscious to the *external plane* (the so-called conscious), which has been kept (or repressed, Freud would say) on the internal plane that will be expressed in *unitive dreams*. But not all myths are the product of this plane; rather, they are always the product of the unitive consciousness that is related to the different planes of understanding, which can add their way of knowing to the original intuition.

In the myth we find the principle of causality, absent in dreams, which tries to explain events, but the myth always resorts to a *spiritual cause*, a resource that from the speculative faculties is shown as magical, but these faculties in their turn do not notice their alienation with respect to the spiritual, which is the product of the materialisation of the mind, of a disconnection with universal Consciousness. And this is much more serious than what is *thought*, since said Consciousness is the very nucleus of our consciousness, that is to say that the alienation is with oneself; this is what mythical thinking wants to avoid at all costs. For certain, this often leads to establishing relationships that seem too magical, but, let us not forget, always connected with the spiritual universe that underlies the world and all events. For this reason we must never rule out its validity, but rather learn from that projection and connection, since our integration with our own consciousness and with the Consciousness of the world depends on it.

In addition, causal relationships of a spiritual order are not always so magical, we find a happy medium between the phenomenal and the noumenal, as can be expected, among the Greeks, particularly in their tragedy, an unequalled expression of that *universal equilibrium*, in which the rationally evolved mind reaches its plenitude, without forgetting and without alienating itself from its spiritual and original side.

Even at the risk of repeating myself, I will say it one more time: The human being, like the rest of living beings, lived *within* the Unity of Everything, in this I agree with Schelling, but I would add: In his pre-rational state his consciousness was an extension of universal Consciousness, even if he did not think so, it simply was so. At the moment, which may have been prolonged in time to extend throughout the species, when he becomes aware of his self and of time and space, he separates and begins his *process of individuation, exteriorisation and alienation* with respect to universal Consciousness. It does not occur to Schelling to think that alienation occurs with the irruption of reason, and, although in other writings he mentions a universal Soul, he never mentions a universal Consciousness. Mythical man, more than intuited, participated in this Consciousness, hence his attempts to maintain a relationship with it (as Schelling noticed), perceived as gods or as a personal God, through rituals and mythical explanations by religious leaders, shamans or priests, who established more or less elaborate religious customs.

All of this shows that the human being has been losing contact with original or universal Consciousness to the benefit of his individual consciousness, which became completely disconnected recently, only two centuries ago, with the decidedly disastrous doctrine of materialism. This disconnection implies the total alienation of the spirit with respect to the Spirit, of consciousness with respect to universal Consciousness. Actually, it is not the *fault* of this doctrine, since it is itself a consequence of the aforementioned progressive process of alienation of our species; materialism would be the height of our alienation. The matter is of the utmost gravity because it implies the alienation from *The Roots of Morality*, from *The Roots of Art* (see these works), and from the roots of our humanity, which explains the dehumanisation of contemporary man.

I will try to make myself understood: man is a rational being, but also and above all a spiritual being, I mean to say moral, aesthetic and religious; without these pillars all rational constructions must crumble. This process of rationalisation and alienation was not necessary or inevitable; *our species could have followed the natural process of the extension of universal Consciousness*. Remember that Schelling spoke of the *natural* consciousness and religion in mythical man. But the human being, thinking more and more of himself to the detriment of the environment in which he lives, and of other species, and even of his neighbour, has followed this process to the point that individuals have remained locked in their individuality. This responds in unison to the process of the exteriorisation of his mind that has progressively been identifying with his external faculties to the detriment of his internal or unitive faculties; hence his alienation.

It will be understood that to make it clear to reason we have distinguished a rational consciousness from a mythical consciousness, but what we cannot do is divide the mind, since, as Schelling had already warned and Eliade confirms, *mythical consciousness is an inseparable part of our mind*. For this reason it would be more appropriate to speak of a mythical faculty, just as we speak of the imagination, with which it is closely related, of emotions, etc. In reality it is reason, particularly its external side, discernment, that divides, separates and excludes, and it is to the extent that we identify with these external faculties that we exclude the internal ones, among which we must include the mythical. And it would be wrong more than arbitrary to separate and unlink this from the religious, artistic or moral faculties or consciousnesses. What we can call consciousness or mystical faculty is only an elevated condition of mythical consciousness. And since it is the one that moves our spirit towards the Transcendent and provides us with the experience and knowledge of it, the function of mythical consciousness will be understood.

But here, in everyday life, mythical consciousness, because it tends precisely towards the Transcendent, has the virtue of taking us out of the burden of the day-to-day, of the domestic jungle, of the malaise of culture, Freud would say, of the boredom of the repetitive, in short, from the elementary stage of survival. All of us, even the most elementary, feel that this is not enough, that there is something more, and mythical consciousness reminds us of it. Let us think of the tales collected by Grimm and Anderson from folklore, which until recently fed children's spirits, transporting them to an ideal, magical world, if you will, but vitally more real than the reality presented to us by naive realism that, despite being the generator of tedium and insipid life, is the very one that judges mythical consciousness to be naive.

Note the parallel between the parable and the folktale, that is, between the mystical language, used by the Buddha, Jesus and many others, and the mythical: Both avoid naive realism by means of a circumlocution that leads us to an ideal reality, that is, more essential. Both refer us to a time which is... timeless and, therefore, transcendent (to reason). "Once upon a time", begins the story. Is not this principle perhaps the "*illo tempore*", the mythical time that Eliade speaks of? And in this way they transport us to that world of Ideas from which they extract the moral message, which is applicable to numerous similar cases, because it is exemplary, because it has *something* universal.

What mythical man does not want to lose sight of is the Cosmos, the universal Order, he wants to remain integrated into it. God, in all doctrines, represents this Order. One of the commandments prohibits swearing in the name of God in vain, because breaking it implies a dismantling of the universal Order, swearing on the Bible, a custom that is still practiced even though it has lost its validity, has the same meaning.

I think that if we apply the "personification principle" that Schelling spoke of to our vision, we would clarify this matter quite a bit. "What are personified are the moral principles or natural phenomena." "The gods would be moral beings each endowed with a moral property." For now, I consider that separating monotheism from polytheism, or religion from mythology, is an arbitrariness that hinders the understanding of the subject. It is arbitrary to separate the mythical from the religious consciousness. Jesus himself is a personification of Divinity, as well as the hundreds of virgins, each of whom expresses "a moral property"; and it would be never-ending to bring to the saints the objects of devotion of certain communities or people, and to the host of angels that inhabit the heavens. Within the context of my philosophy, said "moral properties" would be the *primary manifestations of universal Consciousness*, which would be very clearly expressed in the Greco-Roman religion, where the virtues themselves are gods or are attributes of the gods: Zeus represents Order, Good and Justice, Apollo Beauty and the light of Intelligence, Athena, wisdom, Aphrodite Love, Demeter the vital force that makes Life possible. It is enough to reflect a little on this to realise what we have lost in the West when we stop *believing* in these emanations and when we stop perceiving them.

But this must be clear: when the virtues become attributes of a god it is because they are already personified, that is to say that there has been an inversion, since they precede them, they are the *primary manifestations of the Essence of the Universus*. This is what the spirit perceives when it transcends its individual perspective; it is this that personifies the virtues. The Greek genius, we must insist on this, before personifying them, managed to perceive Justice (with a capital letter) itself, Wisdom itself, Good itself, Beauty itself, but of course, this is an *attribute* of geniuses. Now, understand well, my philosophy at no time condemns or disqualifies the invention of a personal god or of the gods, since they are explanations of the virtues; what is serious is to lose contact with them; it is this disconnection that I call alienation because it leads to dis-Order and Chaos.

The human being intuits, then, this and other manifestations of what he understands by divinity. But, except for very rare exceptions, that is as far as understanding goes, since the Absolute transcends these manifestations. Unfortunately, the Essence of the world is beyond normal human understanding, what he vaguely intuits are its manifestations, only sensitive and spiritualised minds access it, normal people only intuit unconsciously and this leads them to accept an established religion, to believe in it. Hence the difference between religions, which would not exist if people had access to the Absolute.

It will then be understood that this Absolute is the beginning and end of all knowledge. What is more, much more, whoever realises this knowledge has direct and immediate experience of the *primary manifestations* of said Essence of the mind and of the world, which are the spiritual motors of individual minds and of the universe. This explains, if an explanation is required, why reason, which is a derivative of the mind, tends to find unity and reaches relative knowledge when it finds partial unities. Spiritualism in general and humanism in particular are an extension of the mythical mentality. The importance that this represents at this moment, in which the materialistic mentality triumphs, will be understood.

In one of his myths, that of Er the Armenian, Plato makes one of the Fates, the virgin Lachesis, say: "Ephemeral souls, a new cycle" (another reincarnation) "will begin for you as mortals" (which implies the possibility of becoming in another form). "Virtue has no master, each one will participate before it according to what honours or despises it. Each one is responsible for his choice because God is not to blame." (*Rep. 617e*) Cassirer, who has not failed to notice this passage, adds: "in this grandiose vision, in which the capacity for mythical creation that characterises the Greeks and especially Plato is once again summarised, we continue in the field of myth. But, as to the idea of the guilt of mythological fatality, here the basic Socratic idea of ethical self-responsibility is opposed." (*Theory of the forms of myth*) Cassirer, although condescending, wants to see the triumph of reason over mythical consciousness, and this is a dangerous mistake. The value of the Greek mentality, this is what I am interested in highlighting, must be found in the *balanced convergence of both perspectives*.

In traditional mythology from Homer onwards we find, it is true, that the gods are blamed for the faults of humans, but also that they recognise their mistakes, as in the case of Helen, who sometimes blames Aphrodite, and other times admits her lust. Homer himself, purposely, puts this reproach in the mouth of Zeus: "It is to see how men incessantly blame the gods for all their evils, being that they themselves are the ones who bring for their follies their excess of sorrows." (*Odyssey, 32*) Nietzsche, much more perceptive of mythical consciousness, and in defence of it, warns of the danger of Socratic rationalism; which also affects Cassirer. (See *The Greek Tragedy* in *The Roots of Art*) If the mythical mentality is observed *from within*, it will be seen that the duality of personal consciousness and divinity is not such as it is understood by a current dualistic consciousness, to be precise, in mythical consciousness the gods are in the mind, that is why the subject feels that he is being manipulated, and the mind is in the gods.

In Plato we see how the two mentalities converge, the mythical and the rational, we even notice the clash of these two tendencies, because although he accepts the mythical way of thinking, he wants to adjust it to the rational way; hence the disagreement that he has with the poets who accept the traditional myth that is not always exemplary for the mentality that he wants to impose. In my opinion, due to his lack of tolerance, he falls into excess, into an unnecessary puritanism. But what is decisive for mythical man is this inseparable relationship, the gods are not only in consciousness but they are consciousness. Hence, it never occurs to him to think, in the manner of Fauerbach, that they are a creation of man, he perceives, rather than believes, that the mind is a creation of the gods.

We see in Greek thought that the balance leans towards the *individual perspective* but without abandoning divine intervention, that is, the *unitive perspective*. This is another example of the Greek equilibrium, this time applied to the relationship between the heavenly and the earthly on the moral plane. I am interested in underlining this balance that is brought to perfection in Greek tragedy, because it is here where the two mentalities, the two perspectives, happily converge. Although impregnated with the Greek spirit, we find Aristotle already immersed in his *individual perspective* from which he tries to *induce* the Prime Mover, while his teacher *deduced* earthly reality from his Ideas. And since then philosophy has been divided between Platonists or idealists and Aristotelians, whose difference is explained by the two aforementioned perspectives. The idealists, to whom I cannot help but belong, have preserved the essential and characteristic of the mythical mentality: they start from Unity, from the One, the Aristotelians tend towards unity but are already immersed in becoming, surrounded by plurality, enclosed in their individuality; the former come back, the latter go.

But this must be established: The poetic or artistic imagination has, before exercising its imagination, an intuition of something even more real, important and necessary than matter, the power of the Spirit is decisive in its thought and feeling. That the Spirit is represented to it as multiple, in the form of different gods, comes later and is of much less importance. The issue of polytheism and monotheism, about which after 1700 years of indoctrination Westerners never cease to worry, is not fundamental, but rather the a priori existence of spiritual reality found in the world and in the human psyche itself.

We have seen that for Schelling, mythology "is a product of consciousness that incessantly seeks to find itself, to reconstitute itself." This would assimilate him to the *unitive man* to whom I have referred in all my work, since his perspective is similar, so we could say that both observe from a unitive consciousness. Mythical man possesses an incipient universal consciousness, while contemporary man is alienated from the Cosmos, for which reason he consciously lacks said mind that lies latent in him. Hence, the mythical man was *better positioned* to understand the unity of the Whole. In other words, there has been an involution regarding the knowledge of the Transcendent, which is his destiny. So that if contemporary man intends to achieve this knowledge, he must return to the mythical or original consciousness, understood as integrating consciousness, to *realise his unitive consciousness*, which houses the moral, aesthetic and religious consciousness from which he is progressively moving away.

We have to overcome our individual consciousness in all cases. Apart from the usual obstacles presented by the self, with which we "naturally" identify, dragging with it the deep-rooted passions that dominate us like puppets, there is the identification with reason. That man is a rational being is entirely relative, the passions themselves show it. But we have to understand once and for all that *reason is an amoral faculty*, that is, morally neutral, that it can be at the service of the saint as well as of the criminal, and in general it is, precisely, the tool that we use to justify our passions. So that between the self and reason a vicious circle is generated from which it is not easy to get out; especially if we do not want to leave, which is what happens to the vast majority. For Darwin, who knew very well the mentality of animals, including that of the human being, what radically differentiated man from the rest was his moral capacity. That is to say that for him *the human being is a moral rather than a rational being*. This brings our condition closer to the *unitive faculties*. And I maintain that, precisely, what defines our species, by its essence rather than its behaviour, are its spiritual, unitive capacities; although not in contrast to the other species that participate, within their capacities, of the same essence. Then, it is towards this essence that our thoughts and action should be directed. And for this, I will repeat, reason must be at the service of said unitive faculties.

It is I have said that in Greece a mental equilibrium had been achieved in which all the faculties participated at their best. India has known how to maintain this equilibrium; my philosophy seeks to integrate these cultures with the purpose of redirecting our species towards its Destiny that is found in its Origin. Because, understand this: the destiny of man is not the one that he discovers with his technology, his inventions come afterwards, the priority is that he knows himself, only in this way can he choose his Destiny.

The Hindu tradition, for its part, irrefutably proves that evolution, understood as the replacement of mythical consciousness by reason, was unnecessary, since they still coexist today in the most natural way, as they did in Greece where reason, we need not say it, reached its excellence.

In view of all this, summarised here, my proposal is a *Return to the Sources*, to *The Roots of Morality*, to *The Roots of Art*, which implies a *Search for Consciousness* to recover our true consciousness, our universality and reach thus our plenitude.

Part 2

Greece and India

Greece

The Myth of Ariel

Forty years ago, while writing my first book, in a high and snowy range in these mountains where I live, I used to visit a place with a very special aesthetic, character and energy. It is a prominent rock that drops sharply into a vast ravine, at the bottom of which a river runs into the sea in the distance. When the moon passes over on its path, a silvery and uniform horizon is drawn between the dark mountains, imparting a strange sensation of unreality, as if in a dream. But when it is the sun that gilds the scene, the reflection of the sea is such that it forces the viewer's eyes to squint as if reality were too much, and then the gaze moves upwards where it contemplates the brilliance of the snowy peaks that cover the opposite horizon.

On this rock there is a flat surface surrounded by some rocks that a Titan, it would seem, has successfully arranged in an arch. One cannot imagine a better place to erect a temple to Apollo. And today I have come with the intention of relating a story, in which this god is the protagonist, who Ariel had made as my "inner voice" and adviser. The dialogue went something like this:

Jozan - I think, Ariel, we have reached this impasse, when the human being has no values on which he can sustain himself nor any ideals that motivate him, when life itself is considered to be absurd. Everything seems to indicate that he is lost or that he has gone astray at some point. I would like to know the reason for his being lost and recognise that moment to find its meaning in history.

Ariel - Jozan, you can find many reasons and show man his entire history, if he is not ready to change, he will find his reasons not to do so.

There are, fundamentally, two kinds of reasons, those that try to base themselves on truths and those that try to justify behaviour; the former are rare, the latter are common. Since the philosopher always resorts to the former, he is invariably destined to collide with the latter, the pseudo-reasons espoused by the majority.

The human being is a curious animal and just as he has a great facility for discovering the errors of all around him, he finds it difficult to see them within himself; he is able to travel throughout history, even to the remotest of civilisations, to judge the customs of the most distant peoples, before looking at himself.

In history you will find not one but various deviations, just as one would amongst peoples and individuals during their short existence. There are too many twists and turns to follow and still remain focused. I think your task can go a long way towards clarifying man's situation, but this task is more yours than mine. I live in a different age, Jozan, you know, where there are non sequential kinds of moments, in a reality in which events only have meaning if they are exemplary, to the point of being timeless; my vision is thus not historical. This does not mean that I ignore the present situation, but that I know it in another way.

Listen now and try to see how I analyse the loss of man.

In the beginning, man lived in harmony with the environment and with the gods that he respected and venerated. At that time, he rightly paid homage to Gaia, the Earth, the Universal Mother, the oldest deity (preceded only, perhaps, by Chaos). He did so not only because he felt a filial relation to her but also because he owed her the fruits of the earth and all the life that surrounded him; he thus worshipped Life. Temples were raised in her honour in various places, such as Athens, Sparta and Dodona, and in a place that would later be called Delphi.

The origin of the discord with the gods and man's misfortune seems to have begun with the brothers Prometheus, "he who predicts" (calculates), and Epimetheus, "he who sees later" (remembers), children of the Titans (who distinguished themselves more for their brawn than their brains), who had rebelled against the gods who had decimated and punished them. Even though the history of Epimetheus is highly significant, I will not dwell on it at present.

Although Prometheus was not at all wise, he was not as foolish as his compatriots and had his cunning, and when he had the opportunity of taking revenge on the gods, against whom he surely held a grudge since they had prevented his race from being the owners of the Universe, he took it. From the forge of the artful Hephaestus he stole the fire that he would give, without the consent of the gods, to men, whom did not tarry in using this fire to manufacture tools and equipment for their own benefit, regardless of the will of the gods and in detriment to the environment. In this way they began to impose an order alien to the Order established by the gods and to disassociate themselves from them. Gaia was thus slowly forgotten and her holy places neglected. For all these reasons Prometheus was condemned by Zeus and his huge body was chained and laid out in the open to serve as an example to men.

Jozan - But why, Ariel, were they opposed to man's progress?

Ariel - With that misstep you just took, the derailment begins; you have just become the protagonist of the moment that you were looking for.

Jozan - How so? Explain to me, Ariel, what you mean.

Ariel - No matter how much I explain, you will not understand if you do not change your perspective. Try to put yourself in the perspective of the gods, try, like them who are immortal, to place yourself in a timeless and absolute reality. Try to understand the matter here and now, not there and then.

Jozan - What you ask of me is not easy, but I will try. Please continue with the story.

Ariel - The gods do not oppose men except when the latter oppose them. Prometheus was punished for having given men a partial light that gives them only a relatively immediate vision of reality, which leads them to lose their universal dimension. That is why Zeus, who was then concerned about the destiny of humanity, convoked a meeting of the gods of Olympus and told them: "Man has taken Prometheus' torch with strength and assurance, and in his greed and selfishness he wants to see only by its light, without realising that he is condemned to immobilise everything he looks at, because this is the condition of that light. He will see the change with his senses and, wanting to know the reason for the change, he will shatter the objects into smaller and smaller pieces that will in turn become immobilised. It is a vicious circle in which he will get entangled as knowledge acquired in this way advances. In short, he has already acquired this gift, a lot of good and a lot of evil can be done with it, everything depends on whether he uses it for selfish ends and pits it against us, the gods, creating in this way disharmony in the Order that we have established, necessary to his own survival, which will lead to his ruin, or if he uses his knowledge to contribute to the general Order. That light given by Prometheus is not enough and will tend to settle them in their own individuality. It is my all-encompassing and all-penetrating light that they need now. You, Apollo, can grant it to them so that they live in harmony with the environment and with the gods."

To which Apollo responded: "As you know, all powerful Zeus, I revolve around men in my chariot but I fear that my light is too brilliant for them, who prefer the dim lights made for the darkness of Hades. Remember, father, when Semele, a mortal, mother of Dionysus who is present here wanted you to show yourself in your plenitude and divine form and you acceded to it, but she perished, burnt by your irradiation. Men can only contemplate us when they understand their divine nature and become immortal like us." "But, divine Apollo, this is not easy", interrupted Hermes, "believing themselves to be mortal they are constantly prey to fear, and seek temporary pleasures that do not satisfy them, so they go from one distracting desire to another. The fire that Prometheus has given them also contributes to this as it provides them with incessant benefits, which is why they prefer it, without a doubt, to that light which you want to grant them."

"It is true what you have demonstrated -Zeus concluded- but it is them, men, you have to make understand these truths. Find the means to do so."

Without delay Apollo set to work. In the form of a dolphin he leaped on the deck of a ship on the high seas, and forced the sailors to divert their course to a new destination. When they reached port he resumed his divine form, and once the mood of the sailors had calmed down as they had been tense until then, he asked them to accompany him to a nearby grotto where an abandoned temple lay. Once there, he told them: "Here, one knew how to pray to Gaia, our mother of the gods and the mortals, long forgotten due to man's ingratitude. Once it is reconstructed, this will be my sanctuary and since you have known me as a dolphin, you will call it Delphi."

He then explained to them the gods' decision and began to initiate them in the mysteries of religion so that they could fulfil his purpose of imparting true knowledge. It was then that he carved with his own hand, at the entrance of the sanctuary: "Know thyself".

The next day when the sun had lit up the face of the god, he heard one of his sailors call out to him. He came running and, out of breath, cried: "Apollo, Lord of God! What have you entrusted to us? There is a serpent, a great python in the temple ruins".

"Ah! I should have foreseen it. She is a loyal friend of Gaia. She certainly has been guarding the temple ever since it was abandoned. I am afraid that she will oppose my will to make of this place the beacon of an exemplary civilisation. I will have to sacrifice her. But she has loyally fulfilled her mission and we will perform the sacrifice with all honours. Later, you will construct a stadium here to commemorate this noble creature with games, and in the place where she was you will place an *omphalos*, for this will be the centre of the world for centuries. They will come here from all Hellas and from beyond the Hellespont to consult me about what will, unfortunately, always remain a mystery to mortals: their destiny.

That night, after the sacrifice, while Apollo was seated on some great rocks contemplating how the moon poured its magic over the sea, the pilot of the ship approached him and asked: "Tell me, divine Apollo, why have you chosen us for this task since we are not enlightened and we have no other merit apart from having respect for the gods?"

"Make no mistake, noble pilot, you are better prepared for this task than those who spend their lives studying the lives of the gods and comparing them; you have experience. You have seen the angry Poseidon foaming at the mouth many times, you have bathed in it, you have been saturated with divine saliva; you have seen the terrible thunderbolt of the olympian Zeus shine through the darkness and illuminate your pale faces; you have known how to appreciate and venerate the birth of the warm Aurora; you have heard the harmonious murmur of the sirens amongst the rocks in the mist. The spirit grows and is nourished on these experiences. I have also chosen you because your profession has taught you to break with the habits of domestic life that lull men to sleep, while you have acquired the habit of seeing in the dark and searching for faint lights on the horizon.

“Fair Apollo, I can understand the usefulness of those experiences, but not this manner of seeing in the dark.”

“Well, listen attentively to what I will say to you as if you were on your ship trying to hear the reefs in the night.”

“I understand, I am all ears.”

“You will have observed that when you move around in the dark with a lamp you can only clearly see what falls within its beam of light, while the rest remains in an uncertain reality, objects are as if they did not exist until you reach them with your light, it is then that you know them and you can thus establish a relation with other known objects; in this way you gradually discover the circumstance you are in. Now, if the flame that illuminates you goes out, you are suddenly made immobile, without daring to take another step, and you will try to light it again, but if you do not, after a few minutes your eyes begin to get used to the darkness until you begin to see relatively clearly even beyond what the light of your lamp had reached, that is, you begin to have a clearer idea of the whole, although you lose precision in the details. Similarly, on the wide sea you prefer, during the night, not to have a light on board when you want to decipher the profile of the coast to have a general idea of your circumstances, it is then that you resort to the faint light of the Universe that lights up everything equally, but you light a lamp when you need to find some particular object on the ship.”

“Exactly, this is what I do.”

“Now, imagine that the human being lived in a World in which there was only night, it would be very useful for him to have lamps, am I right?

“Very useful, undoubtedly.”

“But it would be very difficult for him to know the reality in which he lives in that way. However many lamps he might have, it would be better if he were to develop the faculty of being able to see at night like sailors can, or like nocturnal animals such as owls or felines.”

“Much better, as you say.”

"Well then, man lives in darkness and, although he might illuminate certain particulars with the lamp of his discernment, between which he has established certain relations and clarified his circumstances quite a bit, he fundamentally does not know the world in which he lives, because he does not see with the light of Zeus that illuminates all things equally and penetrates everything. It is to this light that the eyes of his soul have to become accustomed, but he does not do so because he does not know when to blow out the lamp with which he is accustomed to looking at reality.

He who manages to get used to the light of the gods and can free himself from his individual light, that is, from all selfishness, will see the birth of Aurora in the middle of the night in which he lives. Then I myself will launch my arrow of light that will hit the top of his head, in the very centre, filling him with light. All at once I will injure the hydra of selfishness, freeing him of this great evil; even if it depends on his virtue if the hydra it is only wounded or dies. In any case he will experience a radical change, both in him and all that surrounds him: what he previously took for reality will now seem a shadow; he will see his old values, fears and desires become effortlessly detached from him like dry leaves that are carried away by the wind, and he will see them leave him with an indescribable joy; he will feel that his own body is like a garment, like a mask, in which he will hear himself breathing strangely; he will clearly see his own misdirection and his spirit will find peace by returning to its element and dispersing in him without encountering obstacles or limits."

Greek Spirit and Religion

So much has been written on the classical Greeks that to some it may seem superfluous to add more. I do not believe it to be so. We have derived so much benefit from the little that has reached us from this culture that it is logical to assume that this people had found an inexhaustible fount of treasure. It is not a matter of being able to indefinitely use the material that we have, but of again *finding the same source of inspiration*.

The current spiritual and cultural crisis is proof that we have lost this fount. My intention is to contribute to its rediscovery. I believe we are most at sea in the religious and moral field, therefore, it is in it that I will make my foray into this abbreviated version of the Hellenic spirit. In various earlier works I have written on Greek philosophy and on art in *The Roots of Art*, and on Greek ethics the reader can find more details in *The Roots of Morality*. However, since it would be pointless to write about the Greeks without elaborating on their virtues, I will reiterate this theme.

In order to understand the Greek spirit and all that it created, the first thing that modern man must do is to recognise that he is face to face with something superior. Contemporary man does not do this, instead he looks at it from above like a tourist and this makes the Greek phenomenon incomprehensible. When judging and understanding geniuses: we can only approach them by accepting the humble condition befitting those in the presence of the superior. This should be clear: the *technological level in no way provides the level of consciousness*; in this the Greek has an edge over modern man.

For twenty five centuries sensitive, intelligent and cultured Western man has admired the manifestations of the Greek Spirit, but has seldom bothered to go beyond the surface, to the spirit that underlies this reality. When he has recognised it, it has not really been through a conscious search, but rather through closeness to that level of consciousness, as happened in the Renaissance. By highlighting this psychic-philosophical aspect, I hope to elucidate the Greek phenomenon in its most essential aspect. There is little to say about the other aspects given the number of erudite studies of the last 2500 years. After the awakening of that spirit, however, it has been slowly going to sleep, especially after industrialisation, and in the present age it has became totally alienated.

It is, therefore, very difficult for contemporary man to understand the Greek phenomenon because it is located on *another plane of consciousness*. This is evidently more elevated in the Greek but this is only one way of expressing it, because it is not only upwards that we must look, but also inwards; and this is the most difficult. We should try to understand that the highest states of the spirit are not found at the extremes, but in the balance between the extremes; this balance is the key to unravelling the Greek phenomenon. Our life is a transit between our Origin and our Destiny; knowledge of both the one and the other are necessary in order to recognise the path that we must cover.

The Greeks did not arrive at a religious doctrine, in the strict sense of one that was fully formed. Their brief creative existence, though prodigious like none other, did not allow it. By the time that Plato and Aristotle tried it was too late and already philosophy; the same would happen with Plotinus when Rome needed its doctrine; this irony of Destiny (*Até*), in addition to historical circumstances, has been one of the greatest misfortunes of the West.

To think that the Greek religion was naive, given their high level of creativity, is simply to show our own naivety and ignorance. It is not, therefore, due to a lack of height that the Greeks assimilated the Gods so much to humans, but on the contrary, their level of consciousness and vitality was so high, they felt and knew themselves to be so virtuous that they believed they could assimilate themselves to the Gods. The Gods did not obey a single abstract ideal of perfection, but a great set of ideals so real that the Greek had no doubt that he could put them into practice. The only thing that differentiated them was the immortality of some and the mortality of others.

Reason, as we have seen, is inept at understanding myths. The interpretation that it could give was entirely without concern for the tragedians, artists, religious men and even politicians like Pericles, those who made that exemplary century, and who performed the Greek miracle. The philosophers, as is evident from the study of the historical periods (see *The Spirit in History*), always arrive later, sometimes even when the period has ended, as in the case of the Greeks, to evaluate the results with their reason and draw their conclusions. The miracle had already passed, the original creative impulse, the spirit so to speak, was fading.

It is this air, still laden with myths, which Plato breathes; only a few vapours, the last vestiges of that spirit, would reach Aristotle. I do not mean to say that this genius had no spirit, but rather that this spirit is already placed in another perspective. In order to understand this we should take recourse to my theory of the planes of understanding, levels of consciousness and displacements of the spirit.

The path traversed from the *mythical mentality* of Homer to the rational path of Aristotle is not something that can be taken for granted by the latter. Man does not become a rational animal from then on because he has proclaimed it. If we all had the spirit in the same place as Aristotle we would have come to an agreement some time ago, but evidently the divergences continue.

The "mythical mentality" is the result of the placing of the spirit on a plane of understanding. This configures a place or centre of consciousness that determines a perspective. This place is definitive neither in the individual nor in history. *The Evolution of the Spirit* (see this text), does not happen in a necessary way, there are no epochs of the spirit that have been overcome forever, as Comte and Hegel believed. There is no mentality or an entire "mythic" mind, but only a sector of the mind that provides this perspective. Socrates is a contemporary of Sophocles, while one is rational, the other is "mythical" and this is not to mean irrational, far from it, he transcends reason; therefore he is a genius.

Elsewhere I have said that the *internal plane* (subconscious) has the capacity to produce illuminating syntheses of external phenomena or events. As I understand it, these syntheses would be a conjunction of the plane of intuitions, closely linked to the plane of direct perception, and the internal plane that would, in its own way, interpret what is intuited. In general terms, we could say that when the synthesis is static it would generate the symbol, when there is a sequence it would generate the myth. The instruments used would be those used by what we could call the *mythical mentality*.

In my conception, there has been no positive linear evolution, unless we were to talk of hundreds of thousands of years, but rather shifts of the centre of consciousness towards some centres in preference to others, which are relatively marginalised, forgotten or rejected. This is how mythical mentalities are equated with "primitive" ones, by a "modern" mentality, when the latter is nothing more than a change of perspective through the adoption of another centre of consciousness located, in this case, in the external faculties; the positivist mentality is a result of such placement. Rationalism had already shifted the centre of consciousness in that same direction; positivism takes it to an extreme, in which the internal faculties remain outside its horizon. In this way mythical mentality becomes unintelligible to "modern" man.

Since man does not know nor has known these mechanisms there has been no conscious choice of them in these shifts. If to this we add his ignorance of his *Origin and Destiny* (see this work), we will see why history seems to have been written by a madman.

What we could call mythical consciousness is one of the most beneficial gifts to humanity, for the inspiration received and the multiple arts expressed. This inspiration has the faculty of penetrating the most intimate corners of the soul, where, in contact with the Unity of the world, it imagines the relations of Nature with the universal Spirit.

The unifying and integrating virtue of the mythical consciousness, the closeness and contact with the Consciousness of the world has to be taken into account in the first place. Mythical man aspires, above all, to keep awake this consciousness that allows him to be integrated into Nature, hence his fear of disintegration and alienation from that universal articulation, his fear of God.

In my view, after having been alienated from his own divine Nature, the spirit tries to rediscover it, or rediscover himself, which is the same thing. This attempt is hindered to the extent of man's ignorance of the forces of his animal nature, which with its numerous desires, fears and general inclinations wants and needs to affirm itself for its own survival. This marks a struggle, with the instability this tug of war between its two natures implies for the spirit. The accounts of these struggles, of the search and the ways and means that the spirit chooses in its attempt to recover its original state, are the substance of the epics that the myths recount to us.

Thus animated, the creative powers are fully awakened; only an intelligent reason would be necessary, or, what is the same thing, a reason that is unitive, centred, for them to be made viable, which is what happened in the famous century of Pericles. These are the crucial conditions to produce a period of spiritual apogee.

It is true that in classical antiquity powers were attributed to the gods on which natural phenomena depended, and that modern man has his reasons for discarding this belief. It should be understood that at that time knowledge was not separated into different branches, which is only established with Aristotle; but we are already distant from the apogee. In this respect I understand the reasons of contemporary man, but from there to throwing everything into one basket and labelling it "mythological", giving it the label of having been "surpassed", is a long way. It is to imagine that one has understood all of that knowledge, when the opposite is true; proof of this is the almost complete lack of understanding of the inner reality of today's man. For how does contemporary man recognise his inner world, how does he represent it? Simply, in no conscious way. Since he lives solely on the external plane (discernment) and his internal representations are totally unconscious, he applies these unknowingly, indiscriminately and in a confused, not to say crazy manner, in the occasional fictional heroes, actors, popular singers, football players, etc. that constitute the sad contemporary mythology.

While man has not surpassed his reality of representations, it is necessary that he know the meaning of his internal (unconscious) representations in order to make conscious the reflection of these in his reality. In other words, since he does not know himself in any depth (of what is afar), he should not discard nor negate his internal and personal mythology, as by knowing the meaning of these representations he knows himself, being that some of them, especially morals, are the key to his development.

The irreligious man habitually makes the mistake of trying to understand religious man with his mind and perspective. In this way, if he is accustomed to explaining phenomena scientifically and seeing the useful side of things, as is usual today, he will tend to believe that the religious man of antiquity, the mythical man was on the same quest, only that he had not yet found the "true" answers; but it is not like that. He looked and saw reality differently, and his motivations and interests were very different from those of contemporary man. But unlike him, he saw the spiritual in all of Nature, and this was the most exciting and revealing thing that Nature could offer him (and I, a contemporary, believe that it is still the case). When he makes offerings to the Aurora, it is not, as contemporary man wants to naively believe, "so that the sun rises", but in order to participate in the celestial Order behind which he visualises the universal Spirit. In this way mythical man undoubtedly feels the plenitude of life much more intensely in comparison with contemporary man.

When he discovers a waterfall while walking through the forest, he is not attentive to the transformation of water into vapour, trying to discover the chemical nature of water, but another, spiritual, nature absorbs him, which is manifested as something that lived in water; it is then that a beautiful woman, a Nymph with transparent clothing is seen. This mysterious being produced in him joy, pleasure and perhaps love and filled his life with magic in these moments, like sublime music, like a work of art, thus leading him to a *mystical union with Nature*. If this state can be imagined, it will be understood that for the greatest aesthetic, religious and vital reasons, the last thing that could interest this blessed one was how to resolve the material composition of that element and to be in the place of contemporary man who, because he knows the chemical composition of water, sees in it only water.

Like the artist, the mythical man perceives the thing in itself much more than does the objective man. One is not dealing with a subjective reality as the dual man (objective-subjective) believes, but of an absorption in things and in Nature. But let this be clear, it is not a rudimentary objectivism, an attempt to be objective, but a way of incorporating external reality, within a spiritual reality that encompasses it. He wants to bequeath a teaching that feeds the spirit, that makes man grow internally. He does not speak, then, of particular objective situations that only useful for that case, but of exemplary situations applicable to different circumstances. These are expressed indirectly and hyperbolically through parables, symbols and *Mythology is a moral exercise that strengthens the muscles of the spirit while imparting its exemplary lessons* examples. For this reason mythology occurs in an indeterminate time, avoiding falling into a particularity, which would reduce its exemplary character for all times, it refers to a place that becomes sacred and leaves a record of that event for future generations. This resource is widely used in many fantastic stories that have a similar flavour, but which do not amount to mythology as they do not claim to contain religious truths, and which begin, as all children know, with "Once upon a time..."

The corollary of what has been said is interesting for our purposes, and can be summarised with two clarifications on the Greek religion in general: firstly, as I have already advanced, myths are not a thing of the past and since they are a part of the Eternal, their reality can always be made real; their importance lies in the *possibility of their actualisation*. Secondly, even if Greece has always been recognised as the cradle of our civilisation, *its religion has tended to be overlooked without any thought given to the arbitrariness of this amputation* or the damage that it could have caused in Western culture. This attitude is fundamentally, as is obvious, a consequence of Christianity, which was interested in making use of that culture but not its religion, but it is also due to thinkers, not necessarily committed to Christianity, who noticing the irrelevance of traditional religion in the Greek philosophers do not think it an error to leave it behind, as something that was surpassed during the Athenian apogee. This, however, has been a grave misdemeanour because then they forget other sectors of culture as or more important for civilisation, such as the arts and literature, in which *traditional religion was not only relevant but also reached its highest manifestations*. Let us not forget that all Athenians, even the philosophers, participated in them, while those who followed the philosophers were a rare exception.

The Greek Gods

The myth of the loss of Paradise that is found in many religions is the product of the intuition of a state of higher consciousness. In fact, from an essential perspective, Paradise becomes a reality, everything is in order, men love and understand each other because they still do not think only of their personal interest as they *are not enclosed in their individual perspective*. There is no project nor calculation there as there is no need. That reality is not real, I will be told; well, no and yes, it depends on the perspective of the spirit. It is not real in the usual sense, but as an exemplar it illuminates our aesthetic, religious and philosophical consciousness and our ideas, in short, our understanding of everything. Because, we have to understand once and for all that what is decisive is that the myth is alive in all of us, not that God or the gods "objectively" exist. Since nobody can reasonably prove the objective existence of gods, without finding antinomies in them, as Kant has indubitably demonstrated, nor of course with facts, all these realities remain in our internal jurisdiction. I will not say that they are "psychic realities" in order to not fall into the psychologism of Jung, but rather that they are spiritual realities; and the characteristic of these is, precisely, that they exist as long as they are alive in us. And this does not mean as long as we "believe" that they objectively exist, but as much as they inspire us and make us feel, think, create and act. The Renaissance artist, for example, did not really believe nor was he interested in believing in the objective existence of Greek gods, but they were alive in him. The astute audience cares not if the heroes represented in Greek tragedy are historical or not, because what is important is what they represent, which is what inspires and moves us to the extent that we introvert them and make them part of our aesthetic, moral, philosophical and religious consciousness.

It is reason that has made us divide reality into objective and subjective, and if we think about it (even with the same reason) we will see that what is spiritual does not fit well in either of these two realities. If it is objective, there would be some way to prove its existence; and there is none. If it were subjective the gods would be different in each individual, there would not be common elements in them. And these are so important that they define better than anything the religious spirit of the people. Of course, the belief in the objective existence of the gods influences human beings and their communities but it does not increase our religious consciousness. Reason underpins what has been built at a unitive level, but religion does not live because God exists objectively but because he lives in us.

There are those who believe, and at present I think the consensus is unanimous, that there is a supposed evolution of the moral conscience in its process of independence from the gods, that is, the culpability of man for his actions only concerns the subject. Well, I am not convinced by this any more than the Greeks were; in truth, we find them between the two positions, at times they blame themselves, at others they blame the gods. It should be observed that the characters who blame the gods are not prototypes of integrity; as in the case of Paris and Helena who blame Aphrodite for their actions, even if in other times they recognise their own weaknesses.

In Homer, then, we find both positions and also in Plato and in Democritus. On the one hand the latter says: "One should not be more ashamed in front of other people than in front of oneself." (*frag.264*) and "although you find yourself alone you should not say or do evil." But in another passage he notes: "If one believes that the gods oversee all, he will not commit evil acts, either in secret or openly." (*frag.112*) Voltaire, the great enlightened, for the same reasons as Democritus had twenty-four centuries earlier, believed that "if God did not exist it would be necessary to create him". In my opinion, what is important is not to establish the dependence or independence of man but to see the interaction and, in this way, the integration of the human being with the gods. Thus, there is no "evolution" in the consciousness in leaving behind the gods, there is individuation or alienation with respect to the All, literally disintegration.

I believe that the error, that I would like to rectify once and for all, is that of seeing all reality as subjective and objective. There are realities, and the most crucial ones in knowledge, that are neither one nor the other, but *unitive*. This concept, fundamental in my theory of knowledge, is indispensable for understanding spiritual reality; and the gods belong to this reality. And they will never be understood as objective or subjective realities, as they express *unitive realities*.

According to my philosophical-religious conception, the most basic and indispensable element of polytheism is this: the gods are paradigmatic; each and every one of them has a transcendent function. Since the objective of the human being is to surpass himself as an individual in order to transcend himself and fulfil himself in the Transcendent (see *Origin and Destiny of Man*) the objective of the gods becomes clear. For example, the Beautiful itself, which is an entirely philosophical principle demonstrated by Plato, and which in my philosophy is a *primary manifestation of the Consciousness of the world*, the Greek genius imagines and expresses as Apollo in the masculine, and Aphrodite in the feminine; Beauty is intimately linked to Love and this is another path to the Transcendent.

Amongst the aesthetic Greeks, the artists did all they could to represent that ideal in the most perfect way possible, and they achieved it within human limits through Art; which is another path to the Transcendent. They did it with each one of the gods; very little remains of these works, as of everything from ancient Greece in general, but the little that remains has served and will continue to serve as a paradigm for its perfection.

What is Perfect is Unity (see *The Search for Univ. Consc.*) All religions agree that God has to be perfect; although they might differ on how this perfection is expressed. For example, some say that if he is perfect he has to be good to humans, at least to the good ones, but this interpretation is full of flaws: apart from the fact that history itself proves that it is not so except in mythical stories that are not, precisely, history. If God was concerned with human affairs, given the innate imperfection of our species, he would cease to be perfect.

The personalisation of God is a doctrinal imperfection that makes God imperfect. But the perfection of the Divinity as a paradigm remains intact; and superior men incline towards this. Hermes, who was the intermediary between the supreme Divinity and the mortals, in particular the demi-gods, who are the closest to the paradigm of perfection, must have been an exemplary beauty like a god, and the version that Praxiteles has given us is indisputably perfect. But we must understand that in order to express perfection, we must have an inner perfection, an orderly and balanced conscience.

Can the reader understand the reach of Greek polytheism? In the Greek miracle the gods were only paradigmatic, it was the men or, more accurately, the demi gods who were the actors. These, noble and heroic, do not ask for supplicants from the divinities who perform miracles, they do it themselves. "So did they not objectively exist?" someone will ask me, and I will respond: "no God exists objectively, nor does he come into existence because someone subjectively believes that they exist objectively, they exist when they are experienced unitively, when they transcend the individual, since they are of a transcendent nature."

Man becomes one with Mars when he heroically transcends himself; just as he is truly in love when he feels dominated by a force that is beyond his control, and the Greeks called this force Aphrodite. Aphrodite is a representation of Love and Love is an expression of Aphrodite. If my love is subjective, it is infinitely small, but if I project myself beyond myself through the hand of Aphrodite, it transcends me; it is no longer an earthly love and, of course, it is not only carnal. Aphrodite is the Spirit of Love in such a way that she fills Everything with It. In short, what Aphrodite does is to give Love a universal dimension, which is its real dimension, as *Love is a primary manifestation of the universal Consciousness*. And so it is with all the Greek gods. Praxiteles has also left us the perfect image of Aphrodite.

All the gods and every God (as there are as many conceptions of this as in human beings), are transcendent, and they become real to the extent that man transcends himself. From the aforesaid it can be deduced that the Greeks and their gods can be understood to the extent that one transcends oneself, that is, places oneself on the *level of consciousness* of the Greek, and not, as has been done ad nausea, by reading about Greek mythology. To understand them one has to know about the Greeks in their highest expression, one has to penetrate the minds of their sculptors, architects, tragic poets, philosophers and others without forgetting that they were all religious people.

For 1700 years, Western man has been programmed to *believe* that in general religion is a matter to be resolved with belief or faith. But this is not the case, as this matter is resolved with *experience*. So to understand Greek religion, one has to reach the *experience* of those who made possible the Greek miracle. When a certain number of individuals reach this level, there occurs a renaissance (see *The Spirit in History*). The Italian Renaissance did not take place because the Greek gods were believed in anew, but because a high level of consciousness had been reached that permitted seeing from the same perspective, and the same ideals curiously appeared and with them the Greek gods.

These explanations respond to one of my most cherished aspirations: to generate a New Renaissance, that does not happen through imitation, but through an elevation of the spirit and expansion of consciousness. We should not worry about the gods, they appear on their own accord when we approach them with our ideals and practices of perfection; for this reason the Greek world was filled with gods.

Greek Art

In *The Roots of Art*, I have written about art in general; I will only add the following here: Although the Greeks also created rhetoric, they never liked to say too much; as in their other pursuits, they stuck to the essentials; Greek literature is basic in the sense that the bases are sufficient; every flourish seems unnecessary to the Greek, every ornament an excess, and every excess an imbalance. Without detracting from the literature of later times, like that of Romanticism, for example, to the Ancient Greek it would have seemed elaborate, and in fact we often notice the effort that the artist has made to find the right word, comparison or affect. The Greeks were not only satisfied by what they saw, they were amazed and replete, hence their straightforward language that went to the heart of the matter; it is well known that in the Spartans the language became laconic.

Perhaps because the Greeks discovered the world, what was essential was enough for them. Herein lies the key to their spirit, as their civilisation is not found at the dawn of history; they were the heirs of the Egyptians who had preceded them by several millennia, but the Greek was aware that he was discovering reality as if he were just arriving, awakened into the world. And this was, indeed, the *Birth* of our civilisation. Greek art is basic in the sense that it has laid the bases for all subsequent art in the West. It is basic but it is finished, nothing can be added nor taken away from it, and for Aristotle who expressed this spirit, this is the very definition of what is perfect; and for this reason his art is fundamental, exemplary and imitable. All subsequent art is a variation on the same theme; the theme, the substance and the bases are Greek. The same happens with philosophy as we can see: Heraclitus and Parmenides trace the guidelines on which Plato and Aristotle will construct the foundations on which the construction continues to be built.

I would only like to rectify Eliade's ideas about art who, with respect to the survival of Greek art in Europe, opines that: "If the radically secularised and demystified Greek religion and mythologies have survived in European culture it is because they had been expressed by literary and artistic *chefs-d'oeuvres*." (*Aspects du Mythe, 198*) "The rediscovery of the Renaissance consists above all in the restoration of pure and *classical forms*." I do not deny this aspect, but there is more to it. To express these *pure forms* Renaissance man did not need to re-enact Greek mythology, and he did so profusely. From Corregio to Bernini there are numerous examples. Caracci's monumental *Triumph of Dionysus* in the palace of Cardinal Farnese signified much more than *classical forms*, it signified the triumph of Dionysus. The *Birth of Venus* and *Allegory of Spring* by Botticelli expressed precisely the *Renaissance of a spirit*; these works were commissioned by Lorenzo the Magnificent and supervised by the Florentine court philosopher Ficino, who spoke of "Zeus or God, the God of Pythagoras and the divine Plato." This was far from limited to these *forms*, later Handel, Bernini and many others resorted to Greek mythology when they could.

To separate Greek art from religion is to fall prey to a centuries-old biased interpretation destined to undermine the Greek religion that inspired the geniuses of the Birth and Renaissance, both centred in the *unitive consciousness* that knows little of these distinctions. It is the *same spirit that animates them*, that causes them to be born and reborn. The artist, like the mystic, has a special vision and penetration that transcend reason, which is why the philosophers of reason do not understand them. To think that the Greek tragedies were naive when expressing the myths of their tradition is to reveal our own naivety and ignorance. Geniuses are paradigmatic references, they are there to teach us something that we have not seen or understood; we cannot judge them with our incipient reason.

The *perfect forms* are not born from an occurrence but from the *intuition of the perfection of the Unity*. The Greek ideal of perfection underlies and encompasses religion, art and morality, and is the result of an *elevated level of consciousness*; it is at this level that I am trying to push the spirit, which I want to see it reborn.

Virtues of Polytheism

I have argued that polytheism is the most conducive path to a spiritual life. This should not be interpreted as a "return" to polytheism, for human beings are naturally polytheistic, they always have been. The natural religion of peoples is polytheistic. Monotheism could only be established by a vertical and exclusivist imposition useful for the centralisation of power. Freedom of belief is expressed as polytheism. Therefore, it is not a matter of imposing polytheism but of allowing freedom of belief which, incidentally, also admits monotheism and religious dualism.

My philosophy, as can be seen and will be seen later, is projected towards the realisation of monism. But this experience of the Absolute, as we can see from history, has been the heritage of a few philosophers and mystics and, we can infer, will remain so. The reason for this is fundamentally very simple: few are those who can lead a contemplative, reflective and spiritual life; the vast majority must attend to their immediate, everyday affairs. But we all know that behind these there is something else, something that transcends them. In the moments when we overcome the daily distractions and in solitude contemplate the firmament, we cannot help but feel immersed in an infinite space and time, then we know that we know nothing of where we came from and where we are going. And if we take charge of this infinite emptiness in our soul, we will see that only the spirit can fill it. When we hit the bottom in our consciousness we realise that matter and reasons are not enough; then we either retrace our steps over our daily distractions or we start on the spiritual path; every sensitive and sincere person will choose this path.

I have offered as paradigmatic two civilisations that have been able to fill this space and give a spiritual meaning to existence, and in which monism and polytheism have coexisted harmoniously. A few examples, which I recall at random, suffice to show the depth, dimension and importance of Greek mythology, which I have set out to vindicate.

In Greece, marriage was sacralised by several gods, it will suffice to mention those concerning women: Hera established the marriage bond, but this had to be maintained, and for this we know the importance of the love relationship, which was in the charge of Aphrodite, to which was added the need for reproduction, related to Hera and Demeter, who linked birth with harvests and natural cycles. Next is Artemis, the protector of the newborn, whom she educates from an early age in love and respect for Nature. In this way, marriage and its progeny participated in Creation and attained a universal dimension.

The Charites, who would be the Graces in Rome, divinities of Beauty, dwell on Olympus in the company of the Muses, with whom they sometimes form choirs and belong to the retinue of Apollo, the god of music. The Graces are attributed with all sorts of influences on the works of the spirit and on works of art. They have woven the veil of Harmony with their own hands. They gladly accompany Athena (goddess of female labours and intellectual activity), as well as Aphrodite and Eros and Dionysus. They spread joy in Nature, in the hearts of humans and even in the hearts of the gods. (*Dictionaire Mythologique*, P. Grimal) I do not know if I am understood: Beauty, Harmony and Joy are in unison in the heavenly abode and in our hearts.

Olympus, let it be said accordingly, was not, as contemporary man believes, the mountain that today bears his name. "In the Greek world there were many mountains called Olympus." "Since Homeric times, it has been regarded as the mansion of the gods, in particular as the abode of Zeus." "It is the heavenly abode where the divinity resides." (*Op. cit*. P. Grimal) It is the perfect equivalent of the Mount Meru or Sumeru of the Hindus, which is lost in the Himalayas, beyond time and space.

Religion and Nature

The man of the spirit, alert and elevated, finds himself surprised before the World that is made manifest to him as if everything were new, filled with enchantment and beauty, and charged with moral forces, with something that transcends and underlies him, that moves him and leads him to look at the stars and ask what lies beyond them. When comparing that infinity with the ephemeral reality around him, it seems to be as unreal as a dream in which he must live, a strange reality but full of infinite possibilities in which there is nothing more to create, that is how it sometimes happens to some peoples. It is difficult to say why this happens to one set of people and not to another at any given time. It is easy to attribute it to a Spirit that "alights" on the community, which it stimulates as a cloud that would let its beneficial rain fall on it, but this Hegelian resource of a Deus-ex-machina is a hypothesis that, since we cannot verify it, is suspended in the air only with the breath of illusion. But what is a fact is that sometimes this happens in so many individuals of a society to such a contagious extent that we begin to think of a collective phenomenon.

The reverence the Greeks had for Nature and especially for the earth, as can be seen in *Antigone* and *Oedipus at Colonus,* where it determines the plot of these tragedies, should not be seen as an adoration of the objects in themselves, but as their participation in the Transcendent. A people as highly spiritual as the Greeks intuit that everything is part of a universal Order, and thus they successfully use Nature as a means, and not as an end, to maintain their contact with the gods, that is, with the universal Spirit, which they make plural for a greater understanding of the multiple and varied reality. They make it singular in certain beings, gods who fulfil specific functions. Conversely, these elements or beings are used as signs, figures, doors that lead to the Transcendent.

This connects everything to a *universal moral Order*. In the works cited above we see that in the land of Thebes a traitor to the mother country or a parricide cannot be buried. This naturally means that in order to preserve its sacred nature, this land should not house beings who are outside the moral Order, from which the Greek does not want to be alienated. And in Aeschyus's *Oresteia* we are witness to an entire process of the restoration of Order and accommodation of justice.

The poetic imagination is confused with religion, there is a mythical art, and an aesthetic people *par excellence* like the Greeks needed that artistic expression. Apart from its religious and psychological content, religion needs a poetic and artistic form rich in imagination to be accepted by an exigent people.

Let us reflect on why the Greeks attributed to the gods the origin of the arts, of musical instruments and inventions in general, the relationship they maintained with the *Intelligence in which humans participated*, the link they maintained with the Creative. Each god had contributed one or more of these inventions, which are what have differentiated our species from the beasts; they are the expression of our divine side which, necessarily, mythical consciousness attributed to a celestial and universal origin. The great Ideas also had a divine origin. To Apollo, who played the harp and the flute in an *exemplary manner*, instruments created by the ingenious Hermes, were attributed the two basic principles of the Hellenic mentality: “Know thyself” and “Nothing in excess”.

Orpheus, we know, is the creator of music, generator of numerous legends and of the Orphic rituals of liberation. Orpheus dies at sea and his Lyre is left floating... in the constellation that bears his name. Orion is a hero in the manner of Heracles who performs numerous feats. Also like him, he often loses control and tries to abuse the seven sisters and nymphs, the Pleiades. In order to escape, the Pleiades transform themselves into doves that soar into space. When we look up we see that Orion persists in his attempt eternally. Orion is finally killed by the sting of a scorpion, which is why he disappears as soon as Scorpio appears on the horizon.

The symbolic projection that the Greeks made of their heroes in the constellations of the firmament displays not only a beautiful poetic imagination that aims to keep these paradigms present, but above all, the desire to remain integrated in the Cosmos; this is the most characteristic and edifying feature of the mythical mentality. This projection should not be interpreted only as something symbolic in the modern sense, but in the profound meaning of the symbol. This implies an intimate relation between the soul of the hero and his admirer, between the macro-cosmos to which the former has been integrated and the micro-cosmos of the latter. The Greek participates in the universal Soul; he participates in filling the firmament with his heroes. He is not an individual who decides but the Greek spirit, tradition, the moral order of that people that extends in the celestial order. This is not a purely intellectual decision but one accompanied by a moving religious sentiment. All this is essential to understand the Greek spirit.

Circular and Linear Vision

Two ways of seeing history have prevailed, which can be quite well explained in two geometric forms: one is linear, the other circular. The former is more akin to the Christian conception, the latter to the Hellenic and Indian. It is not, as has been claimed, that the Christian conception has a "historical sense" that the Hellenic one lacks, we know very well that the science of history was invented by the Greeks, in the conviction that the past could serve as a example, and that their civilisation was projected into the future. The difference lies in the conception of the beginning: For the linear the origin begins at a certain moment by the Creation of all things and beings in the space of a few days, in about 4,600 BC. This epoch would coincide with the beginning of the first civilisations, with the idea of history itself. Prehistory does not exist here, neither does the evolution of species nor the prolonged formation of the stars. This conception tends to project human hopes into a promissory future, which in Christianity is placed in the afterlife. The promissory future in this world, as in the case of Marx, is a derivative of this linear vision. So many times has the imminent threat of a final judgment failed that the West now projects its hopes on an earthly future. The historicist theories (of which I have said something in *The Spirit in History*) are a product of the same vision.

This vision responds to a factor that post-Hellenic man does not take into account: the alienation and disintegration that he has suffered with respect to Nature and the Cosmos. The Hellenic spirit experienced this in some way and therefore sought to be *integrated into the world*, its multiple aesthetic, moral, religious and philosophical expressions, from Parmenides to Plotinus, are proof of this. Nature populated by gods, that is, the spiritual reality impregnating rivers, seas, mountains, forests and cities, contributed to said integration. This *integration here and now of man in the world*, which derives from the latent or patent perception of an Order that underlies him, is what forms his *circular vision*. This has tended, at times, to see the historical process as cyclical, which is to take it to an extreme that no longer responds to reality. However, it is convenient to remember that since there is no intrinsic and radical evolution in man, he falls back into the same errors, even if his surroundings, forms of government and means of life change. Man is cyclical and colours history with this character. The cyclical vision points to the essential in man, it is unifying, hence his tendency to pantheism and monism. The linear vision is external and dualistic, for which man is inevitably separated, alienated from the Spirit; the spirit is other, and, if it exists, is in heaven.

The predominantly circular or global vision is found in Greece and India, and in the East in general, where it is still valid. This vision is not presented as antipodal to the historical one, since it only predominates over it. The opposition has been created by the modern linear historical view that ignores the circular view due to the *alienation of the spirit from the unitive faculties*. It is this modern, materialistic, economistic, mechanistic and pragmatic vision that has described as "primitive" a vision that, effectively, has been left behind in history, but not necessarily for that reason should it be considered to have been surpassed, since whoever has "surpassed" it is, as I said, an alienated being. It is this being who has invented the new myth of indefinite progress. I am not pronouncing myself against scientific-technological progress, but rather I am questioning this myth that claims to cure all ills through unilateral progress that, already being the product of man's exteriorisation, exacerbates it by increasing his estrangement from what is most essential. This extreme external progress that implies the conquest of Nature alienates it, establishing a disastrous duality, since man is part of that Organism that he tries to exploit, thus producing an imbalance that is both psychic and ecological.

The circular vision includes material progress, as it is subordinated to internal, spiritual progress, which is gradual, incremental, without urgency, without neglecting what is essential. If this priority is reversed, morality, aesthetics, religion and philosophy decline, which inevitably leads to the decline of man and pushes him to his destruction; even though he believes that he is destroying his "enemies" and is conquering nature.

Considering the two visions, I think it is edifying to establish a balance between them, but for this there should be a displacement of the spirit in Western man (because in the East, particularly in India, he remains, thanks to his religion, quite integrated), towards his *unitive consciousness*, to live in the present in harmony with his environment. Progress would thus cease to be a projection towards a promissory future, be it earthly or heavenly, a mirage that keeps us alienated from our current reality. In this way, fully living our present, without political or religious promises, without daydreams or illusions, history would follow a natural process.

The cyclical vision of history and the universe derives from the experience or intuition of Unity, from whose perspective time and space become circular. The spirit is centred in that space and stopped in that present "time" and knows, or intuits, that this state is correct, that this is the home of the soul. If we talk about evolution, within this scheme, we will be referring to an inner evolution, and this needs nothing more than enough peace to allow a state of contemplation that leads to centring the spirit and unifying Reality. In this state, strictly speaking, time and space have been transcended, this state is prior to time and space; one enters these when one wants to discern that reality.

If man only needs peace for his contemplation, the conditions for his evolution are basic and elemental, and he has had them for a long time, about two thousand five hundred years. But it happens that in purely spiritual expressions, man has not evolved linearly, but has had ups and downs, has advanced and regressed. Indeed, in art and religion, in morality and philosophy, he has not had a linear progress, rather, what he has done is change his core consciousness within his planes of understanding. And in this behaviour of returning to the same planes, after having traversed the others, he effectively shows a cyclical process. This indicates that in his intrinsic and real evolution man retraces his steps. But when he returns he finds different external circumstances, since material, extrinsic progress is without return, it extends out of the circle in all directions. External progress is cumulative, linear, multidirectional, and irreversible. Internal evolution is unitive, circular, centralising or unidirectional and reversible. This has generated two interpretations of the process, which respond to two psychological types; introverts and contemplatives tend to see circularly and cyclically, extroverts, linearly and historically. And in both positions the same mistake is made: that of invading the other reality to interpret it from a particular determining point of view.

My proposal is to accept the different nature of these two realities and seek an edifying balance between them. The matter is not easy because there is no understanding between the two psychological types, which makes a common program difficult. But now that we have left the theoretical plane and contemplate the broad practical scope of the matter, we can become aware of its importance. Where should we direct history? What destination should we assign to material progress? The contemplative man who has had at least an intuition of Unity has these clear answers: man must direct his efforts to reach said Unity.

In my work *Origin and Destiny of Man* this proposal is expressed. But it happens that the executive men, in charge of directing education and government programs in general, are extroverts and ignore the importance of said integration program, so, inverting the order of priorities, they apply themselves to solving the material problems, the means, and tend to forget the ends. From which it follows that the balance we spoke of must be found in the mind of the politician; with which we would return to the enlightened governing ideal. The project is clear, it is its execution that is uncertain.

To deal with these two conceptions from the religious point of view, I think it is opportune to include the erudite studies of M. Eliade, who has his compelling reasons for turning around the paradigmatic myths. In *The Quest*, in a chapter aptly titled *The Fallacy of Demystification*, he tells us that there is no point in trying to demystify the belief of various archaic traditional cultures that the temple is located at the centre of the world. Allow me, before continuing, to rectify this exposition on two points: What he calls "belief" I would call experience, since it is an inner experience. The unitive (not archaic) man rationally knows that every temple cannot pretend to be in the centre, but being in the temple he has the *experience of being centred, unified*. Moreover, it would be as inappropriate as it is offensive to call the thousands of Brahmins and intellectuals who today have that experience when entering the temples they visit "archaic". It is, in fact, part of the Hindu religious life to visit a multitude of temples, and in South India each of the temple-cities has a pole in the centre, usually gold-plated, indicating the *axis mundi*. And this custom comes precisely from the most archaic times, even before temples existed, since it was around the post that the first temples were built. In other words, the experience of being centred is the same, it was always present.

Eliade argues that “it is only by taking this belief seriously, by trying to clarify all its cosmological, ritual, and social implications, that one succeeds in comprehending the existential situation of a man who believes that he is at the Centre of the World. All his behaviour, his understanding of the world, the values he accords to life and to his own existence, arise and become articulated in a ‘system’ on the basis of this belief that his house or his village is situated near the *axis mundi*.

We have seen that the traditional concept is continued and renewed by the Indian thinking that gives it a new dimension and greater clarity. In the moral-cosmic order, the cyclical vision adds the “conception of universal causality to *karma*, which explains the current events and sufferings of the individual, and at the same time explains the need for transmigrations.” (*Myth Et. Ret. 69*). We know that the ultimate goal of the Buddhist and the Hindu is liberation from the cycle of successive lives, for which he has created specific techniques that we can summarise in the concept of *yoga*. Well then, the concept of *karma* grants the aspirant indefinite possibilities of reaching that goal; and for that he *counts on history*. This is cyclical, it is true, but each cycle is made up of eons, so the human being has plenty of time to fulfil his destiny. This Indian vision is not taken into account by Eliade. (On this subject see what I have set out in *The Evolution of the Spirit*).

I have already advanced that Hindu and Buddhist *liberation* should not be confused with Judeo-Christian *salvation*. According to which, “when the Messiah arrives in the world, it will be saved once and for all and history will cease to exist.” We see here an “eschatological assessment of the future.” “History no longer appears as a cycle that repeats itself ad infinitum.” “That is why it is possible to affirm that the Hebrews were the first to discover history as the epiphany of God and this conception, as expected, was followed and expanded in Christianity.” (*Op. cit.*). I think it is necessary to adjust the concepts a bit here: for the Hindu and the Buddhist *everything is an epiphany*, including history, certainly, but the important difference is that this epiphany is not projected into the future but rather is a current experience. It is in the projection into the future and eschatological salvation and in the Judeo-Christian messianic vision that the difference lies. It is in this sense that "the whole of history becomes a theophany." "The same conception enriched by the elaboration of Christology will serve as the basis of the philosophy of history that the Christian, starting from Saint Augustine, will strive to build." (*Op. cit.*). This is where the Christian conception differs from the Jewish one, since the Messiah awaited by the latter arrives, for the former, in the person of Jesus; this is the belief introduced by Paul of Tarsus that the Church would ultimately adopt a few centuries later. The Jews, as is known, never believed that the Messiah had come, they are still waiting for him, but with respect to history there is essentially no difference because Christians believe in a *second* coming of the Messiah, and it is only then that "the world will be saved once and for all and history will cease to exist." Here Jewish and Christian beliefs overlap; the future Messiah fulfils the same function. But it is here where the religions of Semitic origin distance themselves from those of Indian origin, because for those "history is abolished not by the consciousness of living an eternal present (...) but abolished in the future." (*Op. cit.*).

In this conception of the destiny of history, the history of souls is also included; whose definitive salvation will then take place at the end of time. While for Hindus and Buddhists, liberation is a present issue that must be resolved in life (*jivan mukta*). For the former, salvation is eschatological and therefore a belief, while for the latter liberation is current and therefore depends on an experience. This fundamental difference, on which, for the same reason, I must insist, should be well understood and established. Since my philosophy is a product of experience and provides the means to acquire it, it naturally adheres to the Indian conception.

The linear versus circular vision of history and the dualistic versus monistic mentality is what alienated the Western spirit from its centre and Essence. Plotinus made the last great attempt to recover and continue the Hellenic spirit with his monistic pantheism, but it was too late, the Judeo-Christian spirit had already prevailed. The linear and dualistic visions of reality, then, have an importance that until now had gone unnoticed: they have contributed to *alienating us from our unitive consciousness*, that is, from our spiritual faculties, from our nucleus of consciousness, from our Essence. The historicist vision, like materialism and existentialism, are derivative extensions of those visions. I do not deny their partial truths, their contribution to knowledge and social order, but they are tangential, alien, or to put it better, alienated from the essential, for which they have removed the essence of history, they have de-spiritualised nature, the world in which we live, and this is serious. From the religious point of view, the dualistic vision makes God alien to us, that is, we are alienated from the spiritual essence of the World, which is not in the heavens but in our conscience. That is to say that dualism alienates us from ourselves. When the spirit approaches its essence, it is in contact with the Creative and generates periods of spiritual apogee (philosophical, artistic, moral and religious), when it moves away, it produces periods of spiritual perigee (see *The Spirit in History*); the estrangement from our Essence leads us to externalise, to individualise and to alienate ourselves.

Dualism and individualism go hand in hand, they are the result of the same mental process that encloses man within an individual perspective that makes him see the world and all beings as external to him, from that derives from the indiscriminate exploitation of nature, that is, ecological disaster, and the usual immorality towards others.

When man tries to explain the supra-sensible reality from said individual perspective, which he unconsciously assumes, he inevitably falls into heteronomy, into dualism. This leads him to believe in a God external to his consciousness that creates and makes decisions on the world and the destiny of his beings. The personal God is the consequence of a perspective adopted by the spirit, due to an erroneous location of the nucleus of consciousness.

The Cyclical Vision of Time

The tendency to pantheism, the circular vision of reality and the cycle of life, *shared by Greeks and Hindus*, evidently revolves around the experience of Unity; and this largely explains the excellence achieved by these peoples in so many disciplines, then we will see the relationship of this experience with the Creative. Modern man does not know how much he has lost by abandoning the cyclical vision of life, because it leads him to amass and concentrate reality, in unison, and it refers him to his present.

The linear vision projects the thoughts towards the past that has already ceased to be reality, and towards the future, which does not yet exist; both projections alienate him from the present, which is where Reality is hidden, so that he falls into reason that is prey to the coordinates of time and space, whereas the cyclical vision transcends them. I hope it will be understood that I am not talking about external reality, nor internal reality as subjective, but about the oneness of Nature and consciousness. This, and other ideas and concepts that I am forced to advance because they were latent in the ancient Greek, will become clearer in the course of this work.

The cyclical vision naturally obeys a mythical mentality, which is foreign, this is essential to understand, to time and space, and for this reason it appears irrational. Eliade recognises that in Greece the myth inspired and guided epic poetry, tragedy and comedy, as well as the plastic arts "but it is no less true that it was in Greek culture where the myth was subjected to a long and penetrating analysis from which it emerged radically demystified." "Which -he adds- is very serious for the religious historian." But there was not, in reality, a radical change of mentality, but an opening of it towards new fields of investigation. Plato, it is true, was against some myths that he did not consider edifying for the citizens of his Republic, but not against the mythical mentality; he himself, as is known, created myths about which we are still thinking. And it is only in some passages of his work that he is so rationalistic; neither before nor after in his extensive work did he express himself in that way. His last work, the Timeous, is a clear manifestation of that mythical-cosmic consciousness.

If we see it not as an evolution or involution, but as a change of perspective, we will see that the change does not really affect us. We can become independent of the myth, something that Eliade does not want to do because he believes that in it lies the key to the matter, but we can preserve the same awareness that explains reality in another way without alienating ourselves from the circular and cyclical vision of the world, projecting that same vision onto other fields to better understand reality. The cyclical vision of life does not claim (as those who do not understand it want to believe) to be an alleged "scientific vision", that is to say objective, but an integral or unitive vision, hence the inclusion of religion and ritual in it. The presence of religion gives it a transcendent character, but being circular and cyclical, transcendent and immanent, religion and Nature become a single reality.

This is what the Hindus have done, so they can incorporate their myths if they wish, without having a dogmatic commitment to them, by which I mean, without the need to accept their objective existence, because their existence is, in fact, *unitive*. The Greeks tragedians did the same thing, being that they could be entirely rational, more than that, brilliant, for that reason they knew how to get the best possible use out of the myths.

Thucydides, an exemplary historian, that is to say, a complete connoisseur of time and space, had a circular vision of history, but, as a good psychologist, he attributed the cycles to the eternal human vices that were repeated over time. His theory is formulated at the beginning of his work and he insists on it throughout: "Perhaps my work appears unattractive due to the lack of beautiful stories, but I will be satisfied if it is considered useful by those who want to know the truth of the facts and objectively examine the *events that, according to human nature, must necessarily occur in the same or analogous way in the future*. My work is not a piece of writing designed to meet the needs of an immediate public, but was done to last for ever." (*Hist. Pelop War.*)

Since my own work constantly appeals to the roots of man, his psychology, his morals and ultimately his nature, which is what decides human actions, I cannot but agree with our historian. As we contemplate the past and even the present we see that although external circumstances change, man remains the same. Moreover, we see that in times of spiritual perigee he falls even lower than in preceding times. (See *The Spirit in History*). These ups and downs of history are not contemplated by Thucydides, but he has told us a paradigmatic piece of history with its rise and its fall generated by war and this, in turn, by eternal human passions.

Plato shows the cyclical vision by reflecting on systems of government. I will, for its brevity and accuracy, make use of the summary that Ortega y Gasset makes in his *Interpretation of Universal History*: "Aristotle argues this point [forms of government] with

Plato, but finally arrives at a kind of canonical doctrine of political thought which comes to this: the oldest and purest institution is the monarchy, but it degenerates into absolute power which provokes the rebellion of the most powerful men, that is to say, the aristocrats, who overthrow the monarchy and set up an aristocratic constitution. The aristocracy in turn degenerates into oligarchy, and this provokes an uprising of the people who throw out the oligarchs and set up a democracy. But democracy quickly becomes pure disorder and anarchy, swayed by demagogues, and ending by being the brutal oppression of the masses, of what was then called – I am merely translating – the rabble, *okhlos*, and thence *okhlocracy*. The prevailing anarchy then reaches such a degree that one of the demagogues, the most successful or the most powerful, seizes power and establishes a tyranny; if this tyranny lasts, it is converted into monarchy; then the institutions come to bite each other's tails and the cycle of evolution begins all over again. This is what was called the circle, cycle or circuit of the forms of government." "This supposes -adds Ortega- not to believe in any political form, to have experienced that they are all failed and erroneous", it supposes, we would say, that the vices they suffer must be attributed to the men who create and apply them.

Polybius, about two centuries after Plato, writes, and for the first time, a *Universal History*: "Ever since then history has resembled a body, in the sense that incidents in Italy and Libya and Asia and Greece are all interconnected, and everything tends to a single outcome ." Polybius intends to be entirely objective: "The honest man must love his country and his friends..." but "once he takes on the character of a historian, it is necessary to forget sentiments of this kind, since it is often necessary to praise his enemies"; and it really was. We have before us, therefore, a man of objective and rational vision. However, with all his experience and knowledge, which was abundant, he observes the eternal cycle that our species follows, which he attributes, like Thucydides, to the desire for power and the greed of the human being. He argues that the more power rulers acquire, the more they want, and so they abuse their authority to the point that they inevitably find opponents powerful enough to supplant them in government. These in turn cannot be satiated with power either. Then the people rise up against them, and that is how democracy succeeds oligarchy. But even here the desire for power does not cease and greed leads to corruption and the transgression of the laws by the people, so that the state order ceases to function and the appearance of a strong man or a tyrant becomes necessary, who would correspond to what today we call a dictator. The cycle, as can be seen, resembles that described by Plato and Aristotle. For Polybius, all those who manage to govern fall into the same vices that moral conscience does not manage to control: the ambition for power and subsequent greed.

Hindus, surely due to their cyclical vision, have not been very fond of history; it has not ceased to be an inconvenience when studying the past. Its division into four Yugas that go back to a beginning as fantastic as it is remote is well known. The Hindhu vision of time, in its classic texts, is mythical, that is, it is outside of time. As the duration of each one of these Yugas is referred to in years, and even in days, Westerners have taken the trouble to count them up; vain work, we have already said, that of applying reason to myth. Its cycles are not human, they are cosmic and divine, the years are days of Brahman, almost infinite. But they do not become unlimited; they have an end, and in this lies their universal cyclical vision: Brahman itself, that is, the Creator and the entire Creation must disappear so that another cycle can take place; the end of time will give rise to another time.

The theory of the cyclical development of the Universe or of the Kalpas will be expounded in detail in the Brahanda, one of the Puranas. A divine or Brahman day includes a thousand periods (Mahayugas) and each of these is divided into four minor periods called Yugas. The first Yuga called Krita corresponds to the golden age. Here justice and truth reign. It is represented by a bull firmly seated on its four legs. The period is four times longer than the next, and men lived four times longer. Then the process is descending, corresponding to the ultimate Iron Age, which is the one we are living through, which is characterised by man's moral deterioration. The four Yugas add up to more than four million years. These multiplied by a thousand make a day of Brahman, who lives for a hundred years. The last cycle is the one we are suffering, since it falls under the government of Kali, a fearsome goddess who likes blood; and we have seen so much blood in history that we can believe that she still rules. However, the beginning of the Kali Yuga, in 3102 B.C. would coincide with the appearance of Krishna, an avatar of a luminous, ascending and hopeful god, Vishnu, who sleeps on the serpent Sesa, who is infinity itself, and who awakens and incarnates on Earth when humans need him.

Since the human being is such he is in a transition period. The common man accepts what he already is, what falls to him by chance, the superior man knows in his present state that he is not what he aspires to be; he then projects himself onto an ideal in time, onto an ideal past or future. Hesiod, like the theorists of the Hindu Yugas, turns his gaze towards a remote origin and finds, like them, a golden age, where men "lived like gods without sorrow of heart, remote and free from toil and grief." But this period is followed by a progressive decline, which is also manifested in four ages, which, being more imperfect physically and morally, are called silver, bronze and iron. In the latter "might shall be their right: and one man will sack another's city." "There will be no favour for the man who keeps his oath or for the just or for the good." "Envy, foul-mouthed, delighting in evil, with scowling face, will go along with wretched men one and all." However, he makes an exception for the heroic period, as he could not fail to exalt a "god-like race of hero-men who are called demi-gods." "And they live untouched by sorrow in the islands of the blessed." He did not get to know the heroes of Marathon, Plataea and Salamina, but he left them the means to belong to the "god-like race".

The Greek Virtues

Equilibrium

"Superior man is he who has moral talent, and the same can be said of peoples; it is this virtue that structures and consolidates societies. Intelligence is only edifying if it obeys that talent, otherwise idiocy is preferable, that is, the incapacity to do evil." (*The Roots of Morality*)

We know that the virtues in peoples are not acquired in a few generations, so, as expected, the Greek virtues date back to the early days of that civilisation, that is, to the heroic period sung of by Homer; which we will speak of later. We also find them previously expressed by its first great thinkers. From Pythagoras his Golden Verses have been preserved, from which I should extract some pieces because in them we notice the most characteristic features of the virtues that seem to have been engraved in the soul of that people since then: "First worship the Immortal Gods, as they are established and ordained by the Law. / Reverence the oath, and next the Heroes. /

Of all the rest of mankind, make him thy friend who distinguishes himself by his virtue. / Do nothing evil, neither in the presence of others, nor privately; / But above all things respect thyself. / In the next place, observe justice in thy actions and in thy words. / Consult and deliberate before thou act, that thou mayest not commit foolish actions. / For it is the part of the miserable man to speak and act without reflection. / ...a due measure is excellent in these things. / Practice thoroughly all these things; meditate on them well; thou oughtest to love them with all thy heart. / Tis they that will put thee in the way of divine virtue. / When thou hast made this habit familiar to thee. / Thou wilt know the constitution of the Immortal Gods and of men. /Thou shalt likewise know that according to Law, the nature of this universe is in all things alike. / But take courage; the race of man is divine. / Sacred nature reveals to them the most hidden mysteries. / And when, after having divested thyself of thy mortal body, thou arrivest at the most pure aether, / Thou shalt be a God, immortal, incorruptible, and Death shall have no more dominion over thee." I think no Hindu would fail to observe that this poem seems to have been taken from his own sacred texts.

More than one book could be and has been written on Greek morality. As was appropriate, I have devoted some space to it in *The Roots of Morality*, so I will be brief here and instead of refering my work this time I will refer the reader to Aristotle's unsurpassable *Ethics*. Nothing comparable to it has been written on morality, all the virtues are inscribed therein, as well as their antinomies, the vices, in a clear, plain and sure way, so that there is no doubt nor room for different interpretations. I think that its uplifting message is necessary for every educated and responsible person. Moreover, I think it should be taught in all schools as there are no particular beliefs or premises; its teachings are universal. Hindus could benefit a lot from it as there is nothing that opposes their *Dharma*, rather it confirms and strengthens it. Besides, it would also contribute to the understanding of the parallel that I want to establish in this work, and thus to its eventual realisation.

If there is one recurrent idea in Aristotle it is that of *temperance*, to the extent that he pours it into the different philosophical currents that he himself has created, especially in his *Ethics,* where it flows naturally, finding the *golden mean* between the extremes of excess and lack. This concept, nowadays forgotten out of ignorance and to the misfortune of societies, deserves special analysis.

The history of human thought and actions insistently corroborates man's incapacity to stay away from extremes and revolve around the golden mean. It seems second nature for men to accept inherited ideologies or the trends of his age with a certain absolute character, and through his actions he applies them without measure until they become obsolete. In reality they are not the same ones who observe this obsolescence, but the new generations who have another perspective or way of seeing. This makes history follow a dialectical process of action and reaction. In its fundamentals this has little or nothing to do with Hegelian dialectics because instead of being provoked by a supposed Spirit, it is the product of the *incipient reason* of the human being. What we note in this process is a dogmatic acceptance of ideologies, or, a lack of critical consciousness and a vision of nuances, which amounts to the same thing. The dynamics of history are dominated by this *incipient reason* and it is this that has given rise to constant setbacks which have delayed man's evolution. (See *The Spirit in History*)

The most notorious example is found in the Middle Ages in the West. But let us not believe for this reason that incipient reason belongs to the past, today the materialist "truths" go practically unquestioned and are taken to an extreme, and this will lead to a disaster difficult to remedy, and I am not only speaking of an ecological disaster, but of an internal spiritual disaster, the recovery from which will be long and torturous. Just as in the Middle Ages there was a misunderstood and dogmatically applied spiritualism, at present we live in a misunderstood and dogmatically applied materialism. Put in another way, incipient reason is a lack of intelligence to see nuances.

An example of an intelligent race in the above sense are the Greeks who had a particular *instinct-intelligence* to keep themselves within a *zone of equilibrium* with sufficient criteria of their own so as not to fall into dogma and thus avoid extremes. The equilibrium consisted fundamentally between matter and spirit; Nature was imbued with the spirit and spirit overflowed with life. There were no absolute contraries; this is what generated that positive and extraordinarily creative dynamic.

The concept of *sophrosyne*, translated as moderation or temperance is also considered prudence, but this meaning, like a multitude of concepts, has changed since then. For contemporary man, prudence means acting with suspicion, slowly and cautiously, I would almost say that this concept tends to arouse cowardice, odious terms and attitudes for the Greek. *Sophrosyne*, in fact incites courage, it *is* courage. When applying the concept to virile action, Aristotle concludes that the fair measure between cowardice and recklessness is courage. (*Ética Nic. 1107b*). The example is illustrative because it shows us that the Greek spirit is always greater than what we imagine, and in order to understand it we have to *elevate our level of consciousness*. In a similar manner, *Sophrosine* has a relation with the universal Order and the *kosmos*.

I would dare to say that if we understood the basic concepts as conceived and applied by the Greeks, we would be in a position to recover this spirit. Thus, for example, reason or intelligence were not entirely individual faculties, they were also a participation in the *Nous* or universal Intelligence; this alone would change our vision of reality. We could say the same about Justice that is established in the world by Zeus the supreme God. And we have already seen that for Plato the Good, the Beautiful and Love are paradigms that come from on high and are transcendent. For this reason later on we will speak of the real meaning of these Ideas-realities; let us now return to the subject that concerns us.

Sophrosyne is a typical Greek invention that opposes the *habrosyne* that characterises the Oriental luxury still practiced today among emirs, sultans, and the powerful in the Muslim world, whose lavishness disdainfully ignores the poverty of the people. Translating the concept as *equilibrium* seems illustrative to me, as it is a *state of the soul* which is found in tranquillity and repose, without desire or anxiety, or tumult, which is assimilated to *ataraxia*, a state of grace that the stoics ardently sought, and the *shanti* of the Hindus, because peace derives from inner equilibrium as they know well. It is not surprising that in Greece it had become a religious concept, an efficacious means of combating pleasure, sensuality, *hedonism*, a discipline capable of stopping instinctive impulses in order to achieve self-control, the opposite of madness, *aphrosyne*; in short, it became an ascesis that was incorporated into the Orphic cults. In the sanctuary of Demeter in Pergamon, next to the gods of Olympus, are the Orphic gods amongst which one finds *Arete* (virtue itself) and *Sophrosine*.

This personification of ideas and sentiments and even states of Nature was usual amongst the Greeks; Hesiod made a long enumeration of them. The existence of Ideas with autonomy is not entirely an invention of Plato, it was already a tradition; what he did was give it a philosophical explanation. It is important to understand this because, as we have emphasised, the *Universus*, all material and spiritual reality, was imbued with the spirit, populated by gods; as is the case today in the Hindu mind.

Greek wisdom is summed up in this knowledge: *perfection is obtained through equilibrium*. As a result all excess leads to misfortune; this is the main theme of the tragedy, a cultural factor of the first order in Hellenic culture. I sincerely believe that if one does not participate in this sense of innate *equilibrium* that the Greeks possessed, it is impossible to truly understand the spirit of this people, as it underlies their entire being, their way of seeing, acting, their gods, art, laws and city. Their religion and laws are an expression of that instinct, and they function because it underlies them.

Temperance or moderation was the greatest virtue of the Greeks because it is the one that tempers both vices and virtues. It is in the heat of moderation that the Greek forged his virtues. It has nothing to do with lack of character, but on the contrary, it comes before character, it is stronger than it and regulates it to its proper measure to achieve maximum efficacy. But moderation is not something that one can impose on the moral consciousness; it consists of an adaptation to it, and requires an intimate contact of the subject with his interiority. Needless to say, this process leads to and increases self-knowledge, which was another paradigm that the Greek adhered to with religious respect.

In equilibrium and surrounded by equilibrium the Athenian had prepared the necessary conditions for creating. His astonishing creativity in all spheres was the product of a spirit centred on a high level of consciousness. Moral integrity, the capacity for altruism, thanks to which he did not hesitate to sacrifice his life not only to save his city but also to demonstrate to himself his capacity for bravery, which is not just his unconditional heroic sense of life, his need for beauty, in his own body and in his art and his profound understanding of the psyche expressed in the myths, in his religion and literature, and to crown it all his indisputable philosophical capacity are all proof of the shift of the spirit towards what I call the *unitive consciousness*, which comprehends the moral, aesthetic, religious and philosophical consciousness (see my earlier works, especially my *Psychosophy*). When this shift takes place, I repeat, an intrinsic change occurs in man; and every human being should aspire to this.

Heroism and Temperance

The Greeks, who had no other reference point besides themselves as they felt themselves superior to the "barbarians", created their own exemplary beings, their gods. Those who could be assimilated to them were taken to be demi-gods and were placed in the pantheon of exemplary beings. As befits a noble people the highest aspirations were proposed, those that demanded their maximum potential.

What they achieved in their art, philosophy, sciences, in their society and, above all, in themselves, was the result of that titanic project. Their greatest error, however, derived from it: their excessive confidence in their possibilities, their excessive need to realise themselves as heroes. But their excess, let this be settled, was of virtue.

For the Greek it was natural to marry bravery with temperance. The key to the Greek phenomenon is found in this equilibrium and restraint in a vigorous spirit of freedom and transcendence. The Greek intuited that he needed certain internal rules of integrity in this spirit in order to rise up, not in a mad leap that could end in disaster, but on a moral ladder, a psychic order that would temper the ascent, which in no way would distract from his transcendent design but, on the contrary, would remind him of it and serve as a support or vehicle for it.

In principle it would seem to be very difficult to find a balance between the heroic spirit and the Golden mean as one cannot be heroic except in an extreme sense. However, the hero has to experience this extreme in order to know his physical, moral, spiritual and emotional limits. Only by demanding the most of himself, and putting himself in extreme situations can he know how far he is capable of reaching and becoming. And only by traversing the entire horizon of his being can he know his zone of equilibrium, his Golden mean.

He who has not reached his limits can know his zone of equilibrium only with difficulty. Temperance, as the Greek understood it, is inseparable from the heroic spirit. Only a complete person can have integrity. Moreover, when the maximum has been demanded, the Golden mean will be higher as corresponds to the superior spirit. There is no Golden mean to fit everyone. The inferior man will find his zone of equilibrium at a lower level, which will appear fair to other mediocre people like him.

Maurice Bowra touches on a point of great importance, and all who have studied the Greek spirit in depth will agree on how to reconcile temperance, which is the moral response to the Golden mean in actions, with the heroic spirit that leads one to arms. Bowra concludes that the Greeks did not resolve the problem. But the "Greeks" were an entire people and this matter can only be resolved in the soul of certain individuals. The solution that ultimately has to be resolved in the facts is precisely the equilibrium between the moral and vital aspects of man, both of which find their best expression in the Greeks. Moreover, Greek temperance consists, in my opinion, in this equilibrium of such disparate forces. Besides, what kind of Golden mean can be proposed by one who does not know his limits? All those who have not searched for the limits of situations do not know the boundaries of their character, the totality of their being. These extreme experiences are filtered in the soul and this is what shapes temperance. Well tempered steel has to pass through a red hot stage. This exemplary temperance is one of the most precious legacies of the Hellenic genius.

If I insist on this vital aspect it is because it is the design of my philosophy to make of life an art, something finished in an exemplary manner, like the heroes who inspired the Greeks.

Pericles, who knew how to be the best *strategist of this spirit,* makes the meaning of sacrifice clear in his famous speech to the dead Athenians:

"For the whole earth is the tomb of famous men [*those who were so for the Greeks*]; not only are they commemorated by columns and inscriptions in their own country, but in foreign lands there dwells also an unwritten memorial of them, graven not on stone but in the hearts of men."

Bowra gives two examples of the tombstones found amongst the ruins, where he tries to express the true essence of the deceased. But we could extract something more from them as they reveal that difficult equilibrium they called *temperance*: "His father Cleobulus constructed that monument for the deceased Xenophantus, for his courage and modesty". And in this equally moving one: "Archedice, the daughter of King Hippias, / Who in his time / Of all the potentates of Greece was prime, / This dust doth hide. / Daughter, wife, sister, mother unto kings she was, / Yet free from pride." Here lies the Golden mean of the nobles, of Rank and spirit! Modesty together with courage is a surplus of the spirit, a luxury of the soul that only the fulfilled man of integrity can afford.

Pericles understands temperance in this manner "...living in wealth and sumptuousness we use temperance and make a tempered and philosophical life, and we suffer and tolerate poverty without sadness and dismay, and we use wealth more for needs and opportunities than for pomp, ostentation and vainglory".

Do we realise the road that has to be traversed in this 21st century in order to achieve this perfection? Is the importance of reviving this spirit to truly and intrinsically evolve understood? The Golden age of Athens has left us a giant tombstone of white marble on which are inscribed the essential recipes for an exemplary society.

On Life and Death

The Ancient Greek does not strictly have a Paradise, only life in Nature exist for him. It never occurs to him to search for the plenitude of his existence beyond all this, he puts all his energy into this life, he hopes for nothing after death except that his name endures amongst the living. The exuberant energy, vitality and creativity of these people should be sought in their unconditional commitment to life. For the same reason the lack of these virtues in Medieval times and the general lethargy that was produced can also be explained, by the Christian's projection into the other world. For the uninitiated it has to be clarified that even though the heroic gestures might have carried a cross as in insignia, and even though they never were in keeping with the Christian spirit, they are the typical expressions of warrior people who inhabited Europe and whose bellicose spirit was much before Christianity. It is impossible to understand the Medieval ages without balancing and valuing this confluence of opposing spirits at their roots.

The Augustinian aspiration of *the City of God*, never realised by Christianity, if we accept the ideological differences, became a reality in Greece without any external imposition. The gods were never in "the heavens" but there on Olympus and even in the cities and in the countryside. Some had been born in Crete, others in Thebes, others in Delos; and thus they had left descendants who were the grandfathers of these people.

In order to situate ourselves within the Greek mentality it is essential to abandon all notions of a *post mortem* Paradise like in the religions of the Middle East. Death for the Greek was represented as a dream; it is undoubtedly the onirical life that brings forth this idea, and many others linked to religion. But the "dream of death" did not represent any drama, it had no purpose, it was a shadowy world in which the soul wandered and felt strange. It was an unreal world and did not provide any solution, let alone salvation or hope. Nor was the situation presented as eternal; that uncertain moment had to disappear as in dreams.

What was real for the Greek was this life; the only immortals were the Gods. The only option to achieve immortality was to act heroically in order to be like them. Hence the constant bond between men and the Gods; but in this life, where the Gods actively participated; this life was sacred because of this participation, which was mutual and constant, and in this way the Hellene participated in immortality. Socrates reflected on the afterlife at the moment of his death and he did so in an improvised manner without conviction. Perhaps no peoples have aspired so much to immortality like the Greeks but their great vitality did not let them think of seeking it in another life. On this essential point he knew how to find the Golden mean between a purely materialist or biological belief and a spiritual hope that projected him beyond this life. If we ever try to achieve the level of consciousness and creativity of that exemplary race, we have to take charge of that vision of the world and of that manner of experiencing life that leads to that Golden mean.

As I have said, the Greek barely has an idea of death and this is initially surprising in the case of a people who generate ideas *par excellence*, accustomed to leaving nothing in the inkwell, it is fitting that we think of the reason behind this. One cannot discuss the universal reason of the Hellenes, it manifests itself in their entire work so one can infer the matter from it. The Greek expresses the affirmation of life in an unquestionable and paradigmatic manner, and it is noteworthy that Albert Schweitzer (*The Great Thinkers of India*) who searched for this paradigm has not dwelt on it sufficiently.

If there is something that defines the Greek, and curiously it is through the angle from which he is least studied, although it can be explained by the great sacrifice it implies: it is the *practice of virtues*. The Greek intuited that in the *overcoming of the self*-lay the path towards the perfection of the human being; an aspirant of the first rate towards this ideal, sincere and devoted to its realisation, he could not fail to notice that the best levellers of that path were the virtues. Amongst these bravery stood out, where inexcusably (because other virtues can often be fixed by reason at the desk), practice became action and action realisation. Since playing with death became a practice of bravery, the realisation of that virtue was to surrender life in a supreme act of heroism.

It should not surprise us that Aristotle defined man as a being of the polis, if we consider that he wrote this in Attica where solidarity was unconditional; the project of transcendence is in force here and to me there is nothing more propitious for the realisation of a civilisation. Imagine each citizen seeking his own perfection and competing with his neighbour to develop this noble aspiration: the inevitable result is an exemplary society. This competition should be well understood. When one competes to be the "winner" and enjoys the loss of the opponent, one is feeding the ego, and this takes one on a direction contrary to Greek intention where competition is with oneself, and when it is carried out against another it is to stimulate this. This is the radical and abysmal difference between the competition of the inferior and superior man, the latter does not ever forget to judge his self and the former forgets to at all times because what he is trying to do is exalt it. Of course, I am highlighting opposite profiles in order to make it clearer to reason, conscious that there are nuances between them. The Greeks did not ignore it, for this they had created moral mechanisms in order to avoid the usual slippages of the spirit. Discretion, the external expression of temperance is one of them. This allows him to avoid arrogance, which is where the ego escapes the spirit in these cases. Equilibrium, measure, always present in the Greek, were similar resources to maintain the spirit centred on its ascendant path, that is, on the *central or vital plane* to which my *Psychosophy* refers. The difference between superior and inferior man, explained from this psychological structure is that the former has his centre of consciousness transferred towards the plane of central knowledge, while the latter has it towards the external plane, the permanent abode of the ego.

Lamentably the Ionic spirit, his race, character, culture and tradition etc., clashed with that of his neighbours, the Thebans and Spartans in particular, and internecine wars were too frequent, which was truncating the civilisational project time and again, until it ultimately drained that culture.

The tragic sense of life, so dear to the Greek and expressed in an incomparable manner in his tragedy, involves a complex state of the soul, a direct contact with the Transcendent, represented in his Gods, each one provided with the lofty qualities to which the Greek aspired. For this reason, he was always ready to sacrifice his life in the name of principles; introjected principles, experienced, that were predisposed to becoming voluntarily actualised without effort or inner struggle.

Here, as in other aspects of the Greek spirit, it is important to realise that we are dealing with a whole people accomplishing these lofty ideals, they were not isolated individuals. The heroes of the epic or tragedy were the representatives and exemplars that a people tried to imitate. This only happens when there is a high level of collective consciousness and this should be recognised as an exceptional event in history; this is what makes the Greek civilisation and people exemplary. If to this we add the aesthetic sense, that aspiration to a balanced beauty and in that equilibrium the aspiration to be eternal, to be that which time cannot transform (as opposed to fashion that demands change and betrays the instability of a people), aesthetic sense linked, then, to the transcendent, we will see that the Greek spirit was really based in the unitive faculties; the importance for humanity of having a society capable of this realisation will be understood.

My thought can only give certain directions, paths to knowledge that highlight how psychic mechanisms work, develop a theory of knowledge, in short, only philosophical elements, but this will always be very brief and limited if we compare it with an entire civilisation realising this ideal.

The Social Being

The law in Greece (like in India) evolved in a religious atmosphere and was incorporated in the City State. In particular, this took place through social equality from the time of Solon, the political wise man, but, as happens to a people with an elevated and balanced sense of justice as equality given by merit. In the Solonic sense, *Sophrosyne* is understood as equilibrium of classes in fair proportion, so the public offices were under the charge of *the best*. At least this is what happened in theory, we know that politicians manage to get their own way, but in Greece it was applied efficiently because these hierarchies were respected. This, incidentally, is in keeping with my proposal in the political field, *meritocracy,* to which I referred in *The Roots of Morality*.

What we understand today by democracy is not what the Greeks understood, precisely because that sense of *equilibrium* made each individual accept the superiority of the other on merit or made him recognise his own inferiority, especially in the moral order. This established equilibrium naturally in society. The laws made all citizens equal before it, but daily and permanent management of the nuances was established through this particular intuition and recognition. And this is only possible when the people are imbued with an elevated ideal of perfection that they have as a reference and which comes before selfish inclinations; in other words, their *capacity for altruism*, the condition for any superior society. Contemporary democracy that is understood as a system of government in which each one can do and think what he likes, is placed at the antipode of the democracy in which each citizen demands the maximum from himself and not, it should be clarified, so as to acquire more things, but more virtues.

And this is the reason why it is particularly interesting for my philosophy to speak of these people who are exemplary: the change proposed through my philosophy is the same as that of the Greeks, to intrinsically transform man, to develop his greatest qualities.

Following that same ideal, the city of Athens was not only there to make life easier or more comfortable for its citizens but also for it to be exemplary. The architecture of its majestic but sober temples expressed a paradigmatic equilibrium that had to be reflected in the soul of the people. They were surrounded by sculpture that we could call perfect without exaggerating, that expressed the heroic feats of their heroes and housed the gods whose beauty they tried to imitate and whose immortality reminded them of the transcendence to which they should aspire.

The multiple and ductile capacity, that polyvalent intelligence without barriers apt for the varied vocations required in Athens and during the Renaissance is a phenomenon of extreme importance to understand the periods of apogee (see *The Spirit in History*). What this phenomenon fundamentally reveals is the plenitude of man, understood in the first place as an individual and, as a consequence, as a social being. In fact, this social being is one of his personal aptitudes.

It seems almost absurd to us today that the Athenian people would have chosen Sophocles or Thucydides as strategist (or general) to lead an army to war, that is, to task men of letters for this bellicose enterprise, but these people wanted to be represented by personally fulfilled men of integrity. *Their heroes had to have a soul full of virtues,* of which knowing how to fight was a result of physical order: harmony of movement, lightness, dexterity, etc., preceded by a moral order: courage, sacrifice, integrity, etc., that is to say, a good dose of wisdom. Their heroes were not killing machines but those who had these virtues.

From the aforesaid we can gather that in order to produce an exemplary society, the State should be directed to produce fully developed individuals whom the masses can use as exemplars, not those who triumph in only one specialisation. The masses have an ingrained need, surely tribal in origin, of heroes who they can admire. Contemporary society has channeled these tendencies in the opposite direction to that which is needed to produce exemplary individuals and societies.

For the Greek, society, the city, the citizen, were all products of Nature and the gods themselves were inseparable from it, this established an organic and harmonious relationship and from this were born the laws that expressed natural and divine laws. The citizens integrated in this manner in society and in the World, generating incalculable power. The victory over the Persians who had double the number of ships and ten times as many men are proof of this. And the enthusiasm, security, confidence and generosity that this victory generated after the peace in Athens made this the exemplary city that we admire today. And the City-State were thus the field in which the citizen could fully develop his possibilities.

The Universal Being

In the *Universus,* that is, in the spiritual and material whole there are two basic forces, one is creative and, like Bergson who accurately coined this basic idea, we can call the *élan vital*; we also find this idea in Aurobindo where matter charged with spirit searches for it in its development. In *The Evolution of the Spirit* I have commented on both authors so I will not return to them here. The other force is *Order*, and we can give it many names. The Hindus personify it as Vishnu, as he is entrusted with maintaining what has been created. It is well known that in the Hindu Trinity Brahma is the Creator, and Shiva is considered the Destroyer; even if it is understood that the latter does not destroy out of evil but as a necessity of Nature so that it can continue to regenerate cyclically. In my conception this force is not necessary, I believe that Nature decays due to its own imperfection, it sickens and dies; although it does everything possible to live and maintain life by reproducing, adapting and modifying.

The Greeks saw the intervention of some gods in catastrophes, for example Hephaestus in earthquakes, Poseidon in storms, Ares in war. Here too I attribute these forces to Nature's way of being; in the case of war to human nature; even if complex spiritual or psychic factors intervene such as anger, envy, greed, etc., for which the Greeks also had deities.

The natural and psychic reasons will seem more logical to modern man, but what he does not understand is the need of the Greek and the Hindu to stay in permanent contact with the Cosmos, and to remain integrated with All, where there is no separation between the spiritual and the material, where reality is the *Universus*. Psyche, soul and the spirit are one single thing for the Greek; the soul is the principle of life and the creative principle that maintains it; when it leaves the body it dies. But, to repeat, the gods intervene in the psyche because everything is united. Using my language, the gods are *unitive factors*; God, as I have defined him, is the *unitive factor par excellence.*

Modern man does not understand this because his spirit is based in his *individual consciousness* and cannot be integrated into the *Universus*, nor can it understand the integrating function of the gods. The Greek and the Hindu who have the spirit in their *unitive consciousness*, need the resource of the gods to remain integrated in the *Universus*. The greatest aspiration of the Hindu is to achieve the total unification to which my philosophy also inclines; but this is a matter of great import which we will deal with later.

Now I would like to return to the vital and universal, spiritual and material principle of *Order* that as I have earlier expressed is a *primary manifestation of the essence of the World*. In reality, all the Greek gods are there to maintain Order, but some take more delight in this task in relation to men, such as Apollo and Athena, concerned with establishing justice, and Hermes exercising his role of mediator, a fundamental task to keep man in contact with the gods, that is, *unified*.

The Greeks, so fond of equilibrium, could not fail to have a specific goddess for this function: Nemesis is entrusted with avoiding excesses. Her etymology indicates her work: "give to each what is due," she was retributive, compensatory justice. For example, she put a limit on those favoured too much by Tyché, Fortune, she consoled the rejected lover and punished infidelity. She was a personification of the Law, and it is not surprising to see her represented on the coins of the time with the *modius* on the head, which was the *measure* that men in their ambition should not exceed. She was accompanied by the nymph Adrastea, who was the instrument of divine wrath, in a chariot drawn by griffins. In the Louvre there is a statue of Nemesis with the horn of abundance in her arms; a magnificent paradox: abundance (not of much but of good) is a product of equilibrium.

I do not know if contemporary man has the capacity to understand the transcendental meaning of these symbols or Greek artistic invention. Hesiod represents to us a more timid Nemesis, fleeing from this world with Aidos, both covered in white veils, stricken by human perversity; they had their reasons. In Athens a festival in her honour was celebrated: *Nemesia*, a custom imported by Rome, which is not surprising amongst a people who believed in the Law. I confess to the reader that such intelligence on this matter moves me. Lamentably this matter can only be understood unitively, that is, perceiving the religious, artistic, social and psychic relationship and unity in unison; here lies the Greek genius.

Of course, modern man, alienated from his circumstances, only knows of "objective facts," he wants "scientific proofs," without knowing what he is fundamentally missing: the pleasure, the immense joy in being *integrated*. Although it is not to my taste, I will try to be scientific and use anatomy for this purpose. It is enough to study the multiple functions of blood and microorganisms to transport us to a realisation of the force of equilibrium in Nature. When we are hurt microorganisms immediately appear and seek to heal the wound and they leave once *order* has been restored. In a similar manner, when we break a bone cells soon appear, eager to fill the gap and join the separated bone. These cells work ceaselessly to the point of generating a bone spur or a protuberance that would continue to form if other cells did not appear to detain them and establish an *equilibrium*. These simple examples suffice. The entire human body is maintained through an equilibrium; every doctor knows this: neither too fat, nor too thin, neither too tall nor too short, not just proteins, not just amino acids, and not even too much exercise; health is equilibrium. We can say the same of the plants and the rest of Nature: without equilibrium, the universe would be chaos, it would not be a Cosmos; the duration of life and things is maintained by equilibrium. There is, thus, a *universal force* that expresses itself and acts as *Equilibrium*; whether we call it that or Vishnu, Nemesis or Aphrodite, is essentially unimportant. I will again cite from the last verses with which Dante ends his *Divine Comedy*: "The love that moves the sun and all the stars." What is important is that this vision be moving for the reader, so that it moves him to think.

Pericles

In the *The Roots of Morality* I have expanded on Pericles, who I reveal as an *example of an enlightened governor*, which was the great aspiration of the *Enlightenment*, an aspiration I fully share as it is not the forms of government that make for the greatness of a country, but the genius applied to the fulfilment of the human being, prioritising philosophical, religious, aesthetic and moral values over material values. Pericles certainly was concerned with the latter but he put them at the service of the former and thus Athens was exemplary, for its thinkers and artists who, though patronised by the State, could freely express themselves. In the words of Voltaire, the great promotor of the Enlightenment: "I do not not agree with what you say but I will defend to the death your right to say it."

As I point out in said work, their democracy has nothing in common with what exists today, it is actually its antipode, as instead of adapting the culture to the popular level, the people had to follow the high ideals that Pericles and his co-operators put into effect. They rejected the aristocracy as a privileged class but they shared the aristocratic values, they did not accept its political and economic power but did accept its ethics that could extend to all citizens; their "democracy" was based on this. And the miracle was that the people happily accepted these values, something that only happens when there is a high cultural and spiritual level.

We should remember that during the century that bears his name, Greek theatre achieved an unequalled perfection with the Tragedies, it was the greatest attraction followed by the religious festivals that joyfully exalted the spirit of this people. They practiced the virtues with gusto and also died on the battlefield with verve; these people were possessed of moral values and ecstatic with aesthetes. Of course not everything was the work of this great political strategist, his merit consisted in using and exalting the high level of consciousness of his contemporaries.

Plutarch attests that "Pericles was an incorruptible man, immune to wealth and seeing that his country was great, he made it greater and richer; more powerful than many kings and tyrants, he never increased his fortune by one drachma more than what his father left him". This attitude of Pericles is novel when compared to that of earlier rulers and the aristocracy of the Greek states that surrounded him. And, of course it is in stark contrast to the politics of the "barbarian" monarchs, to whom Plutarch alludes. The money and goods saved from useless luxury rebounded naturally for the benefit of the city and the people.

His integrity and other virtues were an example for this people who were loyal to the common program, that "social contract" that Pericles proposed. He was fully aware of the phenomenon of *mimesis* generated not only by his example but also by the plethora of geniuses that surrounded him. He knew that his city for which he had done what he could, would be exemplary until the end of time.

He thus expresses it in his famous discourse to the first deaths in the war: "It is through the truth of works, rather than through bare words that the greatness of our city will be known". "Only she has more fame in the whole world than all the others put together". "Those who live in the present and those of the future will admire us greatly". And he was not wrong, here I am expressing my admiration, and I will not be the last. "And, finally our city is a school of doctrine and a law for all Greece". And for all cultures we could add.

But not only should the citizen sacrifice himself for the city, this in turn completed the greatness of the Athenians. There is no doubt that Pericles wanted the perfection of both; he was very clear about the design and the means to achieve it: "In my opinion the first and principal judge of the virtue of men is the good and virtuous life, and the last that confirms it is an honourable death". This will also be the impression of Plato.

"In doing good, again, we are unlike others; we make our friends by conferring, not by receiving favours" (this seems to be a trace of *Nicomachean Ethics*) "...so that by knowing that freedom is happiness and happiness is freedom you will not flee the dangers of war". "Because a wise and prudent man is more ashamed of cowardice than of death". This extreme morality without sanctimoniousness points to the total fulfilment of the human being. As concerns the freedom-happiness equation, I must admit that it has anticipated one of the central points of my philosophy by twenty five centuries.

The Greek Miracle

I have no doubt that the "Greek miracle" took place because there was *a shift of the spirit towards the unitive faculties,* for the simple reason that when this phenomenon is seen from the unitive perspective, it is shown with crystal clarity. In my earlier works I have demonstrated the different means to produce this shift and reach this perspective. I deal with this matter from a personal aspect, as the relationship of the individual with his own psyche. But this shift occurs at times in various subjects in unison and can affect an entire society with a general elevation of the level of consciousness; it is then that this "miracle" of creativity takes place. Of course, the genius always manages to reach that level and state, even in spiritually sterile epochs, since it knows how to find its creative faculties, but if we follow the rule of the creator of logic, we will admit that "one swallow does not make a summer", a single genius neither defines a society nor makes a civilisation.

When an entire society raises its level of consciousness, we are facing a social fact, but also, and above all, we should not forget we are facing an individual spiritual phenomenon that has spread like a virus. Numerous external, historical, geographical and cultural factors have contributed to it, but these only create the conditions for the spirit to express itself. This is always there, latent, waiting to manifest itself, but evidently there are peoples who have it close at hand and others who neglect it; some who know how to cultivate the spirit and reap the rewards while others neglect it as if they did not know for what it is for. Some individuals, like some peoples, possess an intuition, a particular genius that knows how to extract the most from the circumstances that they have been lucky enough to live through; the Greek undeniably had this faculty.

A vital and aesthetic people *par excellence* made of life an art, and of art the most essential of life: such is the Greek tragedy. (On this see *The Spirit in Art*)

The superior man, the Greek in his glorious times, has the entire *Universus* as a context in his life; for the common man the world is what immediately surrounds him, the quotidian, his "own" and those close to him. Politics interests him to the extent that it affects him, his vision is egocentric, his perspective is individual. The Greek, very particularly, having this universal vision, had the polis as part of this Order. The laws of the State were inspired by this Order, and did not only serve for citizens to settle their affairs by legal means, but above all to integrate them into the *Kosmos*.

The goal of their religion was basically the same; and few religions in the history of humanity have been so effective for this purpose; and this is crucial when judging the Hellenes.

It would be excessive to dwell on Greek inventions: the comedy, the tragedy, arithmetics, geometry, logic, philosophy, historiography, medicine, politics, and the excellence achieved by disciplines that they did not invent, such as the plastic arts or astronomy, as all books cite them. But it seems to me that we take these inventions for granted and that it is worth reflecting on what our civilisation would have been like without them. We would possibly have had to wait until the Renaissance for their discovery and even then it would have been impossible to think of this without the Greek Birth. And one can conjecture what would have become of our civilisation if we had received the entire Greek heritage because, as is well known, we have inherited only a small part of it. I will be told that these conjectures are beside the point as what happened is a truth we cannot change, but what I want is that we realise the importance of that Birth and the need to recover that exemplary spirit, as it is unimaginable what contemporary man with all the technology and external possibilities he possesses could create and form if he had as centred and elevated a consciousness as did the Greek.

I am convinced that "the Greek miracle" was due to the generalised *unitive* perspective that ensured the participation of the citizens and the State in the universal Order. All culture revolved around that superior perspective, that profound experience that few societies and even fewer individuals achieve now or then. For this reason we barely have an idea of what it must have been like to live during the times of Pericles. The genius of this man, who should therefore be considered an exemplary statesman, was to realise this particular spiritual situation of the Attican people, who were in a position to live in that universal harmony. He obtained the means to create the best possible conditions for that spirit to manifest itself in all spheres: artistic, scientific, sports, politics etc. But what determined the current of that civilisation were the highly developed unitive faculties: the aesthetic, moral, religious, and philosophical sense.

Of course, the commercial and economic expansion, which Pericles also knew how to provide, facilitated the task, but we would be projecting our poor present day vision, laying all its hopes on the economy, if we were to explain the "Greek miracle" by its economic conditions. Any modern city is richer than Athens ever was, and there is none, not even the richest, that comes close to performing that miracle. Decidedly, to begin to understand that phenomenon, let alone to realise it, one has to change one's perspective; and this is the most difficult as it implies an intrinsic change in us.

The miracle of Western civilisation was Greece: *the incarnation* of all the muses in the philosophers who reached the sources of wisdom, in the artists who expressed their art to perfection, and in the sages who invented each of the sciences. And the *resurrection* was the Renaissance.

Hadrian

While mentioning eminent makers of civilisations we cannot forget Hadrian, who continued the ideas and works of Pericles in Rome some six centuries later, when Greece was nothing more than a Roman province. The first thing that this emperor observes is the need to stop imperial expansion, which was the prevailing idea among intellectuals such as Pliny the Younger. For this he signs a peace treaty with the Persians on whose borders numerous legions had perished and would perish. During his reign, which would also last a quarter of a century, there was not a single war of aggression. What Hadrian disseminated was culture in its diverse manifestations, and he fundamentally understood this to be the Hellenic culture in which he was educated as a child. I attribute to his government the first resurgence (I will not use the term rebirth because it had survived until then) of the Hellenic spirit. The second resurgence would be that of the emperor Julian, which, as we will see, never came to fruition. If he had followed Hadrian's example, of reaching a peace agreement with the Persians, it is possible that the history of the West would have been very different.

For 12 years Hadrian roamed the vast empire accompanied by architects and specialised craftsmen, leaving temples, theatres, libraries, and various public works that embellished the cities. He did this in Jerusalem, Persepolis, restoring its famous library, hospitals and school of medicine and continuing the temple of Trajan; in Nîmes, France, he builds the amphitheatre that is still preserved; in Athens he builds the greatest temple in Greece dedicated to the Olympian Jupiter, and also a monumental library and numerous other new and restored works. In Rome he constructed the grandiose temple of Venus and Rome, bridges over the Tiber, and Hadrian's villa, an example of Hellenic beauty with a lake surrounded by Greek statues, baths, a library, a room for philosophers, in short, culture in its finest expression. He also laid the foundation of the Athenaeum where philosophy, poetry and rhetoric were taught. And he wrote on philosophy, art, literature, sciences, sculpted and painted, sang and played.

In this prolonged period of peace in an atmosphere of freedom and creativity the Empire reached its zenith in all orders. In words of Gibbon: Within the Empire "the general principle of government was wise, simple and beneficent. They enjoyed the religion of their ancestors." "Toleration produced not only mutual indulgence, but even religious concord." "The devout polytheist, though fondly attached to his national rites, admitted with implicit faith the different religions of the earth (...) this "perpetually disposed him to multiply the articles of his belief and to enlarge the list of his protectors. The thin texture of the Pagan mythology was interwoven with various, but not discordant materials. As soon as it was allowed that sages and heroes, who had lived or who had died for the benefit of their country, were exalted to a state of power an immortality that they deserved, if not of adoration, at least the reverence, of all mankind." This is the cult to merit, so dear to my moral philosophy. "The Greek, the Roman and the Barbarian, as they met before their respective altars, easily persuaded themselves that *under various names*, and with various ceremonies, they adored the same deities." "Within a century or two the Gauls applied to their gods the names of Mercury, Mars, Apollo, &c." (*The History of the Decline and Fall of the Roman Empire*) The advantages of freedom and religious inclusion, as well the parallel with the Hindu tradition are evident.

"What is peace? -Hadrian said- "a tranquil liberty." "What is liberty? innocence and virtue." He could not have made clearer the example of the enlightened ruler, although it might have been in vain because of so many rulers who do not understand the need for the priority of culture and matters of the spirit.

Conclusion

Western history has had, and I hope will continue to have, Greece as its exemplary reference, and it is my objective to contribute to this. With this naturally I want to add that the enlightened of our culture have always had access to the coffer that Athens kept, and still keeps, when in search of the most precious gems of our culture. Pericles's claim that Athens was "the school of Greece", has greatly surpassed his aspirations, it has been the school of Western civilisation and now, with globalisation, it is to be hoped that it will serve as a school for humanity. I am not implying, I hasten to add, that the present Western civilisation become an exemplar but that Athens serves as a school for other cultures, and that the exemplary periods of other cultures, especially those of India, serve our culture. The clarification is necessary precisely because Western civilisation has reneged from this teaching, it has betrayed that school and has placed itself at its antipode, as an example of decadence. We will discuss extensively on this subject; for now the aforementioned clarification will suffice.

Greece is exemplary not only for its virtues but also for its vices. In the coffer of Athens we find, as in the stories of pirates, serpents and other vermin, but which clearly contrast with its gems and serve as a model, as in fairy tales with their morals. But of course the history of Greece is not a "fairy tale", the Greek genius created and practiced all forms of government, its philosophers developed all forms of thought, its mythology covered the most recondite labyrinths of the mind, and using this experience its dramatists shaped the exemplary tragedies that derive from the eternal struggle of virtues with human passions, and its artists expressed them in the purest, most refined and exalting forms.

The Greeks knew these contrasts and their interrelation, which are what constitute the essence of life, and they expressed them so completely that, by their strength, they were left as models to be followed for posterity. And so conscious were they of this that they created a philosophy, and not "yet another", but precisely the model that philosophers would follow and continue to use, and this is so because they did not only search for prototypes in history but in eternal principles. To all this we must add the freedom of spirit, which is part of all the periods of apogee, which allowed this spectrum of possibilities to be opened to its fullest extent, covering 360º of human alternatives. It is worth mentioning that the "Socrates case" is, like him, the exception that proves the rule. We would do well to remember the gods proposed by Plato and Aristotle in order to realise that in Athens anything could be said, as long as it was well thought out and expressed.

When the materialist hears Plato who, in turn, cites Thales of Miletus, one of the seven wise men of Greece: "How can there be people who ignore that the World is full of gods?" Do they think that Thales was not wise and that Plato was naive? What happens to the materialist is that he projects his own vision of the gods who he sees only in his concrete expression, as a statue and idol, while the man of spirit sees it as *an expression of the Spirit*; these are two such different perspectives that there can be no understanding amongst them. The other grave mistake, into which the materialist falls, also through spiritual myopia, is that of believing that the spiritual is reduced to the field of religion, since the frontiers of aesthetics and morality are nothing more than abstractions of discernment. Actually, the man of spirit does not see the world as populated by concrete gods, but charged with spirit, that is, with beauty, love, order and joy and it is this inspiration that leads him to the aspiration of establishing beauty, justice, sympathy, mutual understanding and peace.

For this reason and all that has been said, it should be understood that I am not appealing to the religious in particular, but to men of spirit in general: the artists, those avid for justice, ecologists, those who want to live in peace and happiness. In fact, the religious dogmatics only contribute to misunderstanding amongst men, history and the present demonstrate this. And this happens precisely due to the fact that they are not men of spirit, that is why they need to concretise and materialise the spiritual in rigid laws that they want to impose on others and, of course, acquire power over them. An open-minded materialist has decidedly more spirit than a closed-minded religious one.

The fratricidal wars that led to the decline of Hellas were a consequence of the lack of understanding of the refined Attican spirit, especially by Sparta and Macedonia. The plague that devastated Athens, and finally killing Pericles himself, was decisive; a misfortune that would determine the history of the West. First Alexander's and then Rome's politics of conquest show an externalised spirit looking for external solutions that had little to do with the creative spirit of the Athens of Pericles. Hellas at that time had barely felt the need to extend its dominions to the south of Italy in the Ionic sea, when it could have created an empire as was created by Alexander a little later, but had to attend to more substantial philosophical, artistic, religious and social matters; its spirit was more focused in its creative faculties. I believe that for this reason it was framed in the ideal of the City-State; the same phenomenon, for the same reasons, will be repeated during the Renaissance; and it will be of the same spirit.

This spirit and culture would motivate Alexander and his successors and later the Roman emperors, but they poured so much energy into external factors and extended beyond themselves and their natural borders until they ultimately reached the abyss that would swallow them.

On the Greeks and Hindus

On Greek and Hindu Myths

Hinduism is a vast religious field and it has been able to host all the spiritual manifestations of these people who, in this sense, undoubtedly have been the most prolific on the planet. In Hinduism we find all levels of the spirit and on the highest we find the most elevated that man could reach: the direct relationship with Divinity. Those who have attained this stage in India do not reject the other stages, like those of myths, but integrate them. The architects and artists who execute their temples do the same. It is for this reason that we see the participation of all kinds of animals in Hindu epics and some of them perform such heroic feats that elevate them to being exemplary beings. These deeds of men and animals are also represented on the external facades of the temples.

In general, when a myth is read or heard, only the facts or characters are related as if it were a novel, but that is only the external and superficial part of it. Beyond that express and manifest desire, the myth has the virtue of connecting these facts with a cosmic Order, on the one hand, and with an internal psychic order on the other, closely linked to our moral consciousness. As it is a basic principle of my *Psychosophy*, (I refer the reader to this book) that *there is no psychic order if there is a moral disorder*, the myth acquires a special meaning and has a specific function. Some peoples have been able to know this function and they have incorporated it as a structural part of their culture. This is the case of the ancient Greeks and the Hindus of the past and present, who have shown unequalled psychological and artistic genius to create and express their myths. I will make some connections between them.

It is well known that the Aryans invaded the Indus valley around the 15th century B.C. where they merged with an autochthonous culture. From then on we can begin to speak of an Indo-Aryan culture with its own characteristics. But we would be very superficial if we were to think that only historical relationships were established with transculturation. In the case of religion, it is more correct to speak of an Aryan spirit that inserts itself into the Indian spirit, producing that rich amalgam that today we call Hinduism, full of myths of remote origin that still thrive amongst the Greeks and Hindus, that are expressed in different ways, in tune with the complex context that surrounds them.

In the Aryan spirit, as Max Muller has shown through his philological studies, we find a clear tendency to relate the gods and heroes to the celestial beings that surround us, especially the sun and moon. Before entering into more detail, I will repeat that myths always have a more profound meaning than what is apparent. I believe, and Eliade confirms it, that no culture has adored the sun or moon as such, rather that they are taken as *expressions or symbols of a divinity that underlies them*. This is clear in India and in Greece. Apollo is not Ephebus nor is Vishnu Surya, the sun. They are not the solar disc but, as iconography represents them, they "carry" the solar disc in their hands. They are the light that illuminates the world and also man's intelligence and consciousness. In the same way that no one takes the statue of a god for the god himself, but as a representation of him, the astral beings are also expressions of the Nature of gods that are ultimately intangible, of a purely spiritual nature.

There are different modes of expression and different levels of understanding with Divinity. We should, at the very least, be prudent and respectful of the cultures that we do not understand. One has to be very simple and badly informed to imagine that the Greeks were naive and the Hindus continue to be so. The same myths express different levels of comprehension. A single example will suffice: The mother of Dionysus asks Zeus to be kind enough "to show himself as he is", Zeus tells her not to ask him to do that but, as she insists, he reveals himself. This causes the poor woman to be burnt to ashes because He shows himself as pure Light. This is the Greek god in his essence, and Vishnu in his essence. Khrishna reveals himself as Light (*Gita XI*), as does the Buddha (*Dhammapada XXVI*). That the gods reveal themselves as light is not surprising since the ultimate Reality expresses itself as Light.

This idea of an absolute God will be in India the basis and the objective of its religion. The raison d'etre of Hinduism is to achieve the experience of that Absolute. This is affirmed in religious texts, and this happens some 1000 years after the Aryans invaded the Indus valley, that is, after 10 centuries of the fusion of the Aryan and Indian cultures that had spread over the Ganges valley, in the period when Greece reached its apogee.

The basis and objective of Hinduism will thus be the Absolute, and the life and history of India unfolds, full of struggles, graces and misfortunes, with its heroes, who will be transformed, like in Greece, into mythic and exemplary beings.

The absolute expression of Divinity is Brahman, and even if an extensive philosophy has developed around him, which is what constitutes the Vedanta doctrine, it has barely been incorporated in the world of mythology. Within this, as we shall see, the Creator assumes different names. The prolific popular Hindu imagination has chosen gods who are closer to life and who participate in it. Nowadays there are two main gods in the Hindu religion, Shiva and Vishnu, particularly as Krishna.

Even if countless heroic feats can be attributed to them, they also have their absolute aspect that assimilates them to Brahman, in such a way that the philosopher, the mystic and the artist can apply themselves to the realisation of the Absolute, that is, to the unconditional liberation through them. We find here once more elements for all tastes and levels of consciousness.

Given the importance that the Indian tradition assigns to reincarnation, we will dedicate a specific comment to it later. These quotes are enough here to highlight that this belief was in the Hellenic consciousness, as it is shown in Pythagoras and explicitly in Plato, who tells us in the *Phaedo*: "It is a very old belief that when souls leave this world they go to Hades and that from there they return to this world and to life." (*189*) "When the soul follows the same tendencies as the body", "when it is stained with the same blemishes as the body (after death) it soon enters another body." (*83 a*) In this same work he affirms, as in Hinduism, that the destiny of souls, which are always eternal, must respond to the character and conduct of man. So, if due to his intemperance and lack of modesty, he is assimilated to an ass, he has to reincarnate as an ass or a similar animal. "In the same way those who have loved injustice, tyranny and robbery, will pass into the bodies of wolves, hawks and kites." While the souls that have left the body in all their purity will approach the nature of the gods. (*82 c*) Plotinus, some six centuries later, will come to the same conclusion.

Genesis in India

The versions (since they are many and diverse) of the origin of the Cosmos in the Hindu tradition are born from the sacred books as well as from literature and are intermixed with the mythic. Though far from the origin, *The Laws of Manu*, written around the second century B.C., tell us about Genesis as it was accepted, at least by the Brahmins of that century. "Having decided He alone, the Supreme Being to make all things emanate from his own substance, he forced the waters to rise and for him to deposit his fertile seed therein. That seed became a golden egg (Hiranyagarba), shining like the star of a thousand luminous rays (supernova explosion?) in which the Supreme Being was revealed in the form of Brahma." This idea of "cosmic Egg" is found in the mythologies of other cultures. "Through subtle particles" -the text continues- "that emanated from the being (galactic gas?) the principles of all things that formed this perishable world were created". (*Libro II*) In this way, we see that all that is created participates in the divine substance, that all is sacred. "After having created the Universe in this way, He, whose power is incomprehensible, disappeared again, absorbed into his Soul". "When this God is awake, the Universe performs its actions; when it sleeps, its spirit is absorbed by a profound lethargy and the Universe destroys itself". We see here that God is Creator but not Destroyer, as the "Universe destroys itself". "Through these alternative dreams, the immutable Being, ceaselessly and endlessly makes the group of lifeless or living creatures live or die".

The last period, called the *Kali-Yuga*, which is the present, coincides approximately with the Flood described in the *Satapata Brahmana*. Manu is the name of Noah in the Hindu legend. Manu is the name of those who initiate legendary human periods. The text quoted says that while Manu washed his hands in a fountain of water, he found a small fish who said to him: "Manu, save me and I will save you from the Flood that will sweep away all beings". "What must I do to save you?" Manu asked of the fish. "When we are small," the fish answered, "our existence is precarious because the big fish can devour us. Keep me in this fountain. When I am grown take me to the sea. Then I will be sufficiently big to free myself from all these dangers". When the fish became bigger it said to Manú: "It is now time for you to construct a ship to save yourself from the Flood. When it starts get on to the ship and let the waves carry you along; I will save you later". Manú followed his instructions. After taking the grown fish to the sea, he began to construct his ship. When the rains began, Manu aimlessly set out to sea until the fish appeared to him, now gigantic but which he recognised, and to which he tied his ship. The fish took him to a prominent mountain (that would later be called Sumeru) and told him: "Tie your ship to that big tree". He did so. The waters then receded and Manu found himself alone because all life had disappeared and the fish too. Later tradition would say that the fish had been Vishnu; this will be the first of his incarnations. The fish that we find in Hindu iconography, particularly in the temples, is Vishnu. We will see Vishnu's other avatars as each one of them is a milestone in the history of the *Dharma*.

Manú, then, made repeated offerings to the sea asking for a companion. Time passed and one day a woman came out of the sea and told him: "The sacrifices that you have made have saved my life. Now you can make me your wife through a sacrifice and all your desires will be fulfilled". Manú celebrated the sacrifice. They were the progenitors of the so-called race of Manu which is that of the brahmins, although in tradition it has remained as that of human beings in general. The Manu of the flood would be the first King of India, to whom we can retrace the origins of the mythic "laws of Manu". These were written some 3000 years later but they are said to date back to the first King who with seven sages would have received the Laws directly from Brahman. Now Manu is similar to Moses in his legendary encounter with Jehovah, but the *Laws of Manú* are much more explicit and have been written down: they govern the life of kings, the activities of priests and of society in general, establishing civil and penal laws. These are also the laws to which reincarnation obeys.

As we will see when dealing with the Vedas, the Creator assumes different names, but it will be Brahma who will predominate in the tradition. The Vishnuites will show Brahma emerging from Vishnu's navel, thus making him the supreme divinity, Narayana, who remains impassively sleeping on Sesha, the serpent that had participated in the Creation, when gods and asuras pulled at its ends making it turn to stir the primordial waters in order to extract from them the nectar of immortality; which will ultimately remain in the power of the gods.

On this occasion Shiva had also participated because from those churning primordial waters had decanted evil, a poison, the counterpart of absolute good, immortality. Shiva drinks that poison and digests the evil to make life possible; although considering human history we easily infer that he did not swallow all the evil. However, the poison left his neck blue. All Hindus know this episode. In the Himalayas, home of Shiva and his consort Parvati, a gigantic and strikingly impressive mountain stands, at the feet of whose glaciers I have traversed, which is Shiva himself with his blue neck, Nihil-kant. Far away from there, in Ankor-Vat, Cambodia, I have seen carved in an immense frieze the story of this Creation at the moment when the gods and asuras pull the serpent into the primordial waters. The power of the mythical in the peoples is indisputable.

Parallels in the Epic and Myths

Amongst the similarities that we find between the Greek and Hindu epics it is worth highlighting the need to appeal to divine inspiration, because this custom expresses *the relationship between the individual and universal consciousness* that both peoples felt; as is clear in the invocations of the poets. I have expanded on this subject in *The Roots of Art*.

The similarity between Greek and Hindu culture in the teachings of the epic has to be emphasised: just as Homer had educated Hellas, the Mahabarata and the Ramayana have educated *and will continue to educate* India. And what is curious about the matter is that in both epics we sometimes find passages so similar that they seem to have the same origin.

In Greek tradition there were seven sages held as examples. In order to conserve them amongst the immortals, the seven stars of the Pleiades were assigned to them. In the Indian tradition the Vedic sages were also reduced to seven. These *rishis* were identified with the seven stars of the Great Bear. In the Ramayana, as in the Iliad, the main cause, although it may in fact have been an excuse, in keeping with the poetic version, of the war between the two sides is the kidnapping of a queen of incomparable beauty; Sita is the equivalent of Helen.

The gods are active participants in both epic works, but in the *Ramayana* all the divine, human and animal characters are well defined; they are either good or bad. The gods are all good and act for the virtuous, even if the powers of the demons were granted by the gods before they began to be used in the service of evil. There are no psychological confrontations; there are barely any doubts in acting or later remorse. Even temptations do not exist, as the characters do not obey normal human motivations, but ideals. They are archetypes of the good, the brave, the honest, etc. In the *Ramayana* there is no psychology, there are only pure immaculate moral examples; the idealism is total.

In accordance with the above, Schilingloff observes "that Indian literature has no character who follows an emotional evolution and within whose interior has a conflict of passions; it only knows absolute types representative of an ideal". "The tendency to abstraction converted people into a species of incarnated ideas who, like chess pieces, could move through laws predetermined for a particular type". We can admit thus that literature did not pay great attention to the psychological aspect, rather that its vision, so typical of the Hindu spirit, is decidedly idealistic, like its philosophy. The raison d'être of Indian literature is its example and teachings in which moral idealism alternates with philosophical idealism.

While the Greek gods seem to be more human, with their temptations, jealousies, anger, etc., and we see that some are on the side of the Trojans and others on the side of the Achaeans, the Hindu protagonists act without contradiction, without the weight of conscience, they have a divine perfection. Rama, the greatest hero of the *Ramayana*, is like this; he is not even a demi god, he is Vishnu himself incarnate. Only once do we see him hesitate: when he doubts before accepting his wife, after the latter has lived with her kidnapper, he shows his human side: "in his gaze he expressed admiration, joy, love, anger and pain". This might seem an authorial manoeuvre to show Rama's ignorance over his divine nature, as only at that moment did Brahma inform him of it. Rama's ignorance was necessary for destiny to be fulfilled: the demon Ravana had to be annihilated only by a man. Rama, however, was not as such except at that moment, his powers were divine, without them he could not have destroyed the demon of twenty arms and ten heads that reproduced like the Hellenic hydra as soon as they were lopped off.

Although we do not know if there was ever a direct relation between Greece and India, their mythologies have some common or similar themes: When Odysseus returns to Ithaca, he finds numerous suitors seeking the hand of his wife. Nobody could possess her because there was nobody capable of stringing Odysseus' great bow. By completing the challenge, Odysseus reveals who he truly is. In the *Mahabarata* we again find the story of the suitor of a queen who can only be had by he who can draw the famous bow and cross narrow rings with its arrows. Here, as in the Odyssey, the hero Prince Arjuna appears amongst the nobles dressed in a hermits attire, like Odysseus, only to make himself known after the feat. There are so many similarities that we cannot help but think of a cultural transposition, whose origin we must attribute to India. Logic inclines one to resolve things in this way because the presence of a hermit in a feast of nobles is natural in India where Brahmins, who may be ascetics, are revered, but it seems artificial in Greece where a beggar cannot claim a queen. The fact that the legend is repeated in the Ramayana inclines to support this argument. In the Tulsidas version of the *Ramayana* we have the daughter of the King of Janaka, Sita, who will be given in marriage to whoever could break Shiva's bow. Many suitors try in vain. It will be Rama, the hero of this epic work, who will break the bow "as if it were a lotus stem", and become the one who wins the princess.

Another mythic model is that of the forced absence of the hero for many years during which he performs heroic feats. This model will constitute a classic of the epic that will form part of the universal heritage. The absence of the beloved woman during the time of the adventures is part of this archetype. An exception seems to be in the case of Rama who shares the retreat with his wife but she is soon kidnapped and it is then that the distance is established and the exploits begin, culminating in the death of the kidnapper, the destruction of his kingdom and the rescue of the queen; the parallel with the *Iliad* is undeniable.

In the Mahabarata there was already talk of "Kama, the god of love who carries the most powerful bow in the world and the five arrows with flower tips." In the second version of the Ramayana, written by Tulsidas some two thousand years after the first, we find Kama (Cupid) who, "armed with a bow and arrows of flowers, has managed to dominate the entire universe." We see that Love, both in Plato and his followers and in Dante, is given a universal power.

"The struggle between Garuda (the bird of Vishnu) and the reptile - a very common motif in Indian mythology and iconography - is a cosmological symbol of the struggle between light and darkness, of the opposition of the two principles, that of the sun and the underworld," Eliade points out. Apollo, we remember, kills the python, a subterranean symbol who lived in Delphi where he would establish his famous sanctuary. Krishna, barely a child, kills a serpent with his own hands; the child Hercules will do the same; this same feat reveals the divine origin of both.

"The embodiment of the Cosmic Tree and the Tree of Life in an oak tree by the Indo-Europeans can be traced right back to pre-historic times," and it was the Germanic peoples who developed this myth in the north of Europe. In India this cult is still alive and In full force. Eliade reminds us that "at Mohenjo-Daro one can find a divine epiphany in a *Ficus religiosa*," and he gives us many examples of plant theophanies that are found in Vedic texts: he recalls the oracular sacred oak of Zeus in Dodona, Apollo's bay tree in Delphi and Hercules' wild olive tree in Olympia, to which we can add the olive that Athena sprouted and which grew in the Acropolis of Athens, to gain the favour of the people when choosing the city's patron; the olive is still there in front of the *Erechtheion*.

In India it is difficult to find an ancient tree without offerings and some are used as dwellings by sadhus, thus becoming ashrams. In Europe, particularly among the Celts, oaks were sacred, but this, like all other cults devoted to Nature, was prohibited later.

Dark and Luminous Gods

The parallelism between Shiva-Dionysus and Vishnu-Apollo is undeniable. The first are the gods of darkness, the second are those of light; the first apparently threaten the established order, the second reconstruct it; the former are more distant, inaccessible, the latter are the maestros of the arts and sciences, they are heroic and more human. The deities of the light are an *aspiration* of man, those of darkness are his *inspiration*. But, I must insist, they are complementary. The natural tendency of monism in India leads to the incorporation of the virtues and powers of some gods into others, this does not make the duality cease to exist, but that it coexists in a single God.

Both Shiva and Dionysus are foreign and even strangers to the dominant class that refuses to accept them. Shiva's first wife sacrificed herself in the flames because her father, an important Brahmin, rejected him as a suitor. The ruler of a city imprisons Dionysus as soon as he arrives, as if one were dealing with a dangerous personality; the ruler is later cut into pieces by the Bacchae possessed by Dionysian ecstasy. (Euripides, *The Bacchae*) This attitude is thus explained: Vishnu and Apollo are ascendant, strong gods, connected to the warrior class and to the high officials. Shiva and Dionysus are deities of the people closely linked to Nature, and to the unconscious, to the magical and miraculous. The upper classes would take a long time to incorporate these dark gods who were presented as contrary to their civilisational project, but they would ultimately understand the necessary counterpart that they represented. I infer that if we were dealing with dogmatic mentalities they would not have accepted these foreign deities, but this is not the case; if there was something that characterised this people it was their open-mindedness.

Vishnu is represented, like Apollo, with the bow and solar disc, and likewise he roams the firmament in his chariot. Shiva is identified with Kala, who is time, but he is beyond time and for this reason is called Maha-Kala that designates his transcendent condition.

Both Shiva and Dionysus are sometimes represented with a Phallic image which, given the sexual taboo that the West has inherited from the Semitic tradition, has given them the image of gods of lust; a grave error that leads us to forget their cosmic dimension. The *lingam,* which represents Shiva, is the axis of the universe that is expressed as light and the *yoni,* on which the image usually poses, is the womb of the world. Evidently it *expresses the generative and creative character of divinity*, which is, moreover, the god of the yogis and ascetics; the opposite of a licentious character. The *lingam* would be the equivalent of the finger of God in Michelangelo's famous representation of *The Creation*.

Shiva is also the Lord of the Dance; Hindu iconography has managed to give a cosmic dimension to this singular attribute in its genre. Shiva Nataraja in effect represents the god dancing in a ring of fire, which is the universe, which he moves with his dance to the rhythm of his drum, his foot is planted on a dwarf, the symbol of ignorance; Shiva thus expresses the triumph of wisdom. Like Dionysus he is linked to death and to the cult of the forefathers. Dionysus is also a god of dance and makes the maenads dance frenetically around him.

Dionysus, like Shiva, has his restrictive and ascetic side and like all gods participates in the general Order. This point is absolutely indispensable not only to understand Dionysus, but also the the need within ourselves to experience the core of religion, so that we can also be participants in the same Order; like the Greek gods.

The Dionysus-Apollo duality should be seen as necessarily complementary. Their opposition does not exist for us to opt for one and deny the other, which is what Christianity has done when choosing Jesus, a god who is only luminous, like Apollo. C. G. Jung warns that this unilaterality provokes a disequilibrium in the mind of his patients; for this he proposes to place Satan next to Christ in the heavens (see *Psychosophy 2nd Part.*). A crass error; the only place fit for Satan is hell; let us leave aside for the moment the objective lack of the two, like Jung we can accept them as *psychic realities* in the mind of some believers. To my mind, the invention of Satan is as nefarious as Satan himself. Moreover, all the diabolical works of man are attributed to him as a scapegoat. Evil neutralises the Good, and if the first exists as an absolute (or the duality as absolute) spiritual progress would be a utopia and it would not be possible to manage a civilisation.

I believe that in order to fully understand the religious issue, considering that this understanding is parallel to that of our own psyche, it is necessary to do away with the Manichaean idea that has affected the entire Middle East and, by extension, the West, including Jung. This psychologist would have done well to delve deeper into the religions of the Far East (as I have pointed out earlier) to better understand the psyche. Even today, the Christians pray to Jesus or to the saints when there is a catastrophe to stop the work of Evil. This is the great difference between Satan and Shiva. The latter as destroyer acts through necessity, not to commit evil. In the Hindu myths he is depicted as angry when he destroys; he then returns to a profound state of meditation and absolute peace. Satan is supposed to be Evil itself, he wants to commit evil at all times and knows of nothing else, but it is not he who is prayed to but his enemies. The Hindu, on the other hand, asks Shiva to calm down. The solution cannot be found in the irreconcilable opposites, but in the opposites that are more than reconcilable, they are complementary, and are found in Greek religion and in Hinduism.

Although very distanced by Christian doctrine, in the ritual of wine and blood I see a parallel between Jesus and Dionysus. Blood has been linked to the soul, the most substantial of the individual. It is this potion that was given to the gods in sacrifice. In the ancient Cretan culture, humans were sacrificed and had their blood drawn. As could be expected in such an evolved culture as the Greek, this potion was replaced by wine, considered to be "the blood of the vine, name contemporary poets still use" (Freud, *Totem and Taboo, 175*). To drink wine, then, is to drink the blood of Nature, it is a communion with it. The similarity of this ritual with the Christian sacrament and of Jesus with Dionysus does not need to be highlighted, except that the interpretation given by the Church would vary significantly.

Although Krishna is taken as an avatar of Vishnu, we cannot help but notice an evident similarity between him and Dionysus. Both have the power to attract women who abandon their husbands and their hearths to follow them into the forest; with the former the shepherdesses who hearken to the sound of his flute, with the latter the wives run towards Dionysus and become Bacchae. The symbol, which is what matters, is the same: the women prefer to marry divinity. We can also link Krishna with Orpheus who with his flute attracted not only women but all the beings he appeased, and led them to an abode of inner peace generating an internal and external paradisiacal order. This order is not only an aspiration of desires that imagines a kingdom devoid of struggle and discord, but results from the intuition of the transcendent Order in which the human mind is inspired and by which it tends to establish an earthly order, through laws, rules, etc.; Orpheus, in my opinion, is the personification of the intuition of that Order. Unfortunately nothing remains of the Orphic mysteries.

Let us not forget that all these religious myths that we find in both civilisations are still prevalent in India.

Dionysus and Apollo

As we know, all Greco-Roman mythology as well as the mythology of other religions including the Hindu was devalued, delegitimised and eradicated by Christianity whose interest was to impose its own mythology that, naturally, it does not accept as such. For this reason the West had to wait for the Church to lose its power in order to freely interpret the myths of its cultural past.

Nietzsche was a pioneer in the rediscovery of the meaning and values they contained, and not only this, he contrasted them with Christian myths, proposing a *transmutation of values*, declaring Christian myths and values as *decadent*, exalting the *Dionysian spirit*. Since I have already commented on the work of Nietzsche in *The Roots of Art*, I will not insist on this subject here. I only want to emphasise that I believe that *The Birth of Tragedy* is one of the most enlightening Works of Greek spirit. In this he presents to us the contrary but complementary Apollonian spirit and the Dionysian spirit; a wonderful discovery and accurate judgment with which I fundamentally agree.

In order to understand Dionysus, and Nietzsche, who has a true idea of the god, it is absolutely necessary to shake off the absurd idea of a primitive god. Dionysus is a "primitive" god in the sense of original, primordial, but always existent and present. In fact, man (and all that exists) has an Origin with which he needs to remain in contact, not only to remember it but mainly to experience it. Because, this should always be kept in mind, the Origin did not occur in a concrete past, it occurs permanently. And this experience of the present is so linked to the timeless past, that the experience is one. Although Nietzsche might not mention these mental mechanisms, he converges on the same objective. When the Dionysian emotions are awakened "the subjective disappears until it leads to the complete forgetfulness of oneself". (*Chap. I*). That "intoxicated reality (...) pays no heed to the individual, but even seeks to annihilate the individual and to redeem him through a *mystical feeling of unity* (*Chap. II*). "With the gospel of world-harmony, each one feels himself not only reunified, reconciled, re-incorporated, and merged with his neighbour, but genuinely one, (...) in front of the mysterious *original Unity*" (*Chap. I*). Unfortunately Nietzsche will not use this elevated language again in his later work.

The refined perception of the Greeks led them to adopt as many gods as their spirit needed. This allowed them to make their most relevant actions sacred, if these were rationally contradictory, there was also opposition between the gods, and so every important action had the blessings of a god. Dionysus, surely the most contradictory god of the established order, not only in society but also in parallel on Olympus, is therefore the best example. Just as the Maenads or Nymphs who rendered him homage were the opposite of the beneficent, hearth bound mother, they were also the antithesis of the deity that protected them, Hera, the goddess of marriage, faithful, preserver of order. But if this order was rational and civil, I would say, the followers of Dionysus had their own natural order. Tradition tells us that in this way the same mothers were at times prey to Dionysian madness; they left their homes and domestic obligations and followed the Maenads who with their torches showed them the way towards the wooded hill (not the farming fields) where the cult of Dionysus was celebrated.

Popular legend recounts that these women could eventually end up copulating with the fauns who also attended the ritual. However, Walter Otto in his *Dionysus* affirms with good reason that they did not do so, as the cult was essentially feminine and their relationship was with god and ecstasy was part of this relationship. The fauns were imaginary beings necessary for the myth but did not leave that plane. Those women did not go there to procreate, they had already fulfilled this duty at home, the same home which they had left to attend the cult. Euripides' magnificent tragedy *The Bacchae* confirms Walter Otto's theory, since in it the women kill the man who wants to spy on their private rites.

The way I understand it, this ritual was intended to awaken the primal in its most essential state, possibly the very Chaos that precedes all rational order, which is where the creative, including this order and all order, is born. It was intended to reproduce the state before birth, hence the cult of the phallus and the religious and not the prosaic meaning of the same.

In a Koan, much used by the Zen Masters, the aspirant who is on the verge of understanding is asked: "Who were you before you were born?" Except for the differences between these religions and their methods, which it would be impossible to summarise here, I see a similar intention to reach the essence, and a little beyond, where the first principles are nourished. Not through reason or even intuition but in a lived manner, drinking wine and dancing to ecstasy; an experience that leads one to disconnect with the rational order and connect with the Primordial. Every religion in its most profound, essential and crucial sense has this objective.

The cult of Dionysus is descending and ascending, which implies a double danger, it immerses us in the most elemental of life, in the primordial so that we experience its origin but it has an ascendent end, Dionysus is a god of Hades and of Olympus, son of Zeus, light itself. The first of these double dangers is obviously the most risky as it plunges us into the darkness of Chaos, which is nothing more than Bacchanalian or Dionysian madness but, like Hamlet, Dionysus has a method in his madness. For this a priest who could establish limits and warn of the risks was needed, a guide capable of explaining these Mysteries to the initiates who, inebriated, danced on, letting themselves be carried away by the maelstrom of Chaos until they hit rock bottom with themselves. Then the ascendent part began. In the cult of Dionysus the extremes meet and follow each other, like the *Euroboros*, only in this particular cult one begins with the tail. The ascendant experience is the transformation of Chaos into Order, of darkness into light, of the animal into the spiritual, of man into divinity, the Unity of all and the totality of Life.

Later, the initiates who have had this experience, who would be rare exceptions due to the dangers that we have pointed out, retire satisfied, at the two opposite extremes, which they now know are not, at their point of equilibrium, where they will express the Spirit in Life. Dionysus for his part returns to Hades or to Olympus, to the darkness or to the light, between which as the initiated are now aware, there is no difference.

Disequilibrium does not lie in the natural or corporal sphere, nor in the sexual or even orgiastic sphere, but in the de-spiritualization, because this means leaving the Order; Chaos begins where the Spirit ends, where the gods no longer rule. A society like that of today, without religion or morals, is a hundred times more dangerous and alienated (and of course immoral), as compared to a society that practices the cult to Dionysus as was the custom in Greek times.

If I have written too much in the explanation of this cult it is not because I consider it a path of spiritual knowledge of the first order (not even the Greeks considered it as such, since if it became quite popular, it was not so among the *intelligentsia*), but due to the following reasons: Ever since Nietzsche proposed the name of Dionysus in place of Christ, the Greek god has aroused unprecedented interest. This has led many psychologists and anthropologists to concern themselves with him, but, in spite of this, essentially very little light has been thrown on the resulting religious experience. Dionysus remains in the darkness of Hades. This is comprehensible; studying religion without the religious experience is like learning seafaring on land or topography at sea. Since we will occupy ourselves with Nietzsche's proposition further on, these explanations are necessary. Although I would gladly have done so, I have not found it necessary for the present purpose to elaborate on the other gods of Olympus. I have chosen two opposite gods *ex professo*, Apollo of light, and Dionysus of darkness, in order to cover in some way the spiritual *spectrum* of the Olympians. In order to better complete the same, I will say something about other gods along the way.

Although I essentially agree with Nietzsche, I would like to express my vision in my own words, as I consider the matter to be of the greatest importance. For the fulfilment of his destiny the human being has to transcend himself, and this involves a series of heroic acts, expressed in different ways by the myths of all religions. But the success of this enterprise depends on self-knowledge, because although a doctrine provides a program of action, the subject will not know how to resolve the situation if he does not know himself. He will be able to act correctly by repeating like a parrot all that he has learnt but he will only be able to do so in certain situations, not in all; for this he needs his own criteria; that only self-knowledge can provide. In addition, although he might act correctly, if he does not know himself he will not be able to observe the highs and lows of his spirit, the contradictions that he suffers and, above all, the burdens that accumulate in his unconscious, which will overflow sooner or later spoiling all that he had accrued through good deeds.

Self-knowledge is the path to our inner self, to darkness and to Dionysus. Dionysus is not Evil but the original, the primal, that which is found in the most recondite of human consciousness; when this dark place is illuminated it becomes Apollo. When this light is possessed, and only then, the subject has his own means to act correctly faced with any circumstance. In fact this same light illuminates not only his actions but also his conscience. This is what allows him to *act well naturally*, not through an effort of conscious will contrary to an unconscious instinct that ends up being his latent enemy. It is true that the light is found within and outside; without inner light the external landscape is always cloudy, although if one manages to see it outside, the conscience will also be illuminated as the light is One.

In all religions the different gods express the diverse manifestations or forms of a single Divinity that is only Unity; this is both the unity of all beings and of consciousness. There is no unity in one without the other. In the monotheistic religions the gods are replaced by saints, since these men are deified (to the point that they acquire divine powers), just as the gods are anthropomorphised; in both cases the anthropomorphism is evident. But this is not as serious as imagined by atheists or radical monotheists, as these are steps, means that man uses on the road to his totality. The error occurs when the means are taken as the end, the Son for the Father, for example. In the case of the Greeks, Zeus had the powers of all the other gods, but ultimately in his essence he is pure light. We should not forget that the myths are aesthetic expressions of religions, and that there are myths for different levels of understanding, just as there are gods for different levels of consciousness; not of belief but of consciousness.

What ignorance of religion to believe that there false gods! Not to mention the stupidity that leads to the brutality of fighting for one against the other; a daily occurrence in the historical and contemporary human being. It doesn't matter who is right, much less when reason is sought to be imposed by force, because then reason stops being reasonable and loses all meaning. What is reasonable here is acquiring that Light, which might come from Apollo, Shiva or Vishnu or other gods; each culture has its gods and they are good for them. And this good is measured by the state of harmony, peace and happiness in which they live, as these three virtues are divine attributes; if they have them it is because they are correctly understanding their gods. There are no false gods, even if they are all wrong, they resemble each other, they come closer to the Truth, even if they are only partial truths. The Absolute that all aspire to is beyond them.

The human being adheres closely to the tendency to return to the womb, although the matter is not only biological, this tendency has a transcendent origin; he actually wants to return to his Origin, his Essence, the Universal Womb. The biological womb is a representation, a symbol, an icon, a concrete manifestation of a spiritual impulse that underlies them. Both the cult of Dionysus and Shiva obey this impulse. Our Essence is before, backwards, and after, forwards. The spirit becomes opaque and dark when it comes into contact with matter but it has the germ of the divine; for this reason sentient beings seek the light, and tend to become as transparent as Apollo.

The totality is One. The gods represent the Order that the spirit needs to maintain a relationship with the said Unity. In other words, these are the guidelines man needs to stay in Order. Dionysus and Apollo express the poles of the human spirit, its Origin and its Destiny. Poles of a circle where the ends meet and merge. It is the task of man to go through this circle; by traversing it he fulfils his natural cycle and his Destiny.

The return to Nature is a return to the Origin, to the first principles. It is an attempt to begin again, a *tabula rasa, the search for the Creative*. The Dionysian spirit is one of the great creations of the Greek spirit. This seldom admitted and later repressed religious-psychological-social need, which all societies have, was clearly seen by the Greeks. This *Return to the Sources* that is the Dionysian spirit, is not a return to the past but to the Eternal, it is the soul's need to rediscover itself. It is a necessary rupture with the structures that reason has been constructing. It generates a necessary and almost inevitable change in periods of crisis. This produces a shift of the spirit towards its centre. From there it tries to find other shelters of the spirit, other planes of consciousness, from which other historical periods can begin.

All human beings have a measure of Dionysus and Apollo. The equilibrium between them generates psychic equilibrium. Societies need both for their equilibrium, the sun and the moon, the primal darkness and light as their goal. Dionysus resides in Nature, Apollo illuminates it from above.

The Heroic Sense of Life in Greece

Nothing better expresses the Hellenic spirit than the *cult of the hero*. But *cult* in every sense of the term; as the ceremonies and festivals held for the heroes were taken very seriously and were a part of their religion, and also of the arts and letters; it was also the theme of tragedy, so dear to the Greeks. The cult of the hero was a major part of Greco-Roman culture, and by this I mean the intimate, vital aspect of that tradition; their lives were fulfilled in the cult and the cult was fulfilled in their lives; through this they were so *naturally ready to* sacrifice their lives for their principles. Examples abound, not only in their literature, but above all in their history and their reality.

The cult of the hero should not be seen as an incitement to suicide, we must remember that the Hellenes were very balanced people, and *it is thanks to this physical, psychic and moral equilibrium that they reached such heights in all orders*. Aristotle observes here: "If one is so intrepid and audacious that he does not even fear the gods, he is not brave but mad" (*Gran Ética. 1185 b*).

I believe that it is practically impossible for this ideal to be understood by contemporary Western man who lacks such an elevated paradigm and is motivated by earthly values, and the heavenly ones that he imagines have nothing to do with those of the Greek. The heavenly values of the Greeks were considered to be a mirror in the firmament, that is, in the beyond and on Olympus, which was in plain sight, and thanks to which the Transcendent was refracted in their lives; there is no life in an imaginary "beyond". In Hades existence is vague, dark and also temporary as it vanishes in the mists of time. For the Greek, the hope of eternity resides in the fame that derives from moral integrity in life and the bravery in the face of death. Hence the unavoidable necessity of the ritual of funereal honours; to die without them was to have lived and died for nothing. The recognition of the heroic act was the Greek's springboard towards transcendence; and it was also refracted on this life as an exemplary act for future generations.

One can understand the powerful dynamic that this aspiration can generate in a people, but for modern man it will be difficult to understand this idea of fame. We know that fame today is the growth of personality and those who find it want to enjoy its benefits in life. The Greek hero does not care about the commoner, he is interested in the nobles, especially those of spirit, capable of admiring an exemplary act, as his aspiration is to forge a race of heroes and be amongst the most notable figures; what he seeks is glory. The recognition of his peers begins with the funereal honours with which the exemplary act is consecrated, a paradigm of heroic destiny. Of course the funereal honours are an essentially religious act destined to make the heroic act sacred. The heroic mission of the Greek does not have an individualist character. The hero seeks transcendence in society and fights for it. The general and the captain assume full responsibility for their soldiers and crew members and they all look to society and are observed by it.

After death there remained the prestige, the *kleos*, the imperishable glory. And here we enter another though concomitant field that shows us the Greek spirit projected towards their neighbour, society and culture, an aspiration that constitutes the guiding force of that civilisation. For this reason, Greek exemplarity in this field should be highlighted in capital letters.

Heroic death was celebrated after and even before its consummation, because it signified the triumph of an ideal, the realisation of the human being. Besides the inevitable pain of the loss of a friend or husband was the joy of a success attained. We find these festivities in Homer in the form of the Olympic games in which the perfection of man was also sought.

One must understand the natural ludic propensity or instinct of the Greek who converted everything, even death, into a game. It is said that he also anticipated heroic death with jubilation: On the eve of the famous Battle of Thermopylae, the Persians sent an emissary to the 300 Spartans to discuss their surrender. The emissary was surprised to find them happily playing and competing a day before their certain death; because, as expected, surrender was out of question.

The great Greek paradox is that without expecting anything after death, the plenitude of life is ensured with a heroic death. I believe that the excessive eagerness of the Greeks to die on the battlefront represents the final and supreme desire to assimilate to the gods. This was, perhaps, a delirium, a madness, though sublime as befitted this exemplary people. It is, however, to that sublime aspiration that we can attribute its catastrophe: the Peloponnesian war that spread beyond all measure blindly obeyed that insatiable spirit.

Life seemed too small to the Greek, despite his excellent and multifarious creativity, the virtues that regulated his life were not enough, he had to show his greatest virtue by sacrificing his life for his peers, for that people who were fully aware of being superior and would be exemplars: the conduct of each one had to be uncompromisingly exemplary; the Greek spirit was hyperbolic. This urge for transcendence can only be explained by an intuition or an intimate experience of the Transcendent, which signifies a high level of consciousness. The Greek had placed his centre of reference in the altruist or unitive consciousness, which is precisely where our discipline wants to take the human spirit.

Given the importance of the matter I would like to emphasise the essential part of what has been said: *All virtue is a path to the Transcendent*. Bravery in Greece was rightly taken as a capital virtue, because it undoubtedly manifests the act of going beyond oneself, the ego and individual consciousness. It can be said that it is an external way of transcending oneself, when one takes into account that the external act leads to an internal transformation that is expressed as the *liberty* to leave the self and the *felicity* that derives from it. The impetus, the expansion that comes from the free and happy spirit that moves the hero, is *entirely comparable to the mystic experience of the Transcendent*.

The means that the hero is transported fulfils the very objective of philosophy, as I understand it, and as is understood by the *Upanishads*. However, as behoves the Hindu spirit, this transportation and realisation will be through an internal search that has the advantage of not involving the loss of life (although it does of the ego), and thanks to this, the ability to discern *a posteriori* experience and demonstrate it in writing or verbally. But this does not mean that the hero does not leave a lesson with his example that the

Greek knew how to intuit and value; hence the jubilant celebration that accompanied the funereal ritual.

Fame, understood in the sense that has been exposed, entirely transcends the subject, the ego. The subject knows very well that nothing will remain of him as a person, that he will remain only as an example, that he is the realisation of the virtues whose origin is transcendent, that he is nothing more than an instrument of a divine mandate; this is the work of the superior man. That is why the hero in Greece was considered a semi-god, since he performed his plan in this world as an incarnation of God. In other words, he is an embodiment of the virtues, an actualisation of the primary manifestations of universal Consciousness. The best example of this man-god in the Hindu tradition is found in Rama.

In this way the heroic spirit is brought to its excellence. For this reason it has to be taken into account when explaining the *Greek miracle*, as it helped, like no other virtue, to establish the spirit at that elevated level of consciousness that made it possible. And that *elevated level of consciousness was the result of the excellence to which so many virtues were taken.*

The Heroic Sense of Life in India

If anyone thinks of this heroic sense and does not find a parallel in India, it is because he does not know its history. Apart from the epic period (that corresponds to the Greek), which has been and continues to be exemplary, heroes and heroines abound in all epochs, as this country suffered countless invasions, from which it managed to free itself time and again. We know that the privileged Kshatriya caste took to war as a profession but it is often forgotten that India had entire peoples who were warriors by tradition. The interested reader can refer to the British officer Colonel Tod's *Annals and Antiquities of Rajasthan* (apart from Indian texts if he suspects that these may be apologetic); a kind of encyclopaedia of these peoples with their cities and customs in which he will find countless war stories. Tod reminds us: "There is not a petty state in Rajasthan that has not had a Thermopylae, and scarcely a city that has not produced its Leonidas." Their kings or Maharanas set an example to its warriors with their exploits and these were fearsome.

The origin of these peoples is uncertain, some believe that they descend from the Huns, as their origin is estimated between the 4th and 6th centuries, coinciding with the Mongol invasion. But this theory is not sustained by their facial and physical features; in my estimation the Rajputs are the most gracious people of India. Tod opines that some of them, like those from Jaisalmer, are the descendants of the Scythians and, curiously, the same origin and polyandry is ascribed to the Mahabharata heroes of a far more remote time. The Rajputs have little in common with the rest of the Indian peoples, especially in their tradition of arms, they have a religion of arms in fact. They claim to be the descendants of the sun and this is their symbol.

They were the only ones who offered serious resistance to the Muslim invaders. With reference to these invasions Colonel Tod says: "Scenes of devastation, plunder and massacre commenced, which lasted through ages; during which nearly all that was sacred in religion or celebrated in art was destroyed by these ruthless and barbarian invaders." "The noble Rajpoot, with a spirit of constancy and enduring courage, seized every opportunity to turn upon his oppressor. Every road in Rajasthan was moistened with torrents of blood... But all was of no avail... and dynasty succeeded dynasty, heir to the same remorseless feeling which sanctified murder, legalised spoliation, and deified destruction."

Its most notable leaders are today national heroes. If I were to elaborate on the feats of Prithviraja, Maharana Kumbha, Maharana Sanga, Maharana Pratap and Shivaji, I would attract the reader's attention, but we would be out of the framework devised for this book. A couple of epics have been written on the first, and more should be written on the rest. All of them spent their lives in battle and each one has countless feats. Maharana Sanga had 80 scars on his body, he had lost a foot and a hand, and with the other he continued brandishing the sword. Shivaji, armed like a tiger with steel claws to maul his adversary in hand to hand combat with the head of the Muslim troops, only needs a Homer to equate him with Achilles and Hector.

The history of Chittor, to name just one city, is nothing less than that of Troy. The city suffered three invasions. After an obstinate resistance, when its defenders saw that they could not resist, they dressed in saffron coloured clothes signifying Honour or Death and faced the enemy to the point of extinction. The women, for their part, did not surrender to the invader to suffer abuse or slavery like *The Trojan women* (see Euripides's tragedy), but made an enormous bonfire and all of them, thousands of them, (13 thousand in the second invasion) including the queen, threw themselves into the fire. This custom (*jauhar*) was a tradition amongst these people and it did not just happen in this city. We find a similar example in Jaisalmer. I am sorry I have not elaborated on the history of this race so rich in heroic exploits.

The monarchs and Rajput nobles became civilised; Maharana Kumbha, who beautified Chittor, has left behind certain works and poetry, he played the *veena* and was an expert in Sanskrit. Some dynasties of this race extended their territory outside Rajasthan. In Khajuraho they left the most beautiful temples in all of India, and when they reached the Buddhist lands in Bihar, where they were very generous with the Nalanda University, they adopted Buddhism and generally gave up their warlike habits. They reached Bengal and thanks to them Buddhism survived until the 12th century. Their area of influence extended to Nepal, and I believe that the ferocious Gurkhas found in this peaceful country are their descendants.

The Rajputs managed to make some alliances against the invader, and waged famous battles for the entire country, but not all the kingdoms participated in them. I believe that had they reached a total agreement the history of India would have been very different. However, it is necessary to recognise that many Rajput nobles fought for power and to maintain their own territory and not really for India. In fact India did not exist as a unit, strictly speaking, particularly in those times when the emperors were Mongols and Muslims. If there was a unity in India it was that established by the Dharma, which was not what motivated these warriors. Proof of that is that many Rajputs became captains in the emperor's army and one of them, in the service of Aurangzeb, who was a sworn enemy of Hindus, managed to defeat Shivaji in one of his campaigns. Naturally they have not been immortalised as defenders of the country. In fact, the incessant habit of warfare of these peoples made life very difficult and they ultimately destroyed themselves. We could say the same thing about the Greeks as the parallel is notorious. In my opinion, the transcendent dimension of the heroic act in the *Rajput* hero is not as clear as in the Greek; although in the case of Rama and Arjuna, as we will see in due course, the universal function of heroism is explicit.

The custom of widows throwing themselves onto the funeral pyres of their husbands originates in these people. This practice astounds the Western woman. However, if one considers the heroic life the deceased has led, the wife may well have seemed petty if she did not do so. Admittedly, this custom devoid of that context is senseless.

Of course, heroic life is not exclusive to warriors; I am referring to heroic actions in general. Negotiating the sea, the mountains, the jungle or extremely dangerous circumstances produce the same effect. For this reason in mythology we find the hero struggling with demons with a hundred arms (Ravana), or with dragons (Tristan), or with other terrible beings, because what is important is the exaltation of heroism. Spiritual life, especially that of the renouncer (*sanyasin*) implies heroism; and in this India is unrivalled. Everyone who transcends himself is heroic and this is what is common to all heroes: that they leap beyond themselves to realise their ideal. The difficulty, sacrifice and risk of this act is what produces our admiration.

Following a basic principle in my philosophy to stick to experience, and for the good of the reader, I can assure him that I have not conceived of these ideas at my desk but in the face of the aforementioned circumstances.

In any case, for our understanding it is necessary to know that courage responds to a spiritual and psychic impulse whose origin is a *primary manifestation of the universal Consciousness*: the *élan vital,* and its destiny is the Transcendent. The difference resides in the degree of awareness that can be had of this spiritual dynamic which, even if latent in the valiant, impels him to go beyond himself and only becomes conscious from the *essential perspective* which is that of the Transcendent itself. It should be clear that in this virtue of courage, and we could say the same of any virtue, what is essential is not to make it conscious, if one understands this by the comprehension of reason, but rather that it be a *unitive experience*.

The Greek Tragedy

In *The Roots of Art* I have given several explanations as to why I have expanded on Greek tragedy, but given its importance and scope, I would like to insist on this matter in which our understanding of ourselves and the world we live in is at stake. I have indicated the number of subjects covered by Greek tragedy, but we must necessarily link these subjects with the mental faculties that create them, that is to say, observe it as a psychological fact or even better as a psychosophical fact, for in my Psychosophy the mind is ordered and completed thanks to the transcendent and unifying vision of philosophy; and it is precisely here that it clearly overlaps with Greek tragedy.

I have maintained in this discipline that the true nucleus of the mind is the spirit that moves or, more accurately, focuses its attention on the different faculties of understanding, not only intuitions, reasons and feelings, but also occasional emotional states, memories and irruptions from the inner or subconscious plane. The intuitions, to which priority must be given because they are the creative aspect of the mind, include the numerous specifically spiritual or unitive variants of philosophy, religion, art and morality, in which are inserted perceptions of a mythical order, that is, mythology. It will be understood that I am not talking about a philosophy adjusted to reason, as those who believe it should be scientific have wanted to understand, thereby reducing the broad horizon of this discipline to a narrow vision, but with all its potentialities and nuances. The same can be said of morality, not reduced to an established ethics, as well as a religion restricted to dogmas and allegedly separated from mythology. What is at issue here is a total opening of the mind, but not towards new beliefs without direction, towards the search for novelties, which today they call originality, and has ultimately made modern art sick, but directed towards the encounter with ourselves, with our essence.

Well, the Greek genius knew precisely how to converge in tragedy not only these disciplines, but all the faculties arranged in a universal context. Not simply a play, or literature, or mythology, Greek tragedy is the product of an integrated and integrating mind inspired by the Creative which is the unifying Unity; hence its eternally exemplary character. Myth, in its most acute and elevated aspect, is projected towards the Transcendent in which it is refracted to fall as Fate on humans, that is, on the characters who are victims of said Fate, who, by the same universal context that surrounds them, in turn become exemplary.

Greek tragedy could not be equalled because the intimate and inseparable contact with the Transcendent was subsequently lost, expressed as divinities that were indistinct from their functions: Order, Justice, Fate, the Good, the Beautiful, etc., which granted it a universal dimension and a permanent participation in the Cosmos. And it was precisely what later in the West was contemptuously called mythology, which was even prohibited and persecuted, that had made this supreme art possible, this excellence in the plastic arts, literature, architecture, in short, the most luminous expressions of Greek art.

I attribute to the particular conception of death, and as a consequence of the life of the Greeks, their profound tragic sense and its derivative, tragedy; a unique and incomparable creation of Greek genius. For myths, religion, morality, art and philosophy, that is, all the spiritual faculties converge in Greek tragedy. That is why I consider it to be the most complete expression of the Greek spirit. And this is not only my personal opinion, tragedy had a much greater reception and influence on that people, including the enlightened ones, than philosophy itself.

I think it is because of their belief in reincarnation, which Hindus unanimously take for granted, that makes death something unfortunate but not a tragedy; for this reason they did not see the need, nor it did not occur to them, to develop this literary genre. Although we must recognise that they include the tragic sense of life in the epic in the manner of Homer.

The decisive thing is that they retain the multiple virtues that derive from their mythical religion, which allows them to remain integrated in the *Universus*. This, as the reader will have already understood, is the central theme and the common thread of this book.

Pilgrimages and Festivals in Greece

Two main religious ceremonies keep the cyclical vision of the Greek alive: that of Dionysus and Demeter. In the case of the first, "a god whose periodic deaths and rebirths gave a rhythm to the life of the faithful; the faithful are associated with the divine drama; suffering and enjoying in some way the passion of god, who he identifies with through the mystic orgy" (E. Brehier *Período helenístico*). Dionysus, as we know, is the god of wine, a drug that helped to self-absorb, integrate and identify the faithful and Nature with divinity.

Ortega y Gasset (*Idea del Teatro*) tells us that the cult of Dionysus "has the definitive character of *imitatio dei*. Life, death, passion and the resurrection of Dionysus were represented in the Dionysian dance. The festival was the day of the dead (a day when mead was poured in libation on the tombs of the dead), and this inaugurated the long festival of *Anthesterias*, dedicated to the veneration of the dead. A citizen who appeared as Dionysus, crowned with branches and vine leaves, entered Athens on a ship on wheels; this was the *naval car*, from which derives the word *Carnaval*." In the ritual dance there is more an *identification with the deity* rather than participation, which is the very religious experience. Ortega suggests that this is a "primitive" mode of expression. There is no such thing; in religion, philosophy and art there is no evolution over time, modern art is not better than that of the Renaissance or Greek than Egyptian, they are only different means of expression. Religions, for their part, are measured, or ought to be, by their efficacy in producing a religious experience; the mere understanding of this could change the way of seeing and accepting them, in their fair measure, of millions of believers.

Ortega's interpretation is very correct as regards man's quest to leave behind his daily worries, the encumbrance of life and its monotony, his endless care to prevent misfortune. I would say in my words, to escape from his discernment, always charged with a latent fear that entails suffering and inclines him to search for a way out towards another reality where freedom, joy and spontaneity reign through wine and dance as was part of the Dionysian ritual. But if we attentively observe Ortega's language, full of existentialist scepticism, we will see a basic flaw: "The consciousness of his own relativity is inseparable in man from the postulating consciousness of the absolute. And then there is engendered in him the vehement and *equivocal* desire to want to be precisely *what he is not* (italics mine): the absolute; participate in this other higher reality, bring it to his own needy and limited one, make the omnipotent collaborate in his native impotence." "This duality and contrast -impotence-omnipotence- will accompany man throughout his history." This is true, but we note the change of perspective that leads him to deny the idealism underlying cult actors. Idealism, in fact, maintains the opposite: the human being does not want to be *what he is not*, but precisely, *what in essence he is*. Besides, the desire of being *what he is not* would only be a momentary distraction, a temporary intoxication that would later put him in a depressive state, and there is nothing religious about that. The cult to Dionysus was a religion, that is, it was sustained by the intuition or experience of the devotee that happiness and freedom were real, and that the *identification with the god or the absolute were possible*. Nietzsche, with greater perceptiveness, saw an effective transformation in the subject of the cult.

The importance of the Mysteries of Eleusis in the religious and cultural history of Greece is revealed through the same ritual. We know that in the time of the Athenian apogee, the Eleusian rites were carried out with great fervour and pomp. The pilgrimage went from Athens on the Aegean to Eleusis on the banks of the Tyrrhenian. The reappearance of the goddess Persephone in Spring was commemorated, that is, her annual rebirth and in parallel the rebirth of the harvests; that is why Persephone is always represented holding ears of wheat.

She spent the winter months underground where she was held by her abductor, Hades (Pluto). Demeter, her mother, undertook the desperate and incessant search until she found her. The relationship between the celestial mother, who lived on Olympus, and the daughter, who shared both worlds, had such a profound and complex meaning that was only explained to the *mystes* (initiates) in the *mysteries of Eleusis*.

The ritual repeats the search for Persephone by Demeter: "On the 15th day of Boedromion, or September, the King Arcon proclaimed in the *Poecilo* of Athens, in the presence of the people, the opening of the Eleusinians. During the nine days of the duration of the festival, all warfare in Greece was to cease and business was to be suspended in Athens." "The next day the *mystes* who were standing guard in the Acropolis met in the Ceramico to march to Eleusis." "And then a multitude of youth dressed in linen and crowned with myrtle leaves could be seen marching down the *Sacred Path*." When they reached Eleusis they went towards the "four main buildings that were part of the sanctuary, the temples of Hecate, Pluto and Demeter, with the great square hall called the *hall of initiation*; all built entirely of black marble from Eleusis." "On the left was the majestic Demeter, with her mural wreath and her queen's sceptre. Above it one could read: *I am the celestial light and the origin of souls*. On the right, the sweet grave Persephone, the Reaper, with the sheaf of wheat in her arms. Above it one can read: *I am death and Renaissance. I guard the Winged Crown.*" "In the afternoon of the day of arrival, an important initiation ceremony was performed: *the preparation of Persephone's nuptial bed*." (E. Schuré, *Sanctuaires d´Orient*). After this ritual ended, the dances began. "on the night of arrival at Eleusis, the *mystes* interrupted their dances and rejoicing at the news of the abduction of Persephone. With torches in their hands, they shouted and lamented and roamed all around searching for the goddess. Suddenly, a herald announced to them that Helios had revealed the place where the young goddess was to be found (we should also remember that in India, Surya, the equivalent of Helios, sees all), then the joy, music and dance returned." (M. Eliade, *Initiation, rites, sociétés secrètes*)

So little remains of the private and esoteric initiations in Greece that it would be imprudent to venture further conjecture. "From the beginning those of Eleusis taught the re-ascent of the soul (Persephone) to its point of origin or celestial light (Demeter). Demeter, conceived as Earth Mother and goddess of agriculture, and Persephone, imagined as goddess of the Spring were only the external and popular forms of the cult." "It was a synthetic panorama of the universe, an exercise to explain the origin of the end of life by the history of the soul, sometimes oppressed by the yoke of matter and at other times liberated by the spirit." "It was a vibrant and impassioned translation of the Egyptian doctrine of Osiris and Isis; a translation that was however too elevated for the people to understand, and it was thus always the privilege of a few initiates." (E. Schuré, *Sanctuaires d´Orient*). Tradition recounts that it was a human hero who descended to Hades to rescue the goddess; the myth attributes this rescue to Dionysus, as no mortal could do so without the help of a god. For this he has to reincarnate a second time as Dionysus-Eleutheros and takes the liberated goddess to Olympus, where the festival concludes with the holy matrimony of both, *hieros gamos*.

"It would be naive to want to present in a few lines the essentials of the mystery that dominates the religious life of Greece for more than two thousand years," comments Eliade. "That these elements of archaic religiosity are found at the very heart of the Greek and Greco-Oriental mysteries show their extraordinary vitality, as well as their importance for the religious life of humanity." "These are religious experiences that are primordial and exemplary" "they are of an initiatory essence, i.e. they pursue the spiritual transmutation of the novice." The aspirant "undertakes the initiation with the objective of transcending the human condition and obtaining a higher supra-human mode". (*Op. cit. 243*) "One is dealing with a spiritual regeneration, a *palingenesis*, understood as a *radical change in the existential regime of the initiate*." "Thanks to the initiation, the neophyte acceded to another way of being: he became equal to the Gods, he identified with the Gods." Eliade reminds us that in the late ancient world, "the divinization of man had nothing of extravagant dreams." "Know, then, that you are a God," Cicero wrote (*Repúb. VI, 17*) And in a hermetic text could be read: "I know you, Hermes and you know me; I am You and You are me." This text inevitably reminds us of the famous affirmation of the Upanishad: "You are that," about which we will speak later.

In the *Hymn to Demeter* "the happiness of the initiates in the other world was exalted and the fate of those who died without having participated in the mysteries was lamented". (Homer*, 480*). Pindarus adds: "Happy is he who, having participated in these rites, descends to the bowels of the earth because he knows the end of life and the beginning of the gods." (*Frag. 102, Oxford*) And Sophocles: "Oh! Thrice-blessed the mortals who, having contemplated these mysteries, have descended to Hades; for those only will there be a future life of happiness - the others there will find nothing but suffering." (*Frag. 719 Dindorf*). From which is it revealed, incidentally, that Hades was the place of the dead in general, the fortunate and the unfortunate; although for them there was no fire nor tortures imagined by morbid minds. And in Eleusis itself this inscription has been found: "Beautiful indeed is the mystery given us by the blessed gods: death is for mortals no longer an evil but a blessing."

It is well known that the Greek tradition is heir to the Egyptian; Plato himself admits it. And since this legacy is not rational or philosophical, we can believe that it is mysterious and religious. Let us compare the testimonies that we have on Eleusis with this amazing text found on an Egyptian coffin: "Whether I live or die I am Osiris, / I enter in and reappear through you, / I decay in you, I grow in you, / The gods are living in me for I live and grow in the corn that sustains the Honoured Ones. / I cover the Earth. / Whether I live or die I am barley. / I am not destroyed. / I have entered the Order, / I rely upon the Order, / I become master of the Order, /... / I emerge in the Order.../ I have entered into the Order, / I have reached its limits" (*Coffin texts, 330*)

From the text one can gather that it expresses a mystical union, not only with the gods but also with Nature. I believe that Plotinus, Spinoza and Schelling would also have been astounded by this text. Perhaps the Greeks knew of it; Plato always admits the Egyptian legacy in Greece. In any case the most substantial of the Greco-Roman culture is based on this *unitive and universal vision*.

I am interested in emphasising the vital, spontaneous and joyous aspect that prevails in the Greek and Hindu festivals, which express their way of seeing, feeling and living the Sacred and in expressing its religion. The Sacred generates respect, but not fear, nor guilt nor discomfort. In my opinion, this attitude is a consequence of the *unitive vision* that keeps them *integrated with the gods and the World,* and lets them be *participants of the permanent Creation of the rhythms of Nature*. The cult becomes a festival, what is truly festive is religious; religion does not awaken the pain of existence but the joy of life. *Enthusiasm*, in Greek, means *having the gods within*.

Since in classical antiquity the festivals and rituals followed on from each other frequently and the Greeks actively participated in them, they remained *connected* with the gods and heroes, who were not transcendent and distant in time, but *present*. The gods were there, in neighbouring Olympus, and their presence was necessary in the ritual and the heroes who descended from them were their close ancestors, the founders of their own city or their arts. This made them *participate* in the myth, their own lives were an active part of the myth. The tragedy, in which they also participated, reminded them of the same heroes, and the chorus or chorus leader took charge of leaving a clear moral message, and so gods, heroes and the public lived in constant interrelation, which kept the spirit awake, alert and uplifted.

We cannot fail to mention the Olympic Games whose religious character tends to be forgotten. They took place in Olympia, a sacred place attended by representatives of all Hellas, and all hostilities even during wartime were suspended for this festival.

The first thing the participants did was go to the temple of Zeus, where besides admiring and venerating the gigantic and beautiful statue of the greatest God, created by Phidias and considered to be one of the wonders of antiquity, they could contemplate in the facades of the temple the feats of the model heroes, such as Pelops with his triumphal chariot, or Hercules performing his labours, or Theseus fighting with the centaurs who tried to rape the women, that is, the superior man struggling to overcome passions. These heroes were considered demi gods and for this reason were cult figures. The women who also participated in the games (it is well known that a Spartan princess had twice won the chariot race) made offerings at the temple of Hera.

The winners in the contests achieved glory in life and were richly rewarded, as they were the most perfect in their art that brought them to the level of divinities. Statues were raised in their honour and poets sang of their feats. These praises of Pindarus have been conserved. The edifying stimulus that this pan Hellenic festival awoke in the people will be understood.

Ortega observes that "the only collective behaviour that remained in the West with a certain residual value of an authentic *festival* was the Carnival. Since it had been extirpated from the soul, which was god - Dionysus, the carnivalesque Bacchanal was gradually atrophying and starving until it died in our days." (*Idea del Teatro*) Ortega wrote this 100 years ago, in *our days* the carnival has passed on to the New World and has made a euphoric resurgence in Brazil and Trinidad, undoubtedly due to the high percentage of the population being of African descent; and as I have personally been able to verify, although the primary Dionysian impulse might be manifest, it is realised on a very elementary cultural and spiritual plane. In any case, "the festival is paganism *par excellence*" Nietzsche said, that is, non-Christian. And this brings us once more to the guiding force of this work: in India these festivals with the aforementioned characteristics, as we will see below, far from having diminished, are more relevant than ever.

Pilgrimages and Festivals in India

For Hindus this material world is not sufficiently real if it lacks the spiritual factor. For this reason they seek a metaphysical connection in nature in special places where the material world begins or ends, where the beyond begins, like in the source of rivers, in the promontories on the coast, in the limitless Himalayas. I believe this is the reason why they have made the four cardinal points of their country sacred: in order to make it sacred from one end to the other.

The Hindus, like the Greeks, Romans and those from the Renaissance, were very adept at astrology, and so important events must be in accordance with the order of the stars, in some way, with the *universal order*. Since the rivers are sacred in India, the confluences of great rivers are particularly sacred. As all tourists will have noted, rituals in the rivers are commonplace but just one example is sufficient for our purposes: Every 12 years the greatest festival of India occurs, the Maha Kumba Mela. On the date fixed by the astrologers for this festival in Prayag, everything comes together: the stars, the three rivers: the Ganges, which is a reflection of the Milky Way, the Yamuna and the Saraswati, the latter is a spiritual river that flows into the Ganges, all have their confluence in this place. In no other place can one see so many saints, gurus, sanyasins, sadhus, or people who have renounced the material world. The eminent philosopher Shankara promoted this festival to encourage the meeting of people of spirit. But for the Hindus it is much more than a meeting of mortals: a universal conjunction happens only at this moment according to astrologers; the ritual takes on a cosmic dimension. The pilgrims bathe in the primordial waters as the gods did at the beginning of time. The Westerner does not believe in this order, just as he believes or does not believe in God and he *believes* that this is enough for him. What he does not understand is the need of the Hindu to integrate and to stay integrated with the Cosmos, a need that derives from his developed *unitive consciousness*. He cares not that the sciences can prove the relationship between the micro and macrocosmos, what matters to him is his projection, participation and integration in the *universal Order*. 70 million devotees attended the last Kumba Mela; we need no other proof to verify that religion in India is alive. This festival is a magnificent expression of well understood pantheism or monism, in which a huge multitude tends to be One with All; which is, incidentally, the ultimate aspiration of the philosopher.

The places to which the pilgrims go are called *thirta*, access, a means towards the... Sacred. As always happens when dealing with the sacred, the Hindu takes us to the beyond, as he tries to reach intangible reality, the place, the symbol is not enough. This consciousness allows him to stay away from idolatry. It can seem the contrary to the uninformed observer, due to the awe and even stupor that the Hindu shows before the image, but if he is asked he will say it is the vision of God through which the pilgrim penetrates and is penetrated by the divinity, whose eyes are shining and highlighted with this effect. The images have emerged naturally or have been later placed because the divinity has manifested itself in that place (hierophany).

We find clear examples in the *Lingam* of Shiva. For now, *Lingam* means *sign*, it is never the object in itself but what it *expresses*. It is a symbol whose form alludes to a phallus (a concept that the Hindu avoids). Although it also resembles an egg, which would represent the primordial cosmic egg described in ancient cosmogony; it is, in any case a symbol of creativity and fertility. This sign is seen by Hindus in diverse natural forms, promontories, stalagmites, rocks, etc. that make the place sacred. But as is usual, the sign greatly transcends the forms: it expresses the *axis mundi*, a luminous column whose ends are infinite. Shiva expresses himself in all the elements, and this makes him omnipresent. He has expressed himself in this way in the fabulous temple cities of the South. His expression is venerated as fire in Tiruvannamalai, (*Tejo-lingam*) and in another as water (*Apasa-Lingam*), and elsewhere as ether or as earth.

Shiva lives in the Himalayas. Only one of his fingers has formed a mountain in Tungunnath (and near the summit I have seen an old man with a long beard and huge hands who explained to me how this phenomenon had taken place; a vivid and impressive expression of the myth). On Mount Kailash he remains in a state of meditation; and so the neighbouring mountains take offerings to him: Annapurna means "the one who offers food", Nanda-Devi is "the goddess who offers joy".

I could elaborate endlessly on these sacred sites, their curiosities, anecdotes and others as India is replete with them, but I hope these examples are sufficient to understand the Hindu World, the Unity in which it lives, the exemplary integration of man-Divinity-Nature, expressed as vivid religious art, in short, the dimension of mythic mentality in force in the modern mind, a fact that particularly interests us due to our interest in projecting and prolonging the Hellenic tradition.

Similitudes in Religious Architecture

Greek religious architecture is apparently very different from Hindu, but it still has essential points in common. In general the temple is located in elevated locations, like in India, as evidenced in all the acropolises of Hellas where the sacred edifices were concentrated, or in prominent places, such as the extremes of the peninsulas or on the islands, facing the sun (Apollo) and the distant sea horizon (Poseidon). This undoubtedly indicates an opening towards the infinite, the desire for integration with the gods and the universe. In the spiritual centre of Hellas, Delphi, the *Omphalos* was to be found, *the umbilicus of the World* that was the seat of Apollo. It is still preserved and, curiously, has the form of a *Lingam*.

In Rome, since its origin, Plutarch tells us, there was an Umbilicus Urbis, designed by Romulus himself, which was actually a navel since it was a concavity in which the most representative items were deposited, that is, the Manes and Penates of the city, as well as offerings to the gods. Around this, Romulus himself traced a circle which was to be the limit of the city. This navel was also the navel of the world, so much so that the hollow was called Mundus. It was also the portal to the inner world of the terrestrial organism, to the reality beyond the grave, since it connected the living with the dead, who could communicate on certain ritual days. It is quite feasible that the ideal of the Empire found its foundation in this centre from which this civilisation was to spread throughout the world.

There are no records of temples in Vedic times, but it is known that rituals originally developed around a column that expressed the axis or centre of the universe, it was already established that the correct place for the ritual ought to be the highest part of the area, "as it is from an elevated places that the gods climb to the sky and they like returning to an elevated place." (*Satapata Brahamana III, 1*) Later the temples were excavated and carved out of the living rock, and then built from large blocks of stone that would be sculpted on the outside. The temple was subsequently developed around the original column, and this custom is still preserved. The immense temple-cities of South India always display the pillar, nowadays adorned with gold leaf, which carry the same significance. In the North, the typical temples such as those of Bhubaneshwar and the incomparable ones of Khajuraho, the most important edifice of the complex that has an oval shape like a giant Lingam, the *Sikhara*, rising above the *sanctum sanctorum,* exhibit, in those dedicated to Shiva, a vertically placed Lingam that indicates the *centre of the World*. The Sikhara is topped off with a cone that rests on an enormous pillow, *amalaka*, whose tip is projected upwards, continuing the vertical which is the axis of the World; this is in fact the symbol of the Lingam, which has neither beginning nor end and extends like a beam of light towards the infinite.

The Hindu, more introverted than the Greek, guards his deity or symbol in an alcove in the centre of the temple, sometimes dark and enclosed, expressing its mysterious nature, but the temple is not limited to being the shrine of a god; *it is a micro cosmos*. Around the god to which the temple is dedicated there are other affiliated gods, often those of other sects, who are exhibited since they all are part of a totality. But there is no cloister; the exterior of the temple is the manifestation of those gods: Nature. There has been no shortage of work for the artists as the entire building is covered with sculptures. Firstly, the connection of the deities with Nature is represented; their appearances or avatars, their prowess and legends are represented. Just as the struggle of the gods with the titans is sculpted on the facade of the Parthenon, in the Hindu temple we find the gods fighting against the demon enemies of the universal Order; Vishnu, for example, as a wild boar rescuing the Earth from the primordial waters, or Shiva saving it from a torrent provoked by the Ganga that threatened to flood it. In both cultures, the *heroic sense of life*, expressed in a mythical-religious language, refers to the origin of time and remains engraved as an eternal paradigm.

Then, on the exterior of the temple, humans are carved performing their activities, both in war and in peace, playing instruments or dancing and in some temples in amorous pursuits (*mithuna*). On the lower part we see elephants, horses, monkeys, birds, in short, all life is found there and the continuance of the temple is Nature itself, the reality in which we live. There is no separation; the temple is projected in all directions, as is explicit in those surrounded by four shrines that indicate the cardinal points towards which divinity projects itself. Those of Khajuraho also have balconies from which to contemplate the World from the site of the gods. The opening to the infinite All is like that in Greece, and this similitude, in the spiritual and physical vision, is in my opinion more important than any architectural differences.

In the Buddhist tradition we find that the Stupa, which is in principle a burial mound containing the relics of the Buddha or of his disciples, is also the *axis of the World* around which the universe revolves. In general it is surrounded by fences within which there is a ring road so that pilgrims can move around that *micro cosmos* with the objective, naturally, of *integrating in the cosmic Order*, which is the *Dhamma* or Buddhist doctrine. The fences around the *stupa* have four portals (*toranas*) facing the four cardinal points.

The Christian church points upward towards the sky, but it is closed to Nature as behoves its doctrine. The difference with the Greek and Hindu temples is evident, both the latter try to integrate the spirit in Nature, the former to alienate the spirit from it.

Just as thousands of marvellous temples were destroyed by the Muslim invaders who, as hardened iconoclasts, broke and mutilated all sculptural representation within their reach; and of course they did not take the trouble of asking the Hindus the reason for their icons. The answer would have been that "Brahman has two aspects, *nirguna* (without qualities) and *saguna* (with qualities). If Brahman was only *nirguna*, the world of forms would not be possible." (*Vastu Sutra Upanishad*). It is enough to understand this to end all controversies with the iconoclasts, but we know that it was not only religious fervour that led them to such destruction, as in Christianity, the policy of conquest was behind it. Shankara further clarifies this situation: not only the icons, but "the divinities should be adored as if they were Brahman, but Brahman should not be adored as if here were these divinities." As we can see the Hindu is far from being idolatrous, he well knows the function of the idol.

There will be those who think that if the axis of the world is in one temple it cannot be in another. The first thing that they have to do is understand that logic is entirely inadequate for understanding the mythical mentality, for the simple reason that logic cannot escape the coordinates of time and space, while the mythical spirit moves freely outside these. And it is not as if mythical man "subjectively believes" that he is in the axis of the world, but that being in the axis he concentrates and is *unitively centred in the Universus*, into which he integrates in body and spirit. Can one be so presumptuous as to believe that the Greeks of the Golden Age who made religious pilgrimages to the *umbilicus of the world* in Delphi were naive? Definitely the mythical and mystical intuition has proven to be sharper than logic in matters of the spirit. It is logic that has created the subject-object, subjective-objective duality that has produced a persistent epistemological confusion for two millennia. I believe that the unity that generates the *unitive vision* that I advocate contains the solution of the matter and can intelligently incorporate the mythical mentality and the mystical experience in a post-rational contemporary mind.

The Sun temples are amongst the most famous in both India and Greece. In numerous temples to Apollo the sun entered at daybreak or sunset; in Naxos there is an example. In India some have been preserved, in Greece they were destroyed. The most notable monument, of which nothing remains, dedicated specifically to Helios, in Greece, that was one of the seven wonders of the world (of which five were Greek) was the Colossus of Rhodes. Made of bronze and of such a size it is said that ships could pass between its legs. The statue of Zeus made by Phydias, also colossal and located in the Parthenon, and the Temple of Artemis in Ephesus formed part of these wonders of the ancient world.

Other Similitudes

Prometheus is a legendary Indo-European hero. "His name may have originated from the Sanskrit word *Pramantha*, the swastika, or fire-drill." "The brothers Pramanthu and Manthu, who appear in the *Bhagavata Purana*, may be the prototypes of Prometheus and Epimetheus." (*The Greek Myths*, R. Graves).

The Greek nymphs, beautiful young women linked to the forests and waters, find their correspondence in India. The Yakshis are forest divinities and have their consorts, the Yakshas. The Yakshis are particularly linked to the trees, the mere contact of their feet on the ground generates them and their fruits depend on them; they would be like the soul of the trees, that which animates them.

Yakshis and Yakshas were, at first, small beings, although not as small as the European gnomes, but they grew with the size of the temples, in which they are never lacking, although they would not reach the size of humans. They never lack tropical sensuality, nevertheless, and they are found in love situations and even in erotic positions (mithunas); let us not forget that they are divinities of fertility. Although we find these mithunas in temple friezes from the first century AD. in Mathura and in the fifth century in the Gupta temples, later, under the influence of Tantra, they come to represent the most daring erotic positions, as in Kahurajo and Konarak and, by imitation and without the art of sculpture, in stucco, as added in many subsequent temples. During the Buddhist period, which is a more sober religion and decidedly less imaginative in its myths than Hinduism, the Yakshas and Yakshis became patron gods and servants of the Buddhist cult; in Sanchi there are some magnificent examples. Their significance, more aesthetic than doctrinal, lies in the fact that these minor divinities have served for centuries as an almost obligatory decorative element in Hindu temples. Strictly speaking, when they grow in size often we know not if they are Yakshis or simply dancers or courtesans with their veenas, flutes, drums and such, as in Konarak.

The Apsaras and also the Nagas, serpentine beings of the waterfalls, are assimilated to the Naiads, so dear to the Greek sailors. These deities are related to fertility and are also protectors of life, just as the fauns in Rome kept wolves away from cattle. I can testify that even today the ancient custom, surely of tribal origin, of worshiping the Nagas is preserved and practiced by women wishing to have children. They are generally carved on a heavy stone slab and, curiously, represented as two serpents intertwined like those that Hermes carried on his rod, which has remained as a symbol of medicine.

Courtesans are part of a particular custom that was shared by Hindus and Greeks. They were very liberal women who exercised a discreet or selective prostitution with the upper classes, whom they entertained with their dances or musical instruments. They were educated enough to circulate in the Courts with naturalness and grace; their profession is assimilated to the geishas, of whom we have all heard. In India they were called Ganikas and they came to be supported and educated by the State; in Greece they were known as Etairas. Pericles married one of them who was remarkably enlightened and gifted, and who contributed to his project appreciably, for she lost no time in bringing to Athens renowned philosophers and artists from Ionia, his native country. At Socrates' banquets with his friends they would participate with their music and dances; although not during the dialogues.

Philosophical Conclusions

Plotinus and the Indian Doctrines

I have maintained that the West ought to have followed the idealist philosophical line on the bases of Plotinus's thought. Plotinus unfortunately appears at the wrong time during the period of crisis that would lead to the collapse of the Roman Empire, the inheritor and follower of the Hellenic tradition. More than a thousand years of an unparalleled civilisation on the planet disappeared with the fall of Rome. What I want to highlight are the great potentialities in Plotinus's philosophy, which we come to realise some 18 centuries later, when we see the need for a convergence of Western civilisation, that is, the Greco-Roman and the Indian. Since Plotinus was the most inspired and superior philosopher of Hellenic tradition, he represents a key figure in this convergence.

To situate Plotinus, the Eastern reader can compare him with Shankara, as he enshrined the most substantial of the Western tradition. Unfortunately he never had the resonance he deserved; historical events decided an unfortunate destiny. It is feasible that having been born in Egypt, raised and educated in Alexandria, a cosmopolitan city *par excellence* and bordering the Orient, Plotinus had contact with Hindus or Buddhists. According to Porphyry, who compiled his work and tells us about his life and personality, due to the "desire to experience the philosophy that was practiced amongst the Persians and flourishes in India", he joined a Roman expedition bound for Persia, but his stay was short and in warlike circumstances, and so it is improbable that he received any cultural or spiritual influence on that occasion. A commentator (Jesús Igal) astutely observes that what interested Plotinus was *experiencing* the philosophy that was *practiced in* Persia and India, that is, his interest lay in *experiencing* knowledge; proof of that is that, like the Buddha, he exhorted his disciples to investigate for themselves.

What is certain is that Alexandria continued to be a Hellenic cultural centre, that Plotinus writes his work in Greek, and he is a follower of Plato whom he never fails to cite. His writings, like those of Plato, are sometimes in the form of dialogues, at other times he has the dialogues with himself. This internal dialogue reminds us of the *witness* of whom the Hindus speak, which is also not surprising as this dialogue is inevitable for him who has transcended his self and other faculties which he examines from *another perspective*. This is also evident because he speaks spontaneously without constructing his thought in keeping with logic.

It never ceases to surprise his commentators that, despite his constant interest in philosophy, Plotinus never had clear ideas even after his arrival in Rome at the age of 40. I am convinced that the sudden convergence of his ideas, followed by a startling lucidity, was due to an *experience of the Transcendent*, equivalent to what in India is called illumination (*moksha*). Besides, Plotinus himself admitted that he had had the experience of the Absolute four times.

Another aspect that seems to us to be very *Indian* is that he uses *morality as a way of ascent towards the Transcendent*, which he calls the One or the Good. This morality in his case also implies a moderated ascetic praxis because, without martyring his body, he had no attachment to it. In his daily life he was a frugal vegetarian and was not known to have had any female company. Fundamentally, Plotinus is a mystic and this undoubtedly derives from his experience of the Divinity towards which he aspires to ascend until he becomes One with It, and the means he uses, as we said, is the exercise of the virtues. In all this he is similar to a *yogi*, a philosopher like Shankara, however we easily find his roots in Plato and the Pythagoreans. What Plotinus does is to put the theory of these maestros into practice, and practice into experience. And it is in this experience of the Transcendent that he assimilates himself to Indian doctrines. Since I have elaborated sufficiently in previous works on the philosophical aspect of Plotinus, in which I compared his thoughts with my own, I will be brief here where my interest lies in aligning the basics of his philosophy with Indian doctrines.

As I said when speaking of Plato, one can perceive a duality in him, and this makes me think that his knowledge is the fruit of true intuitions but not of *a total unitive experience*; Plato was not ensconced in Unity, and for this reason he only suggests it in his last works. Plotinus makes a decisive and definitive leap towards what he calls the One and from where he contemplates all Reality. Plato correctly felt that all souls aspired to the Good (*Rep. VI, 505*), Plotinus confirms this, but also maintains that the Good, which with his *unitive vision* he identifies with the One, is the Origin and Destiny of souls, with which he closes the circle of all that exists, as according to him and as in Hinduism, all living beings have a soul.

I do not know if it is necessary to highlight the similarity that this One has with Brahman and with the Mahayana because, just as in the Dharmakaya, the Good emanates kindness (*Karuña*) and through intelligence (Prajna) attracts all beings towards Itself. In all three (and also in my philosophy) we find in the depths of our being a natural attraction towards the Transcendent, that is, the desire to close and culminate the cycle of life. Not only this, the return is also to the Oneself equivalent to the Self, of which Hinduism always speaks.

Between the world of the senses and the One, Plotinus finds two intermediate states; the Soul, that would be the universal Soul, common to Hinduism (Atman), and the intelligible reality (*Nous*) that he takes from Plato. Plotinus terms as hypostasis this complete Reality and divides it into three substances: the One, the Nous or Intelligence, and the Soul of the World, which derive or engender each other through emanation, although they "remain immobile (that is, without change) by engendering these hypostases" (*Aeneid III, 4,1*). In its emanation, the Absolute, the One, like the Unity, Brahman, or the Dharmakaya, does not reduce nor lose anything of its content, it remains the Same, Immutable.

Plotinus imagines, like Plato and Hinduism, a Soul of the World, but it has three modes of being: There is a superior Soul, in direct contact with the *Nous* or Intelligence, another that would be the Soul of the material World, which he also calls Nature, and another that is inferior, which would be the individual souls; each one results from the other. The individual soul that precedes birth, as in Hinduism, on the death of the subject, returns to its original Unity.

As in Hinduism, the particular souls of all living beings participate in the Soul of the world. These souls tend to go back to their origin, to the One, and the most efficacious way for this is through the practice of virtues; hence the fundamental mechanism of Plotinus' ethics. Sometimes the One is identified with the Good of Plato, who also refers to it in his *Timeous*, although not with the clarity and pre-eminence that Plotinus gives to it. In any case, the objective is similar in both philosophers: virtuous actions tend to reach the Good itself.

The One, though infinite, is a totality, it is All; in this it is similar to the Being of Parmenides and the Brahman of Shankara. The One is always the same, it does not disintegrate nor does it diminish when emanating from the created, although Plotinus admits that there is gradual degradation in the process that takes One to matter. Matter does not become evil but it is impure and imperfect; in one image it visualises the soul as if submerged in the mud from which it must emerge and cleanse itself to ascend. As we have seen, I do not agree to this disdain for Nature, which, due to its beauty, seems to me to be an efficacious way to intuit the Transcendent. In any case, in Plotinus there is no division but an extension of the original Unity, there is a continuous order of things, even if the absolute Order is in the One, for this reason the inferior order that is part of the superior, tends towards this.

As in Plato, Love has an important role in this ascent; particular loves are the samples or reflections of a pure Love, just as beauty is a reflection of Beauty itself that attracts and invites one to the ascent. This ascent happens through a progressive purification in which the subject (its soul) becomes aware of its vices, that is, the inclinations of the self which it begins to see objectively. This experience of seeing the self from afar reminds us of the *witness* that the Hindus speak of, and it also reveals to us his knowledge of the instruments of consciousness, to which my theory of knowledge assigns capital importance.

Our philosopher calls purifying virtues those that make this cleansing and consequent ascent possible. The virtues that he alludes to coincide with those of Plato: wisdom, self-control, courage and justice, all destined to overcome corporal ties and the world of the senses to reach the intelligible world. The ultimate goal of the soul is to assimilate to God, whom it identifies with the One.

Plotinus does not fail to warn us that "The greatest of difficulties for the knowledge of the One is that we do not arrive to It through the sciences or through intellection but through a presence that is superior to science. The soul is absolutely not One when learned scientifically; because science is a discourse and the discourse encloses multiplicity." If I were to use my language, I would change two words: presence for experience and discourse for discernment. In this way we "do not reach the knowledge of the One through science or through intellection but through an experience". The last sentence would read like this: "because science is the product of discernment and discernment implies multiplicity (the opposite of the One)". Shankara, as we know, insists on overcoming all duality.

In Plotinus, aesthetics and ethics have such a close relationship to the extent that in their essence they are a single entity, as corresponds to the Greek spirit. It is not surprising that he instructs us by saying that in order to reach beauty we should practise the virtues and thus purify the soul, as an impure soul cannot be elevated and identify with it. In his work *On Beauty* he barely makes an analysis of the qualities of beauty, what he is interested in is guiding the spirits "towards the heavens," and the Beautiful is an efficacious means; the soul recognises this because it is of the same lineage, in such a way that it has a memory of the same, of its essence. What is truly beautiful for Plotinus is not in things, not even in the beautiful ones, but in beautiful acts, in virtues. In other words, the truly aesthetic is in ethics. There is nothing more beautiful than "the face of justice", nothing as resplendent as the "splendour" of virtue, and "neither is the light of the morning or evening" as beautiful as temperance. "Faced with these invisible beauties, those enamoured by suprasensible beauties, the sensitive, feel a stupor, a delightful tremor, love and pleasurable commotion." "For the soul, to become beautiful and good is to be like God, that is one with the Good and Truth."

In *The Search for Universal Consciousness* I have clearly laid down my conviction that the philosophy, including of course that of morality, that Western civilisation should have followed was that of Plotinus. He had been the most substantial filter of the Hellenic spirit, for the first time he had demonstrated the *philosophical-religious monism* in a systematic and comprehensible manner; although we find it enunciated in the origins of Greek thought. In fact, the first Hellenic thinkers intuited what I have called *transcendental or monist pantheism*, which is born precisely of a *transcendental perspective*, which would be that of the Pre-Socratics, of Plato, Plotinus, Spinoza, Schelling (in his *Philosophy of Nature*) and, naturally, is the one that sustains my philosophy.

Personally, I prefer to visualise the process towards Unity as a progressive harmonious integration of the mind in which the exercise of virtues plays a decisive role. This is not, let this be established, a personal psychic process as Western psychology tends to see it, because the person is so because he is disintegrated, when he becomes integrated the individual consciousness disappears. *This process is universal* and, like Plotinus, I see a movement of expansion or diastole, and another that is centripetal or systole, as if the *Universus* was responding to a universal heart. Plotinus also calls this process *self-awareness* (*E.V. 4,2*).

In any case, the Plotinian triad or hypostasis of the One or Good, Intelligence and the Soul is in the soul of all beings, that is, it is in them in force, as a Unity. Just as Shankara calls Brahman "the One without a second", Plotinus calls the Good "the purely One" and, like Plato, "the One in itself", which for me would be "Unity in Itself". (For the difference between the One and Unity see *The Search for Univ. Consc.*). By revisiting the transcendental perspective of Plotinus, I hope to contribute to reviving the Hellenic spirit, indispensable to the new Renaissance that I propose for the West.

For the reasons stated, I am convinced that Plotinus constitutes the connection we need between our past and present, as well as between the East and West. In fact, in Plotinus we not only find the most refined of the Greek tradition but also a parallel with the lofty philosophies of India towards which he had unwittingly drawn a bridge which could have been used by Western culture. Émile Brehier says in this context at the end of the prologue of his unsurpassed work on Plotinus: "And we believed that it was legitimate and even necessary to make a hypothesis about the relations of Plotinus with India, which perhaps others, more competent, would propose to verify". The hypothesis is of the greatest importance because, however brief the relation that he established, a bridge is traced that from the first pages of this work I have tried to widen and level between the East and the West; hence the importance and reach of this subject.

The aforementioned bridge was not completed by Plotinus, but I think that from the *transcendental perspective* that I am showing and what the West has achieved after its long, painful and interrupted climb along the paths of idealism, this task can be completed. The concept of *universal Soul* is superimposed entirely on to that conceived by Hinduism, and the *monist or transcendental pantheism,* to which I have referred, is found with its particular variants in Hinduism and Buddhism. In the same way we see that to gain this experience the practice of purificatory virtues is necessary, an exercise that brings Platonism closer to these doctrines. The similarities should not be surprising as they are a consequence of the same *experience of Unity,* of the One, as Plotinus called it.

A final clarification: I have said that in Plotinus we see a convergence of Western thought in the East. This is one way of saying it and it can be misleading. In fact there is a *transcendent reality* where spirits converge *when they open the wings of the soul*, as Plato had said, regardless of their origin; precisely because that Reality transcends time and space. I have termed the philosophical search for that reality *universal idealism*. Strictly speaking, my philosophy does not converge in the Orient nor vice versa, these are only the spirits that transcend their individual consciousness and converge in the One, in Brahman, in the *universal Consciousness*.

On Life and Happiness

> "La religión chretienne est la religión des tristesses de la vie, des malheurs, des chagrains."
>
> —Goncourt

The fundamental problem that is put together in the work of Albert Schweitzer, *Les Grands Penseurs de l´Inde,* is to disentangle in religious doctrines the affirmative or negative attitude with respect to life and the world, and the ethics that derive from this attitude. I will not comment on this work here, but I will follow this approach, as the position adopted by the human being before reflecting on his life, instructing himself and adopting a doctrine seems decisive to me.

I have not commented on Schweitzer because even if he understands the need to rescue life, generally denied by religions, he does not achieve the necessary transcendent vision to make this objective truly effective. Been an eminent organist, we know that he interpreted Bach marvellously, doubtlessly he felt a calling, and as a doctor he staked everything on going to Africa to help the Africans who needed his science. Besides his artistic endeavous, in the depths of his moral consciousness, he felt the need to help his neighbour, to practise in his own *karma yoga,* which is unobjectionable.

But in order to reach this ideal it is necessary to attend to the philosophical dimension that a *transcendent perspective* grants, indispensable to avoid a common misunderstanding into which all those who condemn religions because they pay no heed to life fall, and also religious men who effectively disregard it. As I have already pointed out when I elaborated my theory of the psyche (see my *Psychosophy*), altruism (like that of Schweitzer) is positive because it is ascendant, but it is only a means that, though it might contemplate the other, does so from an individual perspective. Only by transcending this does one reach the *essential perspective*, from which the spirit descends (so to speak) in order to cooperate with universal life, helping living beings. I believe that this is what the Buddhists like *Karuña* understand, helping others with *prior transcendental knowledge*.

In my conception, it is the action of the *unitive man* who sees and cooperates with the total Order from universal Consciousness. *My philosophy points effectively to the Life of the Universus*, for which individual lives have to be surpassed. It is, thus, an affirmation of Life, but in its plenitude. And this is not an expression of desires, it is an indubitable experience; this Life in its plenitude is real and verifiable. Having advanced these basic characteristics of my vision on this subject, let us see the position of Hinduism and Buddhism.

Mircea Eliade maintains that the "*leitmotiv* of all Indian post-Upanishad speculation is universal pain". This means that not only does man suffer it, but that "pain constitutes a cosmic need, an ontological modality to which all forms are destined to manifest themselves as such." (*Patanjali and Yoga*) And the Yoga Sutras reiterate: "All is suffering for the wise" (*II, 15*) We find this premise in Buddhism as well as in Hinduism: "All is pain, everything is ephemeral" the Buddha concludes. Despite the metaphysical renewal of the Mahayana, this idea is constant: "All that is impermanent is suffering" "All that is felt is suffering," Asanga corroborates centuries later. There is an abundance of quotations, the aforesaid are enough.

It is not necessary to say that Christianity agrees with this basic principle, this world is a "vale of tears;" with the aggravating factor that there is no escape, there is only salvation in the "other" world; besides, (the son of) God himself (a theological contradiction that theologians have conformed to their pleasure and interest), is the very expression of suffering. One has to highlight the radical difference with Indian doctrines as the latter promise us liberation in life, and the experience of Happiness results from this.

My philosophy coincides with Buddhism and Hinduism in affirming that this life, as it is generally perceived and lived by the human being, is an error. For this reason it resolutely is in keeping with these doctrines and the imperious need to eradicate Ignorance, as the *ignorance of the human being about his own essence is what causes most of the avoidable pain and what deprives him of the greatest achievable happiness*. I said it was an error, but not a horror; and it is on this point that I allow myself to differ.

I believe that it is due to the purpose of inducing us to transcendence that the Indian doctrines present this life to us as undesirable, but in the Orient I have not observed that they experience it as such. In any case, this is neither my experience nor my methodology. To me the difference between Ignorance (avidya) and Wisdom (vidya) is too radical, between which I find nuances; our daily life lies between these extremes and it is not always horrible. My philosophy recovers the moments of positive aspects of life that are, in reality, *examples of the Transcendent* in the living. This means that they are not only valid by themselves but they are guidelines, examples, intuitions and even experiences of the Transcendent. They are the moral call, the happy exercise of the virtues, love without presentiments, moments of peace in daily life, full smiles, the sincere embrace of a friend and even the affectionate lick of the dog, in short, *the joy of life*. All this indicates to us that even if living beings, with very rare exceptions, are ignorant of the Absolute, they are not absolutely ignorant. We ourselves are an expression of the Transcendent; all living beings are like this, and although they might not know it, they feel it in certain moments of happiness. Without this important aspect, life would be unbearable. Besides, liberation is feeling happiness in its greatest and purest expression. Where there is no happiness, there is suffering in the form of dissatisfaction, depression, laziness, negligence, indifference, states that turn into greed, gluttony, hunger for power, self-love, violent inclinations, etc. The weight and anguish of existence are an illness of the soul and the greatest remedy for this is the joy of living; possibly the best antidote to suffering and an efficacious medium of transcendence.

Of course, even if I do not share the idea that this life is only suffering, I think that it is indispensable that we be fully aware of the suffering that life implies, especially the suffering that we cause by our desire to live a life of selfishness. The most effective way of attending to this pain is by acquiring the knowledge that one is essentially free from pain, which leads to the lack of desires and fears which are the generators of unnecessary suffering and, obviously, imparting and sharing this knowledge. *It is the liberated man who produces the least amount of suffering*; this is the most positive attitude one can have in life. To live without attachment, yes, but to live. Besides, life presents itself and is experienced in plenitude when there are no ties, when the spirit moves freely in the mind and in Nature.

My philosophy, therefore, does not aspire at any time to end life but Ignorance, what is important, as in the Indian disciplines, is to achieve *Knowledge but with the objective of enriching life*. Whoever has it will decide what do with life, but is not in agreement that "pain constitutes a cosmic need, an ontological modality".

The problem is not in the world outside, but in the mental faculties that keep us in ignorance and make us see our world and peers erroneously; for this reason I have insisted on a *radical change of perspective and on the awakening of other ideal faculties to the knowledge of the primordial Unity*. The Transcendent is constantly revealed in Nature, in the beauty of the world, in the grandeur of the universe and in our Mind. Infinity itself, which more than covers all reality, contains the secret of our existence, it reminds us of our smallness as individuals while permanently inciting us towards the beyond, towards our Destiny: the All.

It is necessary to clarify that the divergences expressed refer to the means and not ends, to the position adopted in the state of Ignorance that, although there is ignorance of the Absolute in it, ignorance is not absolute, because, as I said, the human being has the ability to feel the joy of life.

The moments of happiness are signs of an incipient perception of unconditional Happiness. Incipient, it is true, but a real indication, a latent but living perception of the fullest experience of the spirit that moves and stimulates the body to jump, swim, dance, laugh, expand, transcend its corporal heaviness. These exercises and modes of manifestation are windows to the Transcendent, which remain closed if we cover our whole life with the label of Ignorance. But I have to reiterate that I do not find any divergence as concerns the ends. Greeks, Hindus, Buddhists and my own spirit, we all happily subscribe to the ultimate objective that we can achieve in life: complete happiness. We also have in common that the means to achieve it lie in the practice of virtues. This statement can seem strange to the Westerner who has been indoctrinated in the opposite direction, because the Christian has confused happiness with bodily pleasures for two thousand years now, the search for happiness in this world leads to perdition.

The obstacle, I will say it once more, is not in the World but in our mind, in the identification with our external and worldly faculties. To have the hope of finding happiness in death is a contradiction, an absurdity. Wise men have found it in life, and we know of none who have found it afterwards.

I am very interested in highlighting and, if possible, demonstrating, the vital aspect that goes hand in hand with transcendental knowledge. My intention to cooperate with Indian religions is evident, but for that I find it necessary to rid them of their dark features, their negative side tends to annul our existence. It is not my experience that we need to negate this life in order to attain another where happiness reigns. In reality there is no other life as everything is One. Consciousness reaches its most elevated state when it unifies and understands that it is One, that Life is permanently the emanation of the Unity.

Of course, the detachment from the mundane is inevitable, but the mundane is not the World, it is only the basic, animal, lewd and material aspect of existence. One certainly has to get out of there, but we are not so crass as to ignore the fact that we are also moral, aesthetes, that we have something religious and philosophical, that is, we have something spiritual, something divine. All religions are born of that divine side that we possess. These beings who we call gods incarnated are humans who have fully realised their divine side, who have overcome the self with all the selfish identifications; for this reason they are called *liberated*.

Life and happiness go hand in hand. The Greeks knew this because they had an *intelligence-instinct* for life on the divine side that we possess, for this reason it was not an effort for them to *exercise virtues with joy*. These people are paradigmatic in this vital aspect. I sincerely believe that this uplifting aspiration: *to be as perfect as the gods*, could revitalise decadent religions and retrieve man from his daily, mundane stupor, from this elementary stage of survival.

The Greek, who knew better than anyone the tragedy that living implies, since it was not anguish that he felt, but the tragic sense of life, experienced life lightly, with ease, which allowed him to look death in the face with indifference. This, we must understand, is not an attachment to life but a desire to live intensely. The elevated aesthetic sense and the deep-rooted moral sense are nothing but a consequence of the perception of the Beautiful, the Good and the Vital Impulse projected towards the ideal of perfection, which allowed him to live *in an elevated level of consciousness*. The Greek ideal was to become like the gods who they called "the immortals" and "the happy ones".

The Greek, as we have seen, felt happy when he exercised his virtues and even died happily if his death was honourable and exemplary. Aristotle captures this morality marvellously : "For, ... a man is not a good man at all who feels no *pleasure in noble actions*, just as no one would call that man just who does not feel pleasure in acting justly, or liberal who does not in liberal actions, and similarly in the case of the other virtues..." (*Ética Nic.*) It is clear that one is referring to the already transformed spirit, to the integral and integrated man, to the wise man; his ethics, and mine, point to this stage of the soul. (See *The Roots of Morality*) The evident detachment from life, parallel to the vital impulse and without hopes of reward in the other world, expresses the pre-eminence of virtues in the Greek consciousness. The ludic capacity of the Greeks that led them to make of everything a fiesta or a festival, clearly shows their joy of life; and the result was wondrously positive.

Hindu festivals, which we should take into account as the Dharma is inconceivable without them, besides being remarkably similar to the Hellenes, clearly contradict that life is suffering. The answer is in the Golden mean and this derives from the facts, from the experience that life gives us: life inevitably *involves* suffering, but it *is not* suffering.

In *The Republic* (and not only there) Plato announces these principles that are essential for Greek morality: “One should always concentrate on an intermediate state, always avoiding the two extremes”. “Herein lies the *happiness of man*.” “The happiest man is he who is most just and virtuous” (*Rep. IX, 580c*). We see that Plato’s ethics is directed to transforming man through virtues; these are the greatest good that the soul can harbour, since equilibrium is the regulator of them all. Aristotle confirms to his teacher: “The goal of virtue is what is morally good or noble” (*Great Ethics I, 19*) “And living well means living in keeping with virtue.” (*Op. cit. I, 4*) And *happiness*, that is “the best of human goods” (*Op. cit. I, 2*), is achieved by the exercise of virtue: “Living in conformity with virtues, we can be *happy*.” (*Op. cit. I, 4*) For the Greek, the highest aspirations of man and societies are summed up in these principles: *justice, happiness, wisdom*.

If the Greek paradigm is too elevated for us, we have within our grasp the example of other sentient beings. The perception of the state of happiness is also the legacy of the higher mammals who express this in the games they are capable of improvising; in canines and cetaceans it is already proven; and we have also seen some birds play in the sky.

With this I do not mean to insinuate that this life *is* a joy, there is too much pain to sustain this. I only want to say that the moments of sincere joy show us an aspect of consciousness that lies latent. The pain also makes us reflect on the transcendent, especially when it is caused by the death of the beings that we love and who deserved to be loved for their virtues.

During the time I was writing, an inseparable companion died. He was a dog called Shanti who always live up to his name. For 12 years he accompanied me in my secluded life, he happily shared my walks, if I was lost in thought, he was too, when I wrote, he continued to be contemplative. He never asked for anything, he adjusted to everything, he never attacked anyone but he had courage at opportune moments. His fortitude for pain was exemplary and what can one say about his joy of life! He seemed to possess all the virtues in his nature and exercised them effortlessly. Truthfully I have never known any friend who at some point did not disappoint me; Shanti never did that.

Upon his death I thought that if I adopted the perspective of the Absolute I could be indifferent, but as a human I would have been a psychopath, a demented metaphysician, so I let my heart take over and a profound sadness took hold of me. When life reflects our human condition, I think it is necessary to accept it. Pain is a great teacher, the Buddha said so and the Greek tragedies exemplified it. Wisdom owes much to pain.

The reader will think that this is a personal matter, which I cannot deny, but soon he will see the universal reach of this example. One may think that in a philosophy book one has to put forward notable thinkers, but precisely on this occasion, I think it is opportune to show the matter from another perspective, as it is my intention to show that the virtues that emanate from the universal Consciousness reach other beings than those, and that reason is not necessary to perceive and manifest them. Perhaps because these sentient beings lack reason they are unhindered in spontaneously expressing these elevated sentiments. We humans never achieve Happiness because we search for it in the fruits of vices and not in the fruits of virtues.

The sincere, spontaneous and natural joy of life is an elevated sentiment comparable to the sharpest intuition; besides, it involves a transcendent perception. It is an expression of the free spirit, free from reasons, calculations, desires, fears and the rest; it is a perception and manifestation of Freedom, even if it is transitory. Reason is only useful for writing about happiness, not for being happy.

In short: For Buddhism, Nirvana, which should be achieved in life, generates "a kind of existence full of confidence, peace, calm, blessings, *happiness*, refinement, purity and freshness". (*Milinda Pañha*). And it is achieved through the exercise of the noble truths that are the indispensable virtues preached by the Buddha, guided by the *Prajna*, which is transcendental intuition, and *Karuña*, which is a transcendental sentiment, Buddhist love translated as compassion. For Hinduism, *Moksha*, which is the equivalent of Nirvana, is *Sat-Sit-Ananda*, Knowledge-Existence-*Happiness*, which is achieved through virtues and yoga practices. (We will return to this subject when talking of Hinduism) This means that the ultimate goal, Happiness, and the virtues needed to achieve it, coincide in the Greeks, my philosophy, Hinduism, Buddhism and all living beings seem to feel and sense it. In conclusion, the joy of living is a path to transcendental knowledge. Moreover, it is generated by the latent intuition of Happiness, which is a manifestation of the Transcendent; the universal Consciousness is happy.

On Beauty

On speaking of happiness, I have mentioned beauty, as this is a means towards the Transcendent as well as an end. In fact it is a *primary manifestation of the Essence of the Universus* on which it pours its grace, it is not only prodigious in the world, as can be seen from its infinite variety of forms and colours, but also in our mind and for this reason its aesthetic virtues can be appreciated.

I hold Beauty in such high esteem, and so much do I believe in its efficacy in transporting us to a supreme knowledge, that I find it strange that Hinduism has not incorporated it as one of the yogas. Perhaps it has been for the same reasons that we saw when we referred to Happiness. Beauty, in fact, can create ties to this world because it turns our gaze towards things, but in this same inclination we can observe that our spirit is attracted by beautiful objects because its own spiritual nature participates in Beauty that, like dew, constantly settles on the *Universus*.

I have devoted an entire volume (*The Roots of Art*) to beauty, and for this reason I will be brief here. Besides expressing virtues, I have collected the ideas of philosophers who shared the Idea of a transcendent mission. Some, like Plato and Plotinus, do not fail to mention the participation of all that is beautiful in Beauty itself; "Things are beautiful because of the presence of the Beautiful". "As long as I stick to this principle I do not think I can fool myself." (*Phedo 100 d*). I fully agree with this Idea-reality, since we can distinguish the beautiful from the ugly thanks to that presence that I call essential reference, which lies latent in our consciousness until we acquire the essential perspective; then we know the Origin of the Beautiful. I am convinced that the perfection achieved by the Greeks in art is due to the intuition of said reference, which made that presence evident.

Others, like Schelling, affirm that art is the royal path to the Absolute; Schopenhauer observes that aesthetic contemplation is the only way of escaping the traps of the Will that have kept us imprisoned in this material world. I have also commented and quoted from the artists who rarely philosophise on the beautiful but have a lot to say about it through their art; which is the specific means to express it. The religious scholars and philosophers would be very presumptuous if they were to think that artists know nothing of the Transcendent. Suffice it to quote Beethoven: "All artistic creation comes from God, and is related to man only insofar as he is a witness of divine action in him." (*Carnets Intimes*)

Once more we see the need to return to classical antiquity, as we cannot omit the Greek people who, as aesthetes *par excellence*, felt the need to approach Beauty by all the means at their disposal. We do not need to highlight the perfection of their unsurpassable art, but we should remember that their gods were their prototypes of beauty, and they wanted to imitate them with their own bodies. These people lived in beautiful surroundings, some 2000 isles adorned their celestial and luminous environment, however not satisfied with this they felt the need to surround themselves with beauty. Their land was not very fertile, but abundant in marble which they rapidly extracted and sculpted to express their ideal of perfection. It would be redundant to elaborate on this theme, but this should be clear: *On the high level of the consciousness of this people, beauty had played a decisive role*.

I expressed my astonishment at not finding amongst the yoga's the ideal of beauty, as in India religious art occupies all artistic endeavours, but it has not been given the level of a path of transcendental knowledge. It is surprising, if all is Brahman or if Nature is its body, as expressed in the *Upanishads*, why not see there a means to achieve it? It is true that Brahman cannot be seen or heard, but it manifests itself in all that is living.

In any case, *my philosophy considers all Nature a revelation*. Every beautiful object or being, the grace of beings that run and fly, the call of the flowers, the charm of the trees, the incessant waves and the reflection of light on the limitless ocean, projects our spirit towards the Transcendent, and this very projection is the *aesthetic experience*. Artists know this and with their uplifting music and suggestive paintings, invite us to surpass ourselves. Their desire to express intuitions and sentiments in their art responds to a *vital impulse* that is a *manifestation of the universal* that leads them to participate in the Beauty of the World.

The Search for Unity

The search for Unity or totality is one of the most revealing characteristics of the Greek spirit. We find it already in the Pre-Socratics and it is structured by Plato. Aristotle himself maintained that the ideal of knowledge, the perfect science, is reached when the subject becomes one with the object. This search has been the driving force of idealism ever since. Such is the importance that the Hellenes gave to Unity, which Ortega y Gasset concludes: "One will have to look for the God of the Greeks not in Olympus but in the thought of One." (*El Espectador, I, 38*) This search was not abandoned, although it was interrupted during the Middle Ages, it has been kept afloat and has resurged in more luminous times; and in reality it is this that has constituted the history of idealism in the West. Plotinus, perhaps the highest expression of this trajectory, "collects expressions that suggest to us the tragic thirst of unity beating in things. Its Being is only the trace of Unity." (Ortega, *Op. cit.*)

In the philosophical conception of the Greeks of the Essence of the world one cannot find any being who can be dissuaded by prayers as in no way is the good of humans a topic, as becomes clear from the Good of Plato or the Thought of Aristotle. Perhaps this could seem disappointing to many, but truth is like this and it has the specific function of dissolving illusions. However, I would like to highlight some advantages of the reality that we are lucky to have. If we have a Father who can pardon our sins, our behaviour will tend to remain in an infantile stage, while it is a paradigm that we must attain and in front of which we are alone with our conscience, it places us in an adult situation. And the soaring heights reached by the Greeks are intimately connected with our vehement aspiration to reach the highest paradigms. The gods of the common people were of course different. In the epic period we find, it is true, repeated sacrifices to the gods, however, it was in order to ask them to be favourable to them in their heroic endeavours, not to pardon their sins. In a few words: The Hellenic is an idealist *par excellence* and, like the Indian, tends towards philosophical-religious monism.

Aristotle's God (not the interpretation given by Thomas Aquinas) was the model that our culture should have followed and which had a solid base for a higher religion. An Absolute whose activity is absolute contemplation, towards which all creation aspires, is impeccable from the philosophical point of view. Unfortunately, Aristotle does not provide us with the necessary means to achieve this objective; although he might have left us a solid basis with his Ethics. Not so Plato, in whose work we find various paths, moral, aesthetic and metaphysical proposals very fruitful for this objective. My philosophy revisits these bases and aspires to resume the Greek tradition. Obviously, a God like that of Aristotle will never be popular, but this is not a criteria when proposing truths. This God is like that of Shankara, who is widely known in India; of course the level of consciousness of the Hindus allowed them to soar to these heights. But one of the most interesting aspects of India is that the people have never abandoned the mythic, epic and folkloric aspects which are based on a deep philosophical current that gives them a course and direction, and as soon as we go deeper into those aspects we find a solid base that shores them up. Shankara's *Advaita* fulfils this function. And the same could very well happen in the West, although that current must pass through a sea of prejudices.

It is undeniable that Platonic philosophy was directed towards the Transcendent and that of Plotinus was an expression of the same. The Western spirit had a smooth path to the Transcendent as concerns aesthetics, ethics and epistemology; it is that path that I have followed in *The Search for Consciousness*. I cannot give a summary of this treatise here. However, as I continue to comment on Indian philosophy, my thoughts will become clearer to the reader. I will devote the fourth part of this book to the search for Unity in India.

This is the general idea: The archaic myths of creation express a separation with respect to the original Unity, but they are followed by myths that demonstrate the intention of recovering this Unity; an undeniable manifestation of the *Cosmic Mind* in which evolved societies will seek, not in the past but in the present, the *experience of that Unity*.

Part 3

The Indic Civilisation

Preliminary Ideas

The Medieval Era in Europe and in India

A thick volume would be needed to explain the facts that are of interest to us as we are dealing with two complex cultures over extensive periods of time. Since this is not a book of history, I will try to reduce these facts to what is necessary. The concept of *Medieval*, needless to say, is only applicable to the West, but the period it comprises can serve us as a reference because, curiously and symptomatically, a reverse process is taking place in the Far East, a process of apogee. This is happening, in effect, in India and China and with many nuances in its zone of influence, Indochina. For our purposes I will only speak of what is necessary of India and Europe.

The origins lie in the Middle Ages, for their notoriety and enormous consequences, with the fall of Rome by the hands of the barbarians. But the spirit of the Medieval Era, characterised by Christianity and the political power of the Church, had already been strong a century and a half earlier; the decadence that characterises the following centuries was already in place.

The historical facts speak for themselves: until the 4th century A.D. the West competed on equal terms with the great civilisations of the Far East. After that century the difference is abysmal: while the West regressed to barbarism, India proudly exhibited the fruits of a mature civilisation. And one should not entirely blame the barbarians for the European disaster, as India also suffered them, but with religions, philosophies, relevant industries and creative freedom it could rapidly re-establish itself. China, on the other hand, from the 8th century, that is, during the darkest period in the West, develops one of the most refined civilisations in the history of man. The West had to wait seven centuries to reach this height. Proof of this decadence cannot be more evident: the most memorable periods in the East took place during the European Middle Ages. The period that in the West has been called the Dark Ages, is the luminous or

Enlightened Age in the East. This comparison, that has not really been taken into account due to the well-known Western egocentric vision that has arbitrarily and systematically disdained other cultures, is inescapable when judging the history of civilisations.

We have only to see the idea of the world in the Middle Ages on a map of the earth drawn in the 11th century (C. Sagan *Cosmos*), on which it appears divided in three parts or similar portions, without any detail, formed by Europe and Africa, separated by the single rectangular sea on the planet that is the Mediterranean, and Asia, in order to appreciate the incredible regression signified by the Middle Ages. Eight centuries earlier, Ptolomy had configured a detailed map of the known world including the Indian peninsula. On the 11th century map the earth is flat and in the centre of the disc is found Jerusalem, while in the 3rd century the earth was round and did not have a centre. Albeit that Ptolomy had maintained that the earth was the centre of the Universe, and this suited the geocentric vision of the Old Testament.

Like no other epoch, the Middle Ages is proof that decadence existed then in all orders, that there is no linear evolution in history, rather that there can be regressions. And these regressions are not only in the knowledge of the external world but above all in the internal, that is, *man becomes more primitive*. This explains the inexplicable fact that what has been adopted as a general reference of the world, of its creation, the ethical and aesthetic order etc., is a text written some thousand years before Christ that ignores the entire Greco-Roman contribution, that is to say, all its contribution to civilisation. It should be no surprise that barbarism would rule.

We have only to compare the elementary theatre of the Middle Ages that was reduced to *autos sacramentales* (sacramental plays) in which the life of the holy family was represented (or the *autos de fe*, in which heretics were burnt, and were a public spectacle) with Greek drama, to realise the abysmal fall of the spirit; the miserable life of medieval man with the plenitude of the life of the Hellenic; and we do not need to repeat what we all know: the stagnation of the sciences.

Curiously and symptomatically when the destruction of the Hellenic civilisation began, marked by the Church's ascent to power in 325, in India began an age of apogee known as the Gupta era beginning with Chandragupta in 320. The empire reached its splendour and was consolidated with his son Samudragupta, who would rule for half a century. During the long reign of his son Chandragupta II the empire spread to the Arabian Sea in the west, and this allowed India to have commercial relations with Alexandria and Europe, and to open out to the Indian Ocean taking Indian culture to the coasts of Thailand and the Indonesian islands. The Gupta apogee stretches for more than forty years in the reign of Kumaragupta, and ends with the invasion of the white Huns, relatives of the black Huns who ravaged Europe in the same period. But this invasion does not end with the dynasty.

The Gupta era, lasting 300 years, is the most famous in the history of India for its prosperity on all fronts, especially cultural and spiritual because a resurgence of Hindu tradition happens, and this should be understood not as the imposition of a doctrine, but as a natural process that occurs in an ambience of tolerance and respect. The decline of Buddhism begins although it will still be relevant for several more centuries. It is in this period that Mahayana Buddhism emerges, the pride of universal philosophy, its authors often being protected by Hindu as well as Buddhist monarchs. The premises of Hinduism as we know it today were established then: Shiva as Mahadeva, Vishnu with his incarnations, his consorts and his *vahanas* or animals who accompany and represent them, the festivals, so characteristic of the *dharma*, in which all participate without any religious distinction, all of which is in the *Puranas*, texts that devotees still recite and initiate a new form of religious expression, more under the guidance of poets than philosophers, closer to sentiments than to reason.

The literature of this age is considered to be classic as Sanskrit reaches its perfection in the hands of many poets, especially in those of Kalidas, the author of a world famous poem *Shakuntala*, in which love, treated in its highest form, is the guiding theme. Another fruit of this age is the no less famous *Panchatantra*, a collection of stories and fables that express the ingenious spirit of that time. Curiously, Hinduism sees a resurgence in the same period as Christianity emerges, but their ends will be very different as concerns civilisation.

The decadence of the Gupta dynasty, as we have said, begins with the irruption of the Huns. These nomadic tribes cruelly persecuted Buddhism and this could be considered to be the beginning of its extinction in India, later consummated by the Muslim invasion. But this should be clear: Buddhism, Jainism and later the Sikhs, as well the countless tribal religions, always lived peacefully alongside Hinduism. In every case, hostile relations were foreign. This marks a clear distinction between what can be understood as *Indic civilisation* and foreign cultures, whose intent was never to integrate but to dominate, subjugate and become wealthy.

The fall of the Gupta empire is far from signifying the decline of the Indic civilisation, which renews itself in the first half of the 7th century during the empire of Harsha, spreading to the same limits as those of the Gupta monarchs. Originally Shaivist, he finally adopts Mahayana Buddhism which reaches a new zenith under his protection. For this reason, because of his tolerance, generosity and magnificence he is rightly compared with Ashoka. During his reign the burgeoning Indic culture expands to China. After Harsha, power is disputed by the warriors of Rajputana, who reach their apogee during the 10th and 12th centuries. In the following centuries we see kingdoms and dynasties rise and fall, all of which have left cities and monuments as behoves an advanced civilisation.

Leaving aside its architecture and art, and leaving for later its unsurpassable philosophy, India inherited and developed its scientific research from Greece and discovered in the 5th century that “The celestial sphere is fixed, it is the earth that revolves on its axis, and it is this that causes the rising and setting of the planets and stars” (Aryabhatta) and since then the astronomers could predict its eclipses. I think it is well known that Indians invented the zero, the decimal system and the numerals that in the West are called “Arabic”. The Arabs, as is usual with invading nomadic tribes when they encounter advanced civilisations, were nourished by the knowledge they found. They brought from India to Spain numbers, chess and the famous steel that is called “Damascus”, which they used extensively for their conquests. The Arabs destroyed the icons and the temples, but they were not so foolish as to destroy the books. We know that through them, Europe rediscovered the Greek philosophers, especially Aristotle, and thus they showed that they were a superior culture. One should also remember that the highest and most interesting branch of Islam, Sufism has its origin in India. In any case, Islam’s debt to the Hellenic and Indic civilisations is incalculable. When the Arabs were expelled from Spain, Italy was reborn when by incorporating the Hellenic culture that had lain hidden in Greece.

In the 12th century the Muslim expansion reaches the coveted valley of the Ganges. They are not Arabs but Afghans, Turks and Mongols who had converted to Islam. For two centuries they had limited themselves to looting, but from that time on they insert themselves in the history of India. A sultanate whose power would extend to Bengal installs itself in Delhi. There are no pious believers but ambitious leaders with no other objective but power. Within their territory there does not seem to be any peace, the struggles continue for three centuries.

But India is a huge country and many areas were not affected by the invaders. Numerous kingdoms and dynasties had their moments of splendour, and they attracted architects, artists, men of letters and more, and so the Indic tradition took its course. The surviving temples, monuments, palaces and sculptures show a vibrant civilisation. One only has to visit the ruins of Vijayanagar to realise the vigour and grandeur of that culture.

The catastrophe came with the Timurids, descendants of Timur, the fearsome Tamerlane, Mongols who had converted to Islam and who established an empire that would cover the whole peninsula. This was, undoubtedly the greatest attack on the Indic civilisation; a period of more than two centuries on which it would be excessive to dwell on here. We cannot deny the grandeur and beauty of the forts, mosques and tombs of that period, and we could say the same of the Gothic cathedrals of Europe, but when we view history, the question is: Do these edifices justify the hundreds of Hindu and pagan temples that have been destroyed, and more decisively, the interruption in the development of the Indic and Hellenic spirit with its infinite potential?

Curiously, once more, this catastrophe in India occurs just when the Renaissance is taking place in Italy. When Europe leaves the medieval Dark Ages, India falls into obscurity after a period of luminosity. As we know, the Islamic empire is succeeded by the British-Cristian empire, which will continue the exploitation of India and the subjugation of the Hindus for another two and a half centuries. These are not only historical facts, behind them there is a spirit that is reborn and allows the human being to express it: As if the universal Spirit did not want to leave humanity without hope, it seems to have been displaced (as Hegel imagined, but in a very different age and manner) from the Orient to the Occident. It could be said (and later on we will clarify this affirmation) that the spirit awakens during the Renaissance and later during Romanticism, the spirit that until then had been in force in India.

But if there is something that characterizes the Indic civilisation, it is that its spirit, its tradition, its Dharma never goes out; in the ashes of its history there are always embers that are rekindled with the breath of some mystic or religious leader. The Indic civilization, like an old tree, has grown roots so deep that no invasion has managed to eradicate; it is no surprising that in the middle of the 20th century it began to bear fruits again, and in the 21th it is seen leafy and fruitful once again.

Christianity and Civilisation

If it is known how a civilisation is generated, how it is structured, how it functions, and what it is, it will be understood that to speak of a Christian civilisation is a contradiction in terms. The mere claim to make a civilisation with a single book is not only a contradiction, it is absurd. What defines and makes a civilisation are the ideals and practices of freedom of thought, research and expression in all orders, it is this that produces philosophy, arts and sciences, material and spiritual progress, and mental and physical health. This freedom implies an opening and tolerance towards other customs and races, with their religions, ways of thinking and believing, which lead to cosmopolitanism.

None of these characteristics is typical of Christianity, whereas they were of the Greeks and Romans. Christianity (and the same could be said of Islam in relation to Persia and India), was not born out of a civilisation, it lacked the spirit, contact with the Creative, so when it infiltrated the Roman civilisation, it needed to feed on it, so was undermining it until it collapsed. Later, for more than half a millennium, during which the Church managed to monopolise power and did what it could to impose a *modus vivendi* in keeping with Christian doctrine, civilisation was not possible. Only to the extent that Hellenic tradition resurfaced were some symptoms of civilisation made manifest, that is, the aforesaid symptoms reappeared, not through the will of the Church but in spite of it, as an excess of what it could not contain. We can only speak of civilisation when the excess of the classical spirit was unstoppable, so much so that it swept away a great number of the Church hierarchs. Only then did the Hellenic civilisation take on a Christian hue, but this clashed with doctrine to the point of seeming scandalous from a Christian perspective. Hence the Reformation and the Counter Reformation, which were a return to the medieval spirit, and which again undermined and collapsed the conatus of civilisation. But the dykes had already burst and so the Hellenic current, from the time of the Renaissance, has followed its course as the spirit has been able to act on the periphery of the Church; although the French Revolution was necessary in order to definitively break the Christian dyke.

If, with a great effort we do away with the coercive means used by the Church, we can attribute the success of Christianity to an incomparable psychological resource: the promise of eternal happiness. What man longs for the most can be realised, one just has to have faith, although paradoxically one has to wait for death itself for its actualisation.

If Christianity had been sown, germinated, grown and cultivated naturally in our culture, like other religions within the Roman Empire, that is to say, without coercion aimed at disqualifying competition with propaganda, and annihilating it with more concrete and direct measures, we would have known its strengths and weaknesses. In this way it would have competed with other religions and customs in terms of equality and respect; thus, *the West would have followed a natural course*, but it was not so.

The Greco-Roman civilisation and the entire empire developed in a framework of freedom of belief and religious tolerance that were broken by Christianity. And this happened because, in contrast to other religions, it pointed directly to earthly power and once it was attained it imposed it vertically, with strict governmental, political and judicial measures, to the exclusion of other religious traditions. From beginning to end it tended towards absolute monopoly. Once this was obtained through power and other means, it also imposed education in which it did not allow any competition either; obviously within these conditions, education became indoctrination. The West had lost the crucial factor for its creativity and natural development:

freedom; and it had to wait 1300 years from the times of Theodosius at the end of the 4th century to the end of the 18th century to reestablish it. During the Renaissance, freedom had broken the strongest chains and creativity sprung from liberty itself and this identified naturally with the lost spirit nine centuries before.

Of course, after the excess, when there was a Renaissance of the spirit and the resurgence of our civilisation, the Christians attributed the achievement to themselves and began to speak of a "Christian civilisation", but whoever has the eyes to see history will verify time and again that *the great cultural movements have been the resurgence of the Hellenic spirit* that have managed to overcome the barriers imposed by Christianity. The spirit of Christianity is expressed in the medieval ages, even today as we know, the official philosophy of the Church is that of Thomas Aquinas.

From the first moment, with Constantine, to the last, the French Revolution, the Church was against the sciences and against all spiritual quests alien to the Christian doctrine. In 1752, the great intellectual work of *La Enciclopedie*, the subtitle of which explains its purpose well: *Reasoned Dictionary of the Sciences, Arts and Crafts*, was attacked by the church and especially by the Jesuits (the most learned sect), who through their influence got the French government to ban it. Two years later, the pope Clemente XIII condemned it and included it in the Index of prohibited books.

When the Church reached its full power and could consolidate its ideology, there occurred the darkest age, the most sordid and least creative society in the history of the West. Centuries in which barbarism, superstition, magic, fanaticism, terror and an absence of culture predominated. The Logos and all that derives from it, philosophy and the sciences continue to be Hellenic; and they have survived in spite of so many obstacles.

When speaking of civilisation, it is important to remember that the *Bible* is a book that has emerged from a tribal tradition. All the books born of a great civilisation have tried to adapt to this book. For some, the centre of the world was Jerusalem, for others it was Rome; when speaking of civilisation one only needs to compare these two cities. This adaptation of classic texts to the *Bible*, especially those of Aristotle and Platonism is what let to what is called "Christian philosophy" through which the order of things was inverted. Rome could have absorbed and digested Christianity, it had done so with countless religions, but it was not inversely possible and when this enterprise was carried out forcefully, the inevitable happened: the breakdown of civilisation and the fall of the centres that culturally nurtured it: Rome, Alexandria and Athens in particular and the numerous cities scattered throughout the empire, with their libraries, theatres and an entire urban infrastructure such as laws, aqueducts etc. fell to pieces.

To summarise, it could be said that what caused the collapse of the Roman empire, and Hellenic civilisation that had taken more than a thousand years to build and that had attained unprecedented magnificence, was the reduction of all this culture to a single book: the Bible. There was no longer a need for the 33 libraries that Rome had, that were in reality 66, as all were double, one dedicated to Rome, another to Greece; now just one book was necessary. The burning of the Library of Alexandria, which contained more than half a million texts from all over the known world was necessary for this gargantuan task. This Christian attack, this boycott and lobotomy of our civilisation was more harmful than the invasion of the barbarians. In fact, barbarism was already in place, Rome was decapitated; the Visigoths only gave it the death blow. This is why I have maintained that the Medieval Ages begin with the maliciously provoked catastrophe of the Library of Alexandria. The smoke cloud from this fire covers the entire darkest period of our civilisation and only dissipates in the Renaissance. When the Hellenic spirit was reborn, the first need that arose was to rescue as far as possible from the ashes the classical books, the plurality of manifestations of the spirit that Greece and Rome had produced before the catastrophe.

Having revisited Alexandria's age of splendour, I have come to know that it contained Buddhist texts that were brought by the special envoys of Asoka, the magnificent enlightened emperor of India. These texts alone could have led our civilisation to the highest levels. Just as it happened in China with the introduction of Buddhism, and thus reached its age of splendour, could have happened in the West. In both cases, there was a land of fertile cultivation, an excellent cultural and moral storehouse, which needed a religion with solid philosophical bases. But then everything was destroyed.

In any case Christianity cannot be a universal religion (although Toynbee might call it this for its spread if not for its philosophy) for the simple reason that it only contemplates the fate of human beings. It may spread throughout the entire planet, from which it is further and further away, but this still does not make it universal: its narrow anthropocentric and geocentric doctrine impedes this, it lacks a cosmic vision.

Maybe it is not too late for the West to revisit the spirit of the Hellenic tradition, for that it can incorporate Buddhism or Vedanta, as I am convinced that these doctrines can fully satisfy the religious needs of our peoples, and fill the void left by Christianity. With my work I hope to smoothen this path.

The Latent Force of Unity

There is a fact, which does not seem to have been dwelt on, of enormous repercussions for history, which is the cosmic force and psychological consequences of Unity. I need not repeat what I have said about it, I will only recount that being at the very centre of the mind, being a natural and constant attraction, it leads man to gravitate around this centre. This centre also has a metaphysical dimension that awakens intimate feelings of a religious order; all of which mobilises the human being perhaps like no other force. This inner force has been used with unparalleled success by monotheistic religions in order to bring together adherents and convince them of the need to extend their doctrine and power. Of course, without external forces, the military in particular and politics in general would not have been so successful, but these have depended on an inner force that inclines the faithful to feel part of a unit, a unifying project; an intimate sympathy inclines them to be a part of it.

Monotheistic believers will argue that they are motivated by a true God, but besides the fact that the God of Islam is not the same as that of the Christian, the matter is not reduced to the religious order; the tremendous force of nationalism, that is, the identification with a tradition (which can also be achieved by systematic and prolonged indoctrination), obeys the same impulse that also leads to a project of unification. Moreover, the three monotheistic religions are born from a nationalist ideal, as peoples chosen by God, or who have chosen the only 'true' God, and the subsequent conquest has been an extension of the religious-nationalism to frontiers beyond the original nation.

To those latent forces that have their origin in Unity, psychopathic egoism has been added, which has played a decisive role in said expansions. One thing is the unity common to all and the other is *my* unity or *ours*; from which derive personal advantages accruing from the conquest and exploitation of others, of infidels, enemies, idolaters and other epithets used by reason to justify the actions harmful to the others and beneficial for those in possession of the "truth".

I am referring to the tribal need to belong to a group, party or club in which sympathy is projected and antipathy is generated for the opponents, who become enemies, that is to say, what those who accumulate power, and want to remain in power, and have the support of the masses have to achieve is to make the masses identify with the ideologies they propose, so that they believe that they are the product of individuals, and this is achieved with a few generations of indoctrination. When the people believe this, that this is their tradition, the rulers have already bought their souls; and this process is very difficult to reverse. Well, this is what has happened in the West and in the Middle East.

It will be clear that the internal force that drives unity can be used in various ways; mixed with selfish forces and, taken hand in hand with these, to monstrous aberrations. But in these cases, the spirit has followed a divergent path and has become alienated from the original source. This, needless to say, has nothing to do with self-knowledge, and much less with the knowledge of Unity itself. Indeed, the understanding (experience) of Unity involves overcoming the ego, which necessarily leads to freedom of belief and action and respect for others.

Neoplatonism and Christianity

Neoplatonism was the right answer for Western civilisation, but Plotinus, its greatest representative, who lived in Rome for some thirty years, does not seem to have been aware of the historical situation, as he did not concern himself with Christianity, although he intended to found Platonopolis, to make real the dream of the Republic. It is not possible to imagine how this project would have functioned, but it would have undoubtedly stimulated the high spirit of Athens, the torch that Rome took up, and the one that the West should have picked up.

I am interested in highlighting the thoughts of Plotinus (I have already done so in previous works) because, in addition to being the pinnacle of Greek thought, it is the closest thing I have found in the West to Buddhism and Hinduism, which overlap my philosophy. Plotinus ratifies and seals, enunciating it more clearly, what is the psychic, philosophical and religious essence of man and the reality in which he is immersed, the tradition that stretches back to Parmenides and Xenophanes and reaches its greatest philosophical expression in Plato. The essential had already been said, from then on religion ought to have revolved around this essential Truth: the Unity of man with Divinity. Later can be added the myths, the popular beliefs, the minor gods like the Son, the Mother, the saints with miraculous powers etc., who make folklore and its art.

This is what the religions of the Far East have done with indisputable knowledge: firstly the knowledge of the sages, the backbone or orthodoxy of Buddhism, Hinduism, Taoism and Confucianism, and since orthodoxy is not rigid or dogmatic, later the miraculous bodhisattvas were added, the Immortals, Shiva receiving the Ganges in his locks of hair, the avatars of Vishnú, Krishna as a shepherd boy, etc.

But Christianity did the opposite, it placed his mythology not only in precedence to that essential knowledge, and finally denied it and even persecuted it. This attitude was undoubtedly politically correct as it made all that was mythical, popular, folkloric, superficial and within the reach of the masses, into a first and last "Reality", but from the philosophical point of view, that is, with respect to Truth itself, this was a decisive error that distracted our civilisation to a point where it still cannot find itself. Indeed, as I have tried to show, the Renaissance, the Enlightenment and German idealism, the three great attempts to revive our civilisation in the Graeco-Roman spirit, have failed to steer its course towards its true Destiny.

Neoplatonism, which, like all higher philosophy, appealed to cultured and elevated minorities, could not be assimilated during that time. It arrived a little late. Plotinus was born just after the age of Antonine's ended, where it could have grown and borne marvellous fruit. Perhaps in this case the sombre Middle Ages could have been avoided, I want to say, perhaps a Renaissance could have happened. And although distinct from the Florentine, we can suppose that it would have been more profuse and better supported. Neither Greek nor Latin had to be recovered, the library of Alexandria was full of classics, which were, moreover, in the houses of the patricians, and most of them were lost a century later. There was no need to salvage this knowledge and translate it from the ruins, all Greco-Roman culture was fresh and at hand.

There was a new attempt to reestablish Hellenic culture during the Renaissance. As I have already said what I consider necessary about this period in *The Search for Universal Consciousness*, I will not repeat myself here. Suffice to say that in my opinion the Platonic spirit gave rise to the Renaissance, it was a breath of life that was propagated in multiple branches of knowledge; even Aristotle was seen with new eyes. We have only to remember that the arts were inspired by the Hellenes and Latins.

I will only add the objective of G. G. Plethon who arrived in Florence from Greece in the *quattrocento* (15th century), that is, when the Renaissance, even if already manifest, sought with albeit controversial ideals to clear the panorama that had been obscured for ten centuries. "What is most interesting of Plethon is his imposing prophetic affirmation, when he announces the end of the Hebraic, Christian and Islamic religions and the advent of the Platonic city according to the principles of an idea of the universe where Neoplatonism is expressed as a rite and a law of life." (E. Garin, *L'umanesimo italiano*) That is to say, as a religious and civil rule and order of the West.

Plethon had a vital influence on the Medici, the princes of the Renaissance, and on Ficino, the most important philosopher of the age, who translated his work and also the works of Plato and Plotinus and continued this line of thought. The Reformation and the Counter-Reformation were in charge of putting out these flames of the spirit.

Indic Thought and my Philosophy

It is perhaps unwise to speak in general of Indic thought. Whoever has taken the trouble to examine more than 4,000 years of its development will have seen not only the diversity of thinking, but also the variety of their modes of expression: philosophy, with its different schools, authors and commentators, some more intuitive, others more rational, others more emotional, etc.; religion, which abides by sacred texts, or devotion, or yoga techniques, or ritual, etc.; literature, the epic in particular, with its legendary variants, its myths, its fantasies, its examples, etc. In short, it is very easy to get lost among the branches of Indic thinking pursuing scholarly work, and the result can be sterile.

But if the task of philosophy is to get to the essence of things, instead of following the branches, we go to the roots, although aware of the danger of falling into generalisations, we are going to keep something in hand, which has to do with the essentials of the matter, or, at least, with something that can be useful to us, that opens the doors of understanding.

Strictly speaking, separating philosophy from religion and religion from the Indian epic has a touch of arbitrariness and can even be inadequate. There are common features that outline and configure the profile of the Indian spirit, which I am interested in highlighting because they are also common to my philosophy. And this is what is interesting about the matter, it is not the result of Indian influence, but of a long process that idealism has followed in the West.

Now, Hinduism and Buddhism are idealistic by definition, and my philosophy is superimposed on this idealism. I believe that it will be guides for the reader to anticipate the general features in common that demarcate said superposition. Later we will go into detail and highlight its nuances. The ultimate goal, as I anticipate, is to demonstrate that if my philosophy, which is the result of Western idealism, overlaps with Indic idealism, which has spread throughout the Far East, it is because there is a *universal Idealism*. That is to say that the human spirit, when directed towards the highest peaks of thought, responds to the same intuitions and generates the same ideas.

This is an aspect of my philosophy that has already been explained in previous works. I think, from my own experience, that the history of thought does not fundamentally depend on cultural heritage, on the influence of borrowed thoughts, but on common Ideas of the same transcendent reality that generate similar ideas. That is why I prefer to speak of overlapping ideas, rather than influences. The structure of the human mind is similar in all races and peoples, and in what is substantial and decisive, that is to say, when it philosophises, it is faced with the same circumstances: the brevity of life, its aspiration to happiness, its need to unify to understand, its projection into the afterlife where it seeks the perfection of its aspirations: unconditional Happiness, total Unity, the Absolute. It is from the intuitions of this transcendent reality that the philosopher draws his ideas and not from those who thought about them before. *There is a transcendent vertex that is the Origin and Destiny of all true philosophy*.

This clarification is highly opportune because not only does it explain my way of seeing, but also applies very well to Indic thought. In effect, the similarity or coherence that we find in Indian thinking, in contrast to the disparity that we observe in the West, is due precisely to the convergence of intuitions in that vertex. This, in my opinion, has a sensible explanation: spiritual techniques, which are around 3000 years old in India, have proven to be extremely effective for internal and external knowledge. This means that the thinker is provided with knowledge, and this is not the product of reasoning, but of experience, and his work will not be the product of inductions but of deductions. The Westerner may come to believe that the disparity in his culture is a consequence of his greater creativity; Hegel himself, among other nonsense of which he is so fond, saw Eastern thought to be repetitive for this reason. I think my explanation is more consistent. In Hegel we find, to be precise, a paradigmatic case of an inducer of realities, but metaphysical realities are not induced or constructed, they are discovered.

Then, going back to the subject that brought us here, the similarities of Indic thought with my philosophy, in summary are these: We have just mentioned two of them, both are *idealistic* and are based on *experience*. Both philosophies are essentially *vital*, they are not satisfied with being reasonable, they are to be lived, experienced, they are worthy of the expression of pragmatic spiritualism; if it is not lived, a theory has no value. Both have a *transcendental destiny*, which is why they tend towards the Absolute. And if it is not one's own spirit or soul that experiences this Absolute or Brahman, there is no liberation. This *Liberation* in both conceptions implies *Happiness*; this is also a common goal.

In both disciplines, *the moral path* is unavoidable, albeit that my philosophy tends to see it as an ordering of the psyche, in that any disorder clouds the mind, which is why it does not emphasise the feeling of guilt, but rather the awareness of the mistake and disorder of the psychic order (see my *Psychosophy* and *The Roots of Morality*). *In both disciplines, philosophy and religion go hand in hand*, and both use a transcendental psychology. For certain, overlapping does not mean identification. Since my thinking has arrived from another side by other means, within a different context or tradition, there will necessarily be differences that will be pointed out in due course.

In any case, my philosophy adheres to my own experience and is developed according to it, if it does not coincide with texts from India, so be it, because my commitment is not with them but with what I hold to be indubitable truths. Of course, I will make an interpretation of those works, but with a critical and objective sense, it will not be the usual commentary in India on adaptation to the texts.

Some of them, it is true, have such penetration and scope that they seem, in effect, to be a carbon copy of the Transcendent. They are undoubtedly the work of *seers*, as they are often called, that is, of those who see or have seen, but it is one thing to see and another to express what has been seen, and this is not ignored by the philosophers who comment, those who interpret *what the author meant to say*. In any case, the commentator and those commented on are often seers, they have seen; and this, in my opinion, is what is most characteristic or outstanding of Indic philosophy; if it has not been seen, it is not philosophised.

Strictly speaking, the concept of philosophy is Greek, the Hindu calls it *darsana*, whose etymology comes from, to be precise, to see. And this is the most marked difference that I find with respect to Western philosophy, where too many thinkers venture to philosophise without being clear about the object, even though they know what the objectives are, since philosophical tradition has already established them. And this is where my theory of knowledge categorically adheres to the Indic tradition. Furthermore, my theory, which is based on practice and is directed towards experience, although it seems clear and sufficient to me, is very brief compared to the Hindu one, which has bodily, spiritual, psychological, moral and finally philosophical techniques that have been highly elaborated over thousands of years. I refer to Yoga, which is the great discovery of the Indic genius.

We will return to Yoga, but I would like to proffer this in advance: the constant, highest and necessary Greek aspiration, *know thyself*, carved on the temple portal at Delphi, the most prominent sanctuary in Hellas, where pilgrims from the most remote places went in search of knowledge, finds the most effective method in Yoga. Moreover, as this aspiration is the basis of Socratic-Platonic thought, which is projected to this day, it finds the most appropriate complement in yoga. We already see, in this relevant aspect, how the Indic civilisation can be a continuation of the Hellenic.

Without self-knowledge there can be no personal, social, or international order. Disagreements with our fellow men, which are an inseparable part of human history, do not come from the fact that we want different things or because we want to possess the same things, the disagreement has its roots in the ignorance of our true being. Self-knowledge is the starting point, but it does not end there, if we continue delving into it, at some point we will find ourselves in the field of philosophy.

The true treasure of India is the one that the invading peoples failed to see. From it we can learn the means that lead to inner peace, essential to achieve outer peace. It is the aspiration of all civilised nations to develop in peace, without war. It is enough to reconsider a little to realise that this aspiration is not achievable in societies whose citizens are loaded with violence and greed. India has the means to cure this disease, so ingrained in man. The solution adopted up to now, that of gradually increasing weapons so as to be stronger than one's neighbour, cannot continue. This social Darwinism corresponds to a primitive stage of the human being that it is time to overcome. Every sane and rational person realises that humanity has been walking the dark paths of madness for a long time. It is becoming more and more evident that every project of civilisation, from now on, must be carried out on the basis of moral, aesthetic, religious, in short, philosophical values, which the West has set aside but which India has managed to preserve.

The fact that of all the ancient civilisations India is the best preserved, and in a strict sense, one might say, is the only one to have survived with its distinctive features, should make us think as long and deeply as we can. Faced with this fact, we cannot help but infer that this people possesses the key that every civilisation needs to survive. Also to be found in Asia is the other civilisation that has endured, China, but as is known, by adopting a Western materialist ideology it has renounced its cultural and spiritual past, which has generated a sort of catastrophe similar to the fall of Rome as a consequence of the triumph of dogma and barbarism. From what has been said, when judging Indian culture, one should do so with caution and respect. This is not what the Westerner has done in general; highly convinced of the benefits of his technology and the advantages it gives him over less industrialised countries, he tends to believe that civilisation should follow the path he is following with his machinery. But this perspective lacks the mediacy and scope necessary to appreciate a culture as complex and ancient as the Indian, which is already over 4,000 years old.

The vast territory conquered was not enough for the Persian empire. The Greek genius could not produce more than an ephemeral civilisation. Nor were the organisational spirit and the immense sacrifice of generations after generations enough to prevent the fall of Rome. Persia ends with Alexander; Greece with its internal wars, and Rome with the internal invasion of Christianity and the external one of the barbarians. In view of this, one is tempted to believe that when peoples are conquered by others technologically more advanced, or better prepared for war, their destiny comes to an end. When we look at the catastrophe of the pre-Columbian civilisations, this rule seems unquestionable. But when we study the history of India we see that this law is not fulfilled. India has been invaded, not once but numerous times, by the most fearsome warriors, the barbarians, who devastated Europe, who were their neighbours and intruded on their territory. The Mongols, descendants of Tamerlane, the Timurids, conquered more than half of their territory and stayed for centuries imposing the religion they had adopted, Islam. Nor was the systematic campaign of the English enough to put an end to the Indian culture. That this culture could not be eradicated can only be explained by the depth of its roots.

Unfortunately, for reasons of space, here I can barely mention India's rich historical past, but, as we will see, this civilisation is not explained by past events, but by its tradition, its customs, its *Dharma*, its spirit; it is around these that my comments have to revolve.

On Monotheism and Polytheism

The history of the human being can be defined as the systematic misunderstanding of his *Nature*, although from time-to-time spirits appear who discover its Essence. The edifice of Western culture has been raised within this incomprehension; that is why I am doing this work to clarify and review its foundations. Since I am not unaware that a good part of this edifice has been and is maintained thanks to indoctrination, I think it is also necessary to clarify some concepts and beliefs.

The decisive differences in the wide world of religion must not be sought (as we have been taught) in the different doctrines, there, but in the different levels of consciousness, here, in each one of us. All doctrines pursue the same goal: Unity, to which they give different names; they all point in the same direction, only that they present different paths or means. There are no, let us get this disastrous idea out of our heads, objectively "superior" and "inferior" religions, there are only more or less effective ways, which will be so according to the particular capacities of individuals. Whoever reaches the end of the path, whichever he has chosen, understands the two problems: the different means or doctrines and the other levels of consciousness. Those who have not reached it, can see relatively clearly the levels that are below, those that they have already surpassed, but they cannot see those that are above, however intelligent they are; understanding here depends on experience. Taking sides, then, for one religion or another without having experienced its Essence, which is the current attitude, in addition to being an error, is a sign of ignorance.

A long indoctrination has led many Westerners to believe that monotheism, as seen by Christianity, is the highest rung of religion, and that polytheistic religions remain on the lower rungs already surpassed by it. *Objectively*, monotheism appears as more evolved, the intellect believes it has reached a greater synthesis, *the one* is the first, etc., but this satisfies logical needs that have little to do with Reality.

What establishes the biggest difference between religions is not, as we in the West have been taught to believe, polytheism and monotheism, but between a personal God and an impersonal and Absolute God. Once God has been personalised, he has already been humanised or anthropomorphised, and this has little difference with a multiplicity of gods, since these are nothing other than the different ways of being of the human being with superhuman powers, attributes that the monotheist finds in a single god. By separating these attributes or characteristics, the polytheist expresses them more clearly. Thus, for example, if it is said that God is love, the polytheist represents a god or goddess of love. So for this specific need he addresses this particular god; which is to all intents and purposes the same thing that monotheism does when praying to a particular saint, since, as I have already said, these saints are in no way different from the gods, they are different names to designate the same thing. But the impersonal and Absolute God has nothing to do with these human affairs, he no longer differentiates himself as "unique" in relation to others, but rather he is One.

Christianity itself, as we have seen, with a Son and a Mother of God, and three main divinities that only the force of dogma has been able to compress to make into one, does not, despite its theological efforts, fit into a strict definition of monotheism. In addition, Semitic monotheism has another God who is the greatest demon that could have been inoculated into human consciousness: the Devil himself. If there is something wrong with polytheism, which I am far from believing, all the gods combined could not produce the evil that the Devil has produced. In all of India there is no Devil, he does not exist in any Hindu consciousness; we can hardly guess the *handicap* that this generates in the West, versus the fears that it avoids in India, the freedom of spirit that this means. And this has been put in the most gratuitous and arbitrary way, for the simple reason that the Devil does not exist. For the rest, if he did exist, monotheism could not be proclaimed. The most diabolic expression that religions have produced, the Inquisition, fed on that sick spirit in which the idea of the Devil had settled; the Devil looked for his victims and, naturally, found them.

Nor can Judaism be defined as monotheistic, since it also believes in a Messiah Son of God, so its situation is similar, or it will be when the Messiah materialises, then its theologians, if they want to preserve monotheism, must use resources similar to Christian scholars. Only Islam and Taoism respond to this definition, in them Divinity has no relatives. This does not guarantee, however, that they are therefore superior, this synthesis is only one aspect of the complex and subtle world of the spirit in which logic is inapplicable; there are other aspects, some of which we will consider below.

With the number of similitudes between the Hellenic and Indic spirit especially in the philosophical-religious sphere, I am convinced that if the Hellenic spirit had been allowed to freely develop in the West, the right equilibrium would have been reached between polytheism and monotheism, religion and philosophy that the Hindus had achieved. A monotheism born of the mystical philosophers would have been developed from the gods of popular mysticism, and without discarding the former they would have lived in good understanding. Plato and Aristotle had smoothened the path but they were too rational and they lacked the direct and penetrating vision of the mystic. It is unfortunate that the embassies of Asoka to Alexandria had no resonance. Since the texts of the visitors were kept in the famous library, one can imagine that they perished in the fire of the library.

In Greece and India there is no corner that is not penetrated by the spirit as multiple gods made their appearance; this is the key to understanding these religions, the attempt to fill reality. For this reason, in Hinduism, we see the systematic intention to make God an All and all the minor gods part of Him. The wise men, as we will see, warn us that behind the particular gods there is a formless God, the Absolute.

A faraway God who waits for us after death is too remote to be effective. When the gods are everywhere, when one experiences that even the air is full of spirit (*prana*), when the sun itself and its reflected light are sacred, then the heart and mind are full of spirituality. The superiority of polytheism is undeniable at this point, and it should be repeated that it does not end in plurality but in Unity, which is much more than "one" God, it is the totality and simultaneity of the singular and the plural, it is truly the universal Spirit. Polytheism well understood and developed as in the case of Hinduism implies that totality and diversity. And just as there is diversity in the Nature in which we live I do not see why we cannot accept the diversity of spirits to better understand our minds and the world that surrounds us.

Semitic monotheism, strictly speaking, is born of polytheism, from which all other gods have been discarded and only one imposed. This process was repeated time and again in the Old Testament. Christianity only follows this tradition: when the prophet Jesus appears he is made the only begotten son of God that Moses had imposed over others; although Moses had not been in agreement with this adoption, as is proven by the general consensus of his descendants. And ever since the Church had political, military and economic power, the same tribal politics were put into practice, which was disqualifying and eliminatory till all the gods of Europe disappeared; they did not go much further because the "only" God who sustained the now Islamic nomad tribes who had spread over half of Asia was found.

In effect, in the 7th century another Semitic people adopts this tradition. We know that in the Kaaba there were 200 gods and that Mohammed took out 199 (he left an aerolite that was an old nomadic cult in the desert). Of course, to impose his God (now in capital letters) he had to suppress the other tribes who believed in the discarded gods. One can understand the tribal mentality that governs these religions.

This does not happen in Greece nor in India where the struggles take place between gods, titans and demons, and once order has been established in the heavens, the men religiously accept it and do not quarrel amongst themselves; the religious wars are unknown in Greece, Rome and in all the Hindustani religions.

For this reason, once we reach India we have to leave behind these tribal histories, we are face to face with a full-fledged civilization with its philosophy, art, religion, its codified laws, its organized cities like in Greece and Rome; before they were invaded by this tribal mentality. Rome fell, but not India. Since it is a civilization, in India we find other ways of seeing, thinking, acting with other frameworks only comprehensive from the dominant perspective: monism; born of a transcendental experience. This means that it should be seen from the Transcendent in order to be understood. The entire Universe with its spiritual expressions: aesthetic, philosophical, religious, i.e. with all the gods and with all the art that the human spirit can imagine, but which is an emanation of the Transcendent, of that Unity that underlies multiplicity.

All religions have their *level* of truth, but this *level* is measured by its closeness to the Absolute. Since this is the reference, it matters little if the religion is classified as monotheist or polytheist, what is decisive is that *behind* that approximation, as all that is not the Absolute is approximation, is the Absolute itself. And precisely the three vaunted "monotheistic religions" offer the God—person as the ultimate Truth; Christianity takes this belief to an extreme by taking a person of flesh and blood as God himself. In this way the monotheistic religions have as their final objective an approximation, *a relative truth for absolute,* closing in this way the path towards the truly Transcendent. And since they do so in a dogmatic and condemnatory way they leave the spirits stuck in the middle of the road, *condemning them to* Ignorance.

The Indo-Aryan religions, catalogued by the auto denominated "monotheists", as "polytheists", do not just leave the way open towards the Absolute, but also stimulate it and have it as an ultimate objective; besides, by not being dogmatic and condemnatory, the path or paths (as they are not closed to other paths of knowledge), are mechanically open to the Transcendent.

The plurality of gods implies the plurality of points of view, i.e., the opening of the spirit to multiple possibilities. All gods, if they are one or many, women or men are represented in one way or another, they are paths to transcendental knowledge. But they are just "paths" nothing more, there is none that is entirely true or false. The only true one is the One with my spirit; if I do not have this experience, I will do well in taking gods and doctrines as a mean towards that knowledge which is the only end. As we understand what is expressed, we will have the spirit better placed to understand not just the function of each one of the gods, but also highly refined doctrines like the Buddhist that never tried to be the only truth but simply the best path to it.

For the discerning, the affirmation that "my God is the only true one", is a meaningless simplification, because they know that any god who has made the subject better, more comprehensive, more human and more divine is "true". And, on the other hand, if the god who has been served, even if he is unique, charitable and all powerful has taken him towards evil, violence and misunderstanding of the neighbour is false. It has to be understood that there is no "objectively true" God. If this truth is understood well, the ingenuous task of convincing the neighbour that "my" God is the real one, will disappear; ingenuity that has been manipulated by those ambitious for power.

I am not saying that the God's truth is subjective. The subject is sufficiently more complex, see my work in general. Suffice to say that it is neither objective nor subjective, but *unitive*; I have been concerned in liberating the spirit from the "objective truths" and, more so from the subjective on the path towards the Transcendent.

If God is a person, monotheism is simply exclusivism, and this is the case with the Semitic god who is one in Jehovah in the beginning but latter is different because as we know Allah is not the father of Jesus, and the Christians do not believe that their god has been led to Mohammed. The fierce religious wars are proof of these divergences and the practice of the exclusion of other gods, without taking into account the ignorance of the religious matter taken to an extreme by barbarism. And it is in the name of this "personal God" and this practice of exclusivism that the "superiority of monotheism" is intended.

This should be clear: the monotheism of Judaism, Christianity and Islam that have been promoted as a superior and universal value, is a characteristic of the provincialism of tribal societies. What is correct in civilizations is the plurality of ideas, openness inclusivity and tolerance. When these are in force civilizations develop, for the simple reason that the spirit is free to research and create.

And this has been demonstrated in history. While Christianity imposed its power and inoculated the aforesaid illnesses, civilization was not possible. And as soon as there was a Renaissance of Hellenic civilization and the barrier imposed by the Church could be undone, civilization could again get on course. From then on one could speak of a Christianised Hellenic civilization, but there was never a Christian civilization. The historic example of Islam extends to our days, the peoples subjected to this faith as in medieval times live for it, as external progress is due to what they have borrowed from Indic and Western civilizations.

Monotheism correctly speaking is not personal or exclusive, as in the case of Vedanta and Buddhism where it exists, because they are inclusive and permissive, the freedom to believe in other gods, and this clearly illustrates the understanding of the principle of non-violence that is basic in religious matters. Monotheism achieves its excellence in monism, where there is experience and not the limitation of the belief that inevitably involves dualism that defines the Semitic doctrines.

What I have demonstrated in my philosophy is essential Reality, basic experience, the *essential perspective*, that I consider indispensable in order to begin to philosophize. Without it each one will have his ideas and beliefs that he will disseminate or impose in keeping with his capacity of public control. The most efficacious way to do this as proved by history is through power, political, economic, etc., ensured with conversion by the sword. But this has nothing to do with the truths in themselves, this is not religion but politics. And unfortunately, Christianity and Islam have spread in this way, after having achieved absolute power through the extinction of dissidents, they have been spread as a cultural heritage, an inertia that has been maintained through sustained propaganda and an imposed education.

That God is one with all the virtues or if they are distributed in many gods is not important. He who believes in one god is not more immersed in truth as compared to him who believes in many or vice versa, but rather the one who has introjected the greatest number of virtues because in this way he becomes more wise and divine. He who assimilates the virtues of the gods assimilates them too as was thought by the Greeks and as do the Hindus today. Then and only then, it will be judged if God is one or many; before these final questions are irrelevant because if one is just a human being there is ground to be covered.

It seems to me to be legitimate and even necessary that men express the marvel of Nature through religious art, creating myths, celebrating them as they religiously interpret the world, making it sacred because in this way they integrate their spirits in Reality. Since polytheism has resulted more beneficial for this goal, I incline towards it, I mean it seems more advisable for those who need it or prefer a religious approach. For those who want to see the Reality as it Is, I have offered my philosophy, but in this there are no false and true gods, *there are only levels of consciousness*, increased clarity, a betterment of the gaze in keeping with the perspective adopted. The problem of beliefs is that we construct them out of ideas, and fixed concepts that block our path. My project will be clear and it is the *experience of the Transcendent*, where there are no things, nor ideas nor beliefs nor divinities. The reader will have his opinion and his reasons and he can console himself believing in the promise of his salvation in the next world, but the author can assure him that this is not enough, that it is only an approach; what is important here is the *liberation in life* which is what Indic religions aspire to and this is my philosophy. In this one he will not find any condemnation or threat, only a kind invitation to other forms of knowledge in which he can find the reason for his existence.

On Monism and Dualism

There are two kinds of monotheism, one monistic, and the other dualistic, they are very far apart, there is, strictly speaking, a whole world that separates them; official Christianity has adopted the second, so its claim to be the last rung of the spirit is questionable in principle. Having reached this step, the spirit finds itself before an abyss that it must overcome, or at least consider. But before proceeding with this subject, it will be convenient to define these terms, following the usual distinctions, because there are several varieties of monism and many varieties of dualism. There is even a *naturalistic monism* that reduces the categories of spirit to matter, which is held to be, then, the only reality. I have to leave this kind of monism aside because it is born from an erroneous perspective, the individual one, which leads to the pantheism of the ignorant, blind to spiritual reality, which is what has been called atheistic pantheism. The correct perspective observes the World as a manifestation or emanation of the Universal Spirit, this vision is designated as theophany and corresponds to theistic pantheism.

I understand by *monism* the metaphysical and cosmological doctrines according to which both matter and spirit, the physical and the psychic are aspects of the same substance, Essence, or Spirit that manifests itself in those forms or phenomena; this Essence is immanent in the World. I understand by *dualism* the metaphysical and cosmological doctrines according to which matter and spirit, the physical and the psychic, are substantial or essentially irreducible, even though they find a principle, God, who nevertheless maintains a transcendent position with respect to them. I will therefore stick to these definitions, excluding the other forms that will remain on the margins, in particular the multiple forms of dualism, good and evil, feminine and masculine, psyche and body, etc.

The fact that all religions at some point accept God as a personal being cannot fail to strike the student of religions. It could be argued that it is so because God is like that. But there is an order of priorities that must be taken into account. Experience does not teach God in this way, but as something that transcends all explanation. God is presented as experientially immanent, but logically transcendent. This, I believe, is the original experience of all mystics. However, in not a few of them, later, God begins to take the form of a person. If this happens in those who have had the experience of Divinity, with much more reason it will happen with those who have not. This means that religions based on the original experience, monists, sooner or later begin to count among their adherents believers in a personal God, that is, they become dualists. Buddhism, for example, never doctrinally accepted a personal God, but, in fact, there are millions of Buddhists who worship the Buddha in his personal character. And the same is true even in doctrines that specifically deny this form to Divinity, such as Advaita Vedanta. The Masters of this doctrine admit believers who contradict their principles, expressly or tacitly acknowledging that these believers are of "less understanding", but that they are in a better situation than those without understanding. And there are, as we know, religions such as the Christian and Muslim in which a personal God is sustained by the arrogance of dogma. For this reason many mystics in them have been persecuted or sacrificed for questioning the dogma.

For all this, it is worth asking what ultimately leads men to this belief. Of course, the first answer is that very few have had direct experience of the Sacred. If we ask ourselves why, we return to the previous question. The explanation I find is that, to be precise, the Sacred is inconceivable, but since man needs to have a relatively clear idea of it, he anthropomorphises it. But all this creates a vicious circle of misunderstanding. In the first place, this need generally arises from the convenience of asking God for favours; the first error. Then man himself identifies himself with his body, with his person; the second mistake. And so God becomes the *object* of his prayers; the third mistake. The solution, in my opinion, is for man to make the effort to understand that both he and God are essentially pure spirit.

Whoever has walked these paths without obstacles, whoever has covered a good part of that broad spectrum, cannot help but observe the narrowness of the path and the limited horizon offered by official Christianity, when reading in a prestigious dictionary of the language, Catholic, (that is, according to the canons of the

Church); Faith: "Theological virtue by which we firmly believe, by the authority of the word of God, all the truths that He has taught us." Doctrine: "Set of Christian dogmas." Dogma: "Beliefs that constitute the background of a religion." Can the vicious circle be observed? Faith leads us to dogma, which is the capital point in religion, and doctrine is nothing but a set of dogmas. And experience, which is truly decisive for the spirit, is there no place for it? Is there no way to escape from that vicious circle? So, as the Church has put it, there is not, but is this really Christianity as envisioned by Jesus? That is the question for today's Christian.

The difference between faith or belief and experience is so immense and leads to so many different realities that it is essential to clarify these disparities. Strictly speaking, faith and belief are not realities but abstractions of a possible and uncertain reality; they also have the decisive deficiency of not being able to reach ultimate reality. It will be possible to *believe* in Unity, in Happiness and in Freedom, but we are still very far from those objectives, and since they do not ultimately come true, the possibility is always open that we stop believing or believe the opposite. Belief and faith are compensatory mechanisms of reason, while spiritual experience belongs to another mechanism that encompasses them.

But let us return to the topic at hand and see if we can find solutions there. The greatest religious experience, and all religions seem to agree on this, is *mystical union*, although official Christianity (not made up of mystics, naturally), has not made it a *capital point* as it has made dogma, far from it. It has kept the mystics away (none of them, to my knowledge, ever reached the rank of Bishop) when it has not persecuted them. If St John of the Cross had not escaped from prison, he would still be there, and Master Eckhart died when the Inquisition was conducting an investigation of his work, part of which was condemned shortly after his death. This, to cite only a few known cases; there are no records of the countless mystics who had much to say about religious experience, and why has the Church always gone toe-to-toe with the mystics? Because they have expressed their own experience. And it is not that this was against the sacred texts, but against the dogma established subsequently by the Church. If we take this passage for example: "God and I are one. By knowledge, I take God; through love I enter into God". If Jesus had said this, we would have already heard this quote millions of times in the churches, and thousands of Christians would have reflected on it; but as it was said by another, it has not become official and no one has heard it since Master Eckhart did in a temple. Is what I mean and where I am going understandable?

Jesus was a mystic and since he did not adapt to the ancient tradition, he was condemned by the priests, that is, by the official, dualistic religion. The mystic, if he sticks to his own experience, is monistic; Jesus is a good example of this. *The New Law begins, then, as Monist*, but the lesser understanding of its subsequent representatives, beginning with Paul, the first theologian of the Church, continue with the Jewish dualistic tradition. It is true that Jesus does not leave clear bases for Christianity to take a *monistic* direction, the truth is that he leaves many issues unclear. It is clear what he said, for those who know how to listen, but he left many gaps that were, as is known, filled by theologians, not by mystics. Jesus did not leave behind a philosophy (like the Buddha, or Confucius) not only because he lacked the necessary philosophical genius, but also because he was completely unaware of Greek culture and because in his Jewish culture there had never been a philosophy. An artificial, official and dualistic path was then followed in the West instead of a *natural and monistic* path.

The mystic does not need dogma or even faith, because he simply knows by experience, not by letter, and he is convinced by it, and if he has any doubts, he goes and checks, and in this way confirms in certain points the sacred texts that will be the ones that are being established, and thus, gradually, a particular doctrine is being formed, always having as reference not the letter, but what inspired it, the Creative itself, the eternal Source by which all the enlightened have been inspired. Those who do not have access to it are the ones who need the chains of faith and dogma, to which they must inevitably refer because they have no other source. All disciplines, including religion, need strong doses of positive, creative critic to maintain and revitalise themselves, and those qualified for this are mystics and not scholars chosen by ecclesiastical power.

Whoever has lived the experience of Divinity and then has returned to himself, has had what I have called a *partial unitive experience*; this experience is the most common among mystics. The spirit, in these cases, has moved towards its Centre and has observed from the *essential perspective*, which is the same as Divinity or Essence, and has returned to the *individual perspective*, from which it appreciates what was *previously* perceived as separate. Thus, he believes that he was transported to an *other* timeless reality that allowed him a union with Divinity from which, however, he is now separated by time and space, but this is because he has fallen into these coordinates which he takes as his reality, while looking at the *other* timeless reality as alien, without realising that it is he who has alienated himself from the correct perspective, the unitive one. Within a dualistic doctrine this is the greatest experience, since it leads one to believe that Divinity *is* transcendent. It should not be surprising, then, that spirits like those of Saint John of the Cross and Saint Teresa, after having reached "so high, so high", and "to reach their knowledge, to not understand understanding, all science transcending" (unitive perspective) return to this valley of tears and hear them exclaim: "I do not want this life, I die because I do not die" (individual perspective). And this really is unfortunate, because if they had had access to a monistic doctrine or philosophy, they would have overcome that dualism and the suffering that it created in them, a product of the basic ignorance that Reality is One.

I do not believe that there has been a more important discovery in the history of humanity than the one made by Sidharta Gautama, the Buddha, more than 25 centuries ago; I mean the non-existence of the self; a discovery that Western psychologists still do not fully understand. Without the understanding (experience) of this truth, my philosophy would not have been formulated. But let us now return to where we were.

In the prophetic spirit, the self is identified with the Self (terminology that Buddhism avoids because it does not believe in the existence of either one or the Other), so there is a relationship here between monism (not necessarily pantheistic) and dualism. Now, whoever has known their Centre, tries to maintain this perspective, and this requires training and very clear knowledge. This training is, then, *after* the *unitive experience*, which tries, by means of the same to make total; the practice that Zen calls *seal the Dharma* tends toward that goal. But, the human being is not only spirit, he is also human with all his circumstances, and it is his fate to share this double nature, and he has, then, his temptations, his weaknesses, and for this reason he can feel in certain cases, generally extremes, separated from his true Nature. Faced with the foolishness, wickedness, selfishness, greed, in short, ignorance, (all of them justified with elusive reasons, because no one believes that they suffer from any of these evils) of those with whom the *unitive man* must live and die, and seeing that he cannot change this situation (because the dead might have been raised, but no one has yet been able to achieve the miracle of eradicating stupidity), he feels powerless, abandoned and alone, indescribably alone, infinitely alone, as only God can be, and he falls on his disconsolate self and prays, but *ipso facto* starts to have a dualistic vision, because when spirit is unified it loses meaning, and Unity is experienced or manifested.

That is why Jesus, for example, is heard speaking both languages. We hear him say "I and the Father are one" (*John 10-30*), but later in moments of anguish we see him pray and even exclaim: "My God, why have you forsaken me?" In the first case his spirit is unified, in the second, separated. Language that demonstrates the supreme knowledge of this man, but a man after all; from there to *being* God, there is, literally, a Universe. We also hear: "I am He and He is me." But where is this, in Mark, in Luke? No, in Swami Vivekananda, in a conference given in the U.S.A. 100 years ago. The reader must understand that the language has not been made to express this type of experience, in which the Spirit is the main protagonist, but to resolve the things of this world, so these expressions lend themselves to misunderstandings; and in fact, this has been seen to have happened. Vivekananda does not say "I am God", in the sense that he can create and destroy the Universe as he pleases; I think only someone delusional could exclaim such a thing. What he means is that he is in God and God is in him; that is why he later adds: "None but I was God and this little I never existed", trying to avoid a misinterpretation. I have tried to further clarify this *unitive experience* (although I know that without it the words will always be equivocal). "I do not say: I am the Essence, in the sense that I am God, but, on the contrary, insofar as I am not I, I am the Essence, or, better, the Essence Is." (*The Return to the Sources*)

I do not know if this language suits the reader, but I believe that the most balanced and wise way to manifest the Spirit is by using the safe vehicle of philosophy. If there is something that the philosopher should have learned from the sciences, it is that one can no longer speak dogmatically. I know that philosophical language is the least popular, but I believe that a friend of wisdom is worth more than a thousand devotees who are today for Jesus and tomorrow for Barabbas.

In any case, this language has not only not been admitted but persecuted and condemned by dualistic or Semitic religions, in which it is understood that only God or his Prophet can use it. Thus we see that Judaism condemns Jesus because, not being the Messiah, he is using language that it considers blasphemous. In the same way, the Church has condemned countless mystics because it assumes that only Jesus, considered to be God, can express his Unity, and the same has happened in Islamism, particularly with the Sufis, who have even been crucified, because it understands that there can only be one Prophet, a dogma that prevents mystics from equalling themselves to the Prophet or speaking in God's name. That is to say that in these religions monism is reserved for a single Person. While in the Buddhist and Hindu traditions we see that it has been the monistic experience of multiple sages that have been transmitting and confirming the Dhamma and the Dharma. If this sages would have been born in de West, we infer from what has been said, they would have ended in the stake.

The superiority of monism over dualism lies not only in a more finished and integrating idea, but in that it is the product of an experience that reveals a higher *level of consciousness*, it is the same consciousness that has been integrated and unified. It is the highest summit that the spirit can reach. This is the great leap that the *Upanishads* and Buddhism take, and therein lies their value.

In this experience we find the very roots of Vedanta, from which the immense tree of Hinduism has grown, knowledge to which the great mystics of India have contributed. It is this trunk, in my opinion, which constitutes the orthodoxy of this doctrine, since the branches of that tree are inserted in the monist trunk. Such is the case of Shaivism and Vishnuism, its two great branches with their multiple minor branches.

So, we have that at the roots of Hinduism is the experience of the Absolute or Brahman. The gods are names that try to express that experience or, in the absence of intuitions of that reality, beliefs that tend to fall into dualism. Such is the case of Krishna, a branch of Vishnuism, which for the same reason leans towards the devotional path. Buddhism, for its part, is nourished by the same monistic roots and is born from the same experience, which is repeated, continued and transmitted from knowledgeable master to understanding disciple; hence the fundamental brotherhood of Dhamma and Dharma.

The Philosophical Bases

The attentive reader will know how to extract the essentials of my message from the comments that I will make later, however, to facilitate the task, I will try below to make a synthesis of my thinking. Perhaps this reader will find me repetitive, but I prefer to be so than to run the risk of being insufficiently or badly understood. In any case, this synthesis does not pretend to explain my previous work exposed in eight treatises, but I believe that it will serve the present purpose.

All true philosophy has its foundation in the intuition, expertise or experience of the Transcendent. I say *true* because the Transcendent is permanent and, therefore, Real. Thus, as Plotinus says very well, "we speak of what always exists, that is, not of what some times is and some times is not." (*Ennead III, 7*) I have already clarified in previous works the difference between *intuition, experience and vital experience*; for this reason, I will say only what is essential here: Transcendental *intuition* is a product of the intellect and lasts only a few moments, which allows us to verify the existence of the Transcendent, but since it is so brief, it does not leave sufficient certainty, which generally the thinker seeks to complement with reasons to obtain that reality more clearly. With very few exceptions, the idealistic philosophies of the West start from this intuition. *If this intuition* is more durable and no longer allows any doubt, and it manages to overcome the subject-object duality, it becomes an experience. Vital e*xperience*, as I understand it, definitively overcomes this duality because it incorporates all the faculties, in particular the intellect and the elevated sentiments, so that it *generates an intrinsic transformation of the subject*, a *radical change of perspective* in that the subject disappears and only the *fundamental Unity of the Universus* remains, that is, of matter and spirit. Given the human condition, this *unitive experience* of the Transcendent is not permanent, but it can be repeated because it becomes the natural state of the soul.

The dose of feeling and intellect in these experiences usually differentiates the mystic from the philosopher; the former has the advantage of being able to remain in that state for longer because he can do without reason, while the philosopher cannot do without it, which forces him to leave that state; although he does not lose the *essential reference or perspective* in which he is inspired. Most of the mystics, for their part, by giving priority to feelings, tend to establish a duality with the *object* of their devotion.

This said, I am forced to confess that *my philosophy is based on said unitive experience of the Transcendent*, otherwise I could not be talking about these states of the soul. The absolute certainty that this experience grants to the spirit (not to myself, which has no part), has allowed me to apply it to the different branches or disciplines of philosophy, that is, to psychology, to the theory of knowledge, to metaphysics, to morality, to art and history, which has finished by forming a philosophical system. This means that it could have done without any other philosophy or doctrine entirely. However, it is also part of my philosophy to demonstrate that this transcendent foundation is not exclusive to a particular spirit but *is shared by the entire Universus*, so that we find it latent in all beings and more or less patent in humans who have had the aforementioned intuitions or experiences, which are what lead them to philosophise. That is why I have dedicated a good part of my work to commenting on the authors who ratify the existence of the same Essence of the World on which they base their thoughts. This is what is decisive, the differences that we find between them are not.

To be certain, the differences must be taken into account, and this is what I have done in my comments, where I have tried to rectify the deviations, so that they can flow together in the universal current that my philosophy follows, which, certainly, I consider to be an inevitable reference. In this way, just as I have commented on the most inspired thinkers of the West and the East in previous works, I now propose to comment on Hinduism in particular, without failing to highlight its close kinship with Buddhism, always with the same objective: to highlight the common Source in which all the philosophies inspired by the Transcendent participate, that is, the idealists. My interest is, then, to demonstrate the existence of a *universal Idealism*, which expresses, beyond convergent ideologies, the existence of the transcendent Reality; this is the ultimate goal.

It might be worth clarifying that I am not looking to make a syncretism in this work, nor even an identification or approximation of the concepts, rather to highlight the convergence in the same Source, and, ultimately, to lead the reader to the knowledge of it, that is, to the same experience that has inspired these authors. Because, philosophies like these do not come from the imagination of idle intellectuals, but from experiences that transform the philosopher and compel him to transmit them. They are truths of the soul that we agree with our reason and we love with our feelings.

On Psychology

Throughout my work I have insisted on the need for a psychology with a philosophical scope, that is, capable of reaching the Essence of life, and conversely, for a philosophy that reveals to us the Essence of the mind. Since I have found neither the one nor the other in the West, I have seen the necessity of developing a specific discipline that I have called *psychosophy* (other "psychosophies" have appeared that have nothing to do with mine, with which the reader should not be confused).

Due to the dissemination and influence of Eastern doctrines, also various *transpersonal psychologies* have appeared in the West. I do not know if these projects of syncretism achieve their objective; I leave this concern to the reader. I will only offer a warning about another point of critical importance: this matter that we are dealing with is not resolved by comparisons, analysis, inferences, logical conclusions or syncretism's, but by experience.

In my *Psychosophy* where, as can be inferred, psychology is used as a tool of philosophy, I have made sufficiently clear the differences I have with current Western official psychology. My critique of it does not differ fundamentally from that of Hindu thinkers. Its shortcomings are obvious to anyone who has brought their consciousness closer to the Transcendent, a reality that this psychology completely ignores. It could not be otherwise, since this new discipline, which bears the title of a science and is taught in universities, is a product of medicine and is basically materialistic, which views the mind as a product of the body, so naturally, from this perspective the Transcendent is beyond its horizon.

Since the Transcendent is the theme on which Indic psychology revolves, its superiority, quite rightly, does not fail to stand out. However, it tends to forget, on the one hand, what I have just highlighted: this official Western psychology is recent and the daughter of materialism, and on the other, that the previous psychology that extends from the Greeks to Romanticism, goes, as in India, hand in hand with philosophy, has had a transcendent objective and dimension. What also confuses the Hindu is that during this period the influence of Christianity has been very important, and since this doctrine is very poor in psychology, far from making a contribution in this field, it has prevented its development. It is precisely when psychology becomes independent, and can express itself freely, that the new discipline is born. The first thing it does is to highlight the traumas generated by Puritanism, particularly those of a sexual order.

The fact is that in the West, the concept of psychology changed radically after Freud, who acquired such prominence that all psychology is understood as such. Jung himself, who came to venture into Eastern psychology, goes so far as to say that this is not strictly psychology. And for Freud, this example suffices, "religion is simply the product of a collective neurosis". Aurobindo was right to say, "Freud's psychoanalysis is the last thing that should be associated with yoga." (*Integral Yoga*) (For a critique of the religious vision of Freud, Jung and Fromm see my *Psychosophy 2nd Part*). The result is that this new version of the discipline has come to monopolise and distort the concept, and is entirely unfair with respect not only to Eastern psychology, but also to Western psychology before Freud.

Indeed, it seems to have been forgotten that psychology has always been a branch of philosophy. Aristotle had already advanced a *Treatise on the Soul*, and for all the idealists, particularly Plato and Plotinus, it constitutes a fundamental tool, whose objective is to transcend the animal condition of the human being. And later there has been no lack of spiritualists and recently existentialists with remarkable psychological insight. Eastern idealism has the same transcendent goal; in Hinduism, specifically, it is Brahman, in Buddhism, it is Nirvana. My philosophy, following the Platonic tradition, also uses psychology as a tool or vehicle to reach the Transcendent, which is why it has felt the need to disassociate itself from psychology as it is understood today, and to develop a discipline of the psyche with a philosophical dimension that I have called Psychosophy. In my conception, fundamentally, man is a universal Being, and if he does not experience himself as such, it is due to his alienation. And I believe that it is precisely the specific function of philosophy to generate that experience.

For all of the above and for our purposes, I consider it necessary to distinguish at least two types of psychology: one, which as a daughter of medicine has been divided into two branches, psychology and psychiatry, dealing with mental pathologies, and the other, dealing with the philosophical, which has the Transcendent as its object. The latter begins where the former ends, that is, with the healthy man who is not satisfied with his normality and wants to go beyond himself. This philosophical psychology finds its parallel in Hinduism and Buddhism.

The Hindu understands that the body has life because there is a spiritual energy that sustains it. Strictly speaking, this idea-belief extends to all of Nature and all living beings, so it is fundamental in their thinking. Therefore, all those who want to understand yoga must begin by internalising this transcendental psychology. For the Hindu, everything begins with the Spirit, everything is sustained by It and ends in It. In other words, everything is sacred; he who does not see it that way is ignorant. The air we breathe is not only oxygen, it contains a spiritual energy necessary for life that the Hindu calls *Prana*, the water we drink is not only H2O, it also has spiritual energy, and so with all the rest, everything it is permeated with Spirit; the Mind, as in my psychology, has a universal dimension.

The human body, like that of all beings, has one or more spiritual energies that keep it alive, the soul, incidentally, is essential. The Hindu, particularly after the *Upanishads*, is convinced that by discovering the spiritual energies that underlie the body and the mind (and in this I fully agree) he has to find the Essence of his existence and the reason for being of everything that exists. Philosophy, religion and psychology basically consist of this search. It is not by the discovery of matter, but by what underlies it, that the first principles are found; and this is also a basic premise of my philosophy.

My discipline of the mind has suitable faculties for spiritual reality, which I have called *unitive*, and which are located in the vital, central or direct plane of perception, between the external faculties, particularly discernment, and the internal or subconscious. I have separated the intellect from discernment because it has intelligent or creative functions; if it is put at the service of discernment, it attends to external affairs, if it is inspired by the *unitive faculties* it is ascending. If the spirit, by means of these faculties, manages to ascend to high levels of consciousness, it can have access to intellectual or transcendent intuitions, that is, to have contact with the Transcendent. Thus understood, the intellect is what has made philosophy possible. Sentiments, another internal faculty, can also rise in contact with the *unitive faculties*, or descend if they obey the passions instigated by the body that tends to his satisfaction.

The *unitive faculties* tend to integrate and unify all of reality and all the faculties and, if they achieve their objective in an absolute way, converge in the Unity that is Transcendent or universal Consciousness. It follows from what has been said that in my conception there is nothing outside of the mind or consciousness, if there is something outside of it it is absolutely unintelligible and remains in the realm of imagination or belief, that is, outside the field of philosophy. In other words, the Transcendent is only to the speculative faculties: the discernment or the intellect (in his external function).

I understand that all beings, just as they have earthly faculties to survive, also have faculties to integrate into the *Universus*, that is, in the material and mental totality that everyone senses, feels or intuits; that just as they are individuals, they are part of the whole, and therefore have faculties to attend to both their individuality and their universality. In fact the latter is still latent in all beings, including humans who are in a slow process of evolution and are still far from reaching their universality. That is to say, the human is closer to his animal than to his divinity; moreover, as he is seen today, he is closer to destroying himself by obeying the demands of the former than to saving himself by obeying those of the latter.

For the reader who has not read *The Spirit in History*, I would warn him that this evolution is not linear and progressive, but that it ascends and descends in individuals and in peoples according to the level of consciousness reached in different cultures and times; just as it does not depend on any heteronomous or divine will, but only on the perception, intelligence and good or bad will of man.

According to my vision of mental mechanisms, it is more revealing and illustrative to speak of *displacements of the spirit*, because I consider that it is not enough to observe its movements, but to get on it, so to speak, and observe the perspective it has in each position it adopts. This practice also impels us to get used to looking from the spirit, and this is the important thing, which makes us realise that we are not a self that observes from a fixed place, *but that we are a spirit that moves* endlessly according to different stimuli. So that when we finally identify with it, we can move it at ease through the different planes of understanding, which allows us to know the meanders of our mind, thus eliminating the obstacles that prevent us from evolving and finding the most appropriate way to move it upwards, towards *higher levels of consciousness*. I have called this pathway or *plane of understanding*, which lies subconscious in normal man, *vital, central, or of direct perception*, because from it he sees, intuits, or experiences spiritual reality directly. This whole process can take several years, but the correct insights can shorten the process considerably.

In this process, the spirit does not travel alone, but has to harmonise and integrate all thc mental faculties, for which reason it will use the purest and highest sentiments, as well as its reason, which must accommodate itself to transcendental intuitions, albeit keeping its rational coherence. This coherence and integration is the generator of experiences that are firm steps that lead the spirit towards its total integration. The total integration is in the *Unity of the universal Consciousness*.

On the Evolution of Consciousness

I have highlighted at different moments in my work a matter of particular importance in the history of thought that can be summarised as follows: Scholars, who look at the thoughts of others from the outside, insist on seeking the influence of some authors on others, that is to say, the cultural heritage they have received, and when they find a similarity, they conclude that the idea was not born in the subsequent thinker but in the thinker or thinkers that have preceded him. I do not deny that there can be a cultural transmission, however, those who have developed an entire philosophical system, it is logical to believe, have extracted it from their own ideas that, despite being similar in some points to those of their predecessors, are original, they were born of personal insights. I can affirm this from my own experience, since being predominantly an autodidact, I first had my own idea-generating insights and then, in general, I studied the history of thought in which I have found an overlap of ideas. It has happened to me in particular with Buddhism and Hinduism, to which it has brought me closer precisely because they coincided with my previous ideas. I have had the same experience with authors not so distant in time and space, but oblivious to my information. Thus, for example, it transpired with the experience of the idea of permanently fluent time and the rigidity of reason that is static, and therefore incapable of expressing the constant flow of nature. The idea had already been developed by Bergson, whom I knew of later, and was announced 15 centuries before by Heraclitus and by the Buddha.

Needless to say, it is not a question here of demonstrating the originality of my thinking, but of demonstrating the *theory of the superposition of ideas*, foreign or disconnected in time and space. This can be explained because there is a connection with the same universal circumstances that all humans share, and internal circumstances that are also similar, I mean the mind, which is interested in solving the same problems. In this way, by intuition or personal awareness, ideas that are *original* are born in different thinkers.

Without pretending to make this theory "scientific", I think it is worth considering within this field. A theory has recently been launched that has had an echo in the scientific world and a lot of acceptance in popular opinion; there is something magical about the theory, and this inevitably attracts the common people. It has been argued that when monkeys discover a solution to a practical problem on one island, such as how to split a coconut, soon after on neighbouring islands the same method is applied. This makes me think of my theory that the same external and internal circumstances cause the same awareness to be had in both one and another place not long after.

Going further into the field of science, I believe that my theory can be fruitfully used when studying the evolution of species and of man in particular, since what has generated their evolution has been fundamentally awareness. This theory could apparently collide with the one that explains evolution by genetic changes, but within the former we find a convergence that gives it validity; although I do not know if it will be to the taste of scientists because it is of a philosophical order.

I consider it necessary to take a small detour to understand this matter: I have insisted in my work on the importance of the *primary manifestations of the essence of the world* (particularly in *The Search for Universal Consciousness*), which I have separated to make them more intelligible, but which are emanations of the same Consciousness. I will refer here to two of them to explain the topic that concerns us now: Life in itself and Intuition-instinct, in which all living beings participate from the microscopic to the human.

Life in Itself has been intuited and developed, according to their perception and interpretation, by Schopenhauer as *Will* and by Bergson as *élan vital*, but it differs from them precisely in its intimate and inseparable relationship with the other primary manifestations. If we take it in isolation as energy or *élan* vital, this manifestation could fall within the domain of science, since it affects matter, although only partially, as in my conception it is not only a physical energy but also and fundamentally spiritual, which impacts on sentiments and reason; it is, so to speak, the soul and spirit of living beings. This is not the case with the other *primary manifestations* that are purely spiritual and only comprehensible by the spiritual or unitive faculties, although they affect the entire universe that participates in them, since everything is permeated by Spirit and Intelligence.

Returning to the subject that has brought us here, it would be simplified as such: There is a universal Intelligence that penetrates and stimulates all living things, which receives and understands according to its potentialities or particular faculties. It is a life impulse (*élan vital*, in Bergson's sense) but it is charged with intelligence and elevated feelings that drive beings to transcend themselves, that is, to go beyond themselves and their present condition. This intelligence, which would be intuition-instinct, is not only in the mind but in the cells, starting with the spermatozoa, in the blood and in the organs. Being so, an awareness of the subject would affect its entire organism, so that it would *tend* to generate a genetic transformation. The basis, then, of all evolution would be the consequence of awareness, as long as we do not understand by this an experience limited to the framework of reason, but of multiple organic mechanisms provided with their particular intelligence, which finally generate a genetic change.

Anyone who has read anything about medicine will see that every cell in the body has a certain intelligence on which life depends. We all know that the body has "defences", but it is worth reflecting on this wonderful mechanism: everything we breathe, drink and eat is regulated by the different organs that transmit nutrients through the blood to the smallest extremes of the body. And not only by the best-known organs, bones are not like dry reeds but are living ones that produce white and red blood cells in *measured and balanced* amounts that circulate through the blood along with many other components, and each one of them performs a function provided with *intelligence-instinct*. Thus, for example, if a virus or bacteria or another foreign element enters the body, that is, in the bloodstream, immediately said blood components react in *defence* of the organism and *attack* the intruder in an *organised* way. When we are sick these components are working hard to save us. In short, the *intelligence-instinct* is in each of the smallest particles of the bodies of all that live. The *vital Impulse* and the *Intelligence-instinct*, *emanations of the Essence of the Universus*, make possible the life of everything that exists.

That is to say that the multiple intelligences or intuitions-instincts of the organism reach a tacit agreement in the face of the circumstances of the moment or period and prepare the propitious conditions for an opportune mutation. I have already rejected at the time (in *The Evolution of the Spirit*) the theory of the intervention of chance in mutations, which, paradoxically, is the one that the sciences have adopted by preference, since there is nothing less scientific than chance. I believe that my theory offers a coherent and rational explanation to the phenomena of the *mutations* that could be scientific if tested. At the same time have given sense to the concept of *instinct*, which has been so mysterious to reason.

Going a little further and higher, in previous works I have argued that the awareness of universal Consciousness generates *a radical or ontological change* in the subject, this makes him, ipso facto, an other. This spiritual mutation, however, does not seem to generate a genetic transformation capable of being transmitted to children, since their genetic load is long and heavy. On the other hand, there is the burden of society, of customs and education that is far from being directed at such awareness. But if a good number of humans participate in this experience, it can be contagious and produce a radical change in our species; and this is my proposal for contemporary man. Nevertheless, when we consider his present poor level of consciousness, and the circumstances he has created, we must recognise that he is closer to destroying himself than bringing about that upward change.

On Philosophy of History

Hinduism has not considered it necessary to develop this discipline. It has its reasons, since history inevitably plunges us into the current of becoming, which this doctrine has the purpose of overcoming. Since my philosophy serves the same purpose, I should not concern myself with history, but so many mistakes have been made in it, which have cost so many human lives and the destruction of so much human art and labour, that time and again I have found it necessary to make my critique of it, leading me to deviate from my true objective. But this detour is temporary, and is intended to put those alienated from their destiny back on track, those who cannot leap onto a metaphysical plane without first being made aware of the historical and psychological plane on which they find themselves. This does not mean that the philosopher loses his destiny because of it, because when the spirit is well established in the Transcendent, which is immovable, it does not allow itself to be dragged by said current, it keeps an *essential perspective* from which it contemplates the course of history; history seen and commented on in this way constitutes a philosophy of history. It is in *The Spirit in History* where I develop this discipline as a branch of my system.

Naturally, the *philosophy of history* is an attribute of philosophers, however, all beings are part of the Universe, that is, we participate with our body in the matter of the world and with our mind in the universal Spirit, albeit relatively latently or unconsciously. It is not necessary to clarify that the human being also obeys contrary tendencies, his passions and selfish inclinations. Well then, human history is made from the grouping and variant mixture of these ascending and descending tendencies; in what depends, of course, on our species, since there are natural catastrophes, such as earthquakes, tidal waves and plagues that affect the history of all species. Thus, for example, a tidal wave ended the Creto-Mycenaean civilisation, and a plague in Athens decided the Peloponnesian War and, as a consequence, the history of the West. When the downward inclinations prevail over the ascending aspirations, we observe decadent or perigee periods in history, since the spirit is further removed from the light and attraction of universal Consciousness, while in epochs of apogee it shows itself to be more sensitive and obedient to *unitive forces* and approaches Unity, that is, to its integration.

In his task, then, of shaping a philosophy of history, the philosopher, as I said, must not stray from his reference or *essential perspective*, but he is inevitably forced too often to walk over the rubble, blood and corpses that men have left behind, guided by their passions, by their dogmas, by ignorance of their Essence or alienation from their Consciousness. Aware that history is made by all of us, the philosopher will not seek to straighten the course of history alone, so he will limit himself to pointing out the errors and exalting the virtues, since these are the ones that direct the soul and pave the way that the philosopher has traced on the marine chart of the extensive ocean of the spirit, whose destiny is Knowledge, Liberation and the resulting Happiness.

On Ideas, Knowledge and Life

The ideas we have of things, facts, people, etc., do not fully respond to the knowledge we have of these objects because they are constantly changing and the ideas are fixed. This is a fact of extraordinary importance which I have covered when commenting on Bergson (in *The Evolution of the Spirit*), that he had already noticed this fact, but to which he does not have a clear response. But from where do we get fixed ideas? This is what Plato was asked and answered with his theory of a world of perfect and stable ideas. This is not sustainable but it is close to reality. There is no world populated with ideas, but there is *something* immutable that serves as a permanent reference. Well then, in my conception I have this answer: universal Consciousness is Immutable, and it is through the contact we have with it by means of latent intuitions of the Transcendent that we can form *fixed* ideas about the moving. We are not aware of this process because we look at it from our *individual consciousness and perspective*, which cannot make conscious what is transcendent to it, because we do not know the Origin of ideas and things.

Even at the risk of being criticised by those who already hold their beliefs on this subject, but sticking to the truth that my experience tells me, there is, strictly speaking, no way to know if we have an individual soul or an individual Purusha, but it is a fact that when we transcend our individual consciousness, we encounter a universal Consciousness or Reality, not our soul or our Purusha. Experience, more important than logic, shows us that when individual consciousness is transcended, the spirit expands without limits, the drop dissolves in the Ocean. It does not know all the particulars of the ocean, it does not know all the galaxies, it does not know everything, but it knows that it is universal, One with the All. It does not look through time and space, it does not think, it knows, it contemplates itself; this is universal Consciousness.

What is a fact is that our consciousness has contact with or participates in the Transcendent, hence the elevated ideas and sentiments, a consequence of the *primary manifestations*. That is to say that *the human being has a transcendent capacity that allows him to participate in the constant emanation of universal Consciousness*, that we are constant participants in the Everything. Ignorance consists in the lack of awareness of this, and Knowledge consists in a change of perspective. The "normal" human being has only become aware of his individuality, the realised, total human being, the *unitive man* has become *aware of his universality*.

According to this all ideas and sentiments have a transcendent origin. Bad ideas and lesser feelings are consequences of the alienation of the mind, to be precise from its Origin, they are a consequence of the unhealthy use we make of them. Extreme ignorance is already madness due to the obturation and confinement of the spirit within the narrow dark well of the self, where the light of universal Consciousness or its emanations does not reach.

It is true that, as far as humans are concerned, the spirit cannot remain in this state of absolute contemplation, so it returns, but before entering time and space, it perceives the emanations of universal Consciousness, which is its consciousness, which are a priori to the a priori of time or space and causality that are already in the domain of reason. These secondary a priori are Kant's great discovery and on them he built his theory of knowledge, which is his philosophy, but those first a priori he could not reach them, because they are transcendent to reason. The spirit, then, returns to his body and his circumstances, but the mind is changed, it no longer obeys his individual perspective but his essential, universal perspective, loaded with primary manifestations, for which he feels the need to express them, because they are his own expression, his own emanation. For this reason he feels the desire, the love and the joy of doing Good and establishing Order.

To reach that knowledge, to be that Consciousness, man must transcend himself, and this is, without a doubt, his Destiny. Now, if he returns to his humanity, it is because there is something left to do in it, and that is to open that Consciousness and indicate and pave the way for his fellow men towards that Destiny. If he wants and can, he will stay in It, if he returns, as I said, he will do Good. This is the human cycle that ends when the spirit finds itself.

Hinduism includes the mind as one of the senses; in addition to the five senses, which we all know, is added the mind. It has its reasons, but I am very afraid that this can lead to misinterpretations, which is why I consider it extremely important to clarify this matter; I will use my conception of the psyche for this purpose. On the one hand, this doctrine is certainly right in establishing this relationship, since there is a permanent interdependence between the mind and the senses; these, in effect, see, hear and feel according to the schemes that the mind has configured, and vice versa. But the mind itself has become what it is after a long *process of individuation, exteriorisation and alienation*, which is nowadays ignored (explained in *The Spirit in History*). On the other hand, said conception of the mind restricts it to external or speculative faculties, which, although due to configuration and customs are the predominant ones in our species, are far from filling the entire mind. In my *Psychosophy* I have insisted on the existence of the *unitive faculties* whose function is to harmonically integrate all the faculties, not rationally, on the contrary, to make them independent of the closed triad of the self-reason-memory, which constitute the external faculties with which the human being has come to identify himself.

In this process of dis-identification, the *unitive faculties* cause consciousness to progressively identify itself with the spirit, which is nothing more than an extension of the universal Spirit or Consciousness whose awakening would be its final objective. Certainly, in order to arrive at the experience of universal Consciousness we must recognise that this life, as perceived by our senses and discerned by our speculative faculties, is not enough. Yet this does not mean denying life but having knowledge and control of the faculties that determine our senses. These, then, are not an obstacle on our way to the Transcendent, they are so only when they are at the service of said external faculties. Indeed, when the senses are illuminated by the *unitive faculties*, nature shows itself to be revealing, luminous, and announces the Transcendent, since our senses participate in the light that emanates from universal Consciousness.

What keeps us in ignorance is not Nature or the senses with which we perceive it, but the duality with which we look at it and think. To deny this reality in the name of another is to fall into the trap of duality. In reality, dualism does not exist, it is a resource of the external faculties to differentiate things. If we deny this reality in the name of another, we are assigning excessive importance to speculative faculties. When we discover our *unitive faculties*, this duality is clearly presented as arbitrary and illusory. Reality is One. Unitive consciousness, with which we contemplate the world, is not of a different nature than universal Consciousness, for this reason we cannot describe it or give it attributes, it is the pure Consciousness that illuminates our faculties and our senses.

By identifying with the external faculties, we have divided not only the external world, but also our own faculties so that we are alienated from ourselves. The task, then, is to *unify the mind* until it is centred in its core, where it remains unified; that nucleus is universal Consciousness where there is no duality. This is not a construction of the mind, it is Reality.

It is true that when pure Consciousness manifests itself through *total unitive experience*, all Nature disappears as well as our mind, which is as if absorbed by Consciousness, but this occurs only for moments (which transcend time) and not for that reason are we going to believe that the World does not exist, because although Consciousness is the only permanent thing in everything that exists, it is the Consciousness of what exists and also of our mind. And in coming back to it, we do not need to fall into our usual individual perspective. Neither one extreme nor the other, the correct and *balanced* position of the human spirit is the *unitive consciousness* that knows of the universal Consciousness and keeps *the essential perspective* acquired, the essential Unity that underlies the diversity of the World. And this is where life begins in its fullness. To live intensely is to live in the knowledge and recognition of what makes life and consciousness possible, Nature and Spirit.

If we observe our mind and our behaviour, we will verify the existence and action of the *unitive faculties*. Without them we would never be good or appreciate the beauty of the World, there would be no morality or art, which are means or ways to transcend ourselves. *All the virtues are ascending pathways* because they are *expressions of the primary manifestations of the Consciousness of the Universus*. The spirit must be nourished from them to live fully in the Unity that we are.

A Sketch of the Universus

The human being intuits, sometimes, an *other* consciousness that transcends him, but time and again he makes the mistake of wanting to interpret it with his individual consciousness, with his speculative faculties. He does not fully understand that to reach that one he must transcend this one. For this reason, I also call that which is universal Consciousness the Transcendent. But, as I have already said, it is transcendent only to said speculative or external faculties. Hinduism and Buddhism do not venture to speak of the origin of these faculties and consider that they are innate in our species. In *Origin and Destiny of Man* I have exposed my theory on the genesis of these faculties, which I call *external* because they were formed in their evolution to respond to the external needs of the human being, but, as I explain in that treatise, this evolution implied an alienation. But man has, he has always had, albeit latent, other faculties that I have called *unitive* that are beyond individual consciousness, that incite us to transcend ourselves.

This incitement, however, is not an individual concern, but rather, so to speak, universal, since all beings are encouraged to go beyond themselves, and this is so because universal Consciousness *emanates that attraction*. It is not done voluntarily because it is not a Person who tries to decide on our destiny, none of that, this is an invention and a belief of the external faculties that project their vision into a transcendent being they call God. There is nothing personal in universal Consciousness, nor in the understanding of it, everything is universal; neither is there duality but Unity. It emanates because it is the Creative itself, so it permanently creates the Cosmos and transmits its Intelligence to all beings, who realise it within their limitations, according to their level of consciousness.

In this concern for transcending oneself, sentiments play an important and, for many people, a decisive role. But since the feelings are at the service of the individual faculties that converge in the self, they are projected onto that Person that said faculties imagine; this has been called a religious sentiment, and it is even believed that this Person is necessary to awaken this feeling. Moreover, it is even affirmed that it is essential for there to be religion; and not only those of the dualistic tradition hold it to be true, an authority like S. Radhakrishnan also believes it. (*Indian Phil.*)

The truth is that the religious sentiment exists not because there exists or it is believed that there is a Person in which it can be projected. Fortunately, feelings also have their ability to transcend this limited perspective. *The religious sentiment exists because universal Consciousness emanates Love*. It is from the perspective of this Consciousness, that is to say, from the *essential perspective* that the religious sentiment reaches its plenitude. The ultimate design, then, is not to love God above all things, but *to love all beings from universal Consciousness; to emanate Love like It*.

The importance of this vision (which is the product of an experience and not a belief) will be understood, since it is precisely the faith in a God as a Person that has separated so many times, and rightly so, religion from philosophy. As can be seen, in my philosophy they converge on a higher level, which both feelings and understanding must reach. It is by taking this leap towards the Transcendent that the spirit definitively transcends all individual perspectives and reaches its Unity, which is the *Unity of the Universus*.

In short, to understand universal Consciousness, it is necessary to transcend external faculties and individual feelings. It follows from what has been said that the idea or belief in a God as a Person tends to perpetuate our ignorance of the foundations of our existence. Incidentally, religious sentiment, even at this stage, implies an upward evolution with respect to the materialist vision, which in philosophy is called naive realism. But as we have seen in history, many atrocities have been committed in the name of this sentiment, precisely from a dualistic perspective in dogmatic and exclusivist minds that make relative knowledge an absolute truth; which leads us to conclude that the human being still has a lot to evolve, in his sentiments and understanding.

The understanding of universal Consciousness is not, then, the product of our speculative faculties, but of a *unitive experience*, which implies the prior integration of all the faculties (this is a basic premise of my *Psychosophy*) including sentiments, which it transports to a high level of consciousness, entirely transcending the individual perspective. Said *experience* responds to another perspective: that of the very Essence of the *Universus*, which I have therefore called *essential perspective*.

We cannot say anything about this Essence because it is Consciousness itself, the Intelligence of the world. But we can say what we can behold from that perspective. We can behold in the first place that emanates Life or an energy that generates life, and Intelligence-instinct, Good, Beauty, Love, all virtues that tend to universal Order, to the Perfection of universal Consciousness. These attributes are consubstantial to It, we can account for these effects if we notice in ourselves and in the rest of beings the *instinct or desire for perfection*, evident in healthy and ascending beings.

Then - you will ask - does this Consciousness not have a body or a brain? Well, no, it is an entirely spiritual being and remains in a state of pure Consciousness, of which, however, as I said, we know its *primary manifestations* that are *a priori to time and space*, that is why they are transcendent to reason that depends on these forms. However, these manifestations are inserted in the material and spiritual world. As they are an emanation of the *Creative*, they tend to create, but not this or that in particular, but rather they act on the basic elements of life, producing an atomic combustion, we would say today, that like light and heat generate an infinite number of worlds, beings and particles that are attracted to form celestial bodies, or cells that are attracted to form vegetable or animal bodies; particles that then disintegrate and attract each other again in an immeasurable time, or cells that perish in a measurable time.

Is this universe the body of that Consciousness? Some *Upanishads* (as we will see) maintain that it is indeed the body of

Brahman, although this assertion can be misleading if it is discerned by our external faculties. We could also say, with the same risk, that it is the Subject of the Cosmos, since it is the Spirit that is in all beings. I am talking about a pantheism, which must be differentiated from the naive one, which I have called idealistic because it looks from the Idea, which is the Consciousness of the *Universus*, I speak of a Cosmos charged with Spirit, that is, of the aforementioned primary manifestations.

But - this is an inevitable question from our individual consciousness - if it is perfect, why does it create an imperfect world? One could make this reproach against those who believe in an almighty God who by his will creates heaven and earth, but here there is none; the perfect can only be of spiritual substance, matter cannot be so. Neither can a being who discerns with his external faculties and speculates on mundane and human affairs. Matter, for its part, enjoys *relative freedom*, it is free to the extent of its condition and nature. Absolute freedom is total alienation, madness. Living beings do what they can within their means, but their imperfection is innate, genetic, it is the condition of all living beings. Man's basic imperfections in the natural order are inevitable, the moral or spiritual imperfections come from his identification with the material part of him, while his perfection comes from his identification and knowledge of the Essence of the spirit or universal Consciousness. We have, as Plato said, an animal part and a divine part, the struggle between these two natures can be appreciated by everyone who observes his intentions behind his thoughts.

If I go by my experience, which is what I have done when developing my entire system, I must admit that I do not know why this Cosmos was created; it is those who do not adhere to their experience who venture to imagine and believe in the "intentions" of a Spirit that they do not yet know. The fact is that the universe is here and we are in it and as human beings we are part of Nature, of the *solar organism* in which we live and on which we depend, and *our consciousness is part of universal Consciousness*; these are our external and internal circumstances.

From what has been said, nothing is more natural than worshiping the sun. Not, by the way, as an inanimate thing, but as an *expression of the vital impulse* that is an emanation of the Essence of the world. We know that without light and heat no life is possible, but the sun is not reduced to its physical function. Light is also a source of inspiration and aspiration of the spirit, moreover, the purest and most essential expression of it is light. Light is also another *primary manifestation of the essence of the Universus: the intelligence-instinct* found in everything that exists. I am not speaking, incidentally, of the reason that is a particular derivative of said intelligence-instinct; nor am I limiting myself to animal instinct in particular, I speak of the Cause of Intelligence and instinct. As we have seen, the *intelligence-instinct* is in each of the smallest particles of the bodies of all that live.

In our brief life we are like butterflies in search of Light, the same one that creates the sun and all the stars and illuminates our intelligence. *There is an original creative Light*. I sincerely believe that the stars are the concrete expression necessary to the life that is in the Unity in essence and in power. The same happens with our intelligence, and we know this with certainty when said Light penetrates our brain (literally, in the central and superior part of it) and illuminates our interior, our soul; then we know that our consciousness is an extension of universal Consciousness.

The highest and purest state of our spirit manifests as Light from which Creation emanates; it is strictly speaking the Creative itself. This *permanent Creation* first has to make the stars that generate life, that is, solar organisms like ours of which we are an inseparable part. We are children of the Light, our own body is part of the air we inhale and the water we drink; we are part of the elements that surround us, that penetrate us, that we possess and possess us. It is our *incipient reason* that has made us believe that we are independent parts, it is it that has separated our faculties and thus has alienated us from the *Unity of the Universus*. We are part of the *universal Order*, but our egoism has rendered us disordered.

It follows from what has been said that our essential task is to re-establish our *original Unity* through the unification and harmonic integration of all our faculties, ordered by our *unitive faculties*, capable of also perceiving the *primary manifestations* of the *Essence of the Universus* which, as they are emanations of universal Consciousness, are the lights that illuminate our spirit and indicate the path to follow, towards total identification and unification.

Synthesis of my Proposal

The purpose of this 3th Part of the book is to complete the bridge between the Greek and the Indic spirit to fully enter the wide territory of the *Indic civilisation*. In this I include Buddhism, so first of all I have to attempt to unite this doctrine with that of the Hindu; doctrines that I hold to be the greatest that humanity has created. Of the Greeks I have said enough for my purpose, likewise of Buddhism in *The Evolution of the Spirit*, where I have commented on it in relation to the thinking of Sri Aurobindo, the most outstanding philosopher-mystic of modern Hinduism, and expounded my vision of both doctrines. But Hinduism requires further explanations that I intend to expose in 4th Part of this book.

My proposal is clear from what has been exposed, here and in *The Roots of Morality*. In the spiritual field, Christianity does not present itself as a reasonable option; beyond my arguments and criticisms of so many authors, it has actually shown its ineffectiveness. Since the French Revolution, which abolished the Church's means of coercion and instituted secular education, with which the Church lost its monopoly on education, the decadence of Christianity has increased. In fact, the West in the 21st century develops entirely outside of Christianity.

The Hellenic spirit, for its part, has proven to be an inexhaustible source of creative inspiration, but at the same time it has two shortcomings: one, that very little remains of its legacy, and the other, that it remains the heritage of a civilisation that is not there for us to see it living and acting. But, as I have tried to show, that spirit, with its particular variants, is alive and well in the *Indic civilisation*; thus, I believe that this is where the West should direct its gaze. It is not a question, I think I have already insisted on it, of adopting the beliefs of that tradition, but of seeing and experiencing, as much as possible, that same spirit that has been lying in our own consciousness for 2,500 years and that has been reborn in the epochs of apogee in the West; as I have shown in *The Search for Universal Consciousness*.

I believe, as I have already pointed out, that both idealisms converge in my philosophy, that of the West and that of the East. I clarify, however, that they do not converge in a particular ideology, moreover, I do not think I have created anything. This is not an expression of feigned humility; it is a basic aspect of my philosophy:

the three visions emanate from the same Sources and their currents converge in what I have called *universal Idealism*. The purpose is, therefore, through the convergence of these civilisations, unprecedented in history, which enables cultural exchange with the Far East, to generate a *New Renaissance*, which necessarily has to affect both cultures and have global repercussions.

I am not saying that this has to happen, only that it could happen; I do not participate in those historical dialectics that are projected onto an uncertain future with reckless accuracy, which, like all imprudence, can generate unforeseen and undesirable results. I know very well that what moves people are the promises of a sure salvation or faith in an inevitable future; one only has to look at history, but they have been prophetic speeches, political resources, not philosophical ones. In mass movements, faith in promises has played a very important role, but Renaissances have only come about through individual awareness, which through the process of mimesis produces an echo in society, thus generating the spirit's approach to universal Consciousness. This displacement of the spirits is what generates the apogee itself, the change of consciousness and the transformation of society (see *The Spirit in History*).

I am interested in emphasising the importance of the natural process that the human being must follow or should have followed, important for his mental health and an essential process to achieve his fullness, that is, his transcendence. For this *natural evolution* it is and was equally essential that it be accompanied by a freedom of ideas, beliefs and expression. The intolerance of Christianity and Islam, which does not allow us to go beyond dogma, has undermined and diverted this natural process. The titles of my books express my project: *The Return to the Sources*, *Origin and Destiny of Man*, *The Roots of Morality*, *The Roots of Art*, etc., refer to a reunion with our origins, with our culture and tradition, and finally, with ourselves.

All that has been called heresy, idolatry, witchcraft, alchemy, as well as pagan philosophies, religions, arts and ethics, were psychic, spiritual and intellectual needs, which were persecuted, truncated, diverted or extinguished in the West, with man's consequent alienation from those realities. Eliade never tires of reminding us that initiation rites, found in all cultures, express "existential experiences constitutive of the human condition". (*Init., rites*) Their repression or suppression are attacks against our way of being, they alienate us from our search for the Transcendent, which is ultimately, in my opinion, where they are headed. The bewilderment, disorientation, immorality and dehumanisation of contemporary man is not alien to the *artificial evolution* that he has suffered.

The search for the afterlife and the projection towards the Transcendent that occurred in archaic societies through rituals and initiations (and perhaps other means that we are unaware of) was taken up and reactivated in Greece by the pre-Socratics, in whom we see religion inserted into philosophy, and already on a philosophical plane in Plato, by the Neo-Platonists and by the idealists in general in the West. I refer the reader to *The Search for Universal Consciousness*, where I expose this trajectory from the pre-Socratics to my own idealism. This search, which follows the natural direction of our tradition, was interrupted on numerous occasions and for long periods by Christianity, as we have seen in Part 3 of this work, but it has survived, as I have demonstrated in said treatise.

This search is also continued in India, but what is interesting about the process followed there is that it occurred uninterruptedly, in a natural and homogeneous way. Indeed, there was no clear split or marked opposition between mythology, religion and philosophy, rather these disciplines have been able, in the Far East in general, to complement each other by expressing, on different levels of understanding, the same transcendent reality and thus each one fill the gaps of the others. Very much in agreement with this, Eliade says: "The interest of the mysteries resides in the fact that they show the permanence of the traditional themes of initiation and their capacity to be indefinitely reactivated and enriched with new values." And he adds this, which coincides with the very core of this book that we are developing: "*We find in the Hellenic world the same state of affairs found in India*: an archaic scenario is susceptible to being taken up and used for multiple and varied spiritual purposes, from the *unio mystica* with Divinity to the magical conquest of immortality or the obtaining of final liberation, Nirvana." (*Init., rites 246*) This statement expresses an old aspiration of mine and summarises the raison d'être of this work in which I try to establish the said parallel.

Having been concerned with, as I was saying, this *Search for Consciousness* in the West, adhering primarily to the philosophical order, although not separated from the religious one, my current purpose is *to link our Greek philosophical, religious, moral and aesthetic roots, now forgotten, with the Indic traditions* where the same spirit lives on. In other words, instead of continuing to rescue and decipher the pieces that have remained from the rubble of that exemplary civilisation, my proposal is to turn our gaze towards India. As will be clear to everyone who knows my work, it is not a question of importing a tradition with its local customs and folklore, including its mythology with its particular gods, or even any belief, but of *rediscovering a spirit from which we have been alienated that, since it is alive in India, we can experience*, and in this way make that religious experience our own.

It is not, as is clear from said *Search* that there are not unitive religious elements in the West, in Plato, Plotinus, Ficino, Spinoza and in my own work, they are evident, but the religious experience through philosophy is for a very small audience. Thus, in India it is reduced to only one of the yogas, the *gnana*. The Hindus, with their usual wisdom, have other proposals, other yogas, which also lead to transcendence through more accessible paths, particularly for those with a religious vocation.

There will be no shortage of believers in materialism who will reject this proposal, arguing that they do not need any religion to live. In the same way there will be those, also disillusioned with the religion that has touched them, and believers in the current fashion of dealing with these issues, who maintain that they prefer to speak of spirituality and not religion. The fact is, like it or not, the human being is a religious being; religion is part of the mental structure of our species. The reason for this is, in principle, very simple: Being aware of time, whose origin and end are lost in infinity, man cannot be satisfied with a hundred years (in the best of cases) of life; what lies beyond impels him to think and to know that reality that transcends his lifetime and his reason. Since he does not reach this knowledge, he is inclined to believe in an afterlife that he imagines in various ways, and if he decides not to believe, he will surely feel dissatisfied, incomplete. My proposal is to penetrate the most substantial aspect of religion, or spirit, if you prefer this concept, through knowledge. This is completely outside of all dogma and magical-miraculous resources, moreover, a good part of this work deals with freeing us from these means. I am not speaking of any belief, be it in material or spiritual reality, but of knowledge, of ourselves and of the *Universus* in which we live, and, in my experience, nothing is more important within the multiple options that we have in this world.

What is my proposal? The *Return to the Sources*. I am referring to the idealism that has been a constant and most beneficial force in all civilisations. In *The Search for Universal Consciousness* I have developed the history of idealism in the West, here I am concerned with making a convergence of this idealism with its most refined exponents in the East: Hinduism and Buddhism, that is, with constituting a Universal Idealism.

Buddhism and Hinduism

The Unity of Dhamma and Dharma

Since I am to speak of the Indic civilisation, in which Buddhism is indispensable, my first objective will be to demonstrate the basic unity between this discipline, as a culture and doctrine, and Hinduism. I will begin by sharing a lecture given at a symposium that had precisely the same objective as its aim. This symposium, it should be noted, was not the idea and task of several individuals, but rather representatives of all the countries of the Far East participated in it, since all have incorporated Buddhism or Hinduism in their own way, and in some they coexist amalgamated, as in Nepal, Ceylon, Thailand and Cambodia. The interest was common and unanimous; the scope of the matter will be understood if one considers that practically half of the world's population was involved.

Nalanda University, where the meeting took place, was created during the Buddhist period, but Hinduism was also taught as well as various arts. One of the first universities on the planet, its reputation reached as far as China, from whence students came and subsequently brought this enlightened Buddhism to their country. The University, destroyed by the Muslims in the 8th century, was restored in the XXI century. In this lecture I also announce the theme of this book: the convergence of Indic and Hellenic civilisations.

Lecture at Nalanda University, Bihar, India, January 2018:

"This task of reviving Nalanda University, which involves the project of the integration of *Dhamma* and *Dharma*, seems to me very appropriate for the history of this civilisation and could be a decisive step in the history of mankind. You will understand my pride in contributing, to some extent, to this immense project. For this dissertation I have considered it essential to address four topics:

The first deals with: The relationship between Dharma and Dhamma.

The integration of Buddhism and Hinduism is not only feasible but fundamentally already given. From a philosophical point of view, that is, in their essence, they coincide and overlap. This should not be surprising since historically there has been a permanent interaction between them.

One of the points in which Buddhism and Hinduism apparently differ is the concept of Atman or God, since Buddhism does without it. However, of the six schools accepted as orthodox in Hinduism, three of them, Mimansa, Shankya and Yoga, do not accept the existence of a God. Patanjali speaks of Isvara, it is true, but he refers to him as an object of concentration of the mind, *an entirely pragmatic conception governs Patanjali's system*, says Radhakrishna. We know that his entire system is based on the Shamkya philosophy that dispenses with this idea. Patanjali's conception of God is not dogmatic but rather pragmatic. It is like a working hypothesis, a useful idea in the manner of Kant. Patanjali aims, like Buddhism, at experience and not at belief.

In my view, this is the correct way to face the problem to avoid controversies: the subordination of belief to experience, since only this has the certainty of the existence of the Transcendent. Whereas when certainty is sought by means of belief, that is, through faith, one inevitably falls into dogmatism, which inclines towards intolerance. The tolerance shared by Buddhism and Hinduism, which is a characteristic feature of these traditions, is a consequence of their foundations rooted in experience, and this experience is the same, Unity in Brahman, or in the Nature of Buddha. Differences, disputes and intolerance derive from belief; the danger lies in faith, which takes a means as an end and puts belief before experience. There is a latent danger in *Bhakty Yoga* if it goes outside the limits established by Patanjali.

Buddhism, I believe, prefers to avoid the concept of Atman so that the aspirant does not get an idea and remain on the plane of beliefs. I believe that it uses this resource, with the psychological insight that characterises it, as *an effective means* of transporting the spirit directly to the experience of the Consciousness of the Buddha, which corresponds to the concept of Brahman of the Upanishads, and to the concept of universal Consciousness that is the one I use in my philosophy. That is to say that Buddhism dispenses with the concept of Atman, but the Mahayana speaks of a cosmic Mind, and of the Dharmakaya, which seems to me the most accurate, elevated and sublime idea that human intelligence has created.

Another point in common that Buddhism and Hinduism have are spiritual techniques, which, although they have the same objective as the doctrines and can be complemented by them, are not a religion in themselves, but practices aimed at spiritual experience. Such is the case of Yogacara, the fundamental school of Mahayana. Yoga itself is not a religion and neither is Ch'an or Zen. And the experience to which they tend is the same: Samadhi and Satori are the same. That is to say that if there were doctrinal differences, which to my knowledge there are not, in terms of techniques they coincide in practice and in objective. For all these reasons we can conclude that from a philosophical point of view there are no essential differences between *Dhamma* and *Dharma*, and in fact, the peaceful coexistence that they have maintained for centuries is proof of their brotherhood."

The second theme that I wanted to develop is: The relationship between Dharma, Dhamma and Hellenic culture.

"Three great civilisations have been produced by the human being: the Chinese, the Indic and the Western. At present we are concerned with the common roots of the latter two, that is, the Indo-European civilisation. The Indic civilisation is founded and inspired by the *Dharma* and the *Dhamma*, it is these doctrines or traditions that have made this civilisation possible. Western civilisation is founded and inspired by Hellenic culture, that is, Greco-Roman; it is this tradition that has made Western civilisation possible.

These two civilisations, the Indic and the Hellenic, have suffered invasions from other cultures that have modified their tradition to a greater or lesser degree. Despite the numerous invasions that India has had, it has managed to preserve, thanks to *Dharma* and *Dhamma*, its tradition; so it can be said that this culture has been able to follow a *natural evolution*.

Western civilisation *has not followed a natural evolution*: the fall of the Roman Empire and the advent of Christianity, which did its best to eradicate the Hellenic tradition, the most notable example of which was the burning of the Library of Alexandria, having contained more than half a million accumulated texts of the Hellenic culture, meant a great rupture in that civilisation. Despite this, the West has not been able to do without the Hellenic tradition, it has always been an inevitable reference for philosophy, the sciences, the arts, literature and culture in general.

It is then that Western civilisation takes a different direction to that of India. The fall of Rome coincides with the Gupta era, which begins a long period of flourishing that lasts until the Mongol invasions. That is to say that the Middle Ages in the West, so called because it spans two zeniths, the fall of Rome and the Renaissance, has nothing to do with India. What has rightly been called the dark ages in the West would correspond to a luminous age in India.

The Renaissance in the West was of Hellenic spirit, but many centuries had passed, much had gone in the wrong direction; the westerner could no longer return to the initial path, he was alienated and continues to be so. He is alienated from the universal vision that the Greeks had. But deep down in his heart, the Westerner longs for that integral perception, that universal Consciousness. In Greece the world was populated by gods, the Spirit was present in all Nature. We find the same spirit in the Vedas: "Love for trees, love for mountains, love for rivers, love for the sea." Well then, that integrating vision, that *universal Consciousness* that the Westerner has lost, that he cannot reach because he cannot have the *vital experience* necessary for it, is possessed by *Dharma* and *Dhamma*. In Buddhist and Hindu countries, the Westerner can see and experience that *Unity of consciousness*.

Myths, which were left sleeping in Greece, are awake in Asia, and nowhere are they more alive than in India. In the Christian myth, God creates a world other than himself out of nothing, and then bestows a soul only on human beings. This alone is enough to disintegrate man from the rest of the living beings. In the Hindu myth, Brahman creates a world out of himself, so all beings are animated, they all participate in the same Spirit, in the same universal Soul. The Dharmakaya, for its part, animates and inspires all living beings.

It is a reality that we are Indo-Europeans; and this reality is not only linguistic. The truth is that the more we study this particular, the more we discover our common roots. In the oldest texts that were transmitted orally and later written, in the epic in particular, we find not only common facts, but, what is more decisive, the same spirit.

The aspiration to be like the gods, to become as perfect as them, is the very motor of the Greek of the heroic age that Homer sings about. The most outstanding heroes were sons of gods and some came to be admitted to Olympus. These literary resources were not to entertain the listener or the reader, they were the product of a vehement desire, of a *vital impulse for perfection* that pushed them to be like the gods. These heroes were admired by the public because they were exemplary, the people also wanted to participate in that divine nature. The epic has also been a decisive element of education in India. Here too the gods participated in this transcendent project of the human being, the heroes were also descendants of gods and sometimes the gods themselves.

The Vedic Aryans, like the Greeks, did not show much interest in the future of the soul. Like the Greeks, life for them was bright and joyful. The fullness of life was to be achieved in this life and not after death. In no case did they desire death but rather a long life. Therefore, like the Greeks, they did not have a special doctrine on life after death. And it is this vital attitude that has determined a vital principle of *Dhamma* and *Dharma*: the fullness of life; liberation must be achieved in life (*jivanmukta*), not after death. The Greeks also participated in the belief in reincarnation, although not in an unquestionable way like Hindus or Buddhists, we find it explicitly in Pythagoras, Empedocles and Plato, and even in Rome with Virgil, who expresses the thinking of the time in the age of Augustus.

The epic in Greece corresponds to what has been called the heroic period. The classical period, of apogee, occurs centuries later. In this, as in India, always having the gods as a paradigm, the Greek directs his ideals of perfection towards other branches of knowledge, such as the arts and philosophy.

The difference between Greeks and Hindus is established by their great discovery: yoga. The path of perfection, the most effective way to assimilate to the gods, is through yoga. In the Hindu epic, those who have achieved the powers of the gods have been those who have put yoga techniques into practice, there are some who have become so powerful that they can compete with the gods. And these practices are still in force in India.

In conclusion: the Western enlightened people who have always turned to the Greek past to find their inspiration can find it in the present in *Dhamma* and in *Dharma*. There is no need to keep digging through the Greek and Roman ruins, one can find it here in Nalanda."

3rd Theme: Of the understanding of Dhamma and Dharma

"An issue that has given rise to countless misunderstandings in both doctrines is that of the unreality of the visible world as a consequence of the Buddhist concept of *sunyata* or void, mistakenly rendered in the West as nothingness, and the Hindu concept of *maya* translated as "illusion." If we correctly interpret these doctrines, we will not fall into the extreme of denying this concrete reality, which would lead us to the absurdity of believing that those of us who are present are simply not here, and that we are speaking of empty and non-existent matters. And this happens if we follow the logic of Nagarjuna and Shankara to the letter, who are, to be precise, the most logical expositors of these doctrines.

It is not unusual for the philosopher to fall prey to his concepts in the task of philosophising. To escape this trap, the reader must put common sense before logic. Shankara has no qualms in saying, "Everything you see is unreal." "There is no difference between the waking state and sleep." "*Maya creates everything, the body, the senses, the prana and the ego; everything is unreal.*" And the fundamental idea is extracted from the *Dhammapada*: "*Everything we see is the creation of the mind.*" (*Vivekacudamani*) This should not surprise us since Shankara is a son of Buddhism; it is known that he was first a Buddhist, which is why he uses ideas and concepts of this doctrine over and over again.

But it is one thing to misinterpret reality, and another to create reality. We cannot continue speaking in these terms. We must get out of the tangle of these concepts. We cannot say to modern sciences (today capable of dividing atoms) that they do not know what this reality is. But we can tell them that they are looking from the wrong perspective; thus the incorrect use they make of them. This is where the problem lies, that the sciences use a homocentric and egocentric perspective and ignore the *essential or universal perspective* that the *Sutras* and *Upanishads* use. For this reason, instead of talking about unreality, which is extreme, I have preferred to talk about *perspectives* that gradually transform the interpretation of reality.

Not only have various Western philosophers interpreted *Dharma* and *Dhamma* as denying visible reality. The brothers Asanga and

Vasubandu, of the Yogacara school, accused Nagarjuna of being a nihilist. Sri Aurobindo, less than a century ago, equated Buddhism and Shankara's Vedanta, and accused them of the same thing in the chapter he dedicated to them called *The Cosmic Illusion*. The matter, then, is extremely important and must be clarified. Since I cannot develop this topic here, I refer the listeners to my work *The Evolution of the Spirit*" (I will return to this topic a little later in this book).

And this brings us to the fourth topic that I wanted to address: The difficulty of inserting Dhamma and Dharma into contemporary society.

"All the Buddhist Sutras and the Upanishads are written from the perspective of the Absolute, which is why they are understandable only to those with a high level of consciousness that allows them to intuit the Transcendent. For the rest, the vast majority of human beings, this language is unintelligible, they simply do not know of what they are speaking. In periods of spiritual apogee the number of people of spirit is higher, in periods of spiritual perigee, like the current one, these sacred texts never reach the understanding of the general public. For this *Sat-Sit-Ananda* means nothing: knowledge is vain information, his existence is day to day, and he seeks happiness in the acquisition of things and in increased comfort.

The human being, particularly in the West, has suffered a long and constant *process of alienation* from the Essence of life. All materialism, including his philosophy, is the result of such alienation. Centuries ago man had overcome his primary needs, but in his mind he still has not known how to overcome the *survival stage*; that is why he obsessively insists on his safety and the constant acquisition of things. Consumer society, for its part, encourages that mentality and keeps him at that stage. Likewise, the constant population growth permanently generates new needs, which is why it *tends to perpetuate the survival stage*, which is an elementary and primitive stage in the evolution of the human being. Those who are unaware of their alienation from it, and have not surpassed their *survival stage*, have no chance of understanding, let alone practicing, Dhamma and Dharma.

It seems to me absolutely necessary to clarify once and for all that Dharma and Dhamma do not deny the existence of this space-time reality, otherwise there is no possibility of their insertion into contemporary society. It is essential that they are not seen as a negation of life, but as *projects towards the fullness of life, as eternal paradigms for human action*.

I believe that Dhamma and Dharma are facing a huge contrary current, so it has to be a superhuman, heroic task, to insert them into contemporary society. However, I promise to do everything possible to make this aspiration come true, because I believe that it could be a decisive step in the history of humanity, if *these two universal forces can together push The Wheel of Life.*"

On understanding Dhamma and Dharma

Earlier, when speaking on this subject, I had undertaken to clarify this matter. I will do so briefly because I have already dealt with it in *The Evolution of the Spirit*. In my view, based on my experience, the matter is resolved if we see the landscape clearly and explain it with precise terminology; in short, it is like this:

When the human spirit transcends its individuality and the categories of time and space, the world is, as it were, absorbed by the Absolute, which is Immutable. But human nature prevents the spirit from remaining in that timeless state. Life itself, the vital impulse that animates the Universus, brings it back to life. But then the contrast with the Immutable is dramatic, the mutable is represented to him as vertiginous, the living as unstable, the World as a dream. And here we have the origin of the strange language used by the mystics to whom reality appears as *Maya*, as illusory, as unreal. From the latent intuition of said states of the soul is derived the myth of paradise, the myth of the fall of the soul, and the myth of the reality of this world as a product of the dream of a god and the idea expressed by various mystics that the Divinity sees with the eyes of living beings.

The Spirit then contemplates a World and finds it in Order, luminous and impregnated with beauty; it then knows what I have called the *primary Manifestations of the essence of the world*: Life, Order, which implies universal moral Order or the Good, and the Beautiful. The World appears perfect, the Spirit, which is not the individual spirit, can remain in this state of absolute contemplation... for an imprecise time. But after that state, the spirit *falls* into the realisation that it is looking with individual eyes and hearing with individual ears, and it becomes aware of its individuality. At that moment time and space are manifested and the spirit enters into becoming. It feels like it has fallen from another reality; which has also been expressed in various myths.

Be that as it may, after these ascents and descents, the spirit finds itself living in this changing reality, within this nature, and this is the human condition that we must accept, not as absolute, but rather as it is, relatively unstable and perishable; albeit as a *manifestation of the Absolute*. And this is the essential difference of someone who has been able to transcend his individuality: that a transformation has taken place in his spirit and he has gained an *other perspective*, which I have called *essential*. So he goes back to his individuality, but he no longer has an individual, egocentric perspective, but a universal one; this is what I have called the *unitive process of individuation*. He has acquired *universal Consciousness*, and acts according to the *universal moral Order*, according to the *Dharmakaya*, the *Atman* or *Brahman*. As Shankara rightly says: "*to remain a witness of all transformation, is to know the bliss of Nirvana*." Yes, Shankara expresses this state as *Nirvana*. *Dharma*, *Dhamma* and my philosophy are inspired by this *universal Consciousness* and for this reason they tend towards it and educate the human being to reach this *essential perspective*.

The Buddhist *Sutras* and the *Upanishads* do not speak of this *essential perspective* but they express themselves from it, for this reason they are generally unintelligible to those who do not possess it, but they have that irresistible attraction (for those who are not entirely alienated from their Essence) that generates the latent intuition of the Transcendent. Philosophers who have had the *unitive experience of the Transcendent*, that is, of Unity, when trying to rationally explain that Reality, are forced, for the same reason, which is by definition dual, to use inadequate language or to fall into one extreme or the other; this is the case of Nagarjuna and Shankara. Others fall into logical contradictions, like Aurobindo himself, albeit he has reason to criticise the extreme vision of Buddhism and Shankara (see my commentary on both in *The Evolution of the Spirit*).

I believe I have solved this problem with my theory of the displacements of the spirit, of the levels of consciousness and of the perspectives that it adopts according to the level reached and the level in which it is expressed. This does not mean then that *everything* is relative, since this would be adapting *all* reality to the individual perspective, since the first Reality is the Absolute, the Unity of mind and matter, which is what I understand by *Universus*. But the philosophical effort is only a means to lead the mind to experience; what is decisive is the *unitive experience of the existence of said first Reality*; then comes philosophy; which it does not create any reality, it only intends to express it.

On Buddhism and Hinduism

This is essentially how Hinduism, Buddhism and Far Eastern religions in general are, and how they work:

In the first place, since they know that religions concern only the spirit, the institutions have never seen the need for temporal power and they have left the interpretations to the spirit of each individual. Not even in the doctrine itself is there an imposition, so that, although they have countless rules of conduct and their doctrines are exhaustively elaborated, there is no orthodoxy, indeed, if there were one, they would be composed of heresies; but since there are no impositions there are no heresies. What could be "heresies" they call schools, and in truth they are because each one makes its own contribution to the whole, which develops throughout history and is part of the tradition and is naturally incorporated. In short, they have developed in an atmosphere of freedom of belief and expression.

The last stage of Hinduism is synthesised as the fullness of existence, generated by the knowledge from which happiness (*Ananda*) is derived. Buddhist Nirvana is also described as the fullness of life achieved by transcendental insight, *prajna*, which generates unspeakable happiness. "Nirvana is supreme happiness, infinite joy." Both doctrines call this experience *Samadhi*, although they distinguish different stages within it. Buddhism, always so willing to take the spirit to its extreme, admits a last *Samadhi* in which happiness itself disappears and gives way to unconditional peace. This is typical of its methodology, which always tends to leave no trace of the ego, because if there is happiness, it is supposed, there is a subject who has it. I do not experience it like this, because the pure spirit feels the happiness of liberation precisely from the ego. But we must not remain trapped in these fine disquisitions, Buddhism itself avoids it, as in the case of the *Dhammapada* which identifies Nirvana with happiness.

Both doctrines see the need to control the mind and the techniques to achieve it are very similar, in particular meditation, and both recognise the difficulties of the project. “The agitated and unstable mind falters; it is difficult to control and stop it.” (*Dham. 33*) “To stop the mind, oh Arjuna, is harder than stopping the wind.” (*B. Gita*) Both doctrines tend towards liberation and understand it in the same way, since they maintain that it must be achieved in life: “The wise man enjoys imperishable Nirvana even in this mortal life.” (*Dham. 89*)

Both proclaim helping others, Hinduism even has a path of knowledge for this purpose, *Karma Yoga*, but both recommend the priority of self-knowledge to be prepared for this task and to avoid mistakes. What is fundamental is always to overcome ignorance; and this is not achieved only by helping others: “One should first establish oneself in what is proper; then only should one instruct others. Thus the wise man will not be reproached.” (*Dham. 158*) Both aim, in the first place, to destroy the ego, in it they see the root of ignorance; Shankara insists on this.

Buddhist as much as Hindu ethics have their origins in the *universal moral Order* that exercises its power over everything that exists. This force is dynamic and constant; the law of cause and effect is continuous. Buddhism expresses it as the wheel of life that never stops, that turns eternally. Although everything is in permanent transformation, karma, which obeys that law, is never extinguished, death and rebirth take place over time and inevitably pull along our actions. Everything we do is recorded, all debts are paid sooner or later.

The way to get off this incessant wheel is by achieving the liberation that is reached in life through moral conduct and knowledge. Buddhism establishes the eight noble paths that all obey correct, good and noble conduct. Nirvana is the extinction of karma, not annihilation (as those who misunderstand or are ill-intentioned allege), and the result is peace and unspeakable happiness. It is the awakening of the Bodhicitta which, I believe, is nothing but the *unitive consciousness* to which my philosophy aspires. The path, be it the small (Hinayana) or the great (Mahayana) is fundamentally moral. The practice of moral conduct is decisive, there are no articles of faith or dogmas here, nor regulating deity, only a *universal moral Order* to which the aspirant for liberation must adapt.

The basic concepts of *Dhamma* and *Dharma* in both traditions refer to the same thing: to the tradition founded on eternal universal laws, on a *universal moral Order* that inspires, makes and nourishes the doctrine as well as the spiritual life of its adherents, and both concepts tend towards liberation through knowledge, and liberation itself is supreme knowledge, wisdom.

That is to say that from the beginning to the end, including the means, the structure is the same, they are of the same nature, I would say, because even the behaviours are similar. What separated Buddhism from Hinduism, and later the latter from the former, were external reasons of a historical and political order; although not a State policy, since in these traditions there never was one in religious matters, in the sense of a vertical and exclusive imposition.

As we will see later, in the sixth century B.C. the times called for a renewal, and, as is characteristic of the Indic tradition, it was of a spiritual nature. The entire religious structure was renovated, updated to the needs of the time. There were no radical changes, such as materialistic or skeptical proposals, as would surely have happened in other societies, but rather new ways or perspectives of seeing the same thing, inspired by the same experience. It was not a new species of religion that appeared, so to speak, but the same rejuvenated one.

In the same epoch, as a reaction to the same situation, Buddhism and Jainism appear, and the *Upanishads*. The latter were an updated version within the same Brahmanism that would mature for 13 centuries until it took the structured form of a philosophical doctrine with Shankara, who gave it the name of Vedanta.

Buddhism in the History of the Indic Civilisation

To understand the phenomenon of Buddhism in India it is essential to consider that it is not exhausted in its religious aspect; Buddhism has played an important role in the history of the Indic civilisation, furthermore, the first proper civilisation in India was Buddhist. A brief historical review is necessary to understand the event.

We know that there was a rudimentary civilisation in the Indus Valley when it was invaded by the Aryans, around the 16th century B.C.; only traces of it remain. We will refer to this convergence later when discussing the Vedas. As was natural for it to happen, the Indo-Aryans, who now made up a single people (hereinafter I will call them Indus, since to differentiate them from the American Indians the mistake of calling them Hindus is too often made), spread through the fertile valley of the Ganges and the Yamuna over a span of a thousand years ranging from the *Rg-Veda* to the Buddha and the *Upanishads*. Culture in its various manifestations had progressed and there was already an infrastructure capable of generating a civilisation; thinkers of that stature do not occur in a village.

The little that is known of that time is through the epic; as it happened in Greece with the heroic period. We have certain data, not only from the Greeks, but also from the Indus, from the arrival of Alexander the Great in the Indus Valley. In Taxila, that meeting point between Persian and Indic culture, there is already a university, perhaps the first on the planet. Chandragupta and his renowned minister Kautilya, author of the *Arthasastra* or A *Treatise on the Art of Government*, which will be successfully applied by Chandragupta and his successors, are educated there.

Plutarch speaks of a meeting between the young Chandragupta and Alexander, between whom there was no agreement, but which already shows the ambition and dynamism of the Kshatriya nobleman, who soon after manages to rise to power and begins to extend his reign from Pataliputra. 17 years after the death of Alexander, Seleucus Nikator, who had inherited the Persian west, proposes to recover the Indus area Alexander had conquered with a powerful army, but Chandragupta opposes him with surely more numerous forces, for which he decides give up his attempt. The matter is resolved in a peaceful agreement, by which the Greek gives up the territory he wanted and settles for the payment of 500 elephants. To seal the peace pact he gives his daughter as a wife to Chandragupta.

This episode could be considered to be the beginning of the cultural exchange between Greeks and Indus that will generate the art of Gandhara that will extend to Mathura, where Buddhas stylised in the Greek manner can still be seen today. An economic and diplomatic exchange was also established; Megasthenes, Seleucus's ambassador, will be the first Greek to write with inside knowledge about India; his *Indica*, a work unfortunately lost but much commented on, recounts Chandragupta's period in his capital Pataliputra. Consolidating his power, Chandragupta became the first prominent emperor of India and established the Mauryan dynasty that would last for 127 years. This emperor deserves extensive commentary since his government is held by historians as exemplary, but for our purposes we are interested only as an introduction to the reign of Asoka, his grandson, due to its repercussions throughout the Far East.

The history of the Indic civilisation stands on very firm foundations thanks to Asoka. This emperor inherited an immense territory that occupied the entire North of India and that he extended to Orissa and even further south, to the Andras area. But very soon he changes this military policy for a religious attitude. He becomes aware of the Buddha's teachings and applies them to the vast territory. Asoka promises, setting it in stone, that neither he nor his successors will ever again wage a war of conquest, thus officially establishing the principle of non-aggression, which, as we know, will be basic in Hinduism and Jainism. Although Buddhism becomes the official religion, freedom of worship and expression is established, an ideal that he wants to extend to all peoples. He not only proclaims the basic principles of Buddhism in his famous edicts carved in rocks and marble columns, but also puts them into practice: he creates hospitals for humans and animals, schools, monasteries, which will also serve as art schools, paths equipped with ponds of water and resting places, he has trees planted for shade in the roads, he founds and embellish cities, in short, he creates the infrastructure for his great civilisational project.

As befitted his religion, Asoka forbade bloody sacrifices and enacted laws protecting animals. He himself became a vegetarian, setting an example that would spread throughout the population. Vegetarianism, so widespread in India, may have started then. Jainism, even stricter in this sense than Buddhism, has undoubtedly contributed to maintaining this tradition to this day. Although this religion is not popular or widespread, it has preserved respect for all living beings; an example which the sensitive Hindu mind is apt to imitate.

Convinced that the Buddha was “the prince of peace”, he imitated his example and spread his doctrine beyond his empire by sending missionaries to Macedonia, Corinth, Cyrene, Syria, and to Ceylon, where the Dhamma would find fertile ground, and even to the Ptolemies in Egypt. We can assume that the library of Alexandria kept records of this proposal which, to the West’s great loss, never reached the hands of Plotinus and the Neo-Platonists. We know about these missions because they were engraved in rock in one of his edicts; specifically the XIII.

Asoka did not fail to visit Kapilavastu, the Buddha’s birthplace, where he left an edict engraved on a marble column that is still standing, as well as numerous stupas on the way to this pilgrimage site. He also left, incidentally, edicts on columns at Sarnath, where the Master gave his first sermon and at Sanchi where he built the most notable stupas in India. The stupas, as well as the columns erected by Asoka, were almost all destroyed by the Islamic invaders; only the most notable remain, and in a pitiful state.

The basic principles of Buddhism were recorded, preached and practiced by Asoka: do no harm to and have respect for all living beings (Ahimsa); devotion (Bhakti); service to others; kindness (Daya); charity (Dana); reverence; gratitude; purity of thought; and control of the senses, which is nothing other than Yoga. Tolerance, implicit in these principles, was a particular concern of the emperor. As was respect for other religions, institutions and people, such as Brahmins, ascetics devoted to Shiva and Vishnu, including slaves, who were treated with such kindness that Megasthenes even affirmed that there were none. In one of his edicts he declares that “All men are my children, so I desire their well-being and happiness in this and in the other world.” “My officials are here to fulfil these services.” He was also notable as a patron of artists who beautified his cities, particularly Pataliputra.

This city was completely walled with a length of 14 km by a width of 2.6 km. It had 570 towers and 64 gates and was surrounded by a deep moat more than 150 meters wide. Athens, the most prominent city in the West, had then a diameter of 1.5 km and its walls covered about 6 km. If we compare it with the walls that linked Athens with its port, Piraeus, Pataliputra is five times larger. This was the capital of the Maurya dynasty during which India had its golden period.

It will be understood to what extent this prince of peace exalted the human spirit and established the *necessary moral foundations for all civilisation*. During his reign, India reached an unprecedented spiritual, cultural and social level. H. G. Wells (in his *A Short History of the World*), who devotes ample laudatory space to Asoka, acknowledges that "his reign for eight-and-twenty-years was one of the brightest interludes in the troubled history of mankind." As can be seen, not everything was the work of Asoka, who did nothing more than correctly apply the Dhamma, which already included respect, kindness, service and tolerance for all ideologies and all living beings, principles shared by Hinduism, which is what makes these doctrines truly and legitimately universal. This was engraved in stone by Asoka: "All sects deserve reverence for one reason or another. By thus acting a man exalts his own sect and at the same time does service to the sects of other people. Acting contrary to these principles, man harms both the sects of others and his own."

It has come to be believed that civilisations are built on the ruins of others; Asoka proves otherwise. Civilisations are made by incorporating the legacy of previous cultures; when they are destroyed, the dynamic of history is stopped, and several generations are wasted in the stupid task of rebuilding their culture and reordering their lives. *Asoka's civilising project is exemplary for all humanity*. And it is not only an ideal, the facts demonstrate its effectiveness: the great cultural flowering of the Gupta period was the result of this convergence; the first Gupta princes were Buddhists and their sons and heirs were Hindus. The Dharma embodies the Dhamma and builds the Indic civilisation.

I consider it legitimate and appropriate to compare these leaders of these two great civilisations: Asoka, Pericles and Hadrian. All three ruled for about a quarter of a century, a significant fact because they managed to *educate* an entire generation. The miracle accomplished by them is having incorporated the common people, without any coercion and in an sphere of freedom, that through a process of mimesis they adopted the high values that in current times are only practiced by exceptional people, by *the best*, which etymologically means the *aristocracy*. It is the practice of high philosophical, religious, moral and aesthetic values that generates the periods of human apogee, I mean, of intrinsic and real transformation.

It may be objected that while Asoka laid down his arms to create a peaceful society, Pericles died in battle, but in fact he was a victim of the plague that ravaged Athens, and Thucydides maintains that without this catastrophe the war would have ended in his favour. In any case, Asoka did not face an army as powerful as that of the Spartan; it was an adverse game of Fate. What is certain is that no one was so aware of generating a great civilisation as was Pericles, hence his efforts. Moreover, despite losing his life and the war he left the most illustrious civilisation in the West; and it is not difficult to guess what would have resulted from that exemplary civilising project had it not been spoiled by that bad move of history, if all of Hellas, from Ionia to Magna Graecia, if all the islands, which were already on his side, could have done it. The difference is established by the facts, the crude history: Asoka was able to realise his dream while he was alive, Pericles was not, but what he left behind is still exemplary; this is the enormous force of idealism that both of these visionaries and great statesmen shared. Hadrian's merit lies in having understood from the beginning the need to reign, educate and build an Empire in a state of peace.

We can accept Asoka's superiority over Pericles and Hadrian for his personal piety and in the social field for the propagation of *Dhamma*. One can only imagine what the history of the West would have been if the Greek strategist and the Roman emperor had had a religion as wise, elevated and structured as Buddhism. This reflection leads us to the general purpose of this book: *to establish a bridge between Hellenic and Indic culture*.

Buddhist Culture in the Indic Civilisation

It would be excessive here to attempt to cover the history of Buddhism, which is projected until the 12th century in Bengal. I consider it important to emphasise that its disappearance is largely due to reasons external to the doctrine, such as the numerous and fearsome invasions that India suffered during that period, which exalted nationalism, more identified with the popular ancestral tradition and its mythical gods and local customs. The Huns, relatives of those who devastated Europe, cruelly persecuted the Buddhists, and the Muslim invasion that occupied the entire Ganges valley, the largest area of Buddhist influence, ultimately suffocated it. The de facto disappearance of Buddhism in India was due to this invasion and persecution.

During the first centuries of the first millennium, Mahayana Buddhism was born and grew, with which universal philosophy reached its highest expression, thanks to the genius of thinkers such as Asanga, Vasubandu, Ashvagosha and Nagarjuna, to name the most prominent. On them rests all this sublime theory, which will extend until Japan. India gave birth to its founder and in India these fruits were borne. During the Gupta period, in which Hinduism definitively reappeared, and in the subsequent empire of Harsha, the Mahayana reached its apogee. One more proof of the peaceful and cooperative relationship between Dhamma and Dharma.

The Cultural Centre of Buddhism was the University of Nalanda, to which we have already referred, and which deserves special attention for its greatness in all the fundamental aspects that an institution of this type can cover. It was founded and maintained by the Gupta emperors. Almost everything we know about it we owe to Hiuen Tsang, who came from China to learn the Dhamma; a room in the present University bears his name. He tells us that it contained 1,500 teachers and 8,500 students. Not everyone was admitted; upon arrival, the knowledge of the applicants was examined and seven or eight out of ten were rejected. At the head of the institution were the most renowned Mahayana teachers of the day. Thanks to the magnanimity of the Gupta emperors, teachers and apprentices could devote all their time to their work without needing to earn a living. "The conduct of the teachers was impeccable, their fame reached the most distant countries where they were invited," recalls Hiuen Tsang.

Each king contributed to enlarge and embellish the buildings; as it has been traditional in India with its imposing and replicated temples. The entire University was surrounded by brick walls (current ruins confirm this). It had eight separate rooms; the monks had four-story buildings and, "the roofs were covered with shiny tiles that reflected the light with 1000 hues." It had three buildings to contain its books; one of the libraries had nine stories. In it, in addition to the Mahayana, the Theravada, the Vedas and even Sankhya were taught; in addition to medicine, astronomy and its renowned iconography. The classic mixture of the five metals, which have been used in Indian iconography ever since, has its origin there.

In the 7th century, Nalanda University was destroyed by the Muslims. Its destruction is too similar to that of the library of Alexandria not to establish a parallel between the religions of Semitic origin, harmful to Indic and Hellenic civilisation. Tolerance has been a fundamental aspect of both *Dharma* and *Dhamma*, and it is an indisputable virtue, but the Indus have applied tolerance unconditionally, and this is unrealistic and no longer a good recipe, as it does not apply to everyone. Being tolerant of the intolerant, in effect, is a policy that only benefits the intolerant. The virtue of tolerance must be balanced with another virtue that was characteristic of the Greek. This virtue is *Phronesis*, practical wisdom, prudence, which is what generates the golden mean, the fair measure, and which in turn leads to another great virtue exalted by the Hellenes: justice, consisting of giving each one *what he deserves*.

Considering that in India religion is definitely a matter of spirit and not of institution, we can affirm that Buddhism is alive in that country. It is in the sap of the immense tree of Hinduism, much more than some doctrines that are considered orthodox by intellectuals, but that few know or practice. The Buddha as the incarnation of Vishnu is something accepted by millions and the iconography shows it to be so. There is no place in India that sells religious images that does not have a Buddha. Although it is true that he is not directly worshiped, with the exception of the vast territory of the Himalayas, the spirit of Buddhism runs through the veins of Hinduism. The Buddha remains the paradigm of the perfectly enlightened, which is the highest aspiration of the Indic people. The refounding of Nalanda seems to me a significant and hopeful event; it is also true that the birthplace of the Buddha, Lumbini, with the predictable revival of Buddhism in our day, has grown to gigantic proportions, as all the countries of the Far East and numerous European countries have erected temples that compete for their beauty, which will generate a centre of attraction and diffusion of Dhamma.

Perspectives in the East and West

After wandering through the long history of thought and feeling in the West and the East, this is my conclusion: The disparate and heterogeneous search that occurs in the West is a consequence of the lack of direct perception of the Transcendent. And the similarity in the search that we find throughout the Far East, far from being, as Hegel proposed, due to a lack of dynamism or creativity, is the natural result of a clearer vision of the Transcendent. In other words, that what is "repetitive" is due to the constant convergence of individual spirits in the same universal Spirit, that is, to the fact that they have a clearer objective, which has allowed them to repeatedly hit the target. This is not an opinion, my experience confirms it and it is supported by all my work in which both cultures have contributed and converged. But invariably on entering these two worlds of thought my spirit must adopt different perspectives; that now the reader will know how to differentiate. When I enter the Western world, I find myself with an individual perspective, from which, when the thinker wants to elevate his spirit, he uses isolated intuitions with which, like a pilot among the clouds, he infers the reality that is higher up, getting an idea of it and, with discernment, he establishes the relationships he needs to explain the world at his feet, whose surface he already knows. When I enter the Oriental world, Buddhist, Hindu, Taoist, unless I put my mind in a proper perspective, I simply do not understand what is being spoken of, where I am flying, but as soon as I adopt this perspective, the clouds dissipate and I see the two realities, the spiritual and the material, clearly. I can verify that these philosophy-religions rather than hitting the target look from it; that is the *essential perspective* to which I have tried to bring the spirit of the reader. From it I have written all my work, from it those philosophies become diaphanous.

By following the train of thought of the most enlightened spirits, that is, the idealists of the West, we have seen (in *The Search for Universal Consciousness*) that they tend to converge on a common goal which is the Unity that, as absolute, seeks to unify the external or material reality and the internal or spiritual. Already in possession of this knowledge (although it will already be clear that rational understanding is not enough), I would like to compare my thinking with the monistic philosophy-religions, Buddhism and Vedanta. I have referred to them, I believe enough, in *The Evolution of the Spirit*, where I refer the interested reader, but it will not be too much to insist on clarifying this matter of great importance.

In the Far East this search has been more consistent and homogeneous for the simple reason that its philosophers have been closer to the Spirit and their consciousnesses have not become alienated from universal Consciousness. Political and historical reasons have also contributed. They never had political-religious organisations that dogmatically imposed a faith in opposition to other beliefs, so that the spirit and history could follow a *natural development in an environment of freedom*, an indispensable factor in all spiritual and material evolution. Wars and catastrophes, they had as many or more than the West, but religious wars, that is, for ideologies that concerned only the spirit, they never had. India only knew and suffered this catastrophe with the Muslim invasion, but this could only destroy their temples, it could not reach their spirits. The fact that orthodoxy has been established by those who have had the experience of the Absolute is of the greatest importance and is decisive because partiality, dogma, violence, etc., never came from them, nor can come from them, because they are inspired by absolute paradigms.

For these reasons monism has been a constant in the Far East. There have been different schools within it, but those that have had a marked orthodoxy, never imposed, I insist, have been so by their own moral and philosophical weight, never opposed to religion. For this reason, rather than an orthodoxy, it would be more correct to speak of a main current, of a permanent reference generated and maintained by its notable mystics and thinkers who have been confirming with their experience the experience of their ancestors, which they have been modifying with nuances to this day. One of the last philosophers and mystics who deserves special recognition is Aurobindo, whom I have commented on in the aforementioned work, but who will serve me to establish the announced comparison.

In *Origin and Destiny of Man*, I referred to the origin of man as a rational being at the moment in which he becomes aware of his individuality, of his self, from which he develops his reason and accumulates in his memory what he has learned. Since then, our species has distanced itself from the other species that it manages to dominate, it can organise itself into societies and it seems to improve progressively until it forms the society we know today. Our history, if we can forget all the atrocities committed, is presented as positive; but this is only a part of reality. Various mythologies speak of man's *fall* at his origin, of a descent of the soul at a time when it seems to us that we are beginning to be different from other species. Aurobindo himself in the 20th century speaks of a descent from the divine to the human state, and a contemporary of his, Ramana Maharshi, another enlightened one, that is, one who has reached wisdom, when asked what he thought of original sin, replied that he had his own view of the matter, that "sin consisted in the first thought." The first thought, as understood by my configuration of the mind, would be the human species' awareness of the self and the immediate identification of the self with the body. That is to say that where we humans believe that our progress begins, on the contrary, begins our error, our ignorance.

I would like to clarify this, because without having an idea of Ramana's position, it is easy to say that he is against reason, progress, etc., but we always come up against the same problem: ignorance of the reality that transcends reason. I think my theory of perspective can shed some light on this matter. If you look at it from the individual perspective, it will be difficult to understand; that is why this entire treatise aims to overcome this perspective. Ramana Maharshi, like so many other mystics, has simply remained in the universal Consciousness from which this whole world appears to be a mess, a turbulence, a struggle of conflicting ambitions, a set of banalities, unstable, transitory, etc.; We cannot blame him for his attitude. I consider it entirely legitimate to remain in that state of beatitude which, moreover, serves as an incentive to perceptive spirits. But there are other positions, other ways of passing on the message, such as through philosophy or art. For Ramana, following Shankara's vision, there is only unity in Brahman, for the common man there is only the multiplicity of the world. We cannot opt for one or the other as if the two perspectives were on equal terms, we must never forget that the *essential perspective* comprehends the individual one; this is the abysmal difference, only chosen by whomever looks from the universal Consciousness. I believe that the correct interpretation of these mystics consists in accepting their teachings without emphasising a priori their supposed denial of concrete reality; a posteriori, after having achieved that knowledge, one will be in a position to decide what to do with the world and history.

Personally, I do not believe it is necessary to come to support the non-existence of concrete reality, because this leads to erroneous interpretations for those who see only one side of reality, but I do accept the Maya theory that leads to seeing this world as an illusion, since it is an effective means of approaching Reality. In the *unitive experience of the Absolute*, effectively, the individual spirit and material reality are absorbed in the Spirit, but the human condition does not allow a definitive establishment in that state, there is a return but with another perspective; this perspective, it will be understood, is the human *affair* par excellence.

The Evolution of the Spirit in Hinduism

Since I have devoted a particular commentary to Sri Aurobindo in *The Evolution of the Spirit*, I shall not dwell on him here unnecessarily. I will say something, however, given his relevance in modern thought, and because it should serve as an introduction to two doctrines of the greatest importance. We must recognise three enormous merits in him: first, the incorporation of an evolutionary theory within Hinduism; second, the full acceptance of the existence of the World; third, the identification of Shankara's Vedanta with Buddhism. This identification seems correct to me, and unprecedented within his tradition, which had emphasised the differences more than the similarities. However, he does not do so in order to highlight its virtues, but its deficiencies and thus expose his proposal. In this way he claims, like other eminent thinkers of India, to be the most authentic expression of Vedanta. In his evolutionary theory we can see his education in Cambridge at the time of Darwin, and of other western evolutionists. However, as corresponded to his native tradition, the evolution that he deals with is that of the spirit; the lack of this in Darwin's theory I have pointed out, for my part, in the aforementioned book.

Aurobindo starts from a basic principle that from the point of view of my philosophy would be unobjectionable: "The Absolute manifests itself in two ways, as Being and as Becoming. The Being is the fundamental reality; the Becoming is the effective reality." (*The Life Divine 659*) This, its mutable form, is an expression of its immutable and formless essence. From this principle it follows that the knowledge of one of these two ways of being of the Absolute, to the exclusion of the other, is a half-truth. Starting from this premise, Aurobindo gathers four visions of reality.

Aurobindo refers to materialist vision as the *terrestrial cosmic* one in which life is confined to the material universe. Although he rejects this conception of reality as insufficient, he sees a moral life within it as possible and intellectual development as positive, the "study of the laws of the Becoming" that is, scientific, and even progress towards well-being. He says that in this conception "God, if God exists, is an eternal Becoming." This being the case, we could include in this vision H. Bergson, whom I have commented on in the aforementioned book, and all pantheism that does not reach beyond the Becoming. For Bergson, in fact, everything happens in the Becoming and he is so convinced of it that it does not even occur to him to look outside of it.

The theory that Aurobindo rejects with the greatest emphasis is the one that he calls supraterrestrial, which is the one that would correspond to religions of Semitic origin. He alludes to this conception, without ascribing it to a particular religion, in these terms: "There is first the idea of certain religions, long persistent but now greatly shaken or discredited, that man is a being primarily created as a material living body upon earth into which a newly born divine soul is breathed or else with which it is associated by the fiat of an almighty Creator. A solitary episode, this life is his one opportunity from which he departs to a world of eternal bliss or to a world of eternal misery either according as the general or preponderant balance of his acts is good or evil according as he accepts or rejects, knows or ignores a particular creed, mode of worship, divine mediator, or else according to the arbitrary predetermining caprice of his Creator." "But this", he clarifies, "is the supraterrestrial theory of life in its less rational form of questionable creeds and dogmas." (*The Life Divine, 672*) Then he refers to similar theories, understood within the same perception, which he considers more rational because in them the pre-existence of the soul is admitted, or the existence of different worlds in which the soul is fulfilling its stages of overcoming.

With an understanding and acquiescent air, Aurobindo admits that the very circumstances that man generates tend to deny this world and seek reality in another: the constant frustration and "illusion behind all human effort and earthly tasks, the illusion of the political and social gospels, the illusion of ethical efforts towards perfection, the illusion of philanthropy and service, the illusion of work, fame, power, success, the illusion of all achievement", and rightly adds, "all human, social and political effort always goes in a circle and leads nowhere." "Christian love and Buddhist compassion have not made the world one bit happier," they have only "thrown a few drops of water on the fire of the world's suffering." This skepticism, however, can vanish and be transformed, Aurobindo believes, if we take this world as "the field where a greater motive works", as a "divine Possibility" in the evolutionary process. Aurobindo recognises that the arguments he has just given to understand the reasons that lead to the denial of the world are not those that can motivate thinkers of the stature of the Buddha and Shankara, for which he admits that "there are also higher mental and spiritual bases for the philosophy of the denial of the world", for which "there is only one Reality, the transcendent, the supracosmic".

Although Aurobindo refers to the philosophies that, in his opinion, deny the world, in particular Buddhism and Shankara's Vedanta, in the chapters entitled "*The Cosmic Illusion*", they are the ones that deserve the greatest respect. This theory accepts "only as entirely real the supreme Reality." That is to say, it denies, in his opinion, the Becoming. And since Aurobindo wants to clearly and definitively incorporate this concrete reality, said vision seems insufficient to him because it shows only one aspect of Reality. I would agree entirely with this incorporation, but I would not go so far as to call Buddhism and Vedanta "Illusionism", because although I judge their positions to be somewhat extreme, they have their reasons, as we will see.

Aurobindo does not strictly propose a *new* vision of Reality, but pays it more attention, puts a certain emphasis on concrete reality, too often neglected, without any discussion, by the Hindu tradition. But he did not need to disqualify Shankara's philosophy for this. The facts themselves demonstrate the similarity of both thinkers. While Shankara had left no corner of India unvisited to propagate his philosophy, that is, he had traveled tirelessly through this reality that he apparently considered illusory, Aurobindo, paradoxically, completely disregarded that which he considered real, closing himself off in a room for the last twenty-five years of his life. This paradox confirms that the difference between them does not go beyond the level of theory, and if we put it into practice we would see their roles reversed. In a letter to a disciple, Aurobindo says: "We can doubt or refuse to see the light of day or the sun of heaven (which is what he was doing), because of physical things we cannot be sure (...) whereas in the concrete experience of the divine, doubt is not possible." This letter could equally well have been signed by Shankara. Moreover, when Aurobindo maintains that this concrete world is the result of a game

(Lila) of Divinity for his own entertainment, he implicitly accepts the Mayan theory that makes this reality an illusion for man and only real for Divinity. The explanation of this vital and fundamental similarity in the apparent theoretical dissimilarity is very simple: both thinkers have had a similar experience, and it is from it that they express their ideas, so they may differ in the form of some branches but not in the roots.

There is a point in Aurobindo's philosophy that interests me to highlight because in it my theory of knowledge overlaps with his. Aurobindo refers to "the subliminal", even to the "subliminal being" to express a state of consciousness that appears when "we withdraw behind the veil of our limited personality (which we possess during the state) of awakening". The point of coincidence is this: "There is a state of consciousness that has the power to directly contact the universal, not as our superficial (everyday, normal) being does, which maintains an indirect relationship." But, curiously, he affirms that we come out of this state and achieve a "direct relationship" in the sleeping state and during the "trance", which leads me to suppose that our philosopher had not reached a permanent state of direct relationship, which would explain his tendency to religious dualism, to the (relative) personality of his Divinity.

My philosophy has placed particular emphasis on "the plane of direct perception", which would not be the product of sleep or trance, but the true *centre of consciousness* of the human being in which he can, therefore, definitively establish himself. And this state is reached naturally awake, wide awake. The permanent settlement of the spirit on this plane does not exhaust all its possibilities, it must later negotiate different levels of consciousness. But it is the settlement on this plane that will make one advance with sure steps towards other levels and, in this way, overcome the well-known stage in which a nebulous knowledge of the Transcendent is only obtained through isolated intuitions or perceptions.

Unquestionably, Aurobindo has his perception, which is why he rightly says from his cloister: "Our awakened state is not aware of its connection with the subliminal being, however it receives inspirations, intuitions, ideas, suggestions from it in its will and in its senses that urge him to action." Indeed, the human being receives these *creative impulses* "behind the veil of the waking state", but not on an unconscious plane. Behind the *external plane, the so-called conscious*, my philosophy will say, is the *plane of direct perception*, from which these impulses are experienced, and, at its highest levels, the Creative itself.

What I understand by *universal Consciousness* is nothing but a *unified Consciousness*. This Consciousness could not be identified with Aurobindo's Supermind because it does not perceive any difference with the Spirit, while for Aurobindo the divine Consciousness would be even further beyond his Supermind. Strictly speaking, in his scheme there is no unified Consciousness. This is due to his conception of a Spirit (Divinity) as a Person (Ishwara). Although he purports to assimilate this Person to the Absolute (Brahman) by simply enunciating their equality: "The Impersonal Divine, Nirguna Brahman, and the Personal Divine, Saguna Brahman, are here equal and both aspects of the Eternal coexist." (*The Life Divine 281*) And even less sparingly: "The Divine Being, Sachchidananda, is at the same time personal and impersonal." (*Op. Cit. 662*) With a simple statement he aims to overcome a long and wide controversy. This assimilation is not possible, here there are two degrees of knowledge, two separate consciousnesses according to the level of consciousness of the aspirant.

It is this confusion of consciousnesses that insistently leads him to establish a difference in realities between Spirit and Nature, which manifests itself in a sort of spatial distance. For Aurobindo, an involution of the universal Spirit has been necessary to serve the purpose of the re-ascension of the Unconscious towards the Super-conscious. Thus "the Spirit descends", and likewise, curiously, his Super-mind and Over-mind. So there is no ascension in his evolutionary process without these descents. "In order for the principles contained in the Over-mind and Super-mind of their veiled secret, the being and powers of the Super-consciousness (which is that of Divinity), they must descend in us and elevate us." "This descent is a *sine qua non* for transition and transformation." (*Op. cit. 921*) Aurobindo goes so far as to speak of divine "grace". Strictly speaking, everything is the product of His grace: "We can grant that the forces in action work according to the laws of their movement; but within what the divine Omniscience and Omnipotence has allowed them to grow and act" (*op. cit. 401*); and this already has a strong reek of Christian theology; here he has plunged, dragging the World with him, into an unjustified determinism. His life and his studies in the West had left a mark on him that would disfigure the face of his philosophy. However, Aurobindo does not always fall into dualism, but fluctuates between it and monism: "The Divine Being dwells in everything that exists; we are that in the depths of our soul, the secret inhabitant in our psychic entity, is a portion of the Divine Consciousness and Essence" (*Op. cit. 389*). And in this I would fully agree, which leads me to think that Aurobindo does not notice, when reasoning, the movements of his spirit *between different levels of consciousness*.

Aurobindo, like Hegel, assumes that an involution of the Spirit is the reason for the existence of the corporeal world. "An involution of the divine Existence, the spiritual Reality (and penetration) in the apparent unconsciousness of matter, is the starting point of evolution." (*The Life Divine 683*) "A concrete involution of all that the Spirit is and its evolutionary self-unfolding are the double term of our material existence." (*Op. cit. 681*) This is so similar to Hegel that it leads to the assumption of his influence. However, for Aurobindo said involution is that of an already perfect Spirit that penetrates matter, which originates and maintains its evolution, and allows it to reach greater degrees of perfection. I think this is a misstep taken by both philosophers. From a logical point of view, Hegel is more coherent, since his Spirit needed to evolve, for this reason it knows no rest, while Aurobindo, by making an immutable Spirit suffer an involution, is more contradictory. However, if we stick to transcendental experience (which also transcends logic), Hegel's theory is untenable, while we observe that Aurobindo sins only by going outside the framework of said experience.

Aurobindo warns, very much in agreement with my philosophy, that "in us, as in the atom, the metal, the plant, in each form, in each energy, there is, we know, a secret soul, a secret will, a secret intelligence working." (*Op. cit. 588*) This intelligence, however, has a *purpose*, and this, according to Aurobindo, must, as in Hegel, inevitably be fulfilled. I honestly do not know where both philosophers get this information from, since neither the past nor the present could have provided them with sufficient data to guarantee this inevitable future.

For my part I cannot help seeing the theory of involution as useless, since neither Spirit nor matter need this process. There is no valid knowledge in this theory, neither scientific nor spiritual, since neither can reason prove it, nor is there experience at a vital level to confirm it. And Aurobindo's dogmatic language, which announces this theory without further ado, should not lead us to accept it in the name of his authority, because he has none where there is no external or internal experience. It is not, incidentally, the evolution of the spirit that I am discussing, indeed, the evolution of matter towards life, from this to the mind, and the ascent of this to the Super-mind, seems reasonable and feasible to me. Yet I do not see the need for the gradual descent of the Spirit; being that, as I think, an inspiration and a permanent attraction would suffice, which would grant beings the natural time to evolve in full freedom, to hit or miss, and that would explain their delays and mistakes. For if we depend so much on an almighty God, he could suddenly enlighten us all instead of graduating his help for so many centuries past and future. To explain this unnecessary delay, Aurobindo ventures the theory that God is slowly dosing the spirit we need to reach Him. And in this will of God he expresses his externality and personality, which decidedly do not correspond to the spiritual experience of the Transcendent.

In any case, we must recognise the importance of the incorporation of Becoming into Hinduism thanks to Aurobindo's genius. The step he took is of great importance, because by declaring that *the Becoming is real*, he finds the indispensable bases for an evolutionary theory. Thanks to these bases, he incorporates all those who, in that tradition, sought liberation but were unaware that they were in a common and universal project. This could not have been done by Shankara given the disdain with which he regarded the material world. We must not, however, exaggerate the importance of Aurobindo's theory, to the point of minimising the work and acts of Shankara, who, having made countless beings achieve the same goal, has contributed to the same process of evolution as very few in history. And this is what is decisive in the process: the example that they have left that has led to the experience of others.

Strictly speaking, the idea of evolution of the spirit is implicit in the theory of reincarnation, accepted throughout the Far East, but Hinduism lacked a universal evolutionary theory; Aurobindo grants it this theory. Before him, liberation was an individual matter. What he proposes is a cosmic liberation, the entire universe must converge on God and the evolutionary process of all things must continue until that objective is fulfilled, that is, until the entire cosmos is deified; this theory, without its determinism, is altogether Mahayana. Although this proposal appears philosophically great and sublime, liberation continues to be a personal project, and we know that very few achieve that goal. The philosophies that venture a teleology that must be fulfilled inexorably seem decidedly better structured, but apart from the fact that we have already seen enough failures in this sense, these predictions have nothing philosophical about them; what is truly philosophical is sticking to the truths that conform to reality and not to an expression of desires.

I have observed too often that Hindus do not want to acknowledge their debt to Buddhism; We see it in Shankara, in Aurobindo and even in a current commentator on him, Shejoee Pandey (*Sri Aurobindo and Vedanta Philosophy*), who sees in this philosopher the definitive synthesis that Hinduism needed, and who comments on several Western evolutionists, without even mentioning Buddhism. I believe that the error of so many Hindus lies in continuing to see the stigma of heterodox in Buddhism, instead of accepting it as complementary and part of the same tradition that has been interrelating Dharma and Dhamma and structuring the Indic civilisation. Mahayana Buddhism has, in effect, as we will see below, a project of universal liberation: the bodhisattva vows to be reborn as many times as necessary in order to "liberate every last blade of grass." But he does not venture to proclaim that this has to happen because a God wants it that way, in the manner of Aurobindo, he simply limits himself to doing everything possible to realise this *ideal*.

In my conception there is a dependence of matter on spirit, but it is not absolute; matter is not determined by spirit. It is impregnated with the *primary manifestations*, whose spiritual nature exerts their influence on things and all living beings. However, these, due to their material nature, need to be independent and have the relative freedom to assimilate or move away from said influence that remains latent. In my experience and from what I observe in nature, I do not find a predetermined teleology. In our species it is clear that we can choose to move closer to our *unitive faculties*, which are the ones that perceive the *primary manifestations*, or to move away from them. This occurs in individuals and in societies, which go through states of apogee or perigee, due to their approaching or moving away from *universal Consciousness*. But the definitive triumph of the Good or of the Beautiful, or of Order, cannot be proven; it is laudable as an aspiration of desires, but I consider it imprudent and even dangerous to guarantee it, for this reason my philosophy rejects all determinism.

The Evolution of the Spirit in Buddhism

It is my purpose, then, to point out some parallels on the philosophical plane between Hinduism and Buddhism. Since I have commented extensively on Buddhism in *The Evolution of the Spirit* (where I refer the reader for more information), here I will touch only some points essential for this purpose.

In my view, both Hinduism and Buddhism implicitly contain the idea of spiritual evolution in two basic points common to both doctrines: the theory of reincarnation and that of *karma*. The latter causes all human acts to accumulate in a memory that transcends individual lives and is projected into successive lives. Since both doctrines provide adequate moral means to overcome the ineluctable laws of *karma*, that is, the yogas, which are basically the same, the human being can use them to evolve until he reaches definitive liberation by leaving the incessant process to which he is subjected by the pull of the wheel of life.

The Mahayana Buddhist school has a clear approach and a specific program of action to make the spiritual evolution of living beings effective. Briefly, it is like this: the Buddhist, like the Hindu, aims at the liberation that is achieved through spiritual techniques that include moral behaviour. But once it has been reached, the Buddhist sage or bodhisattva, by means of a vow, rejects the Nirvana that corresponds to him due to his elevated knowledge. The very wise Nagarjuna, speaking of the *bodhisattvas* in his *Treatise on the Transformation of Bodhicitta*, says: "They know very well that all kinds of suffering (which they and all those for whom they sacrifice themselves must undergo) are, in one sense, apparent and unreal, while in the other they are not." *Bodhicitta* is the Mind, I would say universal, that the Mahayana strives to awaken; from this Mind everything is presented as unreal, that is, as Maya; another concept shared by both doctrines.

Said memory differs in its mechanism in the two doctrines: in Hinduism it is the soul that remembers and transfers *karma* to the new born; in Buddhism it is not the particular soul that remembers but rather *karma* is stored in a universal repository (*Alaya-Vijñana*) that is responsible for collecting moral debts. It is not clear in Buddhism how *karma* falls on the particular subject; as I understand it, it extends over the entire species and we all pay the debts of our ancestors. This will not seem fair to the moderately just (the entirely just have already freed themselves from *karma*), but when we look at the historical circumstances in which we find ourselves, we see that it is very reasonable, since we have daily proof that we pay for our historical inheritance and suffer the mistakes of our neighbours. That is why I am inclined towards this theory of *karma*, which applies to everyone; although I must admit that given human psychology and, precisely, the attachment to the ego that most suffer, the theory of guilt and personal payment is a more effective incentive; but this is alien to universal or philosophical truths.

The *Alaya-Vijnana* is the fundamental Idea of Asanga and his brother Vasubandu, creators of the Yogacara school, named for the importance they assign to Yoga; another trait in common with Hinduism, which we must remember. *Vijnana* is usually translated as consciousness, *Alaya-Vijnana* being the term they have chosen to designate *universal storehouse Consciousness*; this, in effect, groups all consciousnesses into one. From what I understand, all the objects of the World acquire their reality by thought (*vijnana*), therefore everything is contained in the *Alaya-vijnana*. This is the common foundation of all the elements of existence. It is the all-conserving Mind, or Storehouse Mind. The raison d'être of the *Alaya-vijnana*, says Vasubandhu, consists in the retribution of our actions. "It is charged with all the elements of phenomenal existence and is the cause of future sensations." "It contains all the seeds of all future life" (*Karma*). "Under the influence of our good or bad acts, our fundamental Mind stores the seeds of future experiences that will contain its retribution." The *Alaya-vijnana* maintains, then, the wheel of reincarnations of each individual indefinitely. "The pre-natal forces (*Karma*) depend on the Transcendental Illusion, but they can never produce a rebirth when Knowledge has been attained" (Transcendental).

Shankara has an objection to this school, "If the *Alaya-vijnana* is regarded as the permanent self, the distinctive feature of Buddhism that there is nothing permanent disappears." (*635*) Indeed, for Buddhism the only permanent thing is impermanence. This, which atomic physics came to discover in the 20th century and which came to obsess Bergson, was experienced by the Buddha in the sixth century B.C. and by all the Buddhist teachers who have confirmed the doctrine. Of course, it does not end there, rather it starts there. The end is liberation or Nirvana; and here is the crux of the matter. What Shankara does not notice is that these philosopher brothers are in search of a concept that designates the first Reality. Shankara looks to a Buddhist principle applied to material reality and not to spiritual Reality, which these philosophers are trying to express. Strictly speaking, no one ever said that Nirvana was impermanent; what the Mahayana does is to adjust this concept. Buddhism is based, as we will see, on an Immutable and Eternal principle comparable to Brahman; it is just that it never goes so far as to make of it a personal God.

Shankara, who owed so much to Buddhism, as we will see later, insists on establishing the differences, since he was in optimal conditions to establish the essential unity between *Dhamma* and *Dharma*. As usual in my philosophy, my interest is not to highlight the pre-eminence of my thinking, but that of the truths themselves, which we find exposed with different terminology in all idealisms, that is, the universal truths in which we all participate. In other words, the true lover of wisdom is not interested in showing his own but in making others wise; this is the very objective of philosophy, and it is what we need most in this world.

In *The Awakening of Faith in the Mahayana*, Asvaghosha, another genius of Buddhism, begins by clarifying that in the text *maha* (great) indicates the greatness of the Essence, of the attributes of the *Tathagatagarbha* and of its influences "that generate good causes and effects in this and the other world". This has a double consequence, both being of the greatest importance. Firstly, *The Awakening of Faith in the Mahayana* is not reduced to a doctrine but rather points to its objective: awakening. Secondly, *Mahayana* should not be understood here as opposed to *Hinayana*; with which Asvaghosha, although he establishes some differences, puts an end to an old (and often sterile) controversy that diverted attention from what is essential, towards which he goes without delay. And this is how he introduces us to the concept of the Mind "which represents the essence of the *Mahayana*." (P.2)

This Mind has two aspects: the Absolute and the relative. "Each of these aspects encompasses all states of existence," because "these aspects are mutually inclusive." They are not, then, two realities but One encompassed by the One Mind. Nevertheless, surely to avoid the misunderstandings of his predecessors, Asvaghosha decides to approach the perception of reason and tries to explain the differences within the Unity, which does not stop being such. "The Mind in terms of the Absolute is the World of Reality (as Unity) and the essence of all phases of existence in its entirety." All things are comprehended by the One Mind, so that they participate in its essential virtue that "transcends all forms of conceptualisation." Hence the term *Tathatà*, whose more correct translation would be, in my opinion, *as it is in Itself*; for it is closed in on Itself (although without leaving anything outside). This makes it unique, incomparable and, as a result, indescribable. Asvaghosha says skilfully: "The term *Tathatà* is, as it were, the limit of all verbalisation, whereby a word is used to end words" (*P.3.C.1.a*).

Tathatà is the name the Buddha used to refer to himself; surely to avoid talking about "I" or "me". Hence the concept *Tathàgata-garbha, the Matrix of Tathagata* where, as in an embryonic state, the capacity for awareness and enlightenment of all sentient beings is found, the "Buddha Nature" that we all possess in a latent state and that the *Dharma* or Buddhist doctrine has as its purpose to awaken. But this *Dharma* is born only from the *Dharmakaya*, which is another name to express the same thing. Thus we read in the *Avatamsaka Sutra* that the *Dharmakaya* "is working on all things to lead them to Nirvana." And Asvaghosha: "Since the Essence of the Mind settles in the *Dharmakaya*, this is called *original illumination*. And the *Avatansaka* adds: "The universe becomes but this Body (as spiritual Unity, the *Dharmakaya*) remains eternally."

These terms, which constitute the axis on which Asvaghosha's work revolves, will remain forever in the Mahayana language. And in this lies the importance of this work: it summarises the previous thinking and leaves the Mahayana philosophy established on foundations as deep as they are solid. In his effort to make it more understandable, our philosopher says that *Tathatà*, which is nothing other than the Absolute, can be regarded in terms of two aspects: As truly Empty and as truly not Empty. "It is Empty because from the beginning it has never been related to any contaminated state of existence, (...) and it has nothing to do with thoughts conceived by a mistaken mind (unenlightened)". We see, then, that he incorporates Nagarjuna's theory of Emptiness but is not content to present only its negative aspect. *Tathatà* is also *not Empty* because the "true Mind is eternal, permanent, immutable, pure and self-sufficient". Asvaghosha boldly takes a fundamental step here by announcing the positive aspects of the Absolute, albeit that this had already been done by Vasubandhu in his own way. We see in this process how the Idea of a cosmic Mind that will inspire the Zen masters, in particular the great Huang Po, is being structured.

The concept of *Dharmakaya*, which will eventually replace that of *Alaya-vijñana*, is an impersonal entity that emanates wisdom and compassion (*prajna* and *karuna*) in the world (I would say in the *Universus*), which is what the human being needs to realise this cosmic project. It is the Absolute or the Buddhist Brahman, also called the Essence of the Buddha. I consider the *Dharmakaya* to be the most sublime and correct idea that philosophy has produced to refer to the Prime Mover. My conception of a universal Consciousness that emanates the primary Manifestations, to which I have already alluded, resembles the Dharmakaya enough to maintain that there is a superposition of Ideas that ratify a fundamental Truth. The Dharmakaya, in effect, emanates *Prajna*, Intelligence, and *Karuna*, Feeling, which summarise the *primary manifestations of universal Consciousness*, attributes in which all beings participate. We then see how Buddhist idealism converges with Western idealism. The next step is to show the convergence of Hinduism with Universal Idealism.

Part 4
Hinduism

The Vedas

It would be excessive to make an exhaustive commentary on the Vedas here, so I will limit myself to highlighting some significant aspects of them. Although the Vedic gods have practically disappeared, Hindus have an evident tendency to preserve these texts as an integral part of their tradition. Moreover, if there is an orthodoxy in Hinduism (we will speak of this later) it is given by the Vedas, considered to have been revealed and therefore sacred.

This already requires some important clarifications, necessary in particular for the Westerner, whose externalised vision does not allow him to understand the need to preserve non-existent gods. However, the key to the matter is precisely there. The Hindu has an *internal vision* and a *particular intuition* that allows him to see behind things, and also beyond personalised and represented gods. It is enough to see the images of the gods that are carried in processions today; one could almost say that they are abstract representations. So many of these celestial gods and those depicted in images are expressions of something that transcends them. The Hindu does not forget or lose his transcendent vision. It is essential that the Westerner become aware of this, not only to understand Hindus, but also the matter of religion in general.

Varuna, god of the heavens in the *Rig-Veda*, is the personification of Order and the one in charge of enforcing it, rewarding the good and punishing the bad. As we will see later, in the mythical-historical order, Varuna has been equated to Uranus, although as executor of the moral Order I believe that it is appropriate to equate him to Zeus. In my opinion, the value of this god lies in the fact that he announces, albeit in a very incipient way, *the universal moral Order*, which in my philosophy is a *primary manifestation of the Essence of the Universus* "The unbreakable mandates are established in you, oh god impossible to deceive." (*Him. 219*) Varuna is all-seeing; his eye being the sun, there is nothing that he fails to see: "The all-seeing one rises, the sun, eye of Varuna." (*Him. 597*) Thus, "Varuna is the witness of everything." Thence, the Hindu intuits that his consciousness is seen from a Consciousness that transcends him, that is, that does not end in his individuality.

Agni, fire, is not a prominent god in the Hindu pantheon, but is an indispensable element in all sacrifices. He is, like Hermes, an intermediary between the Earth and heaven, between men and the gods. In his golden chariot he accepts the sacrifices for the gods. "You are the welcome messenger who carries the offerings to the gods, O Agni, driver of the sacrificial chariot." (*Him. 44*) Additionally, he "is the driver of knowledge" (*Him. 60*) Agni also "knows order" (*Him. 145*) Even today Agni participates in all rituals, "driving evil away from us by his flames". That is why Hindus nowadays draw the heat of a flame to their face with their hands.

A constant that we find in the *Rig-Veda* is the anxiety for immortality, or, what amounts to the same thing, to be like the gods, to reach the world of the happy, as in Greece. In the hymns to Soma, a personification of a probably hallucinogenic drink, which "is the source of inspiration", "the source of happiness", this aspiration is clear: "Where the light is eternal (...) take me to the immortal world, oh Soma", "Where life is free." "Where there is happiness, where there is joy and pleasure, where desires are fulfilled, there make me immortal" (*Mand. IX*)

Vishnu, the Hindu Apollo, becomes an outstanding god in the *Yajur-Veda*, as if his light had been growing, and his importance has continued to increase to this day. On the way, other incarnated gods have been identified with this solar god. All of his appearances have been to save humanity from disaster; in one of them he rescues the Earth itself, sunken in the primordial waters, thus giving birth to life. The *Yajur-Veda* speaks of one of these feats, on which the myth of an avatar will later be woven: in three leaps Vishnu covers the three realities differentiated by the Hindu. "He took a step on Earth, a second step in the atmosphere, and a third step in the heavens." In this way the solar god creates the universe. "I have no words to describe the glory of the *Paramatman*. It is he who created the earth, the atmosphere and the sky."

This relationship with the universe is of extreme importance to understand Hindu mentality, religion and philosophy, since it is this that marks the continuity from the mythical period to the rational period. The Hindu, like the Greek, never disintegrated from the Cosmos, nor followed the process of individuation and alienation suffered by the post-Hellenic Westerner. Since the very purpose of this work is to reintegrate modern man into said universal Order, I consider it pertinent to put forward the living example of the Hindu civilisation.

It should not surprise us, then, to find concepts that transcend the gods, and this is of great importance because they express the tendency towards the Absolute that will take shape until it is reflected in the *Upanishads* as Brahman. One of these concepts is *Rta*, which I am interested in highlighting because it is assimilated to Order, in my philosophy a primary manifestation of the World's consciousness, and which is seated at the very root of universal Idealism. Of course, the concept of *Rta* is not developed or expounded in philosophical terms in the *Rig-Veda*, the oldest extensive text of humanity. *Rta* existed before creation, so we must assume that the universe was in need of said Order to be formed. If so, it agrees with my conception. The order necessarily implies a universal moral Order, something to which not only men but also gods must conform. Radhakrisnan (in *Indian Philosophy*) rightly recalls that the *Greek conception of a moral life as total Harmony or Order* is suggested in the concept of *Rta*.

I have already spoken of the luminous gods common to the Greeks and Hindus. They have always had a particular fascination, respect and affinity for light. *Deva*, who in time came to signify divinity, in the days of the *Rig-Veda* signified brilliant. Once again, it is not about the fascination for an external brightness but about the relationship of that light with an inner light, with intelligence and, ultimately, with an illumination of consciousness. The hymns dedicated to Aurora, who with her chariot precedes her lover the sun, *Surya*, are the most beautiful and inspired by the Vedic poets. The reader should not forget that, according to my vision, the Beautiful is a primary manifestation of the Essence of the World and that this perception is more accessible to poets than to philosophers. Singing and worshiping the beauty of the world is a very effective means of remaining integrated in it. Even today in Benares, I have seen it myself, Hindus repeat the ritual of worshiping Aurora and Surya. It is known that many other peoples, including, of course, the Greeks, practiced this, but the Hindus retain a direct perception and mythical-poetic vision and, ultimately, what matters is that they *feel the need to remain integrated in the World*, and, as I have insisted, *are a living example of this tradition*.

Max Müller, who dedicated his life to translating these texts and commenting on them, coined a term that can help us understand the Hindu way of seeing and intuiting. *Henotheism* means that the believer, in addressing a particular god, sees and feels him as if he were the supreme God. This explains not only the way in which the Vedic hymns are expressed, addressed to the different gods with equal reverence, but also the transformation over time that the Hindu gods followed, who replaced the preceding ones, or acquired a dimension that they did not have before, or that lay dormant, like Vishnu. This finds its explanation in what has already been said: the form that the divinity acquires does not matter to the Hindu, since behind it he always finds a Spirit that is universal and expresses *the Sacred* that he experiences in his soul. (Some Brahmins with whom I have discussed henotheism disagree with the use of this term).

However, henotheism is manifest in the *Rig-Veda,* where there are several creators who, in turn, appear to be unique: in one of the versions, at the beginning of time, only the primordial waters that are identified with Chaos existed. Hiranyagarba is born from them, puts Chaos in order and the universe results from this order. Elsewhere, we find that "He who created the six regions of the universe is Prajapati." (*Mandala I*) In the *Yajur-Veda* it is Vishnu who appears as the Creator, his body being the universe; so in this *Veda* the idea of pantheism is manifest. However, it is not naive pantheism that takes material reality as the only God, since the universe is an extension of the Creator. This idea seems to be common to all the Creators, and it is of extreme importance, since it implies that everything that exists, including, by the way, our species, is an inseparable part of the divinity; hence the respect the Hindus have for everything that exists. Finally, it will be Brahma, implying the idea of self-consciousness in the act of creating, and as a universal spirit (*Purusha*) who will prevail as Creator. Contemporising these last two versions, the Vaishnavite iconography represents Brahma as an extension of Vishnu's navel (the centre of the world). There is, however, a term common to all the creators of the World, they are all *Paramatman*, the great Soul, the universal Soul, an idea that we find in the Western idealists, in Schelling in particular.

So, in India all living beings have a soul, which is like an individualisation of the universal Soul, thus everything is permeated with spirituality. "The *atman* (individualised, particular) is always moving. When life is over, the *atman* leaves the physical body and enters a new one. The *atman* resides in the physical body but is immortal" (*Mand. I*) It should be remembered that the immortality of the soul was accepted by the Christian Church in the fifteenth century, inspired by Ficino's vision who, as a neo-Platonist, accepted reincarnation. The difference lies in the fact that for him, Plato and the Hindus, the soul necessarily pre-exists birth, while for the Church it is born with birth, which is very difficult to prove and believe, since it is half immortal and never ceases to be individual. Hindus accepted the soul as immortal since the *Rig-Veda*, some 3,000 years earlier, and this belief remains unchanged to this day. "The physical body and the atman are together, but their destination is different", because, "The atman reaches high births and low births" (*Mand. I*) Here, the theory of karma is announced by which acts are projected into the future. As all beings have souls, they transmigrate from one being to another. In the epic we find numerous examples: the crow that dies defending Rama's wife explains to him, in his agony, his past life as a human who fell into error; a jackal confesses his mistakes that led him to that state, etc. The ethical scope of this doctrine of essential equality between all beings, and the ecological consequences that it implies, distilled in Hindu culture for 3500 years, can be understood.

The Heritage of the Vedas

The reaction against the *Vedas* in the field of Hinduism itself had its justification. Nevertheless, Hindus have felt the need to preserve them, not only to maintain their tradition (we know that Hinduism is defined more by its tradition than by its doctrine), but also because there were salvageable pieces in the *Vedas* that latently announced a doctrine. The most luminous Idea, the highest concept that we find in the *Rg Veda*, is that of Purusha, who is identified with the Universal Soul, or Paramatman, and with Brahman. This Idea, as we will see, will be the great leap that Hinduism will take over Samkhya. However, we find this Idea at the end of the *Rg Veda* in *Mandala X*, which undoubtedly is a much later interpolation, made more than half a millennium later, that is, much closer to the *Upanishads* than to the original text. It would be an interpolation similar to that of the *B. Gita* in the *Mahabarata*, which would also radically change the dimension of the work. This *Mandala* clearly belongs to another period; so much so that it speaks of the later Vedas: “The gods and sages saw Virat and Purusha and offered a sacrifice in their honour.” “From this sacrifice came the mantras of the *Rig Veda*, the hymns of the *Sama*, the mantras of the *Atharva*, as well as those of the *Yajur Veda*.”

This *Mandala* tells us about the Creation, and even prior to it: “Destruction and chaos prevailed before the Creation began.” The text implies that before even Chaos there had been a destruction, which confirms the belief, held by ancient writings, in universal cycles of creation and destruction that occur after countless *Kalpas* have elapsed. “After the destruction there was neither truth nor untruth.” “There were no worlds then.” Therefore, “The time of Creation became necessary.” Then, “The idea of Creation entered the mind of the Paramatman.” “With the power of his mind He created the origin of the seeds.” And, “With the intelligence of his heart he then created the elements that constitute the universe.” To this the *Mandala* adds a phrase that will be repeated and commented on by the *Upanishads*, and that Shankara will use to support his theory of non-duality: “Brahman alone was there.” “Apart from Brahman there was nothing else.”

However, perhaps to continue the tradition established in the original *Rg Veda*, *Mandala X* also speaks of other creators in similar terms, as if referring to the same thing: “Before the act of creation, only Hiranyagarba was there.” “He is the Paramatman, He is the one who has created the universe.” Actually, Hiranyagarba is the original golden egg referred to in ancient cosmogonies. Although in the text he is also identified with Prajapati, whom the *Rg Veda* announced at the beginning as the Maker: “He who created the six regions of the universe is Prajapati.” (*Mand. I*)

Another concept mentioned in *Mandala X*, which will be reinstated and commented on profusely in the *Upanishads*, is *Om*, although it is still seemingly applied to the old association of sacrifice: “There are five steps that lead to sacrifice.” “The fifth step is the sacred syllable *Om* with whose chant I perform the sacrifice.”

We must recognise, however, that at the beginning of the *Rig-Veda* the key to the ultimate and definitive knowledge had already been announced: "When the *atman* unites with the *Paramatman*, it arrives at the Truth" (*Mand. I*) All the yoga's, all the philosophies, and I believe that all Hindus seek the same end. This Truth is not defined, we only know that, according to the famous statement of the *Rig-Veda*, "The Truth is one, the enlightened (learned) refer to it by different names." (*Mand. I,164*) This affirmation makes of the different visions of the soul of the world and, by extension of all the conceptions of God that the human being may have imagined, a Unity that transcends them. This single assertion, stated 3,500 years ago, was enough to have ended all religious antagonisms, but it refers to the *enlightened* who can see beyond themselves and dogma. That the Hindus have understood this message since then is evidenced in their history, in the tolerance they have had to other religions, which does not come from their apparent submission, but from the deep understanding of said Truth.

The preoccupation with peace and the principle of non-violence, which will not only be commented on in later writings but also practiced throughout India, where even today we can see in all the temples the faithful drawing fire to their faces, goes back to the first verses of the *Rg Veda*: Agni, fire, is "the protector of non-violent sacrifices." (*Mand.1*) "Agni is the non-violent." (*Mand. 8*) And in some verses addressed to the mothers of the gods, thanking the path traced by them for men, we read: "That path is free of violence and is full of love." (*Mand. 8*)

Ratifying this tradition at the end of the *Yajur-Veda* we find this mantra that continues to be repeated to this day: "May heaven generate peace. May the atmosphere generate peace. May the earth generate peace. May the water generate peace. May the herbs generate peace. May the trees generate peace. May peace prevail throughout the universe. May I attain the peace that is truly the truth." What would happen, one wonders, if all of humanity repeated this mantra every day? And in this way the *Yajur-Veda* ends: "O protector! Let there be peace. Let there be peace. Let there be peace." The first invocation refers to individual, personal peace, the second to social peace and the third to world peace. Anyone who has been to India will have heard: "*Om! Shantih! Shantih! Shantih!*"

Decidedly the most inspired and creative *Veda*, as is often the case in historical processes (as I observed in *The Spirit in History*), is the first and oldest, the *Rg Veda*. This inspiration began to decline and the hymns were progressively transformed into rituals and prayers with a supposed magical power or incantations (mantras). The *Sama Veda* and the *Atharva Veda* are reduced to prayers such as these that should accompany the rituals. The reaction of the *Vedanta* was directed against these last Vedas that had been repeating themselves for centuries. It could be said, if we observe the historical process, that Vedanta was a Renaissance of the original creative spirit, but that it substantially modified the content, giving it a philosophical dimension, by making spiritual reality, including all the gods, and material reality converge in a transcendent Unity.

The Decline of the Vedas

There we have the *Rig-Veda* and the *Yajur-Veda*. When we move on to the later Vedas, the *Sama*, the *Atharva* and, in particular, to the *Brahmanas* we find another panorama. Time has passed and so has the creative age. To my way of seeing, *the spirit has distanced itself from the Creative*, it is enclosing itself in formulas and the dogmas appear. The poetic imagination and its beauty disappear and are replaced by rigid formulas, so that the ritual becomes preeminent and indispensable and becomes an instrument of power.

The parallel with the Western Middle Ages is evident at first glance, albeit that it occurred 15 centuries earlier in India. But there are some profound differences. The "power" of the priests in India never led to the slightest violence; a Brahmin could not shed blood, human or bovine; his power consisted in making himself indispensable because so was the ritual. Furthermore, it is very possible that he really believed it given the unconscious obturation of his mind, as happens in times of spiritual perigee (for this phenomenon see *The spirit in History*). There is another factor that must be taken into account: in that period the convergence of cultures becomes evident. Aryans, who dominated in the times of the *Rg-Veda*, now have to temporise with Dravidians, undoubtedly pre-existing, and surely with aboriginal tribes, whose culture was more backward, and thus with other religions with their own gods inclined towards magic, and in general with a more elemental and earthly vision. We have already spoken of Hindu tolerance, deeply rooted among the Aryans. To this we can attribute the fact that these local gods were incorporated into the Brahmanical pantheon. This decadent and chaotic situation generated a counter-current, broadly similar to the

Reformation in Europe (about 2000 years after) which also sought to become independent from the monopoly of the priests.

The mixture of races and cultural confusion at this time produces a reaction on the part of the Brahmins, destined to establish a social and religious order. It is then that the *varna* (caste) system is formulated in which the priests are given a prominent role. I do not know if it is necessary to clarify that although Brahmins are educated in the *dharma*, only a small number of them are priests, and the proportion of these has been decreasing with time. I believe that what the Westerner does not fully understand about the *varnas*, which he has mistranslated as castes, is that fundamentally what defines them is the level of consciousness and education, and not, as he wants to believe by projecting his material vision of society, the level of power over the people. Power has always been in the hands of the *Kshatriyas* who, like the European nobleman, have been warriors and rulers. A *Brahmin* is only superior in spirit because he is closer to the Universal Spirit, to Brahman, and because he knows the texts and techniques that lead to it, and for that alone he enjoys more respect from all members of society. That is why a *Kshatriya* is educated by a teacher or guru, who is necessarily a *Brahmin*. Poor Brahmins are legion and there are even beggars. From then on, the Brahmins have had the function of maintaining the Vedic tradition, the *Dharma*, whose importance in the Indian civilisation has been decisive, to the point that it is reasonable to think that without the continuous weaving of the *Dharma* that civilisation would not have lasted 4000 years, an unparalleled fact in the history of mankind.

In the time of the *Brahmanas*, there was a split and even antagonism between the Brahmins and the Kshatriyas, the warriors and rulers. In one of the myth-avatars of Vishnu, which as we have seen had grown in importance, appears *Rama of the axe*, whose task was to kill all male Kshatriyas, which allowed the Brahmins to appropriate their women, so that they would remain forever extinct. This avatar, which seems to express no more than a wishful aspiration of some priests, is, I believe, the least renowned and least enduring. The subsequent tradition takes another path consistent with an understanding between the Brahmins and Kshatriyas, not between the Church and the State so as to subdue the other classes as in the West, but in the education of the warriors by the Brahmins and the protection of the latter by the former. It is this understanding and interchange that has made it possible to maintain the *Dharma* to this day, notwithstanding when India became independent from the British and, to a certain extent, from the Muslims in the middle of the 20th century, and adopted a democratic constitution that would officially abolish the tradition of the *varnas*, which had been part of the *Dharma* since the times referred to, from the later *Vedas* and the Brahmanas, which span approximately 900 to 600 BC.

The proof that I offer of what has been said is extracted from the same tradition that we find in the epic, which tells, precisely, the story of the most renowned and current avatars of Vishnu: Krishna, in the *Mahabarata*, and Rama, in the *Ramayana*. Krishna instructs a warrior, and Rama, a Kshatriya, retires to the forests of the Himalayas, to lead a virtually ascetic life and to listen to the learned Brahmins who have renounced the material world. This Rama is the opposite of the *Rama of the axe*, for he is an obedient warrior, a disciple and protector of the Brahmins. These retired sages, for their part, are complying with the fourth and last stage that the *Dharma* establishes precisely in those times in which the rigidity of customs was reflected. I am referring to the four ages or stages in the life of man that all Hindus must follow, the *ashrama-dharma*. The first stage consists in the study of the Vedas as a youth; the second corresponds to married life, to being a homeowner and member of society; in the third stage the aspirant gradually withdraws from society and prepares for the fourth stage; in which he definitively abandons the material world to apply himself entirely to a spiritual life (*sanyasin*). It should be remembered that these sages' places of retreat, which were visited by pilgrims or aspirants wishing to be instructed, were called Ashram, and this is the origin of the modern organised institutions that bear the same name today.

These times of the later Vedas correspond quite closely to the transition period in which Greece passes from a mythical to a rational mentality, the time of the pre-Socratics and the tragedians (in this regard see *The Roots of Art*), who incorporate the myths and legends of the epic and of history and give it an unprecedented dimension; a period that will be followed by the strictest philosophy. At the same time, without entirely abandoning their mythical perception, the sages in India will apply themselves to question, rectify and thoroughly interpret the wisdom of the past, and to solve the philosophical-religious problems implied, but with a renewed vision based on their own experience. The phenomenon, also unprecedented, will give rise to different doctrines, some that will follow the Brahmanical tradition, others that will dispense with it and that will therefore be called heterodox, such as Jainism and Buddhism. However, these will not only be integrated into society, but will contribute to the shaping of the Indian civilisation.

A Crucial Time

This theme, which I have already attended to in *The Spirit in History*, in addition to being opportune in our present exposition, deserves, due to its importance, to be emphasised.

History generates circumstances and poses problems that require answers. These take time to mature, which is what the spirit needs to *decant* it to the depths of its being to internalise and make the problem its own. This unification of the spirit with its circumstances generates the idea, and this the concept. The concepts will be clear to the extent of the luminosity of the idea. When the spirit is unified with all its circumstances, both internal (psychic) and external, the result is an Idea, the concept will be Unity, Divinity, the Absolute or something similar.

This Idea rarely appears in history, but there was a time that illuminated the minds of some privileged men almost simultaneously, between the sixth and fourth centuries BC, in India, China and Greece. The causes of this great event are not easy to determine, but there is no doubt that the circumstances were favourable at the time. Centuries of spiritual decantation and maturity had clarified the perception of the most decisive issues for man. Undoubtedly, society must have been organised enough to provide him with the leisure necessary for prolonged reflection. Leisure time has been an indispensable factor in the history of thought, but to transmute it into creativity, a particular genius is needed, which is due to a prior internal transformation. There have been no lack of external reasons to explain the phenomenon of creativity, but as long as it is not understood that inspiration is nourished by the noumenal, one will be speaking without knowledge of the facts.

The truth is that at that *crucial time* the human being and his history reach adulthood. This does not mean that from then on men would become adults, none of that, each one must grow and overcome the trials of his childhood and the whims of his adolescence, and for this he will have to acquire knowledge of himself and education. And in this, in education, this *crucial time* is the inescapable reference. It has been and will be the school of humanity, in it we find the basic structure of civilisations. An *ascending displacement of the nucleus of consciousness* towards *unitive consciousness* happens, from which transcendent intuitions are possible. The universality of these Ideas is a consequence of this.

The concept of civilisation must be seen in the light of the spirit, this is a cardinal point in our theory of history, since the survival of the spirit can far exceed the mortal collapse of the social body. Civilisation should not be confused with the state structure or even with empires. When the Spirit ignites a civilisation, when it has been experienced and incorporated, it remains lit, as only the luminous stars can suffer eclipses, however devastating, prolonged and tenacious the circumstances that caused their decline may be; the Renaissance in Europe is proof of this. But peoples cannot live idly on their cultural heritage, they need to revitalise their dynamism by rediscovering, updating and increasing what they have inherited. Staying in the memory of the past is a sign of old age.

Those who have not had access to the cultures of the Far East should know that what happened in India and China around the 5th century BC is similar in inspiration, greatness and exemplary nature to the process followed in the West in relation to Greece. There are, certainly, notable differences between the three cultures that are due to the idiosyncrasies of their peoples and to minor displacements of the spirit towards specific levels of understanding. Thus, for example, we see in Greece the most developed aesthetic and philosophical consciousness, while in India we observe a pervasive religious consciousness, both being prolific in their mythical imagination turned into the exemplary epics, and in Greece into the unequalled tragedies. China, for its part, generated Taoism and Confucianism at the same time, whose resemblance to Buddhism was such that the subsequent syncretism of the three doctrines occurred naturally. The three civilisations had in common a high level of consciousness and a refined moral conscience applied in a social structure that made them possible.

A reasonable proposition follows: every educated person knows that the cradle of Western civilisation is in Greece, that all disciplines were born or took definitive shape there: poetry, tragedy, comedy, physics, geometry, mathematics, laws with their constitutions, politics and the different forms of government, medicine, geography, history, philosophy with its ethics and aesthetics, its theory of knowledge and its metaphysics, etc. From ancient Rome to the present day all educational institutions have begun with the premises established by the Greeks. Is it not reasonable, then, that *we put back the origin of our conventional time to that exemplary moment*? The year 500 BC lends itself wonderfully to this, since the glorious golden age of Athens begins with the birth of Pericles, Sophocles and Phidias, key figures of that Birth, the seed of all the Renaissances that our culture has had and will have. In this luminous age the two basic sources of all philosophy, created by Parmenides and Heraclitus, also spring up; the value to humanity of these eternal springs is inestimable. It also coincides with the time of Confucius, Lao Tze, Buddha, Mahavira and the highly inspired anonymous authors of the *Upanishads*, who would lay the foundations for Chinese and Indian cultures. We would go back, then, to the origin of the three great civilisations that humanity has produced. The proposal becomes much more reasonable and current in this era of globalisation in which these cultures converge, since neither China nor India have to accept a reference that has nothing to do with their past, and the West has no valid reasons to continue dragging along the mummy of Christianity.

With only nuanced differences, in the same period of humanity in these three cultures, the Spirit is discovered and understood. This event, probably the most important in history, must be remembered and celebrated by all peoples, since the area of influence of these civilisations covers the entire globe. A daily reminder of that paradigmatic era of universal scope cannot be but edifying for the citizens of the world, that new being of man that is already clearly outlined. This adoption would be an important step towards the Neo-Renaissance that we propose and need and would remain as a reference and exemplary incentive for future generations.

After the Vedas

A series of drawbacks which, to my knowledge, have not been highlighted, have arisen from the belief that the Vedas are a product of revelations. In the first place, separating Hinduism from

Buddhism, a separation that has dismembered the Indic tradition, is the *gratuitous dogma* that accepts the Vedas as revealed texts (*Srutis*). This attribution of divinity causes these texts to be taken to have originated in the most remote of times: some speak of 20,000 years B.C., others of 6,000, others of 4,500, others, more objective, revolve around the first millennium BC. Given its character of divine origin, time ceases to have value and it is believed, therefore, that the more remote they are, the more value they have; evidently the intention is to attribute these texts to a mythical time.

The truth is that the pre-Aryan culture of India, which of the Indus or Harappa, developed between 2500 and 1500 BC. I will limit myself to highlighting only some aspects of this culture: Everything seems to indicate that the most outstanding god of that time was Shiva. One of the carved reliefs found in archaeological excavations shows him sitting in the lotus position (*padmasana*) meditating, that is, as Mahayogi or a god of ascetics. This could indicate that yoga, at least in its beginnings, was of pre-Brahmanical origin. On another carving he is represented with three heads, which will be seen again many centuries later in the caves of Elephanta Island in front of Bombay, although some interpret this sculpture as the Trimurti or Trinity formed by Brahma-Vishnu-Shiva, in which case it would not correspond to the relief of the Indus, but it is, without a doubt, an antecedent of a divine Trinity. To my understanding it is only Shiva, although probably representing all three powers. A dancing figure in the manner of Shiva Nataraja has also been found in Harappa, and in yet another we see him with a bow. These images sufficiently prove that Shiva was a pre-Aryan god. There are also figures that seem to express the cult of Mother Earth, which we do not find among the cult of the Brahmins, whose gods, with the exception of Aurora, were all male, women being only their consorts. Also striking among the carvings and figures of the Indus is the representation of the animals that would later be the vehicles for the gods or *vahanas*: Shiva's bull, Durga's tiger, Indra's elephant, etc.

Regarding one of the Aryan gods, I find it illustrative to highlight this antecedent: Robert Graves tells us of Uranus, who became the first Olympian god of the Greeks: "Uranus, whose name came to mean 'the sky', seems to have won his position as First Father by being identified with the pastoral god Varuna, one of the of the Aryan male trinity;" (we have already seen that he was also the god of the sky in the *Vedas)* "Uranus's marriage to Mother Earth records an early Hellenic invasion of Northern Greece, which allowed Varuna's people to claim that he had fathered the native tribes he found there, though acknowledging him to be Mother Earth's son." (*The Greek Myths*). Since Varuna is a prominent god among the Aryans who invaded India, this fact leads us to think that it was the same people or a branch of them that invaded Greece. The similarities that I have pointed out and will point out between these two peoples who, as we know, have common linguistic roots, tend to confirm this conjecture.

We know that of the ancient *Vedas*, the *Rig, Yajur, Sama* and *Atharva*, only a few fragments, some maxims or rituals have remained in force, the rest have been forgotten. The gods to whom these texts are addressed have simply ceased to exist and the few that have remained have been transformed in such a way that it could be said that they are not the same. Only Vishnu is preserved, although with a new dimension given by the later Vedas. It is said that Shiva is a continuation of Rudra, but in this adaptation a fundamental transformation takes place: Rudra is a god of Nature like others of the Brahmins, Shiva, as we saw, is a god of the Dravidians who was gradually introduced. The Brahmins initially rejected him, as is clear from the legend of Shiva's first wife who throws herself into the fire because her father, a Brahmin, does not accept him, but he is eventually accepted into the Hindu pantheon centuries later. In other words, Shiva, who was heterodox, became, after the ancient *Vedas*, orthodox. Rudra was then the one who "nourishes and preserves the universe" (*Rg Veda, Mand. 2*); this function will be entrusted to Vishnu; Shiva will be the destroyer.

Historians and archaeologists attribute the end of the Indus culture to the invasion of the Aryans from central Asia, who conquered the Indus valley and then the Ganges between 1400 and 1000 BC. The oldest of the *Vedas*, the *Rg*, dates from that time. Complicating the accuracy of the dates, however, is the fact that almost all Hindu literature has been the subject of subsequent additions or interpolations. So we find different themes, concepts and modes of expression within the same text. This has led some authors to see a philosophical sector in each of the Vedas called "*Upanishads*".

In any case, what I am interested in highlighting is that what I understand by the *Upanishads*, properly so called, speak of Brahman as the Absolute and belong to a time after 700 BC, in which *another mindset and perspective* reveal an *evolution of the spirit produced by a direct vision of the Transcendent*. This was very different from the previous era in which there were only isolated intuitions, more or less correct, that imagined different gods that in their turn exercised all the powers that were sung to in hymns or directed to in prayers.

The new way of seeing, thinking and reasoning is the one that assimilates Buddhism to the Upanishads. We are talking about a new era in the evolution of the spirit that corresponds, as we have seen, to that of the pre-Socratics and the tragic poets in Greece, to the Chinese thinkers Lao-Tse and Confucius. We are talking of an *awareness* that marks a milestone in history, of a peak reached by man, so high that it continues to be exemplary. This *new perspective of the spirit* differed so much from the previous one that it produced a rejection, not only on the part of Buddhism and Jainism but also on the part of the authors of the *Upanishads*; and this same reaction would not have occurred without such awareness. In the words of Radhakrishnan (in *Indian Philosophy*): "The progress of the *Upanishads* over the *Vedas* consists in increasing the emphasis on the monistic view *suggested* by the Vedic hymns, by shifting the centre from the external to the internal world, in a protest against the externalism of the Vedic practices, and in the *disregard for the sacredness of the Vedas*" (Italics mine). The *Upanishads* themselves declare: "Two kinds of knowledge must be known: the higher and the lower. The lower knowledge is that of the *Rig, Yajur, Sama and Atharva Vedas* (...) The higher knowledge is that by which the Indestructible Brahman is apprehended." (*Mundaka Up. I,4,5*) A euphemism to avoid saying that the higher knowledge is that of the *Upanishads*. The rupture is evident, we are talking about another knowledge and another reality. The old gods have disappeared or lost their value, only the Absolute remains. Illustratively, in another *Upanishad* we see that Brahman has a straw in his open hand that the god of wind, Vayu, cannot blow away, the god of fire, Agni, cannot burn, etc.: the Vedic gods have lost their power. At best, in the *Taittiriya Up.*, which is more condescending to the traditional gods: "Brahman is the Self; the other gods are the members of it." (*I,5*)

In this time of transition, the rejection of ritualism, of the power of the Brahmins, of the marked distinction of castes and other external facts have been highlighted, but, in my opinion, what is fundamental has not been emphasised: *the change of mentality that led to seeing, thinking and feeling differently*. The world appeared different, the Supreme Being had become depersonalised, *the mind had been unified, the Absolute had been discovered*. This is what must be understood: it is not about particular doctrines here, the Absolute does not have doctrines, it only depends, for the human being, on the *level of consciousness* reached.

It will suffice to expose the resemblance between the *Upanishads*, Buddhism, the pre-Socratics and Plato. The *Mundaka Up*. says that by higher knowledge the sage becomes aware of: "That which cannot be seen, nor seized, which has no origin and no qualities, no eyes nor ears, no hands nor feet, the eternal, the omnipresent (all-pervading), infinitesimal, that which is imperishable, that it is which the wise regard as the source of all beings." (*I,6*). Buddhism says: "Empty and calm and devoid of ego / It is the nature of all things: / There is no individual being / That in reality exists." "All beings in the world, / Beyond words they are and expressions, / Their ultimate nature, pure and true, / Is like unto vacuity of space." (*Mahayana-abhisamaya Sutra*). Plato says: "It is more real (the soul) that adheres to what is always similar, to the immortal and to the truth." (*Rep. 585,c*) and in Phaedrus: "That science which is of what the Being truly is," "is colourless, formless, intangible" and "is seen only by understanding." (*247,d*) And Empedocles had already advanced: "It is not possible to approach (the divinity) with our eyes (...) because it is only an august and inexpressible spirit that with rapid intelligence encompasses the entire universe." (*Ammonius, De Inter. 249*). And Heraclitus: "For those who have awakened there is one and the same world" (*Plut. de Sup. 166 c*) I have, therefore, reasons to suppose that Heraclitus's fundamental intuition is that of the Unity that underlies all things, and this Unity is necessarily immutable, in the face of which the becoming becomes patent and even vertiginous. In other words, Heraclitus's fundamental intuition is the same as that of Parmenides, except that the latter remains contemplating the Immutable, as Shankara will do, while the former turns his gaze from that perspective towards the becoming. Heraclitus looked out from this perspective, for this reason he believes that "the soul is immortal, because when it leaves it marches towards what is of its own nature, towards the Soul of All". (*Aetius IV, 7.2*) That is to say that the basic Ideas of *Unity* and of the *universal Soul*, as well as the *immortality of the soul*, not individual, but as a participant in the Soul of All, are already at the origin of Greek philosophical thought. The similarity, not only in the spontaneous and synthetic language, but also in the content of the *Upanishads* is evident. These quotes suffice for our purpose.

It is evident that the *Upanishads*, the Buddhist *Sutras*, the pre-Socratics and Plato are much more assimilated to each other than to the ancient *Vedas*. We see in them a different mind-set, the product of a higher perspective and clearer vision. What the ancient Vedas barely intuited, they experience, what the ancient Vedas sang poetically, they perceive directly; it is this that allows them to take it to a philosophical plane. Now, in addition to these psychological and philosophical reasons, which support my proposal, there are currently historical reasons. Given the obvious obsolescence of religions of Semitic origin, humanity needs to resort to solid doctrines, truly universal, not based on dogmas, but on the *knowledge achieved by a high level of consciousness*; it is this that marks the difference with the Vedas and the similarity between these doctrines. It is essential that this similarity, overlap and tacit agreement in these convergent Ideas be understood.

In truth, although I consider it of great importance to converge Hinduism, Buddhism, and Platonism, my interest is aimed at *unifying human consciousness*, it is towards this destiny that my philosophy points. Moreover, once unified, the understanding of these doctrines becomes clear to the consciousness. And vice versa, I believe that these doctrines, freed from all dogma, can contribute to said realisation; hence my interest in making these discriminations. We are, it will be understood, very far from a syncretistic proposal, since everything is resolved by accepting that Moksha, Nirvana and Satori occur thanks to the unification of the mind, and that this is the *cosmic Mind or universal Consciousness* that expresses universal idealism proposed by my philosophy.

Samkhya in Hinduism

A characteristic that has accompanied Hinduism throughout its long existence, and is essential to understanding its spirit, is that it is inclusive. It is appropriate to see in this attitude the intention of finding truths rather than establishing a closed doctrine. This attitude, which responds more to a philosophical spirit than to a religious one, has enabled Hinduism to incorporate ideas or theories of doctrines foreign to its own, for which, once again, we find the concept of orthodoxy artificial. We have already seen, and will continue to see, the interrelationship it has with Buddhism and the incorporation it has made of theories and concepts of this philosophy; in the same way it has not hesitated to integrate Samkhya philosophy. This has been inserted and extended in such a way in India that we find it in the *Upanishads*, in the *Gita*, in the *Yoga Sutras* of Patanjali, in literature, particularly in the epic and in the *Puranas* that make up the very tradition of Hinduism, and even in less orthodox branches such as *Tantra*, so it is essential when talking about Hinduism.

Samkhya philosophy is so old that it is perhaps the first in the history of mankind. It goes back to the time of the early *Upanishads*, so it would not be orthodox to accept these if not the ancient Vedas, but since there is not even a shadow of a god in the Samkhya system, I do not see the connection with this tradition. Decidedly it is not Samkhya that has accepted the Vedas, which are full of gods, but Hinduism that has incorporated Samkhya philosophy; for this reason it is considered orthodox.

Hinduism, strictly speaking, lacked philosophy, the *Vedas* have nothing of it, and even the *Upanishads* can not be accurately defined as such; we will speak of its particular situation. Hinduism, therefore, needed a philosophy, and this was provided by Samkhya. Hindu philosophy begins to be systematised with Patanjali, who already incorporates Samkhya, and ultimately takes shape with the commentators of the *Upanishads*, who, although they have Vedanta as a fundamental reference, do not hesitate to add the most substantial aspects of the Samkhya system and Buddhism.

The Samkhya doctrine is not what is generally understood by religion, it has a rational character and entirely lacks the devotional component. It is a philosophy, particularly a cosmology and a psychology intimately linked to morality and a theory of knowledge. Reality, for this philosophy, has a substance, entirely spiritual, the *Purusha*, and a material element, the *Prakrti*, which is the universe with all its beings. However, Samkhya stubbornly insists on keeping these two universal components separate, so it could be said to be a philosophical dualism. Notwithstanding, these two elements maintain a subtle but powerful link: *Prakrti*, encompassing living beings, includes their psychic reality, which acts as a reflection of the *Purusha*; much like Plato's view, in which human minds *partake* of Ideas or a fundamental One.

The first thing we observe in Samkhya is its conception of the mind, which is made up of the *buddhi*, which would be individual intelligence, the *ahamkara*, which designates the ego, and *manas*, the organ that includes all the senses. The whole mind, as understood by Samkhya, would correspond to what I have called individual consciousness, which is a part of the mind that attends to specific functions responding to the demands of the material world. I think that by reducing the mind to these speculative faculties too much importance is attached to them. We have already seen that in my conception they are only one aspect of the Mind.

The concept of Purusha would be like the individual Atman or the *jiva* of Hinduism, they coincide in that they are the true consciousness of which the speculative faculties are a reflection. They also coincide in that they act as a spectator, or witness as Hinduism calls it, which makes self-knowledge possible, since it observes the intentions of the self, as well as its unconscious tendencies and recognises its weaknesses. As Patanjali says: "The states of the mind are known because the Lord of the mind, the Purusha is immutable." Becoming is known by what does not become, which is always the same and therefore Is. My conception of the mind and my theory of knowledge coincide entirely with this assertion; as my *Psychosophy* can testify.

I am particularly interested in speaking of the Samkhya theory of the *Gunas*, not only because they are fundamental in this doctrine, but also because they act in a similar way to the *primary manifestations of the Essence of the World* so dear to my philosophy. They are, in effect, energies that precede and underlie the *Universus*, that is, they act not only on the stars but also on the human mind. These energies are the product of a psychology explained from the World Order; a cosmic mentality underlies this theory. The Greeks participated in this Order, it should be remembered, and it is a basic aspect that relates them to the Hindus.

The fact is that Samkhya philosophy has been embedded in Hinduism. The radical difference is that Samkhya refuses to accept a direct relationship between the *Purusha* (Spirit) and the *Prakrti* (matter), while Hinduism has always sought to establish that relationship. However, it has naturally incorporated the theory of the *Gunas*. And the curious thing about the matter is that it has adopted it without altering it, that is, without making these energies come, as might be expected, from Brahman, but rather they belong to *Prakrti*, they are cosmic forces that accompany the universal process, including the mind of the living creatures.

The *primary manifestations* of which my philosophy speaks are similar, then, to the Gunas, present in Samkhya and in Hinduism, but it is necessary to establish the differences to clarify these doctrines. In my philosophy they are subtle but powerful forces that are found both in matter and in the minds of living beings, but the *primary manifestations* are of the very Essence of the world, and they are *virtues* that accompany the *vital impulse* that generates matter and life. While the *Gunas* are expressions of the *Prakrti*, that is, not of the Purusha or Brahman, but of Nature. In this sense they resemble Schopenhauer's Will, since they are blind forces necessary for survival, and are related to the character of living beings. But both are philosophies, they do not conclude in physics, both have an escape route from matter: Schopenhauer finds it in aesthetic perception, in art, by means of which we can escape the empire of the Will, that is, of the weight and necessity of Nature; albeit not permanently (see *The Roots of Art*). Samkhya has, for its part, an ascending path that is the Sattva that allows the spirit to get rid of matter and head towards the Purusha.

In this way, Samkhya announce an evolutionary theory: When *tamas* energy predominates, beings remain in a vegetative or animal state whose life is repetitive. In the *Rajas* state there is already a dynamic that makes evolution possible, but it only takes an upward direction with the *Sattva* energy, whose destination is the Purusha. However, as we anticipated, in this philosophy the Purusha transcends all these states, including the *Sattva*, which are changing, that is, the *Prakrti* in its entirety. The Purusha, like Plato's Good, like my universal Consciousness, is eternal, invariable, always the same. Evolution, according to Hinduism, implies successive incarnations of the soul. And yet Samkhya does not speak of a universal Spirit but of multiple Purushas, although, as we shall see, it sometimes seems to refer to the One, and it is this meaning, that of a universal Purusha, that later Hinduism will develop.

My conception of the *primary manifestations* refers, rather than to the character of living beings, to the spiritual energies that underlie the character and all modes of the mind of living beings. However, they are not opposing forces but complementary. The *primary manifestations* are not a product of *Prakrti* or Nature, rather they are generators of it and accompany it in all its expressions. Although, one can admit that the transformation of the Spirit into matter does not respond to an experience of the mind. A disconnect occurs there, which is surely what has led Samkhya to keep the two realities separate. This position has, therefore, its reason for being, however, given its consequences, it seems to me to be too strict. In my conception there is, admittedly, an inference, but considering the indubitable experience from the *essential perspective* of the *constant presence of said manifestations in the mind and in Nature*, said inference seems legitimate to me. Let me explain: my philosophy admits that there is no experience of the genesis of matter, but there is an indubitable experience of the presence of the Spirit in matter, that is, of a *Unity in the Universus*.

The Gunas in Facts

The theory of the *Gunas* finds its kinship in the theory of displacements and perspectives achieved by the spirit that is supported by my philosophy, from which I will make my interpretation. While it is true that according to the Samkhya doctrine the culminating point of the spirit is found in a pure *Sattva* nature, I would still say, at the extreme of this, as if transcending it, that it would be a mistake to believe that only *Sattva* energy is necessary for the liberation of the spirit. Will, which is a higher faculty, is a characteristic of *Rajas* energy, and it is well known that without this faculty little or nothing would have been achieved or can be achieved by the human being. When there is *good* will, a dose of wisdom (*Sattva*) has *inspired* the will (*Rajas*), thus transforming this faculty into a virtue. In this case the spirit has found a *zone of equilibrium*, which, as we have seen, is part of the line that leads the spirit towards liberation. But, being such a powerful faculty, if the will is badly applied it leads to disastrous results, and this often happens when, instead of being inspired by *Sattva*, it is inspired by *Tamas*. This force is very particular and can be defined as a lack of energy, or as a force that seems opposed to *Rajas* as its power consists in neutralising the other two forces.

This causes the will to be weakened to the extent of the influence of *Tamas*; but lo and behold, this also has its positive function. I will explain: The will depends on a self, on an ego that directs it according to its intentions and knowledge, while *Sattva* energy not only is not dependant on the self, but has as its reference the Spirit itself, which transcends all individual vision. This being the case, in order to receive *Sattva* inspiration, the individual spirit must abandon its self, its individuality, to allow itself to be carried away by the Universal Spirit. And this is where the beneficial action of *Tamas* intervenes, which, I repeat, is rather a lack of action that neutralises the will and becomes positive. As can be appreciated, the positive aspects of *Rajas*, good will, and of *Tamas*, such as the opportune "laissez faire", have a subtle interrelation and establish a difficult game that requires the greatest attention of the spirit, since it is very easy to embark on a single one of these positions thus breaking the necessary balance between them. The "laissez faire" of *Tamas* in turn implies multiple dangers that, naturally, each and every one must resolve in the face of the various circumstances that arise.

Part of *Tamas* energy is the tendency that leads us to leisure. Although it is generally seen as something bad in today's Western culture, it has not always been so. As Ortega y Gasset reminds us, the Greeks knew how to distinguish between *otium* (leisure) and *neg-otium* (business), the former being a necessary condition for philosophy, the latter not. This is understandable, the retiring and contemplative life that the philosopher needs entails a strong dose of leisure (*Tamas*). For the Taoists, not only is a retiring and contemplative life indispensable for correct understanding, a conscious attitude of "*laissez faire*" (Wu Wei) is also indispensable. But, "*laissez faire*" to whom? To the Tao, the Taoists would reply. This is not the place to expand on Taoism (I have already done so in *The Roots of Morality*), suffice it to say that Tao is essentially Order or Harmony, whose equilibrium man must understand. The "*laissez faire*" is therefore a means, a path to the Transcendent, but when there is *Sattva* energy that attracts the spirit upwards. Otherwise, this attitude of letting oneself be carried away by idleness can produce numbness, in its forms of simple lethargy, sloth or moral laziness, with the consequent slide towards vices, from which it is very difficult to get out. To avoid these slippery slopes, the best remedy is usually to resort to *Rajas* energy, to a determined will to get out of that situation, even if it is only by applying oneself to any activity, neutral from the spiritual point of view; then one can think about seeing more clearly, the most important thing in these cases is to get out of the darkness.

The type of life generated by *Rajas* energy naturally offers more distractions or temptations than that of *Tamas* energy, although when it comes to pleasures, it is difficult to separate them, because the two energies are applied to the same end. When gluttony, lust, greed and other deviations are children of the will, one is within *Rajas* energy. As it bestows power and pleasure, it is very difficult to overcome these obstacles. The dangers of *Sattva* are more subtle and, therefore, more difficult to detect, they can lead to a lack of contact with everyday reality and physical needs that, when denied without carefully weighing up the consequences, can lead to psychiatric disorders. Once prey to these, one can believe many things that do not correspond to the spiritual reality in which one believes is living. Also in *Sattva* some defects are acquired, such as "spiritual" pride that can lead some to believe they are avatars or something to that effect. Nevertheless, all the virtues come from this energy or are inspired by it, generosity and altruism, temperance and wisdom, are usually a happy confluence of *Rajas* and *Sattva* energies.

It is no coincidence that those who have and need the *Rajas guna* are called Maha-rajas. In the history of India, the harmonious relationship between the Brahmin, applied to the knowledge of *Sattva*, and the *Kshatriya*, occupied with the *Rajas* tasks of war and government, has been of paramount importance. The warrior could recognise that the ultimate reality is the heritage of the ascetic; this was understood by the Buddha, who, being a *Kshatriya*, abandoned his task as a prince and sought knowledge by leading a reclusive life. And it is around this scheme, it may be said in passing, that the *government of philosophers* should be dealt with. Rama is the perfect *kshatriya* because he has a lot of *Sattva*, which is why he finds out in the end that he is pure *Sattva* (Vishnu), when he has already performed all his feats as Maharaja.

Also Plato, in *Book IX* of his *Republic*, differentiates three types of soul that seek their respective pleasures. One is that of the philosopher who seeks what is always the same, what is permanent, and that generates real pleasure; the second is the impetuous soul who seeks power and honour; the third deals with the pleasures of the body. I cannot help but see the resemblance to the three Gunas to which Hinduism adheres. Although *Tamas* is passive and may not seek pleasure, idleness or laziness is known to incline towards pleasure. The impetuous soul would correspond very well to the *Rajas* spirit, and, most importantly, the soul that seeks the permanent and real is entirely equivalent to *Sattva*.

These differences, we could add, seem to us of great importance, because when responding to different interests these spirits do not really interrelate, they are thinking of different things. I want to say that this is an important cause of misunderstanding among men, not only among the different races or cultures, but also among the different souls or Gunas. So a Greek and a Hindu sage or philosopher are closer and more interrelated to each other than are two Greeks or two Hindus who respond to different Gunas or souls. In my view, these differences are the result of the *position that the spirit has adopted*, determining it to a perspective that makes it see and seek in life what it believes to be more real and satisfying.

In old age, when the *Rajas* energy has been depleted, the spirit finds itself at a crossroads, with one path descending towards *Tamas* energy, and another ascending towards *Sattva*. Following the first it becomes like a baby who only wants protection, comfort, security, etc., following the other, it rises closer to its fullness, to its freedom.

Man must know how to overcome himself because he has a tendency (which can be explained as *Tamas* energy) that inclines him to remain in his present state. This state is not clearly differentiated, since it entails previous states, so many carry infantile states into their youth and even into their adulthood, as psychology has observed, just as in old age there are always vestiges of youth and adulthood. Remaining at these ages when one has reached old age, as is the trend in our times, for the simple reason that *Rajas* energy predominates at this time, is not a positive symptom, nor is it a consequence only of *Rajas* energy. *Tamas* is also in action and providing the incitement not to go beyond this stage, the two forces retain the spirit and impede its evolution.

Sattva energy should predominate in old age, it should predominate at all ages, but this would be too much to ask of man who needs a gradual evolution, to the point that if he makes an effort to skip one of these stages, it is quite feasible that he will fall and damage himself and this pain could make him react negatively and regress. We have the example of young people who want to follow the spiritual path without being prepared for it, who after many setbacks, due to the confrontation of energies because they want to impose *Sattva* energy when *Rajas* predominates, finally give up spiritual life. Because *Sattva* is not an energy that can be known objectively (I believe that my theory of knowledge is correctly applied to the theory of the *Gunas*) but rather unitively, that is to say, it is not enough to know that these states of the spirit exist to follow them, one must *grow* with them, and this growth depends on the *level of consciousness*.

There are, of course, several theories about the character or personality of the human being, but since they lack a transcendent dimension, they do not deserve philosophical speculation. In truth, the philosophical short-sightedness of the authors of these theories is striking: for them, the personality of the human being depends on physiological reasons, and, if they attend to moral conduct, it will be the result of social pressures or customs. In the manner of doctors, they observe man from his individual body and mind, and religion, if they talk about it, is an invention of the unconscious, although they do not explain why it occurs to man to invent it.

The samkhya theory of the *Gunas* opens our mental horizon towards planes unsuspected in the West. The theory of *the will to power*, for example, held in particular by Nietzsche and Adler, expresses a character or way of being human, but not an absolute truth. For yoga, which adopts the theory of the *Gunas*, the will to power would be a consequence of the predominance of the *Rajas guna*, which makes the individual active, ambitious, warlike, etc. Those who hold a hedonistic view of life respond, for their part, to the influence of the *Tamas guna*, which seeks goals that do not require physical, intellectual or spiritual sacrifices. The vision whose greatest aspiration is to approach spiritual reality, and sacrifices everything for it, is the result of the predominance of the *Sattva guna*; and this is what sustains yoga. The theory of the *Gunas*, as we will see, has a moral, philosophical and religious application, so it is understandable that Hinduism has incorporated it in its theory of knowledge and in yoga.

In my conception, man is born and lives on a slope, this is neither a bad nor a good factor, it is simply the necessary factor for the phenomenon we call life to take place. The human being, then, has no alternative, he has to deal with this slope, such is his condition. His animal condition inclines him downwards, his divine condition upwards. As I perceive it, there is a Principle that life and Good emanate from above, but there is no evil principle below, there is only one creative Principle, only one divine light that illuminates Life. Man is not in darkness, much less in sin, but in a penumbra on said slope, from which he can see the light above, or the darkness below. There is, then, no principle of evil that pushes him down, man descends into darkness due to his own ignorance and ascends into light thanks to his wisdom. Finding yourself, then, facing a life that implies a choice and an effort if you decide on an ascending life, you will understand the danger of a force that tends to nullify your energies, that invites or tempts you to let yourself go and obey the most primitive in your nature. But, as will be clear, *Tamas* is not there to generate evil, but as a necessary force for balance. Faced with life, man, as the existentialists had announced (although in a different context) has no choice but to choose, he is, therefore, *an essentially moral being*. In his choice, he must intuit the equilibrium between these forces that are not alien, but consubstantial to him, in order to act correctly.

The Gunas in History

We have seen that Hindus are not very fond of history, so they have not applied this energies in the historical process, however, historical and present facts can be explained, to a great extent, by means of this theory of the Gunas, since, in addition to having a universal dimension, they express three basic functions of the human mind, so intimate that it can be said that they make up the very character of individuals, which is what determines their way of thinking, feeling, seeing and believing.

Each epoch has its preferences intimately linked with its dominant energy (*Guna*), and these preferences are believed to be the model that other epochs should have followed, without seeing the defects that their preferences contain. Defects that will be seen more clearly by subsequent generations, who will react against them by imposing their own preferences, in turn believing that they are *objectively* the best that have ever existed. I am referring, of course, to the mass man who judges the past without knowledge of it. The enlightened man is never satisfied with his own time, and it is he who, with his criticism of the present and his ideals for the future, creates the bases for the following generations.

If the energies (*Gunas*) that drive these preferences or ideals at different moments or historical circumstances are known, the extremes that lead to reaction can be avoided and a middle path or balance between the extremes can be followed more easily, or one of moderate action and reaction (on this dialectic see *The Spirit in History*). When a *Guna* energy prevails, one tends to think and forge ideals according to it, and this is what leads to extremes. For example, in the Middle Ages in the West, the predominance of religiosity apparently indicated a *Sattva* energy, however, the energy was decidedly *Tamas*, which is why the arts and creativity in general were very poor. This energy was probably a reaction to the *Rajas* energy of the Roman period.

Tamas energy is the one adopted by the mass man that is characterised precisely by following the inertia that he inherits or that is imposed on him by the men of power, usually guided by *Rajas* energy. The mass man, if he inherits a religion, is faithful to it, if he receives a tradition, he repeats it, if a fashion emerges, he follows it. The sheep spirit, as Nietzsche called it, suffers from *Tamas* energy; and most are victims of this energy.

Let us take the case of Marxism which underlies a particular psychological type from which a system of thought is derived: Marx, dominated entirely by *Rajas* energy, produces an ideology in which the action of man, production, is decisive, and reacts against contemplative spiritualism. Religion is for him, then, an opium; his position could not be more extreme, and this is explained because he is obsessed with said energy. For Marx, the arts, religion, etc. were dependent on the means of production, that is to say, the *Sattva* energy (which he was obviously ignorant of) depended on the *Rajas*, and the *Tamas*, which at its best is the contemplative life, was intolerable to him. This is why he tried to create an entire society with *rajas* premises that, as it was an extreme, could only be maintained by dictatorships, by force, not by the *balance of forces*. Decidedly, there is no energy that in absolute terms is better than the others; a society cannot be sustained when motivated by a single energy, it is sustained, on the contrary, by the balance of energies.

Within this universal and philosophical context, I would like to descend to our current reality to explain a worrying phenomenon that affects life in general on our planet, which is that of overpopulation, an issue that, naturally, did not affect the Hellenic civilisation, but which particularly concerns the Indian civilisation.

Nothing is more natural than reproduction in living beings. It is not only carnal desire that leads us to it, two universal forces compel it: the élan vital and Love animating Nature. But the latter and the other centripetal forces have lost their validity in contemporary man, hence he fundamentally obeys the centrifugal, external, expansionist, reproductive impulses, to the point that the balance has been broken, and we have exceeded ourselves and overpopulated the planet. This excess has generated not only an ecological imbalance but also an improper social state, which keeps us, due to constantly renewed needs, in the elementary *stage of survival*. This constantly projects us outward, generating a *vicious circle of externalisation and alienation* of our spiritual or unitive faculties.

Needless to say that I am not proposing any form of extermination, but am only pointing out the psychic, social, biological and ecological imbalance that demands some form of control, and that, if not carried out, will end in violent forms of mass extermination.

Except for some peculiar sects, we find ancient texts that stimulate reproduction in all religions, and since these texts are considered sacred, it will be very difficult to admit that they are obsolete in this respect. But it is essential that this conclusion be reached, because we are attacking all life on Earth; including ours. Moreover, since, according to my philosophy, all of Nature is provided with intelligence as even cells and microscopic beings participate in it, the natural order will be in charge of establishing control; but let us not hope for that, because beforehand man will put up a resistance and fight, so Nature has to react excessively to excess, endangering our species. We must not forget that we depend entirely on Nature, which it can entirely do without us. Immediate awareness and appropriate action are essential. Incidentally, we can also explain this phenomenon as a consequence of an energy charged with *Rajas* and *Tamas*, and an alarming lack of *Sattva*.

The efficacy of this doctrine of the *Gunas* is unquestionable. However, in my perception, there are other universal energies to which I have already referred, which, as they are *primary manifestations of the universal Consciousness*, are also an intrinsic part of the intelligence of living beings. These forces are expressed in two directions: one is centrifugal, as in the *élan vital*, which seeks to expand, propagate, reproduce; the other is centripetal, it tends inward, to internalise itself, to unite, to integrate and ultimately leads to the primordial Unity of spirit and matter, that is, to the knowledge of the *Universus*; the Good, the Beautiful, Order and Love correspond to this.The Instinct-intelligence (another *primary manifestation*) can incline outwards, which is what we call an extroverted character, or inwards, which would correspond to the introverted character.

As in the *Gunas*, the correct thing is the proportion between these forces, since some are necessary to the body, others to the spirit. In the universe these forces are clearly shown: there are galaxies that expand towards infinity, just as there are forces of attraction and concentration; here too, balance is what makes possible the stability that is essential to life. For a detailed explanation of these universal energies the reader can refer to my treatise *The Quest for Universal Consciousness*.

Yoga, an Introduction

The recurring and perpetual obstacle that our species finds in its evolution is that each of us looks, thinks and believes using the faculties that we have inherited, with those that we already have, and it does not occur to us to think that we must improve to reach a heightened perspective from which we can see and think differently. And here lies the importance of the great discovery of the Indian civilisation: the yoga. In effect, the first thing it does is to warn us that we have to change, that we are not yet prepared to perceive and think correctly, that we are in an incipient stage that it calls ignorance. And far from ending with a warning, this discipline also provides the adequate means to overcome our current condition.

That we can differ on some doctrinal points, that we do not believe in some presuppositions, or that we do not strictly follow the steps proposed by Patanjali, does not essentially change the matter: which is that we need this discipline to transform ourselves, to be other than as we are. And this, strictly speaking, is what Hindus have done, and even many Buddhists who have adopted yoga according to their requirements and added other techniques. But let us not forget the initial warning: we are ill prepared to understand the essentials of Hinduism and Buddhism in our present condition. If we say "I don't believe in those things", we remain in a state of ignorance.

Yoga deserves special mention when talking about the Indian civilisation, simply because one cannot be understood without the other, because yoga has been inserted into the spirit of all the peoples and races that constitute that civilisation, and in this way into its customs, into the dharma that defines it. As we have seen, in fact, yoga seems to go back to the beginnings of this civilisation in the Indus Valley. Although we do not know what the theories and techniques were like in those times, we can be certain that they have evolved over the centuries. We do know, however, that at the time we have called *crucial*, yoga is definitively reflected in the nascent doctrines such as Vedanta, Buddhism and Jainism, which, although they differ in some theoretical aspects, coincide in the need to practice these spiritual techniques. Yoga, then, is a unifying, common and even defining factor of the Indian tradition.

Yoga deserves particular mention, moreover, because it is one of the least known and most misunderstood subjects in the West. It is known, yes, and even practiced by many, but as expected, the yoga that is known and practiced is the most concrete, palpable and corporal, *Hatha yoga*. But it happens that yoga is a spiritual matter by definition and its objective is precisely to free oneself from the body and from the mind's identification with it, that is, from the ego. This implies a previous radical reversal of perspective since the Westerner is decidedly exteriorised and yoga is a technique of introversion. And to this is added perhaps the greatest difficulty: yoga is not only practiced, it is lived, it is part of a custom, it is a way of life, thanks to which one remains introverted and in this way in contact with the spirit, which is yoga's objective. This makes us see the external world in a very different way, as well as the other species as similar. As all the mental faculties, in particular the spiritual ones, are transformed by yoga, external reality ultimately becomes *something else*.

Thus, for example, *prana yoga* makes no sense if one thinks that one is breathing only air, because for the yogi this is charged with spiritual forces. Likewise, it is not the same to contemplate a forest with its animals (it is often forgotten that its etymology indicates that they are *animated*), than it is to understand that each tree, each being that enables it has a soul. In short, the spirit is a priority for the yogi; practices and works come later to further penetrate that reality. According to my experience and understanding, what has preceded and precedes yoga is the conscious or latent transcendental intuition of the existence of spiritual reality, and this is what has led to the search for the most suitable means to reach that reality; and these means are the yogas. I will not repeat here what is in all the yoga manuals, the list of the techniques and their functions, but we must include historical, cultural and civilisational factors, in the Indian way of philosophising. There are also many other yogas included in these manuals, which usually respond to the particular vision of the guru.

Seeing Hindus and Buddhists to be so introverted, Westerners tend to believe that they are closed in on themselves and forgetful of others. This is what Hegel believed, due to his ignorance of the East, that we should not pay it the attention that the West gives it, and Bergson, who, for the aforementioned reason, believes that "these doctrines are insufficient." (These authors have been commented on in *The Evolution of the Spirit*). Both ignore the fact that there is, firstly, a yoga called *karma-yoga* that precisely consists of helping others, and, secondly, something that Westerners do not fully understand: that these doctrines imply that before helping others one must acquire the necessary knowledge to avoid doing evil in the belief that one is doing good; the yogi can find that knowledge in the doctrines that support the yogas.

Finally, and with good judgment, scholars have separated the Vedas into two: the *Karmakanda*, which deals with sacrifices and ceremonies in general, and the *Jnanakanda*, which, as its etymology implies, deals with the knowledge of matters of the spirit; the *Upanishads* and the Vedanta derived from them. In India, the *Upanishads* constitute the highest authority or spiritual reference that has ever been written, so we must be respectful and cautious with them.

On Knowledge in Patanjali

The obstacle that the reader will surely encounter when reading Patanjali, Hinduism, Buddhism or my commentaries, is that in order to understand them he has to have an idea or intuition of a consciousness that transcends the usual one. Patanjali's purpose is precisely to lead him to that transcendent consciousness by means of yoga, from which he will be able to observe his individual consciousness.

The Samkhya, Patanjali and the Hindu in general presuppose that the reason for being of this world and for our existence is to reach the Spirit, be it Brahman, Purusha, Isvara, etc. Since this world and our existence is material, reaching the Spirit implies a transcendence of our current condition and a transformation. Vyasa explains it like this: Everything that exists serves a purpose foreign to its own, also "the Will-to-be (so it calls the mind, the buddhi) exists for the purpose of another (being or object). On the contrary, Purusha is not designated for another," "it has its own goal." "Everything is done for Purusha." (*Y.S. II,20*)

Just as the Westerner realises the need for experience to know matter, the Hindu has reached the same conviction regarding the spirit. Yoga is a specific technique to achieve the spiritual knowledge that leads to metaphysical reality. Moreover, this technique does not end in mere knowledge, but transports the subject's spirit to said reality. It is literally a *realisation* that changes the ontological situation of the subject. The spirit, in effect, is freed from matter and the mental faculties linked to it, for this reason he calls this experience liberation.

Patanjali takes fundamental assumptions from Samkhya, such as the insurmountable distinction and separation between Purusha (the spiritual essence) and Prakriti (which would become the primordial substance of the universe); the theory of the Gunas; the human mind as a product of Prakriti and, therefore, as part of it and alienated from Purusha, but very contrary to Samkhya, it never occurs to Patanjali to philosophise. He accepts this philosophy and adds the spiritual techniques to achieve those ideals; he is pragmatic.

Patanjali does not deny material or external reality and accepts certain faculties of the mind as conducive to liberation. The mind can be cultivated to the point of reaching essential knowledge. Commenting on this knowledge, Vyasa says: that once attained, "there are no traces of false knowledge," this pure knowledge is obtained, "by cultivating the mind in three ways: by verbal knowledge, by inference and by the practice of contemplation." Vacaspati clarifies, "cultivation by verbal knowledge means by listening to the Vedas" (which implies that he maintains the oral tradition). "Cultivation by inference means thinking." That is to say that he admits thinking when is correct and conducive to the greater knowledge (*Y.S. I,48*) But this is achieved when the mind flows without disturbance thanks to meditation, or, as Vyasa says (*Y.S. I,47*), to "a constant flow of the mind." Here, Patanjali could not have been more concise because, as we know, thought implies a whole mental world, all possible conjectures, all philosophising. But we can infer that if he only grants it a single word it is because he does not assign greater importance to it; it means only that he neither rules out thought, nor promotes it. But when philosophising we must not forget something fundamental that this sage had foreseen: intelligence must be illuminated by the Spirit, that is, in its state of Sattva (*Y.S. II,18*).

The concept of contemplation is equated with a spiritual trance or samadhi. The *Yoga Sutras* speak of a reflection of Purusha in the mind, and that is why it knows, since Purusha is consciousness itself, "The *Observer* is only consciousness." But there is also an inverse reflection, the mind is observed by Purusha, as if it were a mirror that, certainly, remains impassive and unaltered. "Although pure, it sees the ideas that come to the mind" (Vacaspati), hence it is called the Observer, the Knower. I believe that this mechanism of interrelation encompasses the project of yoga, since the objective is to reach that state of purity, of a simple unaltered observer, that is, to become Purusha, "to reach the absolute freedom of the Knower" (*Y.S. II,25*) To achieve this goal, the aspirant must use what Patanjali calls "elements of yoga" (*Y.S. II,29*), that is: body postures, pranayama (controlled breathing), concentration, meditation and, finally, trance or samadhi. Now, all this is the relationship between Purusha and the mind, but no matter how elevated its state (*samprajnata samadhi*), translated as samadhi with support, the mind and the universe are still present. There is a transcendence, since one no longer looks from the self and from the cumulative faculties, but it is not the absolute transcendence that is the Samadhi without support (*asamprajnata samadhi*) in which there are no traces of the world or the mind.

Although it is not my intention to explain the yogas as a manual would do, I consider it essential to say something about the importance of morality as a path to transcendental knowledge, which in my philosophy, as in Patanjali's and in Hinduism in general, has little or nothing to do with helping others with a view to a reward. Rather, the objective is to cleanse the mind and avoid the disturbances generated by immoral intention, thought and action (*vrttis*), since nothing generates as much disorder (in my view) or disturbance in Patanjali, as this. In all these cases the objective is the calmness of the mind that allows contemplation, meditation and correct reflection, which are bridges to other planes of understanding. Among the restrictions that Patanjali advises, non-violence (Ahimsa) stands out as defined by Vyasa: "Do not cause pain to any creature in any way and at any time." The belief in reincarnation as other beings goes hand in hand with this principle. Buddhism and Jainism, the latter in particular and with great emphasis, avoid exercising violence even on insects. The other restrictions are: veracity; abstinence from stealing; abstinence from sex and from avarice; (*Y.S. II, 30*) these do not need explanations, since it is obvious that they stimulate an egoism that goes in the opposite direction to Patanjali's project.

Both in the East and in the West, there has been an insistent fall into the error that leads reason, dualistic by nature, to see all knowledge as objective or subjective. Commenting on the *Sutra IV,23*, Vyasa says, "The mind, itself an object, comes into being in relation to the *subjective* Purusha, through its modifications as the Self." I think Vyasa knows what he is speaking of, but uses erroneous language, as Purusha cannot be subjective, it is *unitive*. I believe that the introduction of the *unitive* concept is an important contribution to the theory of knowledge, that it is neither one nor the other, nor a compromise between the two, but rather a *product of direct perception* (of which Patanjali also speaks).

If we admit the basic overlap (for I have already pointed out other differences) of my concept of *unitive consciousness* with Patanjali's Purusha, it would allow me to differ on an important point in the conception of the mind and its way of knowing. Vyasa (accepted as the most authoritative commentator) says, "He who receives the object reflected in the mind is the Purusha." (*Y.S. IV,23*) And Sadananda Sarasvati translates *Sutra 22* thus: "Identifying with its own reflection in the *chitta*, (mind) the Immutable *chiti* (the Self) acquires knowledge of the *chitta* and the *object* perceived by the *chitta*." In my conception, *unitive consciousness* does not attend to the particular objects that concern individual consciousness (*chitta*), but to the essence of the objects, thoughts and actions, it observes their subtle or spiritual aspect. This is the unitive way of seeing and knowing: to see the essence of the matter directly and intuitively. The individual consciousness perceives the objects of the senses and can even compare them thanks to discernment, but when comparing them it intellects thanks to an intuition that is reflected in the Transcendent, which allows it to see the difference and compare. From this mechanism of reflection the human being obtains *relative knowledge* but ignores *absolute knowledge*. For Patanjali and Hinduism in general, this knowledge is part of Ignorance, and the true knowledge would be that of the Purusha. I think this way of seeing is a bit extreme, I prefer to speak of relative and absolute knowledge.

In my way of seeing and understanding, the reflection or illumination of the Purusha on the *chitta* in its Sattva state, coincides entirely with my vision: it is the inspiration by contact with *the Creative* of the unitive faculties at a high level of consciousness. The reference that derives from this contact is what I have called *essential perspective*. I believe that my distinction between cumulative and unitive faculties satisfactorily explains the total panorama of Mind, since the latter have their origin in and tend toward universal Consciousness. The moral conscience, the aesthetic conscience, the religious conscience and the philosophical conscience, in effect, precede all thought and transcend all cumulative knowledge. Patanjali's *chitta* or mind would be equivalent to the cumulative faculties such as discernment and memory that have the self as their centre, where feelings, desires, subconscious irruptions, etc. converge. The *chitta*, like the buddhi of Samkhya, are born from Prakrti, so they are limited to the material world, but the roots of unitive knowledge are transcendent, just as for Patanjali they are in the Purusha.

The Knower would correspond in my philosophy to *unitive consciousness*. Although this is not individual, it fulfils the same functions since it immediately knows the intentions of the self, which precede the reasons that it gives to justify its actions. Hence the enormous ethical importance that it plays as the very nucleus of moral conscience. The solution to the serious problem of misunderstanding among men is found in the establishment of the spirit in said nucleus. It is also said that the Knower is absolutely objective, and it is, in effect, when the spirit transcends the self and the faculties that it uses, it knows the desires that stimulate it and the fears it suffers. It knows all this, using my terminology, when it looks from the *essential perspective*, from the noumenal to the phenomenal and the mind linked to it. This *essential perspective* comes from the very centre of the mind, which is transcendent. In the apparently supernatural the spirit finds its true nature. Quite in agreement with this, Vacaspati affirms in commenting to Patanjali: "Moksha (liberation) is only the establishment of the Self in its own nature." (*Y.S. II,15*)

In my conception and in my language, it is with this absolute transcendence (*asamprajnata samadhi*) that *unitive consciousness* is embodied, that with samadhi with support (*samprajnata samadhi*) would be consolidated the Reality of the *Universus*, which is not an illusion, but rather reality seen from the *essential perspective*. On this subject, of capital importance, we will return when commenting on Shankara, since it is from this perspective that he develops his philosophy.

Patanjali's God

Ishvara, as Patanjali calls him, means the Lord, but he is a very particular God because he is not the creator of the universe nor does he seem to rule over it, although he possesses all the powers. Despite having powers he does not use them, because if he dealt with the particulars he would lose his absolute status, and Patanjali knows very well the distractions that particulars generate. Later Hinduism, particularly *bhakti*, will tend to forget this observation. "Ishvara is a distinct Purusha, free from all the vehicles that lead to affliction, action and its effects." (*Y.S. I, 24*) He is different from Purusha because he has *always* been free from all afflictions. Certainly, the *bhaktis* will deliver him from this affliction by means of the powers they give to their god; this attribute is an easy resource but difficult to sustain.

Modern commentators, particularly Western ones, have questioned Patanjali's God precisely because he does not possess the attributes that they imagine he must have. In my view, Patanjali errs more by omission (and not only here, due to his terse way of writing) than by mistake. I am inclined to extract the most positive interpretation of this deity: Ishvara has been the sages' reference since the most remote times, since he has always existed (*Y.S. I, 26*), meaning that he could be interpreted as the God that each of the sages reveres, the God in whom religious sentiment or devotion (*bhakti*) is applied. "The culmination of divinity is Ishvara" (*Vyasa, I, 24*) And this feeling has been and continues to be a powerful incentive for man to transcend himself; only that to apply said feeling to himself he needs to personify it in some way or embody it. An abstract God like Brahman lends itself more to be the object of the intellect than of feelings. In any case, if Ishvara represents the archetype of a God who inspires devotion, Patanjali could hardly not propose him as a path to transcendental knowledge, that is, as a yoga. "Feel the omnipresence of God" (*Y.S. I, 23*) is the incentive that Patanjali proposes. Shiva, as the God of the ascetics, would come to express the Lord referred to by our author. It is not the name (personification) that interests but its function. Coming from a technician like Patanjali, I think this interpretation is valid.

Since Ishvara does not obey prayers nor exercise his will over men, the mechanism that Patanjali visualises works as an *instinct of liberation* in the human being; as in Samkhya, this *instinct* exists in nature, in *Prakrti*. This will seem strange to modern man, yet the strangeness comes from his alienation. Totally aside from my knowledge of Hinduism, my philosophy, born from experience, discovers among the *primary manifestations of the Essence* the existence of a universal force I call *Intelligence-instinct*, which in addition to being the *creative aspect* essential to survival, has as its ultimate goal the perfection and transcendence of living beings. I believe, decisively, that I am speaking of the same instinct as Patanjali, only that its origin is transcendent to Prakrti. In the same way, if this force is in all of Nature, it manifests itself everywhere, in our mind and in the life that we live and observe; not only in man. Nature, in my conception, is full of examples of the Transcendent; this should not surprise us since the Transcendent is its *Origin and its Destiny*.

Also, Patanjali has somewhat been criticised for the fact that his God is almost exclusive to Yogis, however, if we think about it, we will see that in fact it is so, since a high level of consciousness is needed to be in touch with that paradigm and use it as a model for inspiration and action.

For Patanjali, Ishvara is one more means, he includes it among the practices that must be observed, how to *remain clean* in body and spirit: *the purifications*, consisting of thinking and doing the opposite of temptation; the study of sacred texts; *the acceptance* of the situation that one is in, so as not to generate desires (*vrttis*). This acceptance, so typical of the Hindu, is very difficult for the Westerner (generally dominated by his *rajas* character) to understand because, precisely, he ignores the disorders that desires imply; disorders that affect *Sattva*. To these practices Patanjali adds: and make the Lord the reason for all actions. This requirement, as we shall see, fully coincides with one of the main messages of the *Bhagavad Gita*. Vacaspati will add, many centuries later, already under the influence of Bhakti, "Making Ishvara the reason for all actions, the other seven accessories are unnecessary" (*Y.S. II,45*)

When speaking of Purusha, in numerous passages Patanjali seems to be speaking of a universal Purusha, but to be exact this is not the case: "The Prakrti is one and the Purushas are many" (*Vacaspati, II, 22*) This raises a philosophical problem to where Mahayana Buddhism has also repaired: if liberation has an infinite scope, a single liberation would be enough for all beings to remain free. But in both doctrines reason ultimately prevails: the liberated is a single subject, a single Purusha. The *Prakrti* is annihilated, but "Though it is destroyed in the Purusha who has attained wisdom, it is not destroyed in the Purushas who have not attained it" (*Y.S. II, 22*) The matter is resolved by facts and reason, however, it does not respond to the experience (samadhi) of the liberated one who has transcended time and space. We are facing two consciousnesses and two realities when they are seen a posteriori by reason; but the liberated one knows that Reality is One. For my part, I have tried to respond to this serious philosophical problem with my theory of perspectives: from the individual perspective, reality is dual; from the *essential perspective*, it is One (see *The Quest for Universal Consciousness*).

Vyasa, very much in agreement with Patanjali's vision of yoga, says: "Moksha (total liberation) is only the cessation of the work of the mind" (*Y.S. II, 24*) This negative conception of liberation (as cessation of the work of the mind) lends itself to misunderstandings, and to forgetting the ends, which are positive: "By suppressing desires, extreme happiness is acquired" (*Y.S. II,42*), "supreme knowledge" (*Y.S. IV,23*) "and absolute freedom" (*Y.S. IV, 26*) There is in this vocabulary a total identification of the means (realised) with the ends, as if the realisation of the former would inevitably lead to the latter. This reminds me of the controversy between the *Soto* and *Rinzai* schools of Zen Buddhism. The first maintains that Dhyana (meditation) is synonymous with liberation or Nirvana, the second maintains that it is a means, that Prajna or knowledge is also needed; I incline towards this position. In my terminology I would say that a *transcendental intuition* is necessary; although it is true that the elevated spirit (through the means) acquires a vision that exposes reality, the eyes (of the spirit) must be open to see, which is intelligence.

Patanjali's constant and insistent purpose is to detach Purusha from Prakrti, liberation itself consists in this detachment and the highest state is achieved with the total disappearance of Prakrti. However, not all Prakrti is bad or negative, the Sattva-guna, which is an expression and a part of it, keeps a permanent relationship with Purusha, and in its purest state, as can be seen from various passages in the text, is confused with the universal Purusha. Ishvara himself, who is the realised, perfect Purusha, has a Sattva side or aspect. This is interpreted as help that he offers to the aspirant, which leads one to think that he has the will to do so, but Vyasa, aware of this, does not take long to clarify that "Ishvara has no purpose," however his presence implies "compassion for other beings" (*Y.S. I, 25*), as if he did not have a will but a feeling. This compassion, which may have been borrowed from Buddhism, does not, nonetheless, reach the importance that this doctrine gives it, nor is it expressed with the clarity of the Mahayana. There is, however, another means of attaining Purusha: "The sacred Word connotes (is inherent in) Ishvara." *Om* being the primordial sound, we can assume that it belongs to Prakrti in its purest state (Sattva). "The repetition of this sound leads to knowledge" (Y.S.I,27,28)

From what has been said it can be deduced that, although my vision leads me to see it and express it in another way and completely dispenses with a personal God, fundamentally it coincides with Patanjali and comes to confirm the truths that he expresses: 1) The human being has *unitive faculties*, essentially equivalent to *Sattva*, residing in Prakrti, which allow him to intuit Purusha, which is actually the Transcendent. 2) This intelligence is due to the emanation or reflection of Purusha. 3) The need for a prior purification through moral conduct, *Tapas*, though I insist on the progressive integration of the faculties, which leads to the Unity of consciousness, while Patanjali insists on the control of the modifications (*vrttis*) of the mind. In both cases, constant vigilance is essential, which comes from other faculties that awaken and stimulate *Sattva* knowledge, which I assimilate to the unitive faculties. 4) The union of the subject and the object, which I assimilate to the aesthetic phenomenon, samprajnata-samadhi. 5) Finally the disappearance (which in my experience is only temporary, while neither Patanjali nor his commentators clarify it) of material reality or Prakrti, correspond to asamprajnata-samadhi, and the absolute knowledge that derives from it, to which I have already referred (*in the Chapter on Ideas,*

Knowledge and Life). 6) In my vision, the *primary manifestations of the Essence* tend towards transcendence because they are the product of the universal Consciousness. All of them tend to perfection because they emanate from the Perfect, they tend to Unity because they come from It. They are *universal virtues* in which the mind of all beings participates to the extent of their potentialities, which is why the *ontological instinct* (entirely positive) exists in man, which Patanjali calls the *liberation instinct*.

Actually, although Patanjali remains limited within the Samkhya scheme, he has already taken the steps towards the Transcendent: Ishvara is transcendent; *Sattva*, in its highest state, resembles Ishvara; the individual Purusha is confused with a universal Purusha; and *asamprajnata samadhi* is the experience of the Transcendent. Only the awareness of the universal Purusha and its identity with the individual Purusha is missing, which will determine a change of perspective allowing us to see from the Transcendent. This is what the *Upanishads* will do.

Patanjali and My Vision

Patanjali's yogas, in addition to being a spiritual technique, as they are generally considered by those who practice one of the yogas and apply it to another doctrine, that is, in a different context, should be considered as a philosophy (*darsana*), because even if it makes use of a preceding philosophy, the Samkhya, it leads it to its realisation. It also has an original theory of knowledge, which implies a spiritual, corporal and moral praxis, all of which has a metaphysical projection.

Patanjali's yogas include two fundamental principles that are often forgotten by Westerners: the interpretation of these texts by a guru and a praxis, which includes various yogas. It is true that Vyasa, centuries later, names up to 12 body postures in addition to Padmasana, which will be incorporated into Hatha-yoga, but Patanjali does not dwell on them, he only cares that they do not imply effort as it is distracting. It has been argued that the set of yoga's that Patanjali proposes constitute Raja-yoga, but this has subsequently incorporated Tantra practices that distort the author's purpose. The multiple yoga's, as we know them today, are branches that have grown after Patanjali. It would be correct, in my opinion, to take the *Yoga-sutras* as a philosophy that implies a practice.

In every sense, Patanjali's psychology is shown to be far superior to modern Western psychology (post-psychoanalysis). This Hindu sage recommends us to control not only the conscious mind, which is very difficult for the Westerner, but also the flow of the subconscious, which is practically impossible for the Westerner. Having noticed this same need, I have spoken of the attention that we must pay to the *irruptions of the subconscious*, which I have called the *internal plane*, since it can become conscious. Which amounts to practically the same thing, but while Patanjali emphasises control, I accentuate a constant observation of our intentions, that is, in their moral aspect. It is, in fact, the ethical errors committed that are most firmly embedded internally and that determine our actions and finally our personality, for as long as the aspirant does not recognise them, they continue to divert their intentions, thoughts and actions. Rather than control them so that they do not express themselves, my ethics prefers to expose them in their nakedness in the light of *unitive consciousness*, in this case *moral consciousness*, until their roots dry up and make them disappear. It is similar to Patanjali's proposal, but I lean towards the path of *unitive knowledge*, which gradually grows the *unitive consciousness* that finally exposes all *indirect knowledge*, such as discernment and the internal plane, which are derivatives of *direct knowledge*. In other words, to awaken the *central, vital or direct perception plane*.

Regarding this, Patanjali tells us that when *samadhi with support* occurs, the union of the subject with the object occurs. This does not contradict my vision, rather it confirms it, only that according to my *Psychosophy*, it occurs because the spirit has moved to the *plane of direct or central vision*, so that it has been centred, has found its true centre, not outside of the mind, but in its very core, which is already *unitive consciousness*. That is why I have highlighted aesthetic awareness, which Hinduism in general has not dwelt on, because it is the artist's own faculty to achieve that state of absorption and transcendence.

My view of the psyche inverts the order established by Patanjali in this regard. For him direct perception and the union of the subject and the object is obtained after a long yoga practice. In my conception, *direct perception* comes first for the mind when receiving the stimulus of the senses, only that immediately after, this vision is interfered with by external mechanisms. The self, discernment and memory move the spirit to the external centre of consciousness to resolve what is rationally perceived; to know, for example, what a lily is, it says that it belongs to the iridaceous family, that it is blue, that it is beautiful, etc. But the order of the factors does not alter the product, in both cases the mind requires the necessary concentration to stop its displacement, I would say in my terminology, which would be the modification of its state (*vrttis*) for Patanjali. There are artists who have the ability, surely innate, to perceive directly, without the irruption of other stimuli from the mind, although we can agree that it is possible that it is not absolutely so. Cézanne said of Monet that "he was a pure eye"; the interpretation that follows is that the relationship between his eye and his mind was *direct*.

With respect to philosophising this I would like to say: there are thoughts that are concurrent, suitable and edifying for the understanding of spiritual reality. Clearly, these thoughts generate movements (*vrttis*) of the mind, a certain alteration of consciousness, but, although the vast majority of *vrttis* distract the mind from its Essence, there are those that attract and direct it towards it. This is not an easy task, as it requires concentration and *fair discrimination*, a basic principle of Buddhism and Hinduism. Well then, this concentration directed towards the Essence, having as its source a *transcendental intuition* followed by correct thought, that is, without contradicting reason, and with the objective of revealing the Transcendent, is what I understand by philosophising proper and by *Gnana-yoga*. This does not mean in any way that reason has the last word, but, as said, the intuition of the Transcendent in which it is inspired. The concepts of Transcendent, Essence, Brahman, Unity or even the Absolute do not explain the matter, except to the extent that one has the experience of what they express. The Creative (another useful concept) illuminates and inspires understanding, and philosophising is derived from this inspiration; fair discrimination consists in adjusting to that beam of light that emanates from the Creative.

That is to say, I do not see thought as something that necessarily disturbs the mind, rather, I try to highlight its *positive aspects* that I consider necessary in the evolution of the spirit. Certainly, Patanjali's proposal that begins with a blank slate offers a clearer picture, while mine is presented as more tangled and therefore easier to fall prey to the negative aspects of thinking, feeling and memories that usually come to mind. But in both cases we need strict concentration and absolute contemplation. The task is not easy in either case, since what we agree on is that the human mind is scattered and alienated from its Essence, which is its objective.

Patanjali takes from Samkhya *the belief* that there are innumerable pre-existing souls that incarnate in living beings. In this way he explains the mythical *fall* of the spirit into matter, from which it has to free itself in order to reintegrate itself into its original state, which is eternal and immutable. Purusha falls into Prakrti and liberation consists in escaping from it and recovering the state of original purity; this task is taken care of by the yoga's. Nonetheless, the belief in multiple souls or in only one at the end of the day does not alter the function of yoga, which is a means. Later Hinduism, as we will see, gave Purusha a universal dimension, equating it to the Absolute.

Introduction to the Upanishads

"Of all the speeches I have heard, not one comes to recognise that wisdom is set apart from all things."

—Heraclitus (*Stob.*)

The times of the Buddha were times of revisionism and no one contributed as much to this as did Prince Gautama. But the prince was from the caste of warriors (*kshatriyas*) and not from the Brahmans, who had until then held spiritual power and through it power over the people. The attack from all the new currents, including the Hindu ones, was so harsh that Brahmanism itself ultimately disappeared. Not so the Brahmans who learned the lesson well; their power from then on would be only spiritual. It is in this epoch of transformation that the great religious-philosophical doctrines of India appear: Buddhism, Jainism and the *Upanishads*. In all of them what would be decisive, in the individual and in the Cosmos, would be moral Order. Then the doctrines that interpret it, the *Dharma* and the *Dhamma*, are born. If before the religious had to perform the ritual correctly to participate in the Cosmos, now they must act morally, otherwise an individual and a universal disorder is generated. This spiritual reality that underlies the material, has, like this, its laws of cause and effect; it is what all Hindu and Buddhist doctrines accept and call *Karma*. By this, the human being is linked to the universal moral Order and obliged to do good and avoid evil. With the new religions, undoubtedly a product of a clearer vision of Reality, the Spirit dominates the scene.

With this brief foray into the history of the Spirit in India, I wanted to highlight the common origin and similarities between Buddhism (very similar, otherwise, to Jainism), and Hinduism. It is from then on that the long pilgrimage of the spirit to identify with the Universal Spirit begins throughout India, which reaches its greatest expression in the Buddhist Idea of the *cosmic Mind* and in Hinduism with the Idea of Brahman or Atman as Absolute.

Hindus have had a particular attraction towards light since the times of the *Rg-Veda*, which is not the product of an organic reflection, but of a particular intuition of the transcendent reality that is effectively expressed as light in the soul, which I understand to be the most spiritual sector of our faculties, *unified consciousness*. I mean enlightenment, known in India as *moksha*, and in Buddhism as Nirvana.

Moreover, this illumination is the culmination of a long search that goes from the *Rig-Veda* to the *Upanishads*. Certainly, said light is not limited to a visual fact, rather it completely transforms the mind of the subject. In my terminology, it produces a radical change of perspective in which the nucleus of consciousness moves from the individual perspective to the essential perspective, which is none other than universal Consciousness. This understanding or experience occurs on the plane of direct perception, which is why it is very difficult to express it, because to do this the subject must resort to the planes of indirect perception, the external or discernment plane and the internal or subconscious plane. In the *Upanishads* we find both, as the language is sometimes rational and at other times a stranger to reason.

For the Westerner, due to a more rational philosophical tradition, this seems less "philosophical" and therefore less "true"; but it is not so. *Truth is direct experience*; language, whether rational or unitive, comes later. Hindu commentators, undoubtedly, have not used this explanation nor this terminology, but having had the same experience they know that the *Upanishads* contain such Truth. For this reason they try to make these texts more reasonable, although they know or sense that they are transcendent to reason.

It is essential that the Westerner understand or at least accept this, otherwise he has to continue to believe that "what is real is what is rational", a false premise that has had an effect on so many intellectuals. Strictly speaking, *what is real is irrational*, I mean, it is transcendent to reason. This is why not a single mystic will be found who agrees with that premise; and what Hegel does with it is to invert completely both transcendent and historical reality to accommodate them to his reason. This is not only my way of seeing (I clarify it because there will be no shortage of those who think that I do so as an "orientalist"), it is what Kant had specifically shown should not be done. For this master of reason, the appropriate means to reach the transcendental or noumenal were intellectual or transcendental intuitions in which, however, he did not believe, surely because he, who had investigated so much, had not had them. All of his inquiry had been with reason, so he had been enclosed within the limits that he himself had drawn. Hegel believed that he could go beyond them and Kant, with his reason, but no one can do that without falling into the errors that this genius had foreseen. I have expanded on these authors in other works, so that for our current purpose what has been said will suffice.

It was then necessary to look for other means, moral and aesthetic ones, for example. Kant ventured into them, but without decisive results, because he did not realise that other faculties more suitable for matters of the spirit had to be used for them, capable of discovering *The Roots of Morality* and *The Roots of Art*; I refer the reader to these works where I show the transcendent capacity of these disciplines. It was also necessary to investigate other faculties of the mind, from another perspective capable of showing its transcendent potentialities, and the usual impediments that man generates that limit or block said capacities; I have dealt with this in my *Psychosophy.*

There are, then, other more effective means, although more subtle than reason, to free the spirit so that it can reach the Transcendent. Albeit they are not the same as those I have just described, India has known specific means for this purpose for centuries, and for which they have developed precise spiritual techniques, such as yoga.

It is a fact that in the sixth century B.C. these techniques were already known in India, the Buddha himself uses and recommends them. It is feasible that the change in consciousness that occurred then was a consequence of these techniques, that is, that the authors of the *Upanishads* had used them. But there are other factors that are not easy to explain, since the experience and language of these authors is ambiguous; there is, in fact, in them a *unitive thinking* and even mythical thinking mixed with the rational. Curiously, the Buddha and Confucius, far ahead of their time, use language that is entirely comprehensive to reason; which in no way means that they are rationalists; the Buddha does not stop making fun of philosophers.

I would like to emphasise, however, that what is decisive is the *level of consciousness* reached. Indeed, what radically differentiates these thinkers from those who preceded them is this level. The Buddha, Mahavira and the authors of the *Upanishads* shared this elevated state of mind which the Vedic poets lacked. So I think that when establishing the orthodoxy of Hinduism, this factor should be considered before any other. The Buddha, let us not forget, is speaking of the same thing and from the same perspective as the *Upanishads*; though he leaves the Vedic gods aside. Moreover, the same feeling of rebellion and superiority with respect to the past and the need for change is also found in them. The *Mundaka Up*. asserts that by considering religion as the observance of rituals (which was what had given power to the Brahmans until then) the confused man remains alien to the highest knowledge. "Confused, believing that the rites inculcated by the Vedas and the *Smirtis* are the highest, they do not understand what leads to liberation." "Only the wise (...) in solitude and silence (...) reach the immutable Self." The aspirant is thus freed both from the ritual and from the intermediation of the priests. But not only the ritual exceeds Hinduism, but also the doctrine: "Two kinds of knowledge must be known: the higher and the lower. The lower knowledge is that of the *Rig, Yajur, Sama and Atharva Vedas* (...) The higher knowledge is that by which the Indestructible Brahman is apprehended" (*Mundaka Up. I,4,5*) The link with the elements established by the Vedas is replaced by the relationship of the individual spirit (*jiva*) with the universal Spirit, Atman or Brahman in Hinduism, the consciousness of the Buddha in Buddhism.

In my opinion, the unity that exists in the *Indian civilisation* lies in a tacit agreement on a transcendent objective, that is to say, that transcends particular reasons, schools, beliefs and ideologies. The firmness of the structure resides in the fact that said unit or objective is indestructible, and it is the foundation of the enormous building that constitutes that culture which, as corresponds to matters of the spirit, is built from top to bottom. In India, the agreement is given a priori by a transcendental intuition that underlies the multiplicity of the *Universus*, already expressed at the origin of that civilisation in the oldest text that it preserves: "The Truth is one but the enlightened give it different names" (*Rg Veda 1,164,46*) This, rightly oft-quoted Idea grants unity, moreover, to the Vedas themselves, which, as all Hindus know, express very diverse ideas, rituals, beliefs and gods.

The Idea had been filtering through the Indian consciousness until it became transparent in the *Upanishads*, which designate it with the name Brahman.

The *Upanishads* are a matter of the first order in the field of philosophy as they deal with the essence of the *Universus*. The problem they present is that the vast majority of humans are not able to understand them, although we can put aside this problem because philosophy in general is the heritage of philosophers who have always been very few. But the *Upanishads* have a particularity that aggravates the matter, and that is that they are not expressed in the usual, I mean, rational, way for the Western philosopher. Far from it, the *Upanishads* use the minimum of reason and their language is spontaneous and synthetic while avoiding marginal speculations as far as possible. Their style is similar to the fragments that the Pre-Socratics have left us, so there has even been an author who maintained that Indian philosophy has remained at that stage of thought and ignored subsequent development (*Julián Marías, Hist, Filos.*). The fact is that, like this author, Western philosophers do not understand these texts either; and this is more serious.

There are several reasons that lead to this misunderstanding. Anyone who has read my work will have found the causes of it, for those who have not had access to it I will try to synthesise these causes, necessary for the understanding of my own philosophy, as well as the most outstanding idealist philosophies of the West, such as Platonism and Neo-Platonism.

The fundamental difference lies in the *plane of knowledge* used and the *level of consciousness* reached, as well as in the *method of knowledge*, all of which generates another way of seeing, thinking, feeling, in short, *another mind*. It will be understood that with these differences the resulting philosophies will be very different. Judging the highest idealistic philosophies, that is, the *Upanishads*, Buddhism, Platonism, Neo-Platonism and my own philosophy starting from premises other than those named is a vain task, since one is not prepared for it.

This radical change of perspective necessarily generates a different language and method that is sometimes unintelligible to the reader. Aurobindo says, referring to the *Isha Up.*: "For the modern mentality this method is null and inapplicable." "Then, it is supported by a number of implicit ideas that are not explicitly manifested, with words that are not directed to the intellect." "So the reader is supposed to confirm his intuitions through his experience." In fact, it is not a question here of reasons but of *intuitions and transcendental feelings or experiences* (vital or integral experiences). *Implicit ideas* imply a certain transcendental knowledge. And this same language is used in practically all the Hindu and Buddhist *Sutras*.

I believe that the eternal error, which has caused so many misunderstandings, regarding the first and last reality, that is, Brahman or the Transcendent, is that the *unitive faculties* are confused with the *speculative* ones, that is, the perception of the former is confused with the ideas that are made by the latter. The Absolute is indescribable because it is the Intelligence itself of the *Universus*, therefore, trying to understand or see behind this Intelligence is a mistake made by the speculative faculties. However, the apperception of Intelligence is indubitable when we penetrate the *universal Consciousness* that includes the *primary manifestations* that we perceive emanating from the Transcendent.

To say that these manifestations are secondary or derivative realities is to apply the speculative faculties to the primary reality, since there is a Unity in universal Consciousness. Thus, for example, the concept of *Ananda* (Happiness) has given rise to sterile controversies. It could be said that it derives from the perception of Brahman, but it is inseparable from it, it is the inevitable feeling that accompanies universal Consciousness, it is part of It. We cannot describe it because it is transcendent, but it is evident because it overflows the heart, it is an inexpressible Happiness.

I have already explained it sufficiently in my work: the Transcendent is to the speculative faculties, to reason, but not to the *unitive faculties* in their highest expression, to the *unified Consciousness* that comprehends the aforementioned manifestations. Brahman, the Absolute, illuminates them so that the content of the *universal Consciousness* becomes clear. This knowledge is not objective because there is no subject here; this Consciousness is recognised exactly by the lack of a subject, there is only Unity in it. Very correctly, the *Brhadaranyaca Up. (III)* says: "It is not perceived but perceives, it is not known but knows." *Universal Consciousness* is recognised because in it time and space are absent, just as speculative faculties are recognised when the spirit moves and *enters* time and space; albeit the one who has not transcended these categories does not know about these displacements.

Since the *Upanishads* are, as we said, often unintelligible without subsequent commentaries, and since I have made use of Shankara's commentaries, I must criticise both in unison. Shankara is also an obligatory reference since tradition has it that he was the one who rescued these texts and selected from more than 100 *Upanishads* the most outstanding that have come down to us. (Tradition says that there are 108, but this is a magical number since 108 are the basic dance poses established by Shiva, illustrated in some southern temple-cities as the number of beads in Hindu and Buddhist rosaries). I do not think it inappropriate to follow the work of this thinker who is closely linked to this extension of the Vedas, to the point that he himself calls it Vedanta. I understand the concept of critique in the manner of Kant, as an objective and constructive analysis, since what matters to philosophy is to rescue the truths that, precisely, abound in these texts. It is not, then, my interest to praise Shankara or, much less to discredit him; what interests us all are the truths themselves, not people or gods. The liberation of each aspirant depends on the path he chooses, and on it he must overcome the external and internal obstacles that he finds in his particular circumstances. The truths themselves become like a general map that is only clear to the philosopher who draws it and where the individual paths are not traced. Philosophy, strictly speaking, does not deal with them, this is the task of literature, which, certainly does not deal with the reader, but with some exemplary individuals that each reader interprets and assimilates in his own way. Aware of this, good philosophies provide the means to prepare and enable the aspirant to undertake these paths that, as they are ascending, require effort and that, inevitably, he must ultimately travel alone; even though he has a guru.

Before commenting on these texts, I wanted to make it clear that it is not my interest to make an exhaustive critique of them, something that has already been done by so many scholars that they are well known and do not need to be repeated, but rather to superimpose the essentials of my philosophy on these texts to show their coincidences and thus ratify the truths they express. But, as already explained, their understanding depends a lot on their commentators, of which the most prestigious or classic are Shankara and Ramanuja.

The latter's dualistic vision is difficult to reconcile with mine, so I have to treat it separately. I sympathise with Shankara's monism, but his extreme way of expression sometimes clashes not only with my vision but with that of the *Upanishads* themselves, so I consider it essential to clarify the differences between these three visions. To these I must add a fourth view, fundamentally assimilated to mine, which is that of Sri Aurobindo. His disagreement with Shankara has been clearly expressed in his capital work *The Life Divine*, which I have commented on at length in *The Evolution of the Spirit*, so here I will only attend to the exposition he makes of the *Isha Up*. Although I have taken some quotes from them, I am not going to comment on the *Chandogya*, the *Brhadaranyaka* and the *Svetasvara Upanishads*, which would require a specific and prolonged exegesis because they spread along branches that I consider unnecessary and repetitive, and not infrequently, out of place. Ultimately, I believe that they do not add anything new to the *Upanishads* that should be dealt with or to the fundamental message of Vedanta, expressed with the greatest clarity in the *Kena*, the *Isha* and the *Mundaka*. These, in my opinion, constitute the obligatory reference when it comes to interpreting the rest of the *Upanishads*, and with which, as we shall see, my philosophy easily overlaps.

The Aitareya Upanishad

If our gaze falls on some *Upanishads* such as the *Mundaka* or the *Mandukya*, we will see a very marked contrast with the *Upanishads* that precede them and we will notice that these texts are the result of a process that may have taken a couple of centuries or more. There has been, then, a period of transition in which we find *Upanishads* not yet detached from the Vedic tradition; such is the case of the *Aitareya*, which should not be surprising since it is part of the *Aitareya Brahmana*.

This text, corresponding to that most remote time, does not strictly speak to us of a theory of knowledge like the other Upanishads, but rather tells us of a cosmogony similar to the old style. This being the case, one wonders why Shankara chose it to comment on. I think this question is the very theme of the *Aitareya*, consisting of the differences that Shankara has noted, which highlight the transition that the *Upanishads* go through.

In my view, Shankara is too strict with the concepts because in the texts that precede this one there is already talk of a first creative principle, such as Hiranyagarbha or cosmic power, or of Prana as a vital force, which were even identified with Brahman, but because they are forces linked to matter, they are not to Shankara's liking, who calls this "inferior Brahman", since what he seeks is the absolute Brahman. Shankara's effort is evident as the text only refers to Brahman three times, while he uses it on every page. I think that Shankara wanted to incorporate a cosmogony in the *Upanishads* and found it in the *Aitareya*, which is really a continuation of the preceding texts and not a refutation, as our commentator claims.

The Genesis that *Aitareya* describes to us has a mythical character and, except for some passages, philosophically it has a relative value. In the *Rig-Veda* the creator is Prajapati. "He created the six regions of the universe, and Brahman, the divine essence thereof, is the Paramataman, the Soul of the universe." It even announces a sentence that we will see in the *Upanishads*: "When the atman unites with the Paramatman he realises the truth." In the *Yajur-Veda* the creator is Vishnu: "It is He who created the Earth, the atmosphere and the heavens." Nevertheless, we know that in all the *Vedas* many gods are sung and prayed to.

The *Aitareya* speaks to us of an absolute Creator: "*Om*! In the beginning there was only the absolute Self." And he said to himself, "I have to create the worlds." *(I,1)* It does not take long for Shankara to bestow these attributes on this Self: "The highest, omniscient, eternal, pure, conscious, free and unrivalled." "He (Himself) created these worlds, the heaven and the earth. (*I,2*) "Then he thought, 'I have to create the protectors of these worlds." (*I,3*) For this purpose he creates the elements which, as in the Greeks, bear the names of gods: Fire (Agni), Air (Vayu), etc. (*I,4*) Later, when man is presented to these gods, "They said: This is well formed, man is truly a creation of God himself." (*II,3*) Shankara adds that "God created man by Himself through his Maya"; but the text does not speak of this concept at any time.

We do not need to follow all the steps of the Creator because this entire Genesis lacks philosophical value. Curiously, to tell us that He is everything, it adds, "This One is Brahman, He is Indra, He is Prajapati, He is all these gods and the five elements and all creatures." (*III,3*) That is to say that the *Upanishad is incorporating the whole world*, even Shankara (I think in a slip) admits it:"*It is the same Entity that has become diversified.*" But he justifies it with a quote from the *Manu Samhita*: "Some call this very Entity Fire, others call it Manu, and some Prajapati. Some call it Indra, while others call it Prana, and still others the eternal Brahman." Which inevitably reminds us of the *Rig-Veda*, "... but the enlightened (learned) give it different names."

Only at the end of the text do we find the expected language: All creatures "are driven by Consciousness, they all have the Consciousness that gives them their reality; the universe has Consciousness as its eye and Consciousness is its destiny, and Consciousness is Brahman." (*III,3*) We will return to this luminous assertion later. However, the *Aitareya* concludes thus, "By means of this Self, which is Consciousness, having fulfilled his desires, he ascended beyond this world, and in that paradisiacal world, he became immortal." (*III.4*) We cannot fail to notice that in this ascent and realisation this God has something personal. It is evident, as I said at the beginning, that this *Upanishad* belongs to a period of transition.

The Prasna Upanishad

We can say that the *Upanishads* are the product of the same inspiration, but undoubtedly there is an evolution in the way of expressing that experience that moves away from mythical, figurative or enigmatic language until it becomes clearer and more precise.

This *Upanishad* is divided into six parts which respond to the questions of the aspirant which are answered by a man of knowledge. In the *Prasna Up*. we still find an archaic language that relates a Genesis to us, although in a much shorter way than in the *Aitareya*. It tells us, "The Lord of all creatures, eager to have offspring (...) he Created a couple: food and Prana, with the idea that these two would produce creatures in multiple ways." (*I,4*) Shankara interprets this Lord to be Prajapati whom he identifies with Hiranyagarba. The *Prasna* then clarifies that "The sun is verily Prana and the moon is food." (*I, 5*) The idea, to my understanding, is that the sun "absorbs all creatures with its rays," and devours them, since Prana is also Fire (*Agni*). But what is fundamental is that "the sun is the life of all creatures" (*I,8*) with which all naturalists can agree.

But as is typical of Hindu thought and of the *Upanishads* in particular, this descent, which explains the existence of all beings, is not enough, there must be an ascent of the creatures to reach the Origin, a search that, surely, implies yoga, “Seeking the Self, through control of the senses, renunciation, faith and meditation, they conquer the sun,” (*I, 10*) which implies the assumption of the spirit towards the Spirit. Those who undertake this quest can reach “the immaculate world of Brahman.” (*I,15.16*) In this way, somewhat suddenly, the *Upanishad* introduces us to the Absolute.

In the *Second Part*, *Prasna* returns to this created world whose creative force is Prana, “he is the creator of space, air, fire, water, earth, mind and senses.” (*II,2*) “All things are fixed like the spokes of the wheel in its centre, which is Prana. (*II,6*) Prana is the womb of the world and “All this world and the one in the heavens are under the control of Prana.” “He is the Lord of creation.”

Everything makes us believe up to now that Prana is the primary reality, however in the *Third Part* it tells us that “it is from the Self that Prana is born.” (*III,3*), and adds that this is fixed to himself as the shadow is to the man who generates it. This is a situation that Shankara takes advantage of to say that Prana “is a false principle, as is a body’s shadow”, but this is not what the *Prasna* says, which only speaks of the intimate relationship it has with the Self. Moreover, it tells us that whoever knows Prana becomes immortal” (*III,11*), which equates to Brahman.

The *Fourth Part* of the *Upanishad* introduces us to the concept of Purusha, which is no longer the individual purusha of the Samkhya, but the universal, the Parampurusha, which is the supreme, immutable Self. (*IV,9*), and “He who realises what has no shadow or body, who is pure and immutable reaches the supreme Immutable Self” and becomes all-knowing (*IV,10*) since the Purusha is the Knower. (*IV,11*)

In the *Fifth Part*, it takes up a theme common to the *Upanishads*, the *Om*, which he identifies with Brahman (with which this concept reappears), but it tells us about a higher and a lower Brahman, which are encompassed by the *Om*. Shankara interprets that the higher one is the immutable Purusha, while the lower one is Prana. To my understanding this creates a duality in Brahman that has no place in an advaita vision. Furthermore he is admitting the existence of the lower Brahman which is the world. If he were speaking of a higher consciousness, which would be the Transcendent, and a lower one, which would be Nature, we could agree.

In the *Sixth Part* the question is about Purusha, to which the sage replies: “Here in the body Purusha resides and from it the members are born.” (*VI,2*) But everything also converges on Him, “Just as the rivers have the sea as their destination and are absorbed by it”, everything that has a name and form “disappears when they reach Purusha. (*VI,7*) That is to say that Purusha and Brahman are a single reality.

In my view, this *Upanishad* is not well structured, since the situation of Prana is not left clear as Shankara claims, and Purusha is abruptly introduced and we are not told about the means to achieve it, although some yoga is mentioned at one point. On the ascending path there are several steps missing. Decidedly we need a Guru to understand it. It also lacks psychology because it tells us nothing about the mental process that we must follow to reach such heights. It does not speak to us of the self and its ties or of the way to transcend it; it speaks to us, strictly speaking, of external affairs, even though it tells us that Purusha is in our body.

I would summarise the similarity with my conception as follows: the *Prasna* speaks of a single primary manifestation that would be Prana, which I can identify with the élan vital, essential to life, but insufficient to awaken the highest feelings (Karuña) or Intelligence, the Prajna about which some *Upanishads,* and Mahayana Buddhism in particular, speak. Perhaps the *Prasna* wants to tell us, as I have done, that the human being must first become aware that *he is part of the solar Organism*, which would lead him to transcend his individual perspective and integrate into the Cosmos. Beyond this, consciousness expands into infinity where it finds the limit of the unlimited and in this way is unified with the All, with universal Consciousness.

The Mandukya Upanishad

If we want to find the radical form of Advaita Vedanta, we must go to the *Mandukya Upanishad*. This form was not Shankara’s invention, as he took this text as a model, to which he not only adapted his philosophy but also the rest of the *Upanishads*, accommodating them to this form that responds to a particular vision of the *Universus*.

The form is categorical, here there is no divinity other than Brahman in its absolute mode; this is established from the Invocation: "I prostrate myself before that Brahman (...) that penetrates all human objectives with its rays of invariable Consciousness that encompass everything." Brahman is identified with *Om*: "All that is past, present and future is verily *Om*. That which is beyond the triple conception of time, is also truly *Om*." (*I,1*)

The text continues with that strange obsession of the *Upanishads* with deep sleep (*susupti*), and I say strange because it is strange when talking about the Consciousness of the world, being an unconscious state by definition. Even though while speaking of the fourth and highest state of consciousness, Turiya, which is equivalent to Moksha or illumination, it says, "That which is neither conscious nor unconscious, which cannot be seen, beyond empirical matters, unthinkable, indescribable." "Turiya is forever everything and the witness." (*I,12*), and "In Turiya sleep does not exist." (*I,13*) Strictly speaking, "when the state of sleep and sleep are overcome, Turiya is reached." (*I,15*)

The *Mandukya* then divides the *Om* into its three components a-u-m, thus falling, in my opinion, into the magic of words, but it concludes: "The *Om* without parts (not divided) is Turiya." And it adds: "*Om* is then, the Self." (*Mat. 12*) And, certainly, "*Om* is Brahman." (*I,25*)

In *Chapter II* the *Mandukya* is applied to the reckless demonstration of the unreality of this world, so much to Shankara's taste. Strictly speaking, it was expressed synthetically in the previous chapter: "There is no doubt that the phenomenal world would cease to exist if it had had any existence. All this duality (multiplicity) is nothing more than Maya, it is actually non-dual." (*I,17*) The seriousness of the matter on which I have already expressed myself here and in greater detail in *The Search for Universal Consciousness* will be understood, where I refer the reader precisely because of the importance of the subject, which I will try to synthesise at present:

It is true, I can attest to it, that when human consciousness integrates, which is what I understand by unified Consciousness, the World disappears, but... for a few minutes or instants (which we ascertain a posteriori since time and space do not exist there). But these instants of absolute transcendence do not prove that the world ceases to exist forever, although it is also true that since then it has some unreality, or becomes a reality in another way, this is what I can come to admit as Maya, but no more.

Seen in this way, it is not legitimate for the *Upanishad* to say: it "would cease to exist if it had had any existence." Nor does Shankara's statement end the matter thus: "There is no such thing as the world that appears and disappears." Strictly speaking, in my experience, the one that appears and disappears (been the human condition) is the absolute Brahman, as only consciousness of Itself, although this must be established, this is the greatest experience of the spirit. For this reason I hasten to clarify that although it disappears as if enclosed in itself, in the manner of Parmenides, *it remains* pouring itself out, emanating existence and its virtues, its *primary manifestations* in the world and in our consciousness; it continues to generate life and consciousness. And I do not think it is necessary to insist on this, precisely because it is, in my opinion, what the other *Upanishads* maintain.

But the *Mandukya* will dedicate an extensive chapter to demonstrate the non-existence of this existence. "As objects in sleep are unreal, so too, and for the same reason, objects in the waking state are also unreal." (*II,4*) "The sage says that sleep and the waking state are one." (*II,5*) In the same way it affirms that the inner and outer consciousness's are false. (*II,9*) Therefore, as expected, ultimately is denying the categories of time, space and causality, that is, everything that reason thinks or imagines, and before that, everything that our senses perceive. "Things that are externally related to two moments of time are pure imagination." (*II,14*) Everything is in reality, or is nothing more than "the Maya of the self-effulgent One, by which He himself is confused." (*II,19*)

The reader will wonder if he himself, and those who aspire to salvation and even those who have reached it, exist, none of that: "There is neither origin nor dissolution, there is no one imprisoned (in ignorance), and no one striving or aspiring to salvation and (not even) any liberated." (*II,32*) In conclusion, "Just as dreams and products of the imagination are seen as unreal, so is the whole universe considered unreal by the *Upanishads* and by the wise." (*II,31*). As can be seen here are included the other *Upanishads*, which is what Shankara also tries to do in his comments, but this is not the case, as we will see.

The Kena Upanishad

As soon as we begin reading the *Kena*, we feel transported to the Supreme Reality: "It is the Mind of the mind, the Life of life." (*I,2*) Shankara justly comments: "The internal organs are not capable of performing their own functions - thinking, deciding, etc.- if they are not illuminated by the light of consciousness. Therefore It is the Mind of the mind." But this does not mean that we can understand the mind with the mind, if we understand this as reason. That is why the *Kena* clarifies, "That which cannot be understood with the mind (reason) but by which the mind is understood, knows that That alone is the Supreme Being, and not this or that god that ordinary people worship." (*I,6*) It could not be clearer: it is speaking of transcendental knowledge, but which, in my opinion, implies faculties with transcendental capacity.

Hinduism, as I believe I have advanced, considers the mind as one more sense. With which I allow myself to differ, up to a certain point, as I will clarify below, since it also possesses *unitive faculties* capable of transcending the senses, without which it would not be possible, precisely, to transcend reason. Moreover, without them the *Upanishads* and philosophy itself would not exist. With the incorporation of *Sattva*, Hinduism already admits a superior spiritual faculty. In my view, I would not say that the universal Consciousness is *a part* of the mind, since it cannot be divided into parts, nor that it is in *our mind*, since strictly speaking it no longer belongs to us, but yes, to be more precise, I would say that we count on a *vertex of the mind* that is open to the Transcendent.

For this reason, the *Kena* continues to say the same about the other senses: "That which man does not see with the eye, but rather that which perceives the activities of the eye." And so with the other senses (*I,8,9*) with what evidently refers to the *Witness*.

In *chapter II* the typical dialogue of the mystic who has seen the Transcendent is established, and his mind is split between the consciousness or mind that he knows (the unitive) of the master and the individual consciousness of the aspirant. Therefore the master says: "He who understands this expression: I know and I do not know equally, knows Brahman." Thus, we do not understand it with reason but we do intuit it with other faculties; it refers to what I understand by *unitive faculties*. In the same way he insists with this apparently paradoxical language, "It is unknown to those who know." (*II, 3*) Which reminds us of Lao Tzu in his Tao Te Ching, "He who speaks of the Tao, does not know it." As what we have already pointed out: he who reasons and speaks of reason does not know of the Tao, which is nothing but the same experience of Brahman. However, the *Kena* adds, "Through knowledge immortality is attained." (*II,4*) That is to say that there is a type of knowledge, a faculty, which I call *unitive*, which has access to the Transcendent. This agrees with a fundamental principle common to the *Upanishads*: "Brahman is Consciousness." (*Ait. V,3*) That is to say that knowledge equals us to Brahman, but it is an intuitive, unitive, transcendental knowledge.

In the third part, the *Kena* reaches a happy accord with the Vedic gods, although highlighting the pre-eminence of Brahman: Indra, fire and air are superior to the other gods because they knew Brahman closely (a privilege forbidden to humans). Shankara explains this phenomenon using his preferred tool, the Maya, "By means of its wonderful power of Maya, It appeared as an object of perception to the senses of the gods." And, curiously, he mentions an entirely mythical narration that recalls Zeus's victory over the titans: "Brahman, after defeating the demons, the enemies of the world and transgressors of divine rules, grants victory to the gods to ensure the stability of the world."

Nevertheless, to show the immense preponderance of Brahman, the *Kena* tells us a story no less mythical than that of Shankara, in which a struggle occurs between the most powerful gods: Brahman appears before them in a form they do not recognise (which also proves his superiority) and asks Agni, Fire: "What power do you have?" To which Agni replies, "I can burn everything on earth." Then Brahman presents him with a straw in his hand and orders him to burn it, but "the Fire could not consume it." The story repeats itself with Vayu, Air, who cannot blow it away either. Indra, the most powerful of the Vedic gods, then recognises the power of Brahman.

Is it necessary to highlight the happy convergence, complementation and integration of the mythical mentality with the supra-rational or unitive mentality, as well as the inclusion of the mythical knowledge with the transcendental knowledge? Behold the genius of the Upanishads!

The *Kena* reiterates Patanjali's assertion, "It is a known fact that the mind tends to go towards Him (Brahman), and that He is repeatedly remembered in the mind." (*IV,5*) I consider this assertion of great importance because it leads us to reconsider and investigate in our minds that instance towards the Transcendent, which is a basic point of my *Psychosophy*. The *Kena* also reiterates our need for concentration and the cessation of the relation with the objects of our senses (*IV, 8*), fundamental practices developed by Patanjali.

In short, "He who knows all this remains firmly established in the unlimited, blissful and highest Brahman." (*IV,9*)

The Isha Upanishad

The *Isha* is also among the oldest *Upanishads*, but it already entirely dispenses with the classical language of the Vedas in which personal favours are requested from the gods (the *Taittiriya* still suffers from this atavism), and is directly applied to express what is essential. It is, strictly speaking, the shortest of the *Upanishads*, since it only has 18 Sutras or verses.

The *Isha* begins like this: "Everything that moves in the world is for the Lord's habitation." Shankara agrees with what has been expressed. In my opinion there are two beliefs here: one, which is an inference that cannot be proven, the other, *the Lord*, if he is understood as Owner, since he would already have a personal attribute of God. These unfounded expressions would be avoided if it were said, "Everything that moves in the world is the habitation of the Self, or Brahman, or universal Consciousness." It continues like this: "Seek protection in detachment." Which is very reasonable, and it ends like this: "Do not covet any other's wealth." In this all ethics and religions agree, so it does not present any difficulties, but Shankara, using his typical language, rectifies: "Do not covet things that are non-existent." "Because no one has any wealth that can be coveted." This is not what the *Upanishad* says.

In *Sutra 5*, the *Isha* comes to say the same in another way: "That moves, That does not move; That is far, That is near; That is inside, That is outside." Which is to say, it is omnipresent, which I take as truth because it is the fruit of experience. Shankara reminds us that this affirmation agrees with another Vedic text (*Brhadaranyaca Up. V, 13*), affirming that it is pure Intelligence, an affirmation that I am interested in highlighting because it is the way of being of universal Consciousness.

Sutra 6 expresses the same experience in consciousness: "He who sees all beings in the Self and the Self in all beings does not feel hate." Which is unquestionable, except that I would have added: because he feels Love for all beings. *Sutra 7* says something similar: "When man by realising himself becomes the Self, what delusion or sorrow can there be for the one who has seen unity?" With which I totally agree, in particular because unity is used here, which is also the Unity of consciousness or unified Consciousness, so dear to my philosophy.

Sutra 8 says: "He is all-pervading, pure, bodiless, without wounds, without sinews, unblemished, untouched by sin, all-knowing, master of mind, transcendent, self-existent; He has ordered objects according to their respective duties from years sempiternal." I agree with the first attributes, but not with this one that maintains that he has always ordered things, since it is an improbable belief. Shankara does not say anything about this paragraph, but Aurobindo comments on it at length because he believes in a divine plan. That he was there before is verifiable, because when the individual spirit discovers the universal Spirit, he verifies it. I even consider it legitimate to infer that he has always been since he is seen to permeate all things, but to think of a divine plan is an inference that does not respond to any experience. For this reason, my conception does not infer that nature or man respond to a pre-established design, for which reason it rejects all pre-determinism. The spirit perceives the emanations of universal Consciousness, but reason verifies that beings and things do not respond directly to said emanations.

At *Sutra 9* we have to stop because nowhere have I found Shankara torturing the text so much to fit it into his view. It is understandable, since the *Upanishad* itself warns us of the danger of a unilateral vision. It says thus: "Those who worship *avidya*, enter into a blind darkness; but into greater darkness enter those who consecrate themselves to *vidya*." Shankara, without hesitation, translates *avidya* as rituals and *vidya* as meditation, when, even those of us who have not mastered Sanskrit, know that the first is translated as ignorance and, by extension, as nature or *prakrti*, and the second as knowledge, Purusha or Brahman. This being the case, it is not worth following

Shankara's arguments which, moreover, are very brief when referring to this particular Sutra. The Sutra pronounces itself negatively and does not offer a solution as both paths lead to darkness.

In *Sutra 12* it comes to say the same thing, only that it reverses the order; here *avidya* is the darker. It is in *Sutras 11* and *14* where we find an answer, which is the acceptance of the two realities, but seen, in my opinion, in unison and as Unity, although the text does not express it in this way. *11* says: "He who knows these two, *vidya* and *avidya*, together, attains immortality through *vidya*, transposing death through *avidya*." I cannot help but see the parallel with the Mahayana which concludes, following the Master's line: "Nirvana and samsara are the same." The Buddha, in fact, had already advanced it: "Everything is, is one extreme, everything is not, is another extreme, the truth is in the middle." I know very well that this language can be somewhat abstruse, which should not be surprising, since we are speaking of the *ultimate Reality* to which few have access; one is speaking of Unity, from the perspective of *universal Consciousness* itself. From this, from the *essential perspective*, Consciousness is projected and includes Nature and Life. This is my vision and it is also, with some differences that I must point out, Aurobindo's interpretation.

The Mundaka Upanishad

> "The Self is not attainable by study, by intellect or by much listening."
>
> —*Mundaka Up. (III,ii,3)*

> "Much learning does not teach understanding."
>
> —Heraclitus (Diog. I,88)

The *Mundaka* (*I,i,2*) tells us that this knowledge has been transmitted to Atharva, and, by succession, it has reached Angiras, who is the one who answers the questions of a venerable family man, with which he begins, to my way of seeing, the well-known dialogue between *unitive consciousness* and *individual consciousness*. The first question presupposes a fundamental intuition: "What is that which being known, all becomes known?" The immediate response is categorical: "There are two kinds of knowledge to be known, the higher and the lower knowledge." "The lower knowledge includes the *Rig Veda*, the *Yajur Veda*, the *Sama Veda*, and the *Atharva Veda*," to which he adds "rituals, grammar, and astrology." While, "The higher is that by which the Imperishable is reached." (*I,i,4-5*) I believe that it is the only *Upanishad* which implies not a break, but a clear distinction with the pass. In fact, the four *Vedas* and their gods will lose their validity after the *Upanishads,* to be replaced by other ideals and new gods, and on the philosophical plane from now on the reference will be the texts that we are commenting on.

In the Mundaka the one who imparts "the knowledge of Brahman, the basis of all knowledge", is "Brahma the maker of the universe." (*I,i,1*) In his commentary, Shankara says that Brahma, according to the Manu Samhita, is beyond the senses, is subtle, un-manifested, eternal, exists in all beings, transcends thought, and is the One who was born independently. These attributes could also be applied to Brahman, but what is clear is that all beings exist in the Creator, that everything and everyone is part of it. I am interested in highlighting this monistic-pantheistic principle that underlies Hinduism and which establishes a basic difference with dualist doctrines. For this reason, the Hindu feels part of Creation, with which my philosophy fully agrees, which insists on the need for this paradigm that completely transforms our attitude towards others, all beings and Nature.

But this pantheism certainly does not end with Nature identified with its creator, Brahma. The same *Upanishad* later makes clear that all reality is encompassed by the universal Spirit, Brahman, "This supreme abode, this Brahman, in which the universe is located" (*III,ii,1*) It then speaks of what I have called *idealistic pantheism*, of absolute Unity, which is the very nucleus of philosophy and the last stage of knowledge. Certainly, the *Mundaka* does not speak in these terms but my interpretation is not forced since it refers to the Self, or Himself that is One with Brahman, which is what I understand by Unity of Consciousness and Unity with Everything.

This *Upanishad* also refers to the supreme Purusha (Param-Purusha) who is here identified with Brahman and Brahma, since the *vital force* originates from Him, as well as the mind, all the senses, space, air, water and the Earth that supports everything (*II,i,3*) The reader will remember that I take this *vital force*, as well as the *Intelligence-instinct (or mind)* to be *primary manifestations of universal Consciousness*. This overlapping of ideas, this testimony, is extremely important.

The sage warns us in his dialogue about this Brahman or Purusha, which "cannot be perceived or grasped, which has no features, eyes or ears, neither feet nor hands, which is eternal, all-encompassing, which is the source of all." (*I,i,6*) Nor is "the Self attainable by study, by intellect or by much listening." (*III,ii,3*) The means he proposes is stricter than the other *Upanishads*: "This Self is not attainable outside of monastic life." Finally, he repeats the most daring message of the *Upanishads*: "Anyone who knows the supreme Brahman becomes Brahman" (*III, ii, 9*), a delicate subject that we will address later.

This *Upanishad*, which I have left for last, because it is the clearest and most categorical, obviously does not need to be contrasted with Shankara's negative vision, since over and again it affirms the existence of Nature and the beings that populate it, as well as its Unity with Brahman; he affirms definitively: "This World is nothing but Brahman". (*II,ii,11*) "Also from the Purusha emerged the gods, human beings, birds and life", and also the Vedas (*II,i,6-7*)

I fully agree with "The knowledge of Brahman is the basis of all knowledge", because in my understanding it is the very nucleus of the Mind, it is the unified Mind, it is the knowledge of the All, the fundamental knowledge, the vertex of the Mind and of all knowledge. However, I do not accept that he "is omniscient in general and knowing in detail" (*I, i, 9*), because for this knowledge he would need to use the forms of time, space and causality, that is, to be rational. Moreover, we know that in order to reach Brahman we must transcend these forms. Which makes us think, if so, are we to find them again in Brahman afterwards? This belief is not derived from experience but from an expression of desires, desires to give God all the attributes, but these human attributes do not correspond to Him.

Again and again we find in Hinduism this tendency to make God a Person, but this is not consistent with the experience of his absolute nature. The Absolute comprehends the relative, it encompasses it, but it does not thereby become relative, the general encompasses the particular, but if it becomes particular it ceases to be general. Nor does the Whole need the sum of the particulars. The Mind only knows the universality of Itself, it does not know of this self or that self. The inclusive solution, adopted by not a few commentators, that Brahman is Impersonal and Personal is also wishful thinking that may conform to feelings, but contradicts logic and experience. We will, of course, return to this subject when addressing the *B. Gita*, because there God as a Person is evident, but I wanted to emphasise that this tendency is found in the *Upanishads*, where, although they try to define the ultimate Reality, give it, some times, relative attributes.

I have before me the *Svetasvara Upanishad*, whose dualistic vision is undoubtable, but I consider that it would be repetitive to insist on the same thing. On this subject I believe the comment that I will make on the *Bhagavad Gita* will suffice.

The Bhagavad Gita, an Introduction

The spirit that has before it the Transcendent and wants to make it intelligible resorts to dialogue naturally, it does not adopt it as a literary resource, it is almost impelled to adopt this mode. The explanation is simple: the spirit meets two consciousness's, one universal, the other individual, which determine two perspectives. That one has a clear picture, although it is... unintelligible. However, when he turns his gaze towards the sensible world, a multitude of new ideas and feelings are presented to him, although they obey a way of seeing, thinking and feeling entirely different from what is usual for being human. Then the contrast between the two consciousness's and perspectives arises. If the subject wants to rationalise the experience of the Transcendent, he will begin to question the Consciousness that he knows, and it will try to answer him, and in this way a dialogue is established from which, if done in an orderly manner, a philosophy is derived. I myself, in my first work *The Return to the Sources*, found myself faced with this particular situation that led me to a dialogue with my inner speaker. There is nothing new in this, Plato's famous dialogues obey the same need.

The one who knows, moreover, knows the way because he has travelled it and realises that the questioner has gone astray, then he feels the need to pave the way for him, to indicate the different paths of knowledge towards the Transcendent. If he points out and paves all the paths that he considers conducive, he will set up a philosophical system. This is what I have sought, but I do not believe that these are the only ways of knowing, that is why I am commenting on Hinduism and Buddhism, which I hope to complement with my work.

There is another path, less rational, less elaborate, more direct, which spontaneously expresses its vision of the Transcendent. This is the case of the *Upanishads* and of numerous Hindu and Buddhist *Sutras*, and it is the habitual language of mystics who do not want to rationalise too much, either because they do not have a philosophical training, or because they know that reason never fully explains the affair. Thus, they prefer to use examples or parables, which are not always clear and can be interpreted in different ways; which is precisely what has happened with the *Upanishads* and very particularly with Jesus of Nazareth whose message was completely distorted. Hence, on the one hand, the necessity of philosophy and, on the other, the danger that it implies when it falls into the hands of pseudo-philosophers who do not have the experience of the Transcendent and fill the gaps of their ignorance with their imagination, personal interests or wishful thinking.

Certainly, albeit that these mystics have seen the same thing, not all have seen it with the same clarity, nor have had the ability to express it adequately, nor the opportunity to do so. Indeed, we will never know the number of geniuses and wise men who have remained anonymous. We know, for example, that the Inquisition did not tolerate those who said they were One with God, which is precisely what the mystic experiences. Others did not have the time to fully mature their experience and leave a solidly established doctrine, as is the case of Jesus, while the Buddha, in addition to his natural genius and culture, had 40 years to preach a doctrine that could no longer deviate much from its foundations.

Moreover, we have already pointed out that in India, by tradition, thinkers do not launch into philosophising before having acquired an experience of the Transcendent, so they tend to be mystical-philosophers, hence the height of these philosophies that we are commenting on.

And there is another natural consequence that derives from the knowledge of the Transcendent: whoever has reached it feels the imperious need to transmit that knowledge, since he notes that everything that the human being does is mere groping in the dark because do not know their destiny (see *Origin and Destiny of Man*). He knows that all the disagreement between men, all the wars, all the suffering they generate comes from their ignorance; hence the desire to show them the path that leads to liberation.

Hindu authors, who start from different experiences and beliefs, not only interpret the texts according to them, but also translate them in their own way. Unfortunately, given my poor knowledge of Sanskrit, I am not in a position to judge their translations, but in many cases their bias is evident when it comes to the monistic and dualistic vision or the impersonality or personality of Divinity.

We know that in India there is no institution or collegiate of scholars that establishes orthodoxy, rather, if there is something orthodox in the Hindu Dharma, it is the freedom of belief and interpretation of matters of the spirit. The Dharma itself is tied to the ancient principle: “Truth is one but the wise give it different names.” Note that by speaking of those who know, is not to suggest that there are different opinions that lead to scepticism, but that there is a Truth that is seen and expressed in a different way. And what is common in all Hindus and Buddhists is precisely the aspiration to reach that Truth, likewise in all authors to express it.

I share the belief that there are different ways to achieve it; I myself have exposed different ways of knowledge, and Hinduism proposes various yoga’s. It is not, therefore, my intention to point out the contradictions, but rather to contribute to reaching said Truth. Certainly, I have to highlight the differences to better outline my ideas, which are naturally the clearest for me and which I consider to be the most conducive, but I do not think they are for everyone, since human beings are motivated by different reasons, feelings and circumstances.

The Truth is that there is an experience of Freedom through Knowledge that generates inexpressible Plenitude and Happiness; in this my experience and ideas overlap with Hinduism. In the most orthodox current of Hinduism, the Creator is by definition, given by the *Upanishads* and by tradition, sealed by its greatest exponent Shancaracarya: absolute Existence-*Knowledge*-Happiness (*Tat-cit-Ananda*). In the *Taittiriya Upanishad*, in which Brahman is held to be the creator of Himself (*Chap. VIII*), Brahman and *Knowledge* are spoken of as inseparable (*Chap. V*). It is also defined as Truth-*Knowledge*-Infinity. (*II y*) In the words of Shankara (commenting on the *Kena Upanishad, IIa*), answering an objection he says quite aptly: “Brahman as a mere substance (implied to be objective, not psychic) without consciousness would contradict the Vedic texts.” These texts come to identify the Creator with *Consciousness*: “*Knowledge*, Happiness, Brahman” (*Br.* III ix 28.7) “Brahman is *Consciousness* itself” (*Ai. V 3*) It is more. It is even argued whether Brahman, being pure Intelligence, could have created something material and impure: the world, but the *Consciousness* of it is not even raised (*Brahma Sutras 2.1.4* Likewise, in Patanjali’s Yogasutras, Isvara is identified with “absolute Existence-*Knowledge*-Bliss”. Patanjali goes so far as to affirm that "Omniscience is not even a prodigy for Isvara" (but something natural). The *Katha Upanishad*, in which the Self is spoken of indistinctly as Brahman, says: "The *Intelligent* Self is neither born nor dies." To which Shankara comments: "*The intelligent* One (Self) is (Immortal) because its *conscious* nature is never lost" (*Iii 18*). One can understand my interest in approaching this *Knowledge*, awakening this *Intelligence*, exposing *universal Consciousness*.

The Bhagavat Gita

The *B. Gita* does not speak for a personal God or for an impersonal God, or for something in between, rather it tries to encompass both. Krishna affirms that he is unborn and will not die (*IV, 6*), which is to say that he is eternal as an impersonal God. However, he has the ability to be born as a human (or as an animal with supernatural powers, since he is Vishnu) when his appearance becomes essential. The solution is typically Hindu because it incorporates the mythical tradition of the epic that already speaks of the avatars, but without neglecting the infinite, purely spiritual, absolute and eternal Brahman.

The solution is given in general with the theory of avatars but it has several drawbacks. It would be reasonable if it were Brahma, the Creator, who sends the avatars, but for the Vishnuites, Brahma is born from the navel of Vishnu who sleeps in eternal peace on the serpent whose extension is infinite. He awakens only to incarnate as an avatar and perform his feat; then he returns to his bed where he is cared for by Lakshmi, his consort. Some of the text says that everything that happens in this world, including our lives, thoughts and actions, is what Vishnu dreams of, so he would be the Creator in this original way, even if he used Brahma as an extension of himself. All this is very suggestive, imaginative and beautiful, but obviously we are very far from a feasible or philosophical knowledge.

If we leave aside the genesis of the avatar and we observe him already incarnated, he would have to be born with all the corresponding endowments, but this does not seem to be the case, leaving mythology aside, with the avatars we know. Rama realises his divine status after having performed all his feats. In my conception, the theory of avatars does not hold, although it can be useful to countless believers, and for this reason I do not deny or reject it. But I lean towards the ascending path of man rather than the descending path of God; among other reasons because in one way or another it implies a personal divinity with interests, intentions and will, which has no place in my philosophy.

I am closer to the Greek conception of the heroes who, through their merit, reached their *divine nature*, as expressed by Plato, and for this reason were considered semi-gods. I am fully aware that effort and merit can lead to that realisation without the direct intervention of a supposed divine *grace*. I say direct because divine intervention, if we call the emanations of the Essence of the *Universus* so, is in everything that exists and its emanations are perceptible, but it is up to each living being to discover them.

The theme of *grace* that expresses the will of God is found here and there in the most diverse Hindu texts. Sri Aurobindo believes that enlightenment depends on it. In Ramanuja it is taken for granted because everything depends on the will of God. Shankara seems to be speaking of the direct intervention of Brahman when he says that "The Lord distributes according to the merit or lack of merit of the individual soul" (*Br. Sutr. II,1,34*), but he does not take long to clarify that He acts "like the rain that helps the different seeds to sprout according to their particular nature"; a beautiful and accurate comparison that resembles my way of seeing this capital issue in the order of knowledge. These authors agree with the *Gita* in that "partiality and cruelty are not attributable to Brahman", but to the karma that each one generates by his acts. For the *Gita,* it is not God but rather "*the Purusha* (individual spirit) causes the experience of pleasures and pains." (*XIII,20*)

The *Gita* has undoubtedly been the book from the Orient that has been most commented on, not only by the most prominent Hindu thinkers but also by Western orientalists. The difference that can immediately be observed is that the latter judge it more objectively while the former are more willing to accept it as a whole, since they are more religious and are believers in their tradition. It is not that some are ignorant and others wise, here (among the most prominent) none are naive. In any case, apart from the fact that I would be a recidivist, it is not my intention to add another exhaustive commentary on the text, rather, as I have already advanced, to put my vision in parallel with the essentials of this work, with the aim of making a contribution that I consider to be edifying.

The problem that the Sutras offered, as we saw, is that they were very concise, so they needed to be explained by a guru. The *Gita* solves this problem by being quite explicit and putting a guru as the main protagonist of the work. This resource had been used by some *Upanishads*, but in this case the guru is God himself, which completely changes the situation, since, as the reader must suppose, God is not mistaken; it is the "word of God", as Christian priests say when quoting the Gospel. Before such authority the believers kneel and accept. But we are also the critics less disposed to accept a dogmatic language, which we evaluate according to our own experience. For the rest, curiously, the *Gita* is not considered as having been revealed (*Sruti*) but rather as part of the tradition (*Smirti*), albeit that this does not seem to have affected its prestige, so much so that it is probably more cited and respected than the rest of the *Vedas*. The obstacles that this text presents come from the author's ambition to cover the entire religious spectrum incorporating different doctrines.

It is not my interest to dwell on a scholarly study that would explain the cultural historical background of this process; I will highlight only what is essential for the aforementioned purpose. The *Gita* establishes its foundations in the *Upanishads* and in yoga, which had already incorporated the elements of the Samkhya that we have indicated. But in its time the need to express the same reality with feelings was evident, a strong religious feeling had been awakened. This is not simply an addition, decisive consequences result from it, since it almost inevitably leads to devotion, which in turn requires an object and thus a personal God. The latest *Upanishads*, such as the *Svetasvara*, already show this duality, thereby distancing themselves from the early or original *Upanishads*, which had precisely reacted against an extreme religiosity that showed, as we have seen, its decadence. The reaction turned towards direct experience through intuitive knowledge, it was a more philosophical tendency than religious, more intellectual than emotional, although it took the highest aspects of the intellect (*Sattva*) to reach the Transcendent and to explain it; hence its particular language.

The sentimental reaction, far from ending with the *Gita*, grew in crescendo in the following centuries until it reached pre-eminence as evidenced by the *Puranas* and the bards of the south of the peninsula. In other words, as most would expect, it became more popular. The Brahman of the *Upanishads* was incorporeal, absolute and only accessible to minds capable of abstraction. In the Gita we find it again, but the protagonist is already an incarnated being, more accessible, more human. And in short, in this lies the success of this work: having incorporated the previous intuitive wisdom, plus the spiritual techniques, to which is added devotion (*Bakti*) to a more humane God.

Hindu authors, perhaps all of them, agree that the *Gita* surpasses the Samkhya doctrine because it establishes a relationship between the Spirit (Purusha) and Nature (*Prakrti*), which in fact had already been established by the *Upanishads*. In principle we can all agree with this, but if this Spirit is a Person, that is, part spirit and part matter, it seems to me to be an easy resource that is far from resolving the matter. Indeed, the most difficult issue to resolve in philosophy is that same relationship, that mysterious space between Spirit and Nature, a space that is easy to fill with hypotheses or beliefs, but not with experiences.

The Samkhya is not at all naive and knows well what it is speaking of, and is sincere in recognising the distance that separates the two realities, the Purusha from the Prakrti. However, as we have seen, it establishes a subtle relationship that is much closer to reality, that is, to the experience from a very elevated but not transcendental perspective, which is the reflection of the Purusha in the highest part of the intellect, the Sattva. This proximity, it should be clarified, is not achieved by intellect alone; a prior moral purification is essential, as Patanjali, Plato, Plotinus and the author of these lines believe. The *reflection*, in my vision and terminology, would be the equivalent of *transcendental intuitions*. That is to say that although the spirit has not reached absolute transcendence (asamprajnata samadhi) it has a contact and relation with and, relative but undoubted, knowledge of the Transcendent. The Samkhya expresses its theory from this *level of consciousness* and keeps to this experience that is real and verifiable.

Then, from this perspective, Samkhya intuits and perceives that Purusha is immeasurable, infinite, but as it returns to its individual perspective, it ultimately believes that the spirit does not transcend the subject, and that therefore there are as many Purushas as there are living beings. It does not occur to it to think, though sometimes it is hinted at, of a universal Purusha of which the individual Purushas would be an extension, as the *Upanishads* and Vedanda in general will hold, which nevertheless preserve the individual souls who are the subjects of karma.

The *Gita* not only incorporates Samkhya, but claims to have been created by Krishna: "Two kinds of disciplines in this world were created by Me in remote times: for the samkhyas the discipline of knowledge, for the yogis that of work." (*III,3*) Moreover, the step towards a transcendent purusha has already been taken, the Parampurusha is Krishna himself: "Everything that is sattvic, rajasic or tamasic comes from Me," and adds that the path to wisdom consists of "freedom from *Prakrti*, the cause of matter."

On this fundamental point I allow myself to differ from both Samkhya and Hinduism, although I do not reject in an indeclinable way, as we will see, the theory of individual souls. According to my vision and experience there is a universal Spirit or Consciousness of which living beings are an extension. In truth, I do not perceive an individual or particular soul but a body and a mind animated by the primary manifestations of universal Consciousness. And I consider that the idea of an individual soul comes from the perception of what is reflected in individual consciousness. In reality, it was not the spirit that was born and died, but rather our body and our speculative faculties. That is to say that the spirit that lives in us at our death reintegrates into the universal Spirit; I believe that the perception of this reality is what leads Hindus and Buddhists to believe that they will not be born again, since the spirit remains integrated into the universal Spirit.

My experience does not tell me that those who have not perceived this integration have to be born again with the previous karma, that is to say, that they have to continue with the same soul. It does not tell me that there are separate, individual souls that have existed forever and will continue to exist, I only see a universal Consciousness that nourishes my individual consciousness. I have no means of proving that there are eternal individual souls that carry a karma; although I think it is a healthy and uplifting belief. Those who say they remember their past lives speak of an experience that is foreign to me; therefore, faithful to my methodology, I do not express my opinion.

The *Gita* speaks of a universal Soul but incorporates many theories which it does not pause to explain. If that soul is Krishna's, it is not Consciousness that I am speaking of. At times it speaks of his Person, at others of an impersonal God, at others of Brahman itself, so that there is something for all tastes, except for the taste of the philosopher who finds it difficult to digest antinomies. One explanation, which I do not think was in the mind of the author or authors, since the *Mahabharata* shows this diversity, is that it was written for different audiences or for different planes of understanding to conform to the majority. I simply believe that it has been written by a religious mind-set without paying attention to the philosophical demands. The fact is that it has effectively reached the most diverse intelligences and characters, so that it has become an obligatory reference when it comes to understanding the Hindu Dharma.

Vivekananda apparently solves the problem of the *Gita's* contradictions by calling it "the most complete model of religious syncretism and synthesis of spirituality." (*Phil. Ved. XI*) However, he emphatically pronounces himself against a personal divinity: "We no longer have here (in the *Upanishads*) the crude idea of a personal God nor the even pettier one of a God who sits down to judge." "All that talk about God wanting this or that and getting angry and happy is mere childish talk without meaning." (*Gnana Yoga*). I think that in these cases he is speaking of Christian dualism, although he rejects all dualism: "Dualistic ideas have reigned in the world too long, and this is the result." "Dualism is the religion of the masses in all parts of the world." This is ultimately his vision: "God is a person only in appearance, he is actually an Impersonal Being." (*Op. cit.*) This, incidentally, is not the interpretation of the baktis of the *Gita*.

Hindus definitively refuse to criticise the *Gita* (and their sacred texts in general) in a way that would expose their contradictions, they only make a comment (bhasya) in which they incline the text towards their particular vision. And since they all do the same, I am inclined to see in it a common mentality that tends to be an inclusion or incorporation, which starts from the premise that they are different ways of knowing that lead to the same end. According to Krishnananda (a philosopher whom I was fortunate to listen to, meet and read, and whom I hold in higher regard than his teacher Sivananda who made an apologetic of all the gods and Hindu texts and never a criticism), when I asked him why he taught Advaita, being that so many gods were worshiped in the temple of the Ashram (The Divine Society), he replied, "there are different *degrees of understanding*, that is why we offer different means", which is what I would call different *levels of consciousness*. The Hindu tradition admits all kinds of gods and aspirants. There is in the Indian mentality (the Buddha is a clear example) what we could call a *spiritual pragmatism* by which priority is given to the achievement of the objective before the means, although these differ. Since the *Gita* offers all the means it finds in the tradition, we can see in it a kind of liberation manual that all types of aspirants can use. What is difficult for the Westerner to understand, because he has not lived it, is that Hinduism is defined more as a tradition than as a doctrine, and the *Gita* is a doctrine that responds to that tradition.

The Karma Yoga of the Gita

There is another aspect or task that the *Gita* incorporates, with which my philosophy agrees more because it is more vital, which is action closely linked to morality. Certainly, morality was always present, but it was a prohibitive morality and, from a vital point of view, it was negative, consisting more in not doing than in doing. The *Gita*, from the beginning to its emphasis at the end, encourages an active morality, a proposal that has become one of the fundamental yoga's of the Dharma: Karma yoga. Albeit, as with all Hinduism, this action is also directed towards transcendence, instructing man's activity in this present existence; it is not only renunciation, but also action, although this implies, as we shall see, a renunciation.

In the particular circumstances in which the plot of this work takes place, the action indisputably clashes with the principle of *Ahimsa*, by which, the reader will remember, "no one can be killed or injured, not even by words, under any circumstances". Indeed, Krishna encourages not a worker to go to work but a warrior to kill, and not one but many. It is true that the warrior, Arjuna, had unjustly lost his kingdom, but if we accept this argument we already slip into relative morality and abandon an absolute moral principle. The *Gita* is very earthly when ordering the fulfilment of political and social duty, although within a religious context, within an order established by the karma that must be fulfilled.

Being already on a relative plane the interpretations can be highly varied. Gandhi, for example, thanks to whom many westerners learned about the principle of *Ahimsa*, made a translation of the *Gita* into Gujarati, his native language, and in his commentary interprets the entire Kuruksetra war that occurs in the poem as a useful allegory to develop the other more substantial themes that make up the work. For him it represents the eternal battle between the countless forces of good and evil that becomes personified as virtues and vices. It should be remembered that for Gandhi there was no liberation in life, since he considered an attachment to egoism to be very entrenched in man, which is why it only disappears with the death of the body. Moreover, he maintained that this is the teaching of the *Gita* that, however, clearly expresses liberation in life. We cannot say that he did not know the *Gita* but it is beyond doubt that he did not know liberation. This is the result of someone whose fundamental principles were *Ahimsa*, utter detachment, and unconditional surrender to God. It seems that for Gandhi, as for so many *baktis*, the path of knowledge (*Gnana*) has some attachment to the ego, as if the spirit wanted to know for it and not for itself. Gandhi's emphasis on internal purification leads him to apply it to politics; he wanted a collective purification, and the answers were in the *Gita*.

In the famous salt march that he led, the rebels carried the *Gita* in their hands, as a weapon of defence. Gandhi was undoubtedly a politician whose action he understood as Karma yoga, that is, for public and not personal interest. In this way, it leaves the moral principle intact, but, in my opinion, it denatures Krishna's message that commands the fulfilment of the duty of the warrior, the karma that weighs on him. Gandhi's interpretation of the text definitively does not hold up. The *Gita* incites to fight. Very much in the Greco-Roman fashion, Krishna tells Arjuna: "If you refuse to fight this just war, you will incur a sin." (*II,33*) "For an honourable person, infamy (into which he will fall for not fighting) is worse than death." (*II,34*) "If you die, you will gain paradise; victorious, you will enjoy this world." (*II,37*) The message is addressed to a warrior, "A kshatriya can have no greater good than a just war." (*II,31*) However, the same Krishna says that, along with other virtues, he makes the spirit of non-violence grow in all beings. (*X,5*) It is not surprising that *Ahimsa* has been interpreted in various ways.

It is noteworthy that at the time of the struggle for the independence of India from British rule, the *Gita* was present in all the leaders of the moment, although they differed on this delicate point that we are dealing with: the use of violence, which in my opinion, is unquestionable in the text. This is how Tilak, the original leader of the movement, and Aurobindo, with his brother, understood it. The later considered the *Gita* to be as important as the manufacture of bombs. For this reason Gandhi called them extremists, and with whom he never came to an understanding. For Tilak, a sadhu (who has given up life) was one thing and a politician another (which implied that Gandhi wanted to be both) and this is in accordance with the tradition determined by the *Gita* that asks each one to fulfil their task according to their condition. In fact they all contributed to independence and they all fulfilled the *Gita*... in their own way. Tilak stood his ground as a politician without worrying about Ahimsa; Aurobindo abandoned politics and became a sadhu; his brother decided on violent action and ended up being hung; which surely must have influenced Aurobindo's decision. Gandhi embraced poltics but did not forget Ahimsa, although he could not help hurting with words. In any event, the validity of the *Gita* in the 20th century is unquestionable.

Nonetheless, from an ethical point of view, the contradiction is still valid, so that we are left with only one example, that of Arjuna, and with a relative morality that, evidently, can be interpreted in different ways. What is undoubted is that *Ahimsa* is a paradigm that is still very far from being realised given the condition of contemporary man, immersed in the survival stage. Now, all those who aspire to the Transcendent must keep this in mind, because as Patanjali well knew, killing and wounding generates a *vrttis* that is very difficult to appease.

The *Gita* not only proposes action but also includes the most extreme, the very antipode of the contemplative state proclaimed by Patanjali and Yoga in general: warlike action, where apparently *vrttis* is taken to its greatest expression. We have expressly paused to consider the heroic spirit, in which we conclude that in its highest state it leads to the Transcendent. Because the heroic acts imply, paradoxically, a disposition of the spirit in which, though the external action is pure agitation (*vrttis*) because of having overcome the self, the soul finds neutrality and serenity (*shanti*). I believe that this is the very essence of this capital virtue: courage.

In a command contrary to that of Aristotle, who maintained that "Action is good, but contemplation is better", Krishna tells us that "Action is superior to inaction. A man cannot even maintain his physical body without work." (*III,8*) And even without the body, since Krishna confesses that He himself must work incessantly (*III,22*) "If I do not work the worlds would not be." (*III,24*) In the same way, referring to men: "To promote the good of the world, they must work." (*III,20*) For the *Gita*, work is like an expression or extension of what I understand by the Creative: "Work is creation manifest, bringing beings into existence." Work has a universal dimension, "Brahman in His totality is the Self and all work." That is, the Spirit and permanent creation.

Krishna insists throughout the *Gita* on the necessity of not being tied to the fruits of work. We do not need to cite the numerous quotes to understand his insistence, because if the proposal is to become like Him, there is nothing better than to imitate his labour: "Activities do not affect me; I do not desire the fruits of action; whoever knows me is not subject to the karmic reactions of work." (*IV,14*) "Those persons are wise whose actions are free of desires and whose work has been consumed in the fire of knowledge." (*IV,19*) That is to say, Shankara clarifies, that this work "has been realised without selfish motives". With profound psychology, Hinduism seeks liberation through self-knowledge and not in reward; furthermore, this is seen as a sin: "Free from all expectations, controlling the mind and self, giving up possessions does not incur sin." (*IV,21*) Work should not be done for the individual but as a sacrifice to divinity. (*IV, 23*) And even if the one who makes the sacrifice concentrates on the act that is Brahman, he reaches Brahman. (*IV, 24*) But Brahman is not a divinity in the beyond, "Brahman in its totality is also the Self in all work."

That is to say that human labour must be realised as an arm of Brahman, it must be seen as participation in a universal project. "He who does my work (...) will come to me, (*XI,65*) and will reach perfection." (*XII,10*) Krishna even says that "the renunciation of the fruits of labour is superior to meditation." (*XII,12*) Actually, as Shankara interprets correctly, what is involved is the "renunciation of all desires."

If in the *Upanishads* Brahman was reached by knowledge, in the *Gita* Brahman is reached by work in the consciousness of Brahman (or Krishna). In the *Gita* there is no renunciation of life, and life implies work; the renunciation is of the reward, because in it there is an ego that desires it. The "good deeds" that are performed in view of a reward in Paradise are an illusory and selfish mercantile transaction that keeps us in ignorance.

In short, work is another means towards transcendence. The *Gita* incorporates this original path of transcendental knowledge that we can effectuate in our daily life; our habitual work is transformed into Yoga.

The Wisdom of the Gita

Krishna, according to Hindu cosmology, lived at the beginning of the age of Kali which, curiously, coincides with the history of humanity (earlier is considered pre-history), about 5000 B.C., he then appears at the time of the Kuruksetra war, roughly contemporary with the Trojan war, around 1200 B.C. The written version of the *Mahabharata* dates to approximately 500 B.C. The author of the *Gita*, some 200 years later, who introduces himself as Sanjaya, is in any case very far from having heard the dialogue between Krishna and Arjuna, but he uses an apparently magical device typical of the Mahayana sutras that were written more than 500 years after the Buddha, but they speak in his name, like Krishna, saying at the beginning, "This is what I heard" (*That I heard*), to which he adds, "By the grace of the poet Vyasa (the supposed author of the *Mahabharata*) I heard these words of secret silence. I heard the mysteries of yoga, taught by Krishna, the Master himself." It is appropriate to remember that the author of the *Ramayana* moves to the time and place of Rama before beginning his story. We could also call it miraculous inspiration, but the phenomenon is explained by the basic principle, common to Buddhism and Hinduism, that whoever reaches the knowledge of the Buddha or Brahman becomes a Buddha or Brahman.

The *Gita* reveals itself, like the *Upanishads* and the Buddha, to be against rites, it speaks of those "whose minds have been enslaved by the words of the Vedas that command the rites." (*II,44*) The value of the *Gita* with respect to the *Upanishads* consists in incorporating the human mission, life in the Spirit and this in life. It is, in its own way, a *vital spiritualism*, as I have called my philosophy, because it seeks this interrelationship at all times.

Krishna appears to us as the manifest Absolute, he is Brahman and Brahma. Krishna is everything and he possesses all powers, "My powers have no limits." (*X,40*) "All that is glorious, good, beautiful and powerful is part of my splendour." (*X,41*) "The Imperishable, the Infinite, the Transcendent, the non-manifested, the Omnipresent, the Imponderable, the Immutable, the Permanent, the always One" (*XII,3*) are synonyms of his Being, since those who worship these modes of being reach Him. These concepts express his transcendent side, but it does not end there (as Shankara claims) but rather he is projected into the universe as Spirit and is the generator of what exists.

Krishna maintains, in effect, that "In the universe there are two modes of being: the perishable and the imperishable. The perishable are all the beings of creation, the imperishable is the immutable." (*XV,16*) That is to say that he is speaking of a universe, of *a single reality* made up of two types of beings. Perishable beings participate in the immortal, their spirit is part of the Spirit. "A spark of my eternal spirit becomes a living soul in this world; around it are the senses and the mind." (*XV,7*) In this fundamental point my vision coincides entirely with the *Gita*, this universe impregnated with Spirit is what I understand by *Universus*. The spirit, in fact, is not only in human intelligence, "The splendour of the light that comes from the sun, the soft light of the moon, the brightness of the fire, know that they come from Me." (*XV,12*) It is not, incidentally, that he provides light like the keeper of a lighthouse, nor that he "waters all the plants and herbs" (*XV,13*) like a gardener, but rather that he causes the constant generating spiritual of the universe: "I am the source of all things, the evolution of everything comes from Me."

In the manner of the *Upanishads*, He tells us, "When one sees the multiplicity of beings residing in the One and the plurality proceeding from the One, he becomes Brahman." (*XIII,30*) He who is emancipated has achieved a mental or spiritual state of balance, "he does not hate any being, he is friendly and compassionate; he has shed the sense of possession and selfishness." (*XII,13*) "He is beyond good and evil." "He is the same with the friend as with the enemy, as when faced with honour and dishonour, fame or infamy; he remains silent and satisfied with what he has, he does not regret or desire. (*XII,17-19*) Evidently he is talking about a state of absorption in the contemplation of the Transcendent.

From what has been said it can be deduced that the *Gita* does not deny this multiple reality but rather points to the integration of the multiple in the One and acquires the very vision of Brahman; this is what I mean by *essential perspective*. Furthermore, "The Supreme Being dwells in bodies." (*XIII,31*) This point is extremely important, since we should not look for Him in the heavens but in ourselves, since He is in all beings, the Atman is in all the individual atman. Expressed in my language, everything is and lives in the universal Spirit, everything is the same universal Consciousness. I think that at this point I am saying the same as the *Gita*, although it insists on the need to be free of Prakrti, which is the cause of matter, in order to reach the supreme objective. (*XIII.34*) It also entirely share Patanjali's vision on the Gunas (*Chap. XIV*), a vision that is thus definitively incorporated into Hinduism.

On the Danger of Sentiments

In the history of the ideas of Hinduism we clearly observe that after the luminous period of the Upanishads, in which intelligence dominated the scene, feeling have been gaining prominence until today. But as is typical of the Hindu mentality, there is not rejection of one by the other and rather inclusion. Thus, for example, Tulsidas, in the 16th century, puts in the mouth of Shiva the difference between Gnosis and Bhakti. In principle, he ends up accepting both as valid ways of knowing, but, responding to the spirit of his time, he leans toward the second, believing that the light of intelligence can be easily extinguished by the wind of passions, while in devotion the soul finds a safer refuge. It may be so for those of a sentimental nature, but I have my doubts. I consider feelings as highly variable in nature and capable of moving within the broad spectrum between love and hate.

I accept that one has to control one's thoughts, but if thoughts need control, what can we say about sentiments! Once a feeling-born belief is adopted, one's thoughts just go in the direction they are told to go. When we put a faith first and foremost, the rest, which we fill with reasons, is apologetic; one only has to look at the history of Christian doctrine. Rationalism was necessary to end this, which systematically set out to put sentiments aside; another extreme, it is true, but one that was indispensable at the time. It seems that what is most difficult for human beings is to maintain a balance in the golden mean, which is a natural virtue that the Greeks had; hence the solidity of their philosophies and the perfection of their art. The *Upanishads*, like rationalism, kept the doors of sentiment closed, with the *Gita* they are opened, and since then countless faithful have entered through them, and continue to enter.

In the 20th century, Swami Prabhupada reduces Vedanta to *Bakti* or devotion to Krishna, who then ceases to be an incarnation of Vishnu, rather Vishnu comes to make different expressions of Krishna. Isvara for his part is reduced to a function of Krishna, he will be "the supreme controller". Since it is not Isvara who inspired the Vedas (as Patanjali maintained), "He (Krishna) divided the Vedas into four, then explained them in the Puranas and He (not Vyasa) wrote the Mahabharata." Nor will Brahma be the Creator, "Krishna is the cause of all things." He reminds us that in the eleventh chapter of the Gita, Brahma is designated as the grandfather. Thus, "Krishna is the creator of the grandfather", "He is the original creator, the creator of Brahma".

Since Brahman is said to be like the rays of the sun in the *Brahma-sutra*, Prabhupada concludes that Brahman "constitutes the luminous rays of the Supreme Personality of Godhead," as he likes to call Krishna, and thus translates the term *Bhagavan*, who is rendered by all translators as *the Lord*, who appears countless times in the *Gita*, because he believes that his God is the Supreme Person.

Prabhupada warns us that "certain people with little intelligence", (among whom we must include Shankara), "consider the supreme Truth to be impersonal." The impersonal Brahman is the incomplete comprehension of the Complete Whole, just as is the conception of *Paramatma*" (the universal Soul). The logic that he uses to sustain this belief, daughter of his sentiments, is original, since it contradicts all the philosophers who have dealt with the Absolute: "If He were formless, or if He were less than His creation in any way, He could not be complete." And so, as Krishna is material and spiritual, he needs a planet to live on, and in fact he lives on "the supreme planet called Krishnaloka", which is in a spiritual sky, but according with what have been said has to be (also) material, in which there are several planets, albeit that on the supreme one, "only the devoted enters." "The truth is that whoever accepts the principle of Bhakti-yoga and accepts the Supreme Lord (Krishna) as the *summun bonun* of life (...) can approach Him in the spiritual sky."

Prabhupada concludes his *Introduction to Bhagavad-Gita*, from which I have extracted all these quotes, thus: "In present times, people are eager to have one scripture, one God, one religion, and one occupation." The scripture, incidentally, is the *Gita*, the God is Krishna, and the one occupation "is to render service to the Supreme Personality of Godhead". And he adds a single mantra: "Hare Krishna, Hare, Hare, etc." He assumes only one interpretation, his own. We must believe this author because he "descends from a disciple succession" that comes from Krishna to him, passing through Brahma, Narada, Vyasa and Madhva, among 32 other gurus. It is not hard for us to sense a strong whiff of Semitics in this interpretation: it is dogmatic, sectarian, and exclusivist. His project is not hard to infer either: we replace Christ with Krishna, and the matter is finished. Of the virtues that have accompanied the Dharma from the *Rig-veda* to the present day: tolerance, freedom of belief, the plurality of gods that converge in the One, of the diversity of texts, in short, of the truth with different names, there remain no vestiges.

The reader will be able to excuse this detour, but it seemed to me the best example of the danger implied by the pre-eminence of sentiments, since from it, as I said, subjective interpretations, arbitrary translation and reasons in general are derived. And this is not only a theory, this belief, built in this way, has thousands of followers in India and in the West. In any case we must thank the gods that Mr. Prabhupada did not have enough power to persecute heretics.

I have no objection to the surrender of the aspirant to the God of his devotion, and much less to the religious sentiment that has a specific function, but who is that God, what functions does he fulfil, what attributes does he have? Knowing this, obviously, should precede said devotion; and this belongs to the field of knowledge.

Intuitionists, Intellectuals, Devotes and Animals

Probably the most common mistake among thinkers is to project their vision on a philosophy that is considered to be the best and even the only true one, indeed, with the right to be exclusive. The clearest and most common example is found among supporters of intellectual knowledge and supporters of sentimental knowledge. What they do not seem to take into account is that they respond to a psychological type, to an innate tendency that is configured by character or, as I prefer to express it, by a distinct innate location of the spirit. So what is easier and more natural for some, seems wrong or inappropriate to others. The sentimental will be inclined towards devotion, the intellectual towards intellection. And asking the sentimental person to follow the path of intellection is asking them to change their character, which is practically impossible, and vice versa. Vivekananda purposely says, while speaking on another matter, that trying to change a person's character is like trying to straighten a dog's tail.

There is no path truer than the other, it is only more effective if it responds to the character of the subject. The devotional path is not superior, as the bhaktis proclaim, nor is the philosophical path superior, as the intellectuals believe; they are distinct paths to the same end. That is why the Hindus, given their long experience, have created different Yoga's. Both tendencies have their dangers: the intellectual will tend to fill the gaps in his knowledge with reasons, the devout with beliefs, but the gaps can only be filled with experience.

The same could be said of the intuitionists, such as the followers of Ch'an or Zen who advocate immediate perception and expression, without realising that this means of knowledge responds to the Chinese and Japanese mentality, which is gifted for that means but not for philosophy. While the intuitionists have their raison d'être, since spiritual knowledge is ultimately resolved by a transcendental intuition, this it can be produced by different means of which we are not fully aware until we transcend them. In any case, we must recognise their valuable contribution. Japanese aesthetic perception, capable of appreciating in the small expressions of Nature its transcendental Unity (see *The Roots of Art*), and thus blowing away the cloud of Maya in an instant, is a way of knowledge of the first order.

An understanding between these psychological types should not consist in being *tolerant*, but in accepting that the other may also be telling truths that one is not capable of understanding. Likewise, the followers of the one and of the other will be inclined according to their mind and nature. The lack of understanding of the other ultimately responds to the most widespread defect in the human being: an individual or egocentric perspective.

The natural and ancestral misunderstanding among the rest of mortals in which selfishness reigns supreme will be understood. All the violence that exists in the world is a consequence of this, and since there is no understanding, issues are resolved by force, and the one who wins is usually the strongest or most malicious. Here there are no longer truths, the facts decide reality; this is how history has been written. The truths only serve one, insofar as they are imposed on another, they are only excuses to establish our egoism.

The philosophies and religions that are imposed by means of force, whatever the degree of violence, express the antithesis of the spirit that illuminates those disciplines, they express the ignorance of that spirit. The primary purpose of the disciplines of the spirit, as I see it, is to make man overcome the survival stage inserted in his mind. The majority suffer from this state, from which ingratitude, envy, greed and the rest of the vices that keep our species in the animal stage are derived, and even lower than the higher mammals, for more reasons and devices that they may have. Since reason without spirit, that is to say without morals and without beauty, makes man worse than beasts.

The Brahma Sutras

Aware that with the *Upanishads* we are left with a collection of nuances, Badarayana, to whom the *Brahma Sutras* are attributed, proposes to make a synthesis of all of them; hence the value of this work. Unfortunately, not being a philosopher, it occurred to him to do it in the form of sutras, in the manner of Patanjali, so that, once again, we find ourselves before a text that must be interpreted. And this is what several commentators have done, the most prominent being Shankara and Ramanuja, whom I will try to comment on, with the natural and constant purpose in my work of expressing my vision.

It is certainly not my intention to demonstrate that my thinking is superior to that of these great visionaries, but rather to make it clearer to many who do not fully understand doctrines as lofty and complex as these. Thus, it is not about Hindu or Buddhist truths, this must be clear, but universal truths of which we must all become aware. What I can assure the reader is that in no case should I twist the text to adapt it to my perspective, since I am not obliged to accept any dogma, be it mine or of someone else, so if I find any disagreement, I will declare it, without further ado, as such. I believe that the stature of a philosopher is measured by his unconditional adaptation to the truth.

Anyone who has read the *Upanishads* will most likely wonder if there is not a text that has summarised and unified them. This text exists and not only the curious but also the most prominent Vedanta commentators have resorted to it, but the reader will soon realise that it is not what he expected. The *Sutras* in general, like those of Patanjali, are composed of aphorisms that serve as a guide for the teacher who, it is assumed, is already well acquainted with the content of the text that he will be able to explain and develop according to the questions or doubts of his disciples. Some *Sutras*, such as several Buddhist ones, are more explanatory, but the *Brahma Sutras* are perhaps the most succinct ever written, thus continue to raise doubts about the very texts they intended to summarise, so that their commentators have had to go back to the *Upanishads* to interpret and comment on them; that is to say that we find ourselves with the same disadvantages that we had before consulting them.

In my opinion, the problem should not be attributed only to the brevity of the aphorisms, but to the previous disparity of the *Upanishads*, which, since they are accepted as revealed, are supposed to say the same thing. And the truth, as I see it, is that they speak of the same thing but do not say the same thing; and that is why even today they continue to be interpreted in different ways. Seen in this way, the case is not very serious because they express what is essential, which is the existence of a transcendent Reality. The diversity is due to human nature, heterogeneous by definition, and to the limitations of the speculative faculties from which inappropriate language is derived. There are many human faculties and the combination of them multiplies the diversity to which must be added the character, education and life experiences of the expositor. Let it be clear that I am not speaking of a relativity of knowledge but about forms of interpretation. If the Absolute did not exist, I would not have written a single line, and I think that Eastern and Western idealists would say the same. The problem was already stated and is still valid: "the enlightened (learned) interpret it differently."

The basic problem, which will remain valid until the end of time, is the relationship between Spirit and matter, already posed by the Samkhya philosophy: the different nature of spirit, Brahman, and matter, which this doctrine resolved by keeping them separate. Mindful of this, the author of the *Brahma Sutras* begins with this topic. Not surprisingly, Vedanta's first effort had been to discover Brahman and to give it prominence as indispensable a priori knowledge, and on this all the *Upanishads* agree. The problem lies in the link to the universe; it is there where the nuances in the interpretations begin. Even so, we cannot help noticing that the link also coincides in fundamentals: Brahman is a substantial part of nature, it is in living beings and it is expressed in human consciousness. The goal, then, is already given by the *Upanishads*, the target has been displayed and, if we follow these texts carefully, we will see that each one of them, in their own way, hits the target.

The interpretation of the universe also depends to a large extent on the character of the person, if his tendency is spiritual, he will tend to see the world with disdain, if he is vital, he will tend to assign importance to life. The error is in exclusivism, the solution is in tolerance and the elasticity of interpretation. Now, if he is a materialist, it is because he suffers an alienation in consciousness with respect to the Origin, in this case we can do little for the subject, since he is not even an aspirant to knowledge.

We said that the *Brahma Sutras*, because they are so brief, lend themselves to different interpretations, but even before, in the same translation, their commentators feel inclined to add words to the text, either to make it more intelligible or to accommodate it to their vision; the fact is that they ultimately denature the original. Thus, already in *Sutra 3* we read in the original: "The scriptures are the means to correct knowledge." And in *Sutra 4*: "That is its main purpose." But both Shankara and Ramanuja add, in addition to other remarks, that "*only* through its intermediary can Brahman be known", and, incidentally, they justify it by resorting to a particular passage from the *Upanishads*, according to their vision. Needless to say, those of us who have reached this knowledge independently of the *Upanishads* cannot agree with this addition, which wantonly introduces unnecessary dogma. If were to accept it, we would condemn the Buddha as ignorant, considered to be the perfect enlightened one not only by Hindus, but also by the plethora of enlightened teachers and philosophers who have developed his doctrine.

And so the *Brahma Sutras* are composed and recomposed by their commentators who constantly refer to the Vedanta texts to justify their interpretation. This being the case, and since we have already referred to those texts in their salient aspects, and we have to speak of their most notable commentators below, we must pass over the Brahma Sutras, even though we will consult it eventually.

Shankara

We have seen that the *Upanishads* have the experience of Brahman in common, they draw their inspiration from it and want to lead the aspirant towards it. This experience is the one that unites them and the one that gives them that strange immeasurable power, but, as is only logical, there are some differences in the interpretation. It is logical because we humans perceive Brahman at the very apex of our consciousness, which is transcendent to our reason and sentiments. But when it comes to explaining the Transcendent, in the attempt to make it intelligible to third parties, the use of reason and sentiments is inevitable, and these, as we know, are highly variable according to our nature and determine our philosophical or religious expression and the nuances between these disciplines.

Before commenting on Shankara, we must recognise that he is speaking of the greatest experience attainable, of the Light of lights, of the Mind of minds, of the Absolute; the respect for this mystic-philosopher on the part of so many commentators who have intuited this transcendent reality is understandable.

It follows from all that has been said that Brahman *only* "in the beginning was nothing but the absolute Self." (*I,1*), but Shankara wants to remain in that beginning prior to creation, which is not only impossible, but contrary to the *Upanishads*, except the *Mandukya*. For this reason, when the *Isha* (*12*) says that "Into a dark blindness they enter who worship only the Unmanifest", Shankara interprets this to be Hiranyagarbha (who would be like a Demiurge creator of Prakrti), "Then, if Hiranyagarbha were absolutely real, the worship of him would not be denounced." What he wants to achieve with this inversion of characters is to disassociate Brahman from this world. But in the *Aitareya* it is clear: "I have to create the worlds." (*I,1*) "He created these worlds." "Man is the creation of God himself." (*I,ii,3*), etc.

In Shankara's commentaries on the Vedic texts he does not fail to quote the *Upanishads* and the *Gita* as proof of his *advaita* view, as if they confirmed his theory. I will provide only the most repeated ones, extracted even from the *Mandukya Up.* itself, which contradict it: "He who sees all beings in the Self, and the self in all beings. (*Isha, 6*) (*Ma, 4*). "Indivisible, and yet existing in all beings, as if divided." (*Gita, XIII,2*) (*Ma,1,2*) "All this is nothing but Brahman." (*Mun.II,11*) (*Ma.7*). "The Self, in truth, is all this." (*Cha.,VII*) (*Ma.7*). Incidentally, there is never a lack of, "That is you." (*Ch.VI*) (*Ma.7*) 201. "He is never seen, but he is the Witness." (*Br.III.23*) (*Ma.7*) "He who sees the Lord existing in all beings." (*G.XIII,27*) "He who leaves this world without knowing the Immutable, is miserable." (*Br.III*) In every case it is evident that reality is not being denied. Thus, for example, "he is existent in all beings", which are, naturally, existent. He who leaves the world leaves something existing. And the Witness is of *something*, etc. If "All this is Brahman", *All is*, too. It is not because Brahman exists that things are not, but that they exist because of Brahman. In my terminology, I would say, precisely, that they exist for this reason, as I have expressed it: *It is universal Consciousness that grants Being to all things* (*The Search*).

I do not think it is necessary to insist on this, as this theory is untenable, Shankara ultimately contradicts himself when commenting on the most inspired, serious and coherent *Upanishads* such as the *Kena* and the *Mundaka*, and we have already seen that in the *Isha* he is even forced to alter the translation. And, it should be clarified, do not imagine and believe that by being immersed in the Absolute this philosophy is superior, because it is not. The reality is that we cannot remain in that state of absorption in the Absolute for the simple reason that it is Immutable, and our human condition, and that of all living beings, is mutable by nature (not even Ramakrishna could remain in that state). Do not imagine and believe, then, that it is due to a lack of penetration (*insight*) that we propose Brahman inserted in Nature as Reality, but because *It* is so. To be precise, *the permanence of Brahman can only be constant by the presence of its Consciousness in our consciousness and in the World.*

Shankara rightly tells us that "it is good to find that all the *Upanishads* propose the unity of all the *selves*," (*Ma.3*) because indeed all the *selves* find it in Brahman, but this does not mean that only Brahman exists, and implicitly holds that the selves exist. *Everything Is in Consciousness, everything Is by Consciousness.* It is, moreover, logical, but it will already be clear that logic is not enough; it only confirms one's previous *life experience*. This is the Real; otherwise I could have said just that and saved myself 40 years of writing my Enneads.

Right from the introduction that he makes in his comments on the *Upanishads*, Shankara diverts our gaze towards the panorama that he wants to present to us. Thus he tells us in the *Brhadaranyaka*: "Notwithstanding that the Being is completely different from the universe -free from name, form and action, eternal non-dual, enlightened and free- He appears to be associated with the diversity of action, agent and result that it is exactly the opposite of Him." This opposition creates a duality that, in order to deny it, one is left with no choice but to annihilate one of the parties.

Shankara, not surprisingly, proposes an absolute monastic life and, incidentally, agrees with the *Brhadaranyaka Up*. where the desire to have children is rejected. This, in addition to contradicting the classical Hindu Dharma of the four stages of life that has proven to be very effective and healthy, has also proven to generate traumas that have led to imbalance, as we can see in so many Christian monks who were deprived of carnal relationships when young. It is clear that this proposal goes against our nature.

In the introduction to the *Brihadaranyaka*, Shankara states without further ado: "Samsara is evil by nature." And, "This universe, through ignorance, falsely superimposes itself on Being." The Maya, then, is not an insufficient perspective as I would call it, but it is *false and evil*; and this is an extreme. This world is not *the opposite* of Consciousness, but its material expression, it is as if we were saying that our individual consciousness was contrary to our body. This creates incompatibility, dissatisfaction, anguish and finally contempt for our life and everything living, for birds, for flowers, for everything beautiful and for all living beings, and eventually makes our existence miserable.

What class of society can we create in this condition? I will say it one more time: real Happiness, the one that is born from our virtues, as Plato and Aristotle thought, is a means, perhaps the best vehicle towards unconditional Happiness. That which is a manifestation of Brahman is also a means to reach it, it is a ladder that has been laid out for us. There is no duality, just two ways of being, one absolute, the other relative. And I would not say one spiritual and the other material, since all matter, as we can verify in ourselves, is impregnated with spirit. There is a Unity of Spirit and matter, which is what I understand by monism proper.

Shankara himself acknowledges that the *Upanishads* "speak of two types of Brahman, the Nirguna Brahman or Brahman without attributes, and the Saguna or Brahman with attributes (*Brahma Sutras I,11*) The latter is the product of ignorance (which would include that of Ramanuja), only the former leads to liberation. I entirely agree with him because Saguna keeps us within the speculative faculties alienated from Brahman. Now, once the supreme knowledge is reached, it occurs to Shankara to remain alienated from the universe, it does not occur to him to apply that knowledge to the world. Considering this, my philosophy uses the acquired knowledge that grants the *essential perspective* that it applies to the world. That is to say, it pours the Essence, which is Brahman, over all beings. This totality is what I have called *Universus*. Let it be clear that it is not I who pours over that vision, but Brahman, who had already poured and continues to pour from the Origin. Since my spirit meets the Spirit that was already there, and now knows that This is its Origin and perceives its emanations, it is natural for me to infer that it is the origin of all beings: "That from which these beings are born, by which they live after birth and where they enter at death. That is Brahman" (*Tait. 3,1*)

When commenting on this same Sutra (*I,11*), Shankara alludes to his way of seeing intuition. This would be for him: "a mental modification", corresponding to Patanjali's concept of *vrtti*, for whom it is what must be avoided to undertake yoga, but, curiously, Shankara gives it an ascending function by saying, "for this mental modification (which generates intuition) ignorance is destroyed." I say *curiously*, because this assertion contradicts not only Patanjali's theory of knowledge and system, but also his own, so we are not surprised that (to my knowledge) he does not return to insist on this point. We know that for Shankara Brahman is only revealed by the scriptures (*Brahma Sutras I,3*) or by the grace of God (*Viveka. 3*), with which he would be admitting a God as a Person, which also contradicts his system. But said assertion would be entirely in accordance with my theory of knowledge that assigns the greatest importance to intuition, and for the same reason, develops this conception extensively. I will try to summarise: For Shankara and Hinduism in general, in order to reach Brahman it is necessary to transcend the whole mind. In my conception, man possesses innate and natural faculties, albeit purely spiritual, suitable for knowledge of the Transcendent. But to reach them the spirit must move and move the nucleus of consciousness towards the *unitive consciousness* that makes the *transcendental intuitions* accessible. So it is evident that at this point we are speaking of the same thing: said *displacement of the spirit* is equivalent to the *mental modification* to which Shankara refers, and both produce the same effect: the transcendental intuition that leads to Brahman.

Shankara maintains that Brahman is also the self of each being, but that this self remains isolated from our understanding, while my understanding tells me otherwise. Universal Consciousness or Brahman are absolute and remain immutable, it is true, but if we turn our gaze and enter into time and space, that is, into life, and we observe it from the perspective of the Transcendent, we see it *sub specie aeternitatis*; this is the vision of the *unitive man*. By not perceiving these intermediate and intermediary spiritual faculties, Shankara remains isolated like Brahman was before Creation, and it does not occur to him, like Brahman, knowing himself to be alone, to be many and integrate into the world: "I will be many, I must project myself into the world. Then he projected himself into the worlds." (*Ait. Up. I,1,1*) Where he continues to be.

Shankara and the Taittiriya Upanishad

Although the *Taittiriya* is possibly the oldest of the *Upanishads*, since it seems to have been rescued from the *Yajur-Veda*, I have postponed it until now because it lends itself to criticising Shankara's extreme vision, which by covering the entire universe with the cloud of Maya not only denies Nature and life, but also contradicts this and most of the *Upanishads*. The *Taittiriya* begins thus: "Salutation to That (Brahman) who is of the nature of knowledge, from which the whole universe was born, in which it dissolves and by which it is sustained." This introduction not only summarises this particular text but also the essentials of all the *Upanishads* and Vedanta philosophy.

Shankara is both known and criticised for presenting this world to us as Maya or illusion, and even as non-existent. This vision is so untenable that it leads Shankara to fall into permanent contradictions. He himself agrees with the *Taittiriya* that "Brahman is the Self of the knowing subject", that is to say that the subject exists. Elsewhere he tells us (*Tai. I,11*) that "Brahman is omnipresent because it is the material cause of space" (and air emerges from space and life from the elements), that is, all of Nature. And in the *Gita* (*II,6*), "That (Brahman) having created the world, entered it", quoted by Shankara himself. However, when he wants to prove that Brahman is not limited by time and space (with which I agree since it is transcendent precisely for this reason), he affirms that "objects that are an effect are unreal", "in reality there is no such thing as an effect". It is understood that he wants to remain in the vision of the Absolute, since he knows that the moment he thinks of an effect he leaves said state, but he does not say so, rather that every effect does not exist. It is understood that he wants to induce us out of the causal world, but he does not tell us that this belongs to the speculative faculties that are foreign to Brahman, but rather that the world is not real. I agree that "Its reality is absolute" (*Tai.II*), but that does not imply that there is nothing relative. In short, his vision, his philosophy, his method and his reality are absolute; but his language is contradictory.

In the same *Taittiriya* he argues, "Since all products (effects) issued from Brahman, such as space etc., are perceived, it is a matter of common experience in this world that whatever has been produced exists, for example, the clay is the cause of the pitcher and the seed of the sprout. Thus, Brahman exists, since it is the cause of space, etc. And no effect that is produced in this world has been produced by a non-existent entity." "But they are perceived, therefore Brahman exists." This argument also "logically demonstrates the impossibility of creation from nothing." (*II,6*) All this is very logical, for this reason the causes and effects follow one another, but they do not only prove the existence of things, but also, by the same inverted logic, the existence of Brahman itself. That is to say, he uses the created to demonstrate the existence of the Creator, without noticing that at the same time he is demonstrating the existence of the created.

There is another point on which we will see Shankara trip repeatedly, and that is the Absolute, I will not say that the Absolute becomes a personal God in his work, but that sometimes he acquires a personal tinge when he is granted certain attributes. That Brahman penetrates everything (is all pervasive) is true, since it is perceptible in us and in beings in general as a *vital force* and other primary manifestations. It is also true that "none of the conscious souls are different from Brahman." (*Tai. I,11*), that "Brahman is truth, infinite knowledge" (*Tai. II,1*); we know it because we can experience it. But Shankara supposes, by belief and inference, since no one can have experience of it, that "there is nothing, however subtle, or hidden, or far in the past or future that cannot be known by Him." "Therefore", (by *logic*) "Brahman is omniscient." Moreover, this follows from the text "He knows the knowable, he is called the first, the great Person". But this text to which he resorts for support is, to be precise, a dualistic *Upanishad*, the *Svetasvara* (*III,19*) And he even goes so far as to affirm that Brahman "thinks through all minds", which remind us Hegel's Idea. With this affirmation he not only presents us with a Personal God but also one who thinks through all people; here we are very far from an Absolute.

To this he adds another attribute or personal condition, "We have said that Brahman is truly omniscient; therefore it is but reasonable" (again reason) "that he is capable of desire". (*Tai. II,6*) When he himself had said, very much in agreement with Buddhism, that "Desire must be the origin of Karma." (*Tai. I,VI,2*) Referring to Supreme Bliss, he tells us: "This Bliss is directly experienced by one who is versed in the Vedas, is free from sin and untainted by desire." (*Tai. II, 8*) And later, (*III, 10*) "To achieve unity, logically, no vestiges of any desire or desirer can remain." Brahman, it follows from what has been said, should not desire, and by applying these attributes, he denatures it. However, he himself meets the obvious objection: "So Brahman has unfulfilled desires, like us?" "No", (he answers) "because they are pure by virtue of their identity with Brahman." That is to say that to justify that attribute, he adds others; which is the usual resource of believers in a personal God in the manner of Ramanuja: God possesses all the virtues and attributes of perfection simply because he is God and would cease to be if he did not have them. But all these are reasons that obey aspirations of desires that become beliefs; and it is, ultimately, dualism and not Advaita. Shankara does not appear to take into account Patanjali who very wisely reminded us that "Isvara has no purpose."

A pure Consciousness, as I conceive it, cannot have desires, nor can an Absolute have this attribute. We could concede that it is omniscient, but in another way, not as a subject that knows about the particulars that occur within time and space, but rather encompasses them in its transcendent Unity. What is more, experience itself tells us, because when we reach it we know nothing of the particulars.

Shankara states that "Brahman is omnipresent because he is the material cause of space, etc." (that is, of nature) and, "none of the conscious souls are different from Brahman." (*Tai. I,XI,4*) We see here that two types of knowledge are superimposed: that Brahman is the cause, etc. belongs to cumulative knowledge, since it speaks of cause and effect and, therefore, we can *believe* that in fact it is so or not. It is not certain knowledge because it is not unitive and experiential, but that "none of the conscious souls are different from Brahman". The experience of the omnipresence of Brahman is, inversely, the consequence of our internal experience, of our consciousness becoming One with universal Consciousness, which is *Unity of Spirit and Nature*, which is what I understand by *Universus*. On this fundamental point experience and philosophy overlap and confirm this, as do practically all the *Upanishads*. And the *Gita* will come to ratify this same Idea-experience: "Know that the individual soul is also Myself."

As for the other attributes, which are the substantial ones granted by Shankara: Truth, Infinity and Bliss, I agree entirely. Of the latter, the *Taittiriya* says with great acuity, "This Bliss (in which everything participates) is a particle of Supreme Bliss, which is natural, it is like foam that has separated from the sea and into which it submerges again." "Then there is no difference between Bliss and the being that is blissful, there is no duality." (*II,8*) and so it is in effect: Knowledge reveals the Truth and generates an inexpressible happiness, which is not that of the subject but, as Shankara says, is an infinite sea (Spirit) in which the spirit dissolves.

The *Taittiriya* reminds us that "*Om* is preeminent in the *Vedas* and permeates all words." Indeed, almost all the *Upanishads* refer to *Om* in similar terms and with the same attributes. The *Chandogya Up*. summarises it like this: "All words come together in *Om*." (*II,23,3*) Personally, in a state of absolute contemplation, I do not perceive a sound so low, but rather as the faint percussion of crystals, or as the running of a small stream between stones. But in any case, it is a fact that for Hindus *Om* is the primordial sound, as evidenced by current musicians, who, before beginning their recital, are inspired by *Om* and even tune their instruments accordingly. The *Om* would be, for the *Upanishads*, like the creative spirit of the words: "From Brahman (which is *Om*) in truth, all the *Vedas* are nourished." For Patanjali, the author of the Vedas will be Isvara, and in the *Gita*, naturally, it is Krishna. In all cases, *Om* is not an isolated Absolute in the manner of Shankara, but is projected into the World and is perceptible in man.

I agree on the need to overcome the speculative, or *cumulative or external* faculties as I have called them, which are linked to the self and memory. Shankara does not put it that way, but the mechanism is the same. Albeit that he (and he is known for it) uses radical language: there is only the absolute Brahman and there is only knowledge or ignorance, and the human mind belongs to this. For my part, I perceive that all the faculties are impregnated or illuminated by universal Consciousness (Consciousness of Brahman), only that we cover or shadow them with our self, which determines an *individual perspective* that, effectively, is the opposite of the universal one. But when we meditate or contemplate, sometimes a ray of light filters through and leaves a mark on our *unitive faculties*, which remains engraved in our *unitive memory*. Hinduism does not mention this *memory of the unitive faculties*, but my experience tells me that it is real and very conducive to knowledge because it helps us to remember the luminous moments in which we have perceived something transcendent and in which the self was not present.

Without much effort I can superimpose my conception of *universal Consciousness* onto this Brahman that is "of the nature of knowledge". "Brahman is *gnana*, knowledge." (*II,1*) I could concede that "Brahman is the Lord of all minds", that is, of consciousness's, so that universal Consciousness would be Brahman. This is an essential point in my philosophy, universal Consciousness is not a heteronomous being, thus I agree with Shankara when he maintains that "Brahman is the Self of the knowing subject." (*I,11*) And also when he categorically affirms that "None of the conscious souls are different from Brahman", (*I,11*) since for my part I have insisted that *universal Consciousness is the very core of our consciousness*. Albeit that I have emphasised the integration of all our faculties through the awakening of the unitive, spiritual or intuitive faculties, in order to reach the Unity of consciousness, which is the *Unity of the Universe*, that is, the *Unity of Spirit and matter*.

The Vivekacudamani

We could say that in the *Vivekacudamani* Shankara decides to make his own *Upanishad*. As usual, he recommends the submission and faith of the disciple to the master; accordingly, in this work he establishes the usual dialogue like the one we have seen in the *Upanishads*, although, as in the *Gita*, the master forgets sometimes his interlocutor and the exposition becomes a monologue. It is interesting to highlight this because it is typical of the *centred spirit*. The master promises to teach him the method used by the sages who have reached the other shore (an image widely used by Buddhism) (*43*), Vedanta being the most effective means to overcome mundane life (*44-45*) The only cause of births and deaths consists in ignorance of the Atman which is covered by the Non-Atman (*47*)

In the first topics that he deals with in this work (from *1 to 20*) Shankara warns us of the difficulties involved in liberation, which he already identifies with immortality. Neither ablutions nor donations, nor *pranayama*, nor correct actions, nor work, “nor 10 million acts”, can generate that state; although he clarifies later (*19*) in order to agree with the *Gita*, since it is not a matter that worries him much, the importance of “renunciating the fruits of labour here and after”; this after, I infer, is the hope of reward in the other world. The just discrimination, the six treasures of the virtues and the desire for liberation that he proposes seem to be taken from a Buddhist text.

In topic *3* he tells us that only by *the grace of God* can we obtain the rare advantage of being born as a human, aspiring for liberation and finding an enlightened master. And he further emphasises, “The sword of discrimination that can cut the Maya must be stimulated by the Lord.” (*147*) I maintain that this is an improbable assumption, but what interests me to highlight is what I have already pointed out at another time: that if God deals with particulars, he ceases to be absolute, he personalises and humanises himself.

In topic *20* he launches his explosive statement, which has since been spoken of so much: “Brahman is real, the universe is unreal.” The correct discrimination for him consists in this distinction. We could concede that it was an error in the choice of the term, but he later insists: it is due to “ignorance that one takes the unreal body for real.” (*138*) And, still later, “the unreal world for real”. We will speak of this later when dealing with Maya. Suffice it to say for now that it is not reasonable or even possible to interpret this statement in absolute terms, since it would not even have been written nor would we be reading it.

Shankara surprises us when he says that "Among all the means of liberation, devotion is supreme." However, as expected, he defines devotion as the vehement desire to know our own Atman (*31-32*), that is, he makes bhakti a *gnana*. He speaks of the capacity for dedication and devotion (*26 and 31*) but with a purely intellectual meaning, not an emotional one, since the first consists in the concentration of the intellect, and the second in the passion to know our real nature. For Ramanuja, as we shall see, it will have a very different meaning.

To escape from the "horror of everyday life" (*44*) and overcome identification with the body, which for him is "a despicable dirty matter" and to "reach the other shore" (*43*) it is necessary to become aware that Atman and Brahman are one. (*56*) Once Brahman is attained the scriptures (as in Buddhism) are unnecessary. (*59*) Lin-Chi, the great Zen master, also spoke of burning (symbolically) the scriptures: "To see that the causal relations are empty, that the heart (which is the mind) is empty, and that the Dhamma is empty and in one stroke decisively to cut it all off in order to transcend all, and to have nothing further to seek, this is burning the scriptures and statues."

The highest state of the sage consists in the disappearance of the subject-object duality in his consciousness, "then he knows the bliss of Nirvana." (*70*) (It is not necessary to remind that this concept is Buddhist.) In my opinion, he is taking a false step here, because if we remember Patanjali, who is more precise on this point, this was not the last stage, but *samprajnata samadhi*, with whom I agree since it is common among artists to transcend said duality, but it is rare among them to reach Nirvana. Decidedly there is another leap left, which is the disappearance of the universe (*63*) *asamprajnata samadhi*. What keeps us tied to Karma is the strong tether of desire. (We know that for the Buddha it was desire who drove the wheel of life and generated the transmigrations).

For Shankara, the three qualities (the Gunas, which he accepts as understood by Samkhya, *111-121*) belong to the ego, not to the Atman. However, I consider it important to point this out, because like Patanjali (as we had already noticed), in its purest state *Sattva* connects with the Transcendent. In a similar way, Shankara says: "Pure *Sattva* is the state of grace, is the realisation of the Self". (*119*) And he ratifies it later: "Pure *Sattva* is the cause of liberation" (*174*) This confirms my theory that the mind possesses transcendental faculties, but it contradicts Shankara's conception once again, since we have already seen a similar error when speaking of intuitions. We find this contradiction shortly after: "The body, the organs, the mind and the ego, all modifications and objects of the senses, all pleasure and pain, the five elements, the whole universe...all this is the non-Self." (*122*)

Although he contradicts himself, Shankara insists on denying the body, the universe, life and the mind. For him, following the *Upanishads*, there are only three states of mind, waking, sleeping, and deep sleep. It does not occur to him to think of a supra-conscious state as Aurobindo will do in the 20th century (I do not know when this idea was born in India), being that he only had to superimpose the Sattva onto a higher consciousness. I think that my conception of the mind with its different planes of understanding at different levels of consciousness fills this gap sufficiently. Nonetheless, I will be more explicit later.

The first thing the aspirant must do, for Shankara, is to discriminate between the eternal and the non-eternal. This seems entirely correct to me as a principle of all philosophising, although I must emphasise that this same principle is found in Buddhist texts, as fair discrimination. It is known, although not well remembered, by the Brahmins that Shankara embraced Buddhism before Hinduism. It should not surprise us then that they are similar on several essential points. The fundamental one is the apparent negation of this world, and that is why Aurobindo puts both within the same denomination that he calls *Supra Cosmic conception*, in the chapter on *Cosmic Illusion*, in his *Life Divine*. We already referred to this when dealing with Aurobindo, and I have expanded on this subject in *The Evolution of the Spirit*. In the same language used by the Buddha he tells us that "it is ignorance that from a time without beginning generates birth, disease, old age and death." (*146*) Perhaps the most Buddhist thing about Shankara is his monastic proposition, which is, curiously, one of the reasons why Buddhism was abandoned in India, as it did not agree with the Hindu Dharma.

Shankara warns us about all the evils that the ego generates, which he separates from the *atman*. He feels the need to attribute the spiritual experience to "someone", who will no longer be a subject incidentally, but a cognisant, which for the same reason, he calls "Knower", which he identifies with the *Atman* (*Topic 101*). He does not strictly deny the existence of the ego (like Buddhism) but he is fully aware of the illusory world in which he lives. "The ego, by identifying with the body, becomes an actor." (*Topic 104*) Therefore it "feels enjoyment when the objects of the senses are pleasant and feels miserable when they are unpleasant. Hence the states of joy and misery are experiences of the ego; but these states do not occur in the Atman that lives in absolute bliss." (*Top. 105*) The path to liberation begins by overcoming the sense of ego (*Topic 27*), with which I fully agree as it determines our *individual perspective*.

"The ignorant think it is his body. The cultured man thinks that it is the soul that perceives the body, the wise man thinks that it is always the Atman." (*160*) The Atman, for him, "is the source of all beauty, strength, love, intelligence and goodness wherever they manifest." (*Topic 106*) If we only change the concept "Atman", for "*Dharmakaya*", which emanates Karuña (love, goodness) and Prajna (Intelligence, transcendental intuition) we will see that we are facing the same content with different labels. And that source is ratifying the same emanations that I perceive from universal Consciousness: the Good, the Beautiful, Love, the Intelligence-instinct. We are definitely speaking of the same thing, only that these emanations are poured into a real world, moreover, *they are the ones that grant it reality*. If we only change the *absolute* meaning of Maya and interpret it as *relative*, we will see that our vision is the same.

Shankara admits that the intellect is a reflection of (universal) Consciousness, but since it is a transformation (expression) of *Prakrti*, it cannot be Atman (*185*). We see that he is still locked up in the schemes of Samkhya. For him, the identification of the Atman with the intellect is the cause of ignorance, (*201*) but it does not occur to him to think that it could be the other way around because for him the intellect is enclosed in a watertight compartment that is Prakrti. In my experience all the faculties are free, particularly the intellect, which can be identified with the ego, which is usual, or with the Atman. So I agree with him when he says, "As long as one has some connection with the ego, there is no possibility of liberation." (*289*).

Shankara uses contradictory language: on the one hand he goes so far as to admit that all this world is nothing but Brahman, (*231*) but immediately afterwards he says that "If this universe is real the scriptures would be falsified"; (*232*), and yet we have already seen that it is not what they say. Then he solves it using Buddhist language; "This universe must be unreal and false, like dreams." (*234*) He tells us "that which manifests itself in different things with name and form but remains the same, is Brahman." But afterwards: "he leaves this universe." (*289*). Then he tries to clarify: "all these changes of nature are unreal because of their transitory nature." (*350*). If we understand the unreal in this way, we agree. We know that the Buddha viewed nature as incessant change. He tells us with full awareness of Consciousness: "Its nature", (that of Brahman) "is pure intelligence." (*135*) Indeed, experience dictates that it is pure Consciousness, albeit Consciousness that knows and contemplates Itself, as Aristotle intuited. To which Shankara seems to agree when he says:,"Atman is the witness of the Self, It knows the Self." (*216*) But for the same reason, it cannot be distracted by attending to human affairs, as Shankara sometimes affirms.

Nevertheless, as we progress in reading the *Vivekacudamani*, the contradictions are disappearing, and reality is unifying. It is as if the master himself were changing his language; as if he had used it to put himself within the reach of his disciple, that "in the twinkling of an eye" he comprehends Reality. From then on it is the *transformed* disciple who speaks, and in him there are no longer dualisms. All the objections we had made to him now seem useless; the one who knows now is the disciple who soon exclaims what we anxiously awaited from the master: "This universe is identical to Brahman." (*406*) "My nature is pure Consciousness." "It is the Consciousness of Brahman (...) seeing this world as a dream." This Consciousness is that of the liberated in life, the *jivanmukta*, because "as a result of this knowledge one becomes free even in this body." (*418*) He who is liberated in life does not worry about the past, the present or the future; he sees the sameness everywhere; he remains the same in pleasure or pain; he remains as a witness; and finally he does not know the difference between the world and Brahman. He knows that it is Brahman. (*428-447*)

The enlightened one exclaims: "I do not act; I do not change; I have no purpose; I am eternal". (*515*) This being so, we could go back and reproach the teacher: why then would Brahman have any purpose? To assume this is to go beyond the ultimate human experience. Which Shankara should we believe? Disputes have continued to this day, but I believe that the *jivanmukta* disciple has the answer: "Supreme Happiness is to be satisfied with emptiness." (*522*) This is more than an influence, it is the very experience of the enlightened Mahayana. The enlightened one "sees the multiple in the one" (*525*); which is the *Unity of consciousness*, of the *Universus*, in my philosophy.

If we believe the master of the *Vivekacudamani* more, the criticisms we have made are still valid. For the rest, we cannot forget his comments on the *Upanishads*, which follow the logic of the master. I think Shankara's logic starts from the following confusion: he assumes that the truth has to be one, which leads him to assimilate the ultimate reality with the unique truth without a second one. But the ultimate reality, although it encompasses everything, is not everything, there is an extension, a prolongation of the Spirit in the matter that is the universe, which takes multiple forms, although impregnated in its essence with Spirit. There is effectively an absolute Spirit that is not modified by said extension; this is what the disciple declares. Said impregnation is experiential because we perceive it in our consciousness. So we can say that just as the core of the universe is the Self, so is the core of our consciousness. Universal Consciousness and the nucleus or vertex of our consciousness are the same or of the same nature or Essence. The *Chandogya Up.* expresses it this way: "He, the One, said to Himself: I have to allow myself to be many, I have to allow myself to grow. And thus, from Himself He projected the universe; (...) and penetrated into each being". "Of all things He is the subtle Essence. He is Being. And That is you." It could not be clearer: we are of the same Essence, we participate in Unity.

Shankara would come to be the equivalent and continuer of Parmenides' Idea, whom he certainly did not get to know. Both express the Absolute in the most radical way, as the only Reality and with (relative) exclusion or oblivion of the universe and living beings. This has its reason for being: the undoubted experience of the Absolute. However, while the Absolute is sustained as permanent, the universe, though impermanent, is also sustained. And living beings have both natures, one divine and the other human, as Plato, a follower of Parmenides, would say. Plato also saw our lives as shadows, he also had his Maya, but these shadows *participated* in Reality itself. Shankara not only intends to remain isolated, to which absolute silence and absorption would correspond, but he does not stop reasoning to demonstrate that only the In Itself exists; it comes to be something like proclaiming loudly that only silence exists.

We are all Brahman, in Essence. But just as the individual spirit becomes universal, our individual spirit also becomes multiple, in order to attend to the material reality that diversifies and multiplies. This leads the subject to move away from his Essence and even lose contact with it, and this alienation is, incidentally, ignorance. From this, which gives him an *individual perspective*, he has to resume his ascending path towards the *essential perspective*, which is, effectively, that of Brahman. I think that this conception of consciousness if we call it Jiva-atman or individual soul coincides with Shankara's, but not in terms of the extension of universal Consciousness in matter, in the universe. In conclusion, *universal Consciousness* is immanent to Nature including my mind, which is what I understand by *Universus*; or rather, my consciousness participates in the *Consciousness of the Universus*.

Notwithstanding these caveats, Shankara's Brahman is shown to be correct from a philosophical point of view and responds to a great Truth, for which he deserves the greatest respect. Moreover, there is no doubt that he is speaking with knowledge of the facts, that is, from experience. Albeit that he responds only to the fundamental Truth and remains locked in it in the manner of Parmenides.

Transcendental experience shows Brahman as described by Shankara. Those who criticise him grant Brahman attributes that it does not have and that are not consistent with experience. This certainly satisfies reason more, but reason has no part in the matter. Nevertheless, we can apply reason, not to Brahman, but to its relation to Nature without contradicting the experience of the Absolute. Then, the correct thing is to adapt reason to experience and not vice versa, otherwise the Absolute ceases to be so ipso facto. Shankara does not agree to accept any attribute of Brahman; although he admits that it is "absolutely real", an attribute of perfection par excellence. Also, according to our experience, we can say that it is an absolute present, since it manifests itself only in the present, although not a present in relation to the past and the future, that is, in the becoming. Shankara calls it the "one without a second", so we do not contradict it if we call it the One, like Plotinus, or the *absolute Unity*, as I prefer to express it.

Ramanuja

For my commentary on Ramanuja I have taken his *Vedartha-sangraha* as the main reference because in this work, in addition to commenting on the *Upanishads*, he expresses his own philosophy. Ramanuja begins by acknowledging his worship of "Vishnu the omnipresent Supreme Being." For this reason and to be in agreement with the Upanishads, he uses the resource of identifying him with Brahman: "Narayana (Vishnu) is the supreme Brahman" (133 ff.) Thus, the Brahman of the *Upanishads* would apparently only change in name, but it also changes its nature as here it decidedly becomes a Person, which is why its absolute attributes become questionable. However, he maintains that "Vishnu is presented throughout Vedanta under different names, such as the Soul of all, the highest Being, the most radiant light", etc. He is also expressed as the Controller, according to the *Brihadaranyaca*, which he quotes repeatedly. This assertion is quite arbitrary, since the classical *Upanishads* that we have seen never mention Vishnu.

Unsurprisingly, he speaks out against Shankara's vision. Although he does not mention it he speaks of "Some engaged in the explanation of these passages" who hold that "Brahman is an undifferentiated Consciousness, eternally free and self-luminous." That, "the entire universe consisting of an endless plurality ranging from Ishvara to creatures is unreal." That both, the master who imparts the knowledge and the knower (the disciple), are "only a phenomenal illusion." Likewise, "the scriptures and the knowledge derived from them are unreal." It is true that Shankara lends himself to being interpreted in this way, but, as I have already mentioned, I do not think he has reached that extreme.

Ramanuja proposes to demonstrate with reasons the existence of Brahman-Vishnu as a Person with all the attributes of perfection, "with the total exclusion of bad attributes" (*V-sangr.49*), which is usual in dualistic conceptions. But we know, thanks to Kant, that all the demonstrations of God and of his attributes present antinomies and are therefore invalid. The explanation is simple: The Transcendent is to reason, therefore this is not the faculty to demonstrate it. What is appropriate is to show it, to express it, as the *Upanishads* do. They had already warned: "The Self is not attainable by study or by intellect." (*Mund. Up.III,ii,3*) In Ramanuja we find a "therefore" on every page, being that this forced logic leads nowhere and adds nothing to the *Upanishads*, which he never tires of quoting as "proof" of his logic. He himself, like Shankara, creates his own objections, to which he has the answer prepared beforehand. For the same reason, I have avoided this language. I do not think that in my work, even though I have given it a philosophical format, there is a "therefore". Elsewhere he maintains that the Vedas declare the infinite attributes of Narayana: "Knowledge, infinite joy, and infinite purity." "Similarly, there are thousands of *Srutis* that describe him in a divine form that carries wonderful weapons (...) that has countless servants (...) and a divine home that contains all the objects..." that is, they speak of a highly personalised god who, nevertheless, has supreme powers, so that "all beings are subject to his control." (*V-sangr.197*)

To reinforce his arguments, in addition to the *Upanishads,* Ramanuja uses *Smirtis* texts such the *Mahabarata* and the *Ramayana*, the *Puranas*, in particular and naturally, the *Vishnu-purana*, an the *Agamas* (songs of mystic poets in vogue in his time), and, of course, the Gita, because, he supposes, are all inspired by Vishnu, which for his purpose he has endowed with the character of *revealed* (*Sruti*); albeit that he extracts from them the paragraphs that agree with his ideas. As he expresses it: "As the Vedas are endless and their importance cannot be fathomed, the great sages, commissioned by the Supreme Being, collect the value of the Vedas and in age after age compose the *dharma-sastras*, *itihasas* and the *Puranas* (...) for the benefit of humanity." (*V-Sangr. 232*) In this way one can conclude that "The fires are Vishnu. The forests are Vishnu. The rivers and seas are Vishnu. The worlds are Vishnu." (*Vishnu Purana VI,v,72*) In short, "the whole universe is his body", is repeated ceaselessly. "In Him were submerged (I think he means potentially) the great elements in his subtle form." "He, then, brought into existence the totality of this concrete world from those elements." "Then the supreme Brahman entered the said entities as souls." (*V-Sangr. 236*) Said subtle elements "constitute what has been called *Prakrti*. The sum total of individual beings is called Purusha." "Both constitute the body of the Supreme Being and are his ways." Although I could agree with this, since I perceive that universal Consciousness is in my consciousness, otherwise I would not perceive it, this conception in the time of Creation that Ramanuja makes is an inference, not an experience. To prove the veracity of his cosmogony, he profusely uses the *Chandogya Up.*, with which he effectively agrees: "Being alone, all this was in the beginning, only one, without a second." (*Cha.VI,II,1*) Then Brahman said to himself: "Let me be many, let me grow. (*Cha.VI, II, 3*) Then he became many, all that exists, which is his body." "All this is in truth Brahman, everything originates, subsists and dissolves in Brahman." (*Cha.III,XIV,1*) All this cosmic process is carried out, according to Ramanuja, as a sport (*Lila*) (*V-sangr.220*).

In his exaltation of Narayana, Ramanuja does not hesitate to minimise Shiva: "In the times of *Tamas*, Agni and Shiva are praised. In the times of *Rajas*, Brahma is praised. In the times of Sattva, Hari (Vishnu) he is praised. (*V-sangr.131*) Not for this reason he fails to quote the Svetasvara Up.: "He, who is the great sovereign of sovereigns, the supreme God of gods;" (*Sve. VI,13*) been that this *Upanishad* refers to Shiva. It seems that the harmonious Hindu trinity is a later belief.

At the beginning of his *Vedartha-sangraha*, Ramanuja summarises the path to be followed by the aspirant: "After acquiring the knowledge of himself and of the Supreme and having fulfilled the stages of life, he should apply himself to meditation and the worship of the blessed feet of the Supreme Person." That is to say that the last stage is not knowledge as understood by the *Upanishads*, (although Ramanuja maintains that he is speaking of the same thing), but "worship which, performed with immeasurable happiness, leads to reaching the Supreme." (*V-Sangr.1*) We can observe that in this pre-eminence of feelings there has been a change of faculties, but instead of presenting sentiments to us as another way of knowing, as Patanjali does with equanimity, they are presented as superior and even unique. However, Ramanuja does not fail to cite in his defence the *Upanishads* that hold that liberation is obtained through knowledge, such as the *Taitiriya* (*II,1*). "The knower of Brahman reaches the Most High." In my opinion, the *Upanishads* speak of another type of knowledge, the intuitive-intellectual, of what I understand by transcendental intuitions, and as we have already seen, bhakti, as a way of knowledge, begins much later, with the *Svetasvara* and the *Gita*.

But Ramanuja insists: "The means to reach Brahman is para-bhakti." However, we must recognise that this concept has a particular meaning for him: it is not plain and simple devotion, it implies "a supreme attachment" and a "clear perception", that is, it entails knowledge. The term bhakti means a "particular form of love" and love a particular kind of knowledge *(V-sangr.238*). And this knowledge is the experience of joy. (*V-Sangr.240*) This is explained because Brahman itself is joy (*V-Sangr. 241*) Although my means of knowledge of the Transcendent are not devotional, rather, by my own character or nature I am not of the sentimental type and, above all, because these means imply an object of devotion, I agree in that the discovery of the Transcendent (Brahman) generates an indescribable joy; although I also attribute it to the experience of feeling freed from the self and its attachments, to Freedom.

Regarding these means of knowledge, I believe that Ramanuja projects his personal experience and gives it an exclusive and universal character, since there are probably as many means as there are people, although, it is certainly the task of the philosopher to propose and pave the true paths of knowledge. On this point, Ramanuja correctly warns that everything depends on the subject's conception of himself (*V-sangr.245*), because if he identifies with his body, his search and experience of happiness will be transitory and subject to karma. Incidentally, Ramanuja repeatedly quotes that part of the Gita, somewhat isolated in this text, but which all bhaktis have used: "He who serves me by following the path of unconditional bhakti, transcends these qualities (of Prakrti) and reaches self-realisation." (*Gita XIV,26*). The Gita, which seems to have encompassed everything, lends itself to it: "I am indeed the one who enjoys all sacrifices (performed to other gods). (*Gita,VII,24*) Also, "Lord Bhagavan Narayana, being worshiped through various rituals, rewards the worshipers with the objects of their desires." (*V-sangr.1285*) Ramanuja is convinced of the efficacy of these means and does not hesitate to conclude his Vedartha-Sangraja by saying: "Therefore, only the knowledge that is of the nature of supreme bhakti is the means to attain Bhagavan." (*V-blood.251*)

Ramanuja makes a mistake very common among philosophers, which is to believe that what he has not achieved does not exist, and this leads him to make successive errors that he tries to justify with reason, imagination and his aspiration of desires, thus building a reality that cannot be perceived. I know very well that from an individual perspective, which inevitably leads to a dualistic vision, it is inconceivable to be aware of something if it is not external, as if the object did not exist without the subject. However, if we look closely, we will see that our first reality is our consciousness; and this is what we experience with universal Consciousness in an indubitable way when we remain only with It. And it is, as Shankara rightly and knowingly says, self-luminous, for when the world disappears there is only light and awareness. There is no subject of that light, as Ramanuja infers, who would not understand what I mean by *unitive knowledge* thanks to which subject and object are perceived in unison, or rather, the object is perceived directly and immediately without any mental elaboration, which is exactly what Patanjali calls *samprajnata-samadhi*.

It is logical that the Absolute cannot be perceived with a dualistic vision. This vision can only vaguely intuit the Transcendent, it is to be expected then that it attributes supernatural powers to a Being like those that a human being would have if he could. But with these attributes it is being built, and the Absolute, obviously, cannot *be built*. It does not *have* light but it Is light, it has no consciousness, it Is Consciousness. It is as Shankara says according to the *Upanishads*, Being (*Sat*), Consciousness (*Sit*) and Happiness (*Ananda*), and that does not define or express a personality, as Ramanuja insists on demonstrating. Thus, for example, he tells us that God created the world *out of* love. He cannot know that, he is pretending to know the *intentions* of God, the psychology of that Person that he adorns with attributes that he imagines. He feels something, but he does not know it; he has a feeling but not knowledge; and this is what happens to the bhaktis, compelled to believe, not to understand; although they say, incidentally, that theirs is the superior knowledge.

In my conception, the Consciousness of the *Universus* emanates Love, and this is experiential. Now, I know not why it does it, because I perceive its manifestations, not its intentions. In the same way, Ramanuja tells us that souls and matter are modified and evolve under Brahman's control; this is also a belief and not an experience.

Ramanuja observes that the world is imperfect, to which we all agree, but God is not affected by such imperfections nor is he responsible for evil; this is due to accumulated karma, however, for him it is God who governs Karma. Again, we can, perhaps, experience karma, but there is no way of knowing if a God rules it, and if he rules it we should admit that he wills or allows evil that He could prevent.

In my view there is no evil in Nature, much less an evil being in action (as Christianity, a relative of Manichaeism, thinks) but rather a natural insufficiency of matter. Evil manifests itself when the human being adheres to said insufficiency. Matter is imperfect, only ideas can approach perfection when they are assimilated to Unity. For the same reason, man is perfected when he assimilates to Unity emanations that are virtues accessible to our species.

Ramanuja negates the Maya theory and fully accepts the existence of this world. But this is because it is simply the only world that he can perceive, because he has not had an *experience of the Transcendent*. This is a point of capital importance because it deals with the greatest philosophical, religious and psychological experience. I have talked about it in all my work, but since we are dealing with Hinduism, we can take Patanjali as a reference, who refers to it as *asamprajnata samadhi*, an experience that leads to the disappearance of the material world and the appearance of the pure Spirit and the Consciousness of the same that I have called universal and Shankara calls Brahman. Without this experience it is not possible to understand mine or Shankara's work.

Note that I am not criticising him only from my point of view, as we have seen, Ramanuja has not reached the samadhis that Patanjali has as his objectives. That is why he goes so far as to affirm that Shankara's Brahman cannot be known, and, in disagreement with my philosophy and Shankara's, that there can be no *pure consciousness* or a pure state of consciousness and this is proof that he has not transcended his individual perspective. He tells us, contradicting the *Upanishads* and the *Gita*, that complete liberation occurs only when the soul leaves the body. Krishna opines otherwise: "Absorbed in Brahman he surpasses this world, even here, in the world." "Because his heart knows Brahman, his happiness lasts forever." (*V 19-21*)

It is not surprising then that Ramanuja believes that the only source of knowledge of the super-conscious are the scriptures, which come from others who have had the experience; although he attributes it to divine grace. While he admits that intuition coupled with devotion can bring us closer to knowledge, it also depends on such grace. In short, for Ramanuja, everything depends on God to whom he has awarded infinite powers and attributes. While for the *Gita,* "God does not care about anyone's sin or merit" (*V, 15*), for Ramanuja God intervenes even in our dreams that are pleasant or unpleasant according to our karma, since it is God who directs karma. God, then, ultimately becomes a useful and easy resource to explain with reason, which accommodates his wishes, and the complex reality that we think, feel and live.

Ramanuja does not even go beyond the dualistic vision in which the subject remains separated from the object; belief in a personal God necessarily follows from this view. Therefore there can be no pure Consciousness, the consciousness of Consciousness, *Consciousness itself*, which is the fundamental experience that manifests Brahman (Shankara) and which expounds my philosophy.

From what has been said it follows that Ramanuja has not had a direct experience of Brahman, that he has not transcended his individual perspective. However, he has the merit of getting rid of the ghost of Maya that shadows the world, and thus recovers its full existence: Nature is the very body of Brahman. In this way, spirit and matter are incorporated and unified in an organism that participates in a single substance and that depends on a supreme Mind.

In this it resembles, at first glance, my conception, particularly when referring to the "supreme Mind", which seems synonymous with my universal Consciousness, but when we sharpen our eyes, we see that the similarities are chiefly in appearance. We soon see that all the attributes that Brahman grants correspond to a Person, with all the contradictions that derive from it and that I have already commented on. Thus, for example, Brahman deals with what happens in Nature or *prakrti*, so that earthquakes, plagues and the long series of misfortunes that occur on the planet would be in his charge, and being that these reach both the just and unjust, the serious problem of the morality of the Lord is posed.

I do not believe that the universe is a *modification* of Brahman, as Ramanuja maintains, but an extension like the light from the sun, which gives light and heat, which generates life, but, like Brahman, continues unperturbed. Brahman does not remain the same because of the powers it possesses, as Ramanuja infers, but because its nature is spiritual. Undoubtedly, universal Consciousness (Brahman) has the capacity to produce matter and life, but without a will and a reason, since this would imply a personality that is inadmissible in my conception.

The incorporation of Nature as part of a whole is a step beyond Shankara, but Ramanuja has taken a step back that is of extreme importance and seriousness that fundamentally contradicts the great discovery of the *Upanishads* maintained by Shankara, by holding that an identity with Brahman is not possible. With this, Ramanuja makes us descend and land, and although he speaks of liberation, he does not know what it is about, which is why he projects it into the supposed other world. His conception resembles what I understand by salvation and does not respond to the concept of liberation, as experienced according to the *Upanishads* and Shankara. Shankara's mistake in omitting Nature is great; Ramanuja's is extremely serious because he omits the utmost experience of consciousness.

From what has been said it seems that my philosophy falls somewhere between Shankara and Ramanuja, but in no way should this be understood as a syncretism, since it was conceived and written independently and prior to knowledge of these doctrines. Furthermore, I have no commitment to any text or author, my commitment is to philosophy understood as an expression of the truths that are expressed in consciousness in its highest and purest state. These truths are neither Eastern nor Western, they are beyond time and space, they are universal. All my philosophy is a deduction from the knowledge of the first causes, as in the case of Plato and Plotinus, it is not the product of an induction as in the case of Hegel and Ramanuja. I have already purposefully said when commenting on Hegel that the First Principle is not constructed, it is discovered, and from it both the *Universus* and the philosophies that explain it are derived.

Ramanuja and the Brahma-Sutras

As happens to trees, which become more rigid in their adulthood, usually happens to philosophers who, in their eagerness to be stricter, allow themselves to be carried away by reason without realising that by doing so they are hardening their spirit. It is quite common, we notice it in Plato and even in literati who, as they become framed within a system of thought, lose their spontaneity and original freshness. By nature or character Ramanuja's tendency is to follow the devotional path to connect with the Transcendent, which he visualises as a Supreme Person. The problem that presents itself is that he does not remain on the plane of sentiments but rather he tries emphatically and repeatedly to prove his emotions with reasons, without having previously overcome his *individual perspective*; and it is from this perspective that he judges the *Brahma-Sutras*, and interprets the *Upanishads*.

Ramanuja cannot know the Transcendent directly, but rather tangentially, because he can not leave behind his reason, which constantly leads him to establish dualities, since the Transcendent is, precisely, to reason. In his commentaries on the *Vedanta* texts he is correct when he quotes them but rarely so when he comments on them. Whoever wants to approach Brahman as a Person can make use of Ramanuja, but he does not need so many reasons but rather to follow the path of sentiments. Now, whoever wants to know the *Upanishads* in their Essence will do well to follow Shankara, who has indeed seen Brahman face to face; but without falling into dogma or extremes and following his own experience. However, as can be seen, there are very few who can overcome the ego-reason-memory trio, so it is only natural that Ramanuja and his Bhakti followers have many adherents, and Advaita few. But the number of followers does not imply or demonstrate knowledge, except that derived from feelings, which is not the specific problematic of the *Upanishads*. Sentiments as a way of knowing, as we have already pointed out, arise later, we see them appear in the latest *Upanishads*, which show another way of seeing and, naturally, of feeling. Ramanuja was born in another era, that of the *Puranas*, already very far from the *Upanishads*.

Ramnuja, therefore, cannot understand Advaita precisely because Advaita is by definition non-dual, it is direct, intuited, not inferred knowledge. It is not surprising, then, that the first thing he does in his commentaries on the *Brahma-Sutras* is to inveigh against Shankara's vision. When he maintains that Brahman is non-differentiated, what he means, exactly, is that if it is differentiated or compared, one is already outside the perception of Brahman itself, that is, one is in the realm of reason, in the individual perspective, and not that of Brahman, which is what I mean by *essential perspective*. From his *individual perspective*, Ramanuja infers, then, that Consciousness (Knowledge, the Consciousness of Brahman) is by nature that which reveals an *object* and a "knower." (subject) (*Br.-Sut.1,1,1*) So he concludes that a non-differentiated *object* cannot exist. And... yes, as an object it cannot exist, within the schemes of reason, but precisely what the *Upanishads* want to say is that it Exists (Sat) when there is neither subject nor object. Which shows us that Ramanuja has not even reached *samprajnata samadhi*, much less the *asamprajanata samadhi* that Patanjali already spoke of, which is precisely the *samadhi* on which the *Upanishads* are inspired.

And so we see Ramanuja fall again and again into the same error: "Again, Consciousness cannot be Existence (Sat) because this is an *object* of knowledge." (*1,1,1,3*) Therefore, he concludes, they cannot be One, which is what the *Upanishads* insist on. The *Tait.II,1*, for example, and the *Brih. Up.*: He who thinks "He is one and I am another, does not know." (*I,4,10*) And, "He who differs from Him, goes from death to death." *(IV,4,19*) Everything seems to indicate that this is the fate of Ramanuja.

What experience proves with evidence, not inference, of the Transcendent (Brahman) is that it *Is pure Consciousness*, independently of everything, for the reason, as I said, that *It contemplates Itself, It knows Itself*. This experience of what *Is in Itself* cannot be understood by a dual mind. Therefore, naturally, Ramanuja tells us that "pure Consciousness can never be experienced." (*1,1,1,6*) And I have the duty to warn that he is denying the greatest experience of human consciousness; and this is serious. This leads him to torture the most obvious statements, such as: "In the beginning there was only Existence, One without a second" (*Chan. VI, 1, 1*), saying that "this Existence is inconceivable without attributes."

It would be excessive to follow Ramanuja through his 500 pages of commentaries on the *Brahma-Sutras*, which I have to reduce to their essentials. From his perspective, naturally, he cannot conceive of the liberated in life (jivanmukta) who has become One with Brahman. Thus, the *Sutra* (*4,1,19*) says, "Having destroyed good and evil by experience, Brahman is attained." To which he adds, "only at the death of the body is Brahman reached". Although it is true that this agrees with the *Sutra* (*4,2,18*) that tells us, "the connection continues as long as the body lasts." And undoubtedly with the *Chandogya Up.*, "Surely there is no cessation of pleasures and pains for the one who is incarnated." (*VIII, 12-13*) And, "As long as he is not free from the body, he must wait." (to be One with Brahman) (*VI,14*) In my opinion, this is wrongly stated, since it is not a matter of the body, but of the spirit, which has undergone an absolute change of perspective, and since then has known to be One with the universal spirit (Atman). With a beautiful and accurate comparison, Shankara exemplifies the phenomenon: The jivanmukta is consummated in life, as the pitcher is finished on the potter's wheel, but it continues to turn until its inertia ends; when it stops, the body dies. *The Brahma-Sutras* end by saying: "There is no return for liberated souls" (after death). Shankara and Ramanuja this time agree.

Aurbindo and the Isha Upanishad

I have dedicated a special space to Aurobindo in *The Evolution of the Spirit* where I comment on his evolutionary theory expressed in his capital work *The Life Divine*, so on this occasion I will limit myself to his interpretation of the *Isha Upanishad*.

That Aurobindo has made an extensive commentary on the *Isha*, is due to a simple reason: this *Upanishad* responds like no other to his cosmological conception which radically differs from that of Shankara, because while the latter condenses all reality in Brahman, the former incorporates the concrete world, Prakrti and even Avidya. This incorporation is not entirely clear in some *Upanishads* and there are those that lend themselves better to Shankara's version. In any case, I think that Aurobindo's interpretation of the *Isha* is entirely legitimate. Moreover, I think that whoever wants to intelligibly understand the message of the *Upanishads* in general, in the light of a modern Hindu thinker with undoubted experience, should resort to this little treatise. In effect, it is more of a treatise than the usual commentary that is made of these texts, consisting of interpreting each paragraph in particular. Aurobindo takes the *Isha* as a basis and, without contradicting it, presents his own vision separately.

Aurobindo's God is not the Absolute closed in on Himself as in Shankara or Parmenides, but everything is born and converges in Him. For now he warns us that "The Vedantic idea of God, Deva or Ishvara, should not be confused with ordinary notions attached to the conception of a personal God. Personality is generally conceived as identical with individuality, and the vulgar idea of a personal God is an individual magnified like man in his nature but greater, vaster, and all-powerful." This idea, which would correspond to that of Christianity, is therefore discarded. He also disagrees with this doctrine stating that "Immortality does not mean the survival of the self or the ego after the dissolution of the body." "Immortality means the consciousness that is beyond birth and death, beyond the chain of cause and effect, the consciousness of the Lord Himself, the supreme Purusha." He tells us of a "Higher Self that is neither born nor dies." At the end of his chapter on immortality, Aurobindo goes hand in hand with the Mahayana Buddhist conception, although he does not admit it, he is speaking of the mission of the bodhisattva: "Having realised his own immortality, the individual still has to fulfil God's work in the universe. He has to help life, mind and body in all beings to progressively express Immortality and not mortality." For, "birth in the body is the closest, most divine and effective form of help that the liberated can give to those who are still tied to the progression of birth in the lower world of Ignorance."

Following the oldest Hindu conception, he tells us that "the Universe is the body and action of the Lord." "In the universe there is a constant relationship of Unity and Multiplicity." And also when he states, according to the *Rg Veda*, that "The Divine Personality manifests in various forms and names to the individual soul." "The Divine materialises in mind-form before the multiple consciousness and helps it in its return to its own Unity." "The nature of Brahman as we see it manifested in the universe is absolute calm and passivity, purity and equality within, sovereign and inexhaustible activity without." All this agrees entirely with my experience, my idea of Mind and Cosmos, as well as when he expresses that "he is a self-aware Absolute." And, like Plato, he affirms that divinity "is incorporeal, formless and indivisible."

Commenting on *Isha Sutras* 6 and 7, he says with undoubted knowledge: "The Lord permeates the universe as the cosmic Soul; He enters into every moving object, as to knowledge as Brahman supporting individual consciousness and individual form. He manifests as the Jivatman or individual self in the living creature." "If the mind is pure, bright and peaceful, the correct reflection takes place; if it is impure, disturbed and obscured, the reflection is distorted and submits to the false action of Ignorance." And he concludes this chapter by stating: "The beginning of wisdom, perfection and beatitude is the vision of the One." I fully confirm this, what is more, we are speaking the same language. The following chapter ratifies: "Matter is only a role of life, Life a role of Mind, Mind a role of Truth or of the causal Idea that represents the truth of existing in all possible mental forms; Truth a role of Sachchidananda, and this the self-manifestation of an unknowable supreme Para-Brahman or Para-Purusha." We see here the fundamental leap, which the *Upanishads* had already taken, over Samkhya, thanks to which the multiple purushas are absorbed in a universal Purusha.

On the other hand, Aurobindo tells us: "All things have already been realised in Brahman. It freely contains within itself all eventualities as well as all potentialities. Everything is already realised in It." One could accept this assertion, but this inference that every act was potentially in Brahman cannot be proved. If we follow this Aristotelian logic, which comes from the contemplation of Nature, we must accept it, but Brahman has a spiritual Nature, and we cannot know if the latter contains the former.

In no case, in my opinion, does Avidya complement Vidya, as Aurobindo sustain, since Ignorance is what always prevents us from perceiving the Being of Consciousness and Nature. Aurobindo, following an equivocal reasoning, seems to see it as a product of the sum of Nature in Spirit, since it is Spirit, Consciousness, that invades, floods and permeates Nature. I think the error comes from identifying Ignorance (Avidya) with the awareness of multiplicity. It is true that ignorance leads to seeing *only* multiplicity, but it is not by adding this to Unity that it becomes existent, it is not thanks to matter that Brahman and Vidya become reality, but, conversely, it is *by virtue of awareness of universal Consciousness that Nature attains its Being*. At the end of this chapter dedicated to Vidya and Avidya, Aurobindo seems to see it this way (although he does not rectify his definition of Unity as non-existence" independent of Avidya): "The perfection of man is the total manifestation of the Divine in the individual through the supreme agreement between Vidya and Avidya. The multiplicity must become aware of its Unity, the Unity encompasses the Multiplicity."

For my part, I consider the leap taken by Aurobindo towards Nature and Life to be a decisive advance, a leap, moreover, that had already been taken by the *Isha*. Fundamentally, therefore, I agree with him, although I have some objections that I will detail below, not to his vision itself, but to his rational interpretation. In his reasoning, in effect, Aurobindo comes to forget the experience of Brahman in Himself, to the point of calling it empty, in the equivocal sense of the term, as nothing, as lacking material existence to be. Indeed, Commenting on *Sutra 9*, which is, as we have seen, the one that Shankara avoids because it goes against his conception, and the one that marks the opposite direction that Aurobindo takes, he tells us, "Multiplicity is implicit or explicit in Unity", with which we would agree, but he adds, "Without it Unity *would be a void of non-existence* or an impotent, sterile limitation of the state of indiscriminate self-absorption or blank repose." This serious delusion, very probably following Hegelian logic, leads him to contradict the condition of pure Existence (Sat) of the Spirit. Hegel, in effect, who had never had an experience of the Transcendent, seeks, for the same reason, to give meaning and existence to the universal Spirit through the existence of the world; with which he inverts the order of knowledge and things. That is to say, since he does not discover it or see it in Itself, he constructs it by observing its work in human thought and history. This is not the case with Aurobindo, who starts, apparently, from an *essential perspective*, but when trying to explain his vision rationally, he sometimes goes astray, as in this case.

In the aforementioned equivocal paragraph, he confuses or does not understand a basic principle of the Mahayana, the concept of the Void, about which I want to make a fundamental clarification: there are two basic visions of the Transcendent: one, it occurs in the background or nucleus of consciousness, that like Patanjali we can call *asamprajnata samadhi*, which is, in my experience, *the perception of Consciousness in Itself*, pure. The other, when this Consciousness is poured into the world, before applying the categories of time-space-causality, that is, a priori to these a priori categories necessary to reason, there is the perception of what underlies material reality, that we can call the Spirit or Consciousness, since it is not matter but *is appreciated as Reality between things and in things and before them*. This experience is, I believe, what the Mahayana calls the *samadhi* of the Void. Actually, it is thanks to this experience that we continue to know the presence of Consciousness (of Nirvana) in Nature, and *it is thanks to it that Nirvana and Samsara become One and the same*. I believe that Lao Tze participates in this same experience: "The use of a vessel depends on its empty part." In the same way, "the use of a house *depends on the empty space* that remains between the walls". (*Tao Te Ching 11*) This is not, incidentally, a curious way of seeing, but a total inversion of perspective generated by the direct vision of the Void, which for Lao Tze is an attribute of the Tao "His emptiness is for the Tao his effectiveness. It never fills up." (*Op. Cit. 4*) He is seeing the first and last Reality in Himself, without any attributes: the Void; that it has nothing to do with nothing, and in no case with "a void of non-existence"; decidedly here Aurobindo derails. I believe that Chuang Tzu is clear about this great matter: "The Tao cannot be expressed with words or with silence. In that state that is neither that of words nor that of silence, its transcendental nature must be understood."

We then have two transcendental unitive experiences, which I can testify, in which Hinduism on the one hand and Buddhism on the other have repaired, which are complementary and converge in the *Unity of the Universus*. If Aurobindo had clearly seen the aforementioned Buddhist (and Taoist) experience, he would not have made the errors indicated. I consider this complementarity of extreme importance because in it we see, once again, the immense benefit of uniting Hinduism and Buddhism, which obey, moreover, the same vision, genius and insight typical of the Indian mentality.

General Commentary

On Spirit and Matter

I can verify in the *Upanishads* and in their commentators a permanent conflict between the Creative and the Creator, between Brahman and Brahma or Hiranyagarba or Prajapati, which does not end up being resolved, as if the shadow of Samkhya continued to fall on Hinduism. Hiranyagarba comes to be translated as Cosmic Mind, and Brahma as Consciousness. In the *Brhadaranyaka* (*II,6*) we are informed that this same *Upanishad* has been transmitted by Brahman to Hiranyagarba by direct *revelation*. This alone lends itself to serious objections. The same *Upanishad* insists that Brahman cannot be known and now tells us about this transmission. Of course, we are told about revelation, that is, about dogma, then we fall into belief and leave experience, which is the firm foundation of the *Upanishads*.

Hinduism does not entirely detach itself from Samkhya by maintaining a distance and difference between the ultimate Reality, Brahman, and the Creator, Brahma. Brahma comes to be like Plato's demiurge, who is in charge of shaping this universe while Brahman, the Supreme Being, remains separate and Immutable.

Shaivism, which as we have seen has a remote origin, only took shape as a doctrine much later with the mythical-religious literature of the Puranas. Already warned that the Supreme Being cannot be occupied with particulars, and influenced by the Tantra tradition, it presents a solution that conforms to its followers, prone to turn their devotion to a female deity, who would be like Plato's Demiurge. In this way, Shaivism leaves Shiva inactive meditating in the Himalayas, while his consort is in charge of Creation. If we take into account the long folkloric tradition of Shiva, on the one hand, and the serious requirements of the *Upanishads*, on the other, to which we must add religious sentiment, the proposed solution appears reasonable and balanced; the enormous number of supporters it has should not be surprising.

Vishnuism, also loaded with an ancient mythical tradition and without ignoring Vedanta, finds its own solution: the Creator will be the classic Brahma, but he will come out of Vishnu's navel, which leaves him as the supreme divinity, Narayán, who sleeps for eternity on Sesha, the serpent that represents infinity.

The reader will surely be surprised to see that in my conclusions the mix of doctrine with these mythical stories. But if this is the case, it is because he has forgotten that Hinduism uses all the mental faculties in its projection towards the Transcendent, so it would be arbitrary to reduce it to one of them. Hinduism cannot be limited to rational schemes. Moreover, we have already seen enough to attest that *the first principles and the last truths transcend reason*. So that reason is already a descending path, it is what is deduced from these transcendent truths, and what interests us is the ascending path. It may then be thought that we can dispense with philosophy, but this would be the opposite of what I mean by such, which is to pave the way towards these first principles. The conclusions come later, and they also carry the same ascending intention by making it reasonable for us to take that path. In my opinion, the intermediary Being in Creation, which is constant, is unnecessary, in addition to generating an inevitable duality. I believe that the theory of emanations that I propose and that which the great Plotinus had already expressed, avoids that unnecessary step.

In my experience, this intermediary being does not appear, but rather *pure Consciousness* emanating, pouring into the Universus its virtues, among others, *the vital impulse*, which would be the function of Brahma. Furthermore, I am reluctant to believe that anyone has had the *experience* of Brahma or Hiranyagarba and am inclined to think that it is the result of an *inference*. And I hasten to clarify that this does not alter the essence of Hinduism (or Buddhism) which is the experience of the Consciousness of Brahman (or of the Buddha) and of the unity of Atman (as consciousness) with Brahman or universal Consciousness. Brahman does not need hands and not even reason, because only if he dealt with particulars would he need them. Of course, in my conception, all personal gods are no more than a human projection.

I think Buddhism has the obvious and correct answer: "If the world had been made by Isvara, (this includes all gods as a Person) there would be no change, no destruction, no suffering, no calamity." (Asvaghosha, *Buddhacarita*). This would imply, we can add, that he participates in some way in the feelings of mortals, which would question his virtues. "If Isvara -continues- acts with a purpose, it cannot be said that he is perfect, since all-purpose implies the satisfaction of a desire. And if he acts without a purpose he would be like a baby or a madman. So he concludes: "The idea of Isvara proves to be false before all rational arguments." (*Op. Cit*).This arguments, needless not to say, are applied to all dualistic doctrines. It is appropriate to remember that the Isvara proposed by Patanjali, who with his habitual wisdom had surely considered these possible objections, "does not create, nor has any purpose."

The great contribution of the *Upanishads* is the pre-eminence of the Absolute, but still they and their commentators remain tied to the old Vedas and their gods to a greater or lesser extent, and Brahma, a personal god, is a remnant of that tradition. I admit that the majority of human beings need to personalise the expressions of the universal Spirit, and it seems to me very good that they do so, since we cannot ask everyone to be philosophers with mystical experiences, but when it comes to philosophising the intervention of personal gods they constitute an obstacle to the understanding of the Absolute.

Later I will refer to the problem of revelation in general, now I would like to highlight the particular drawback that it presents in the interpretation of the *Upanishads*: if they have been revealed, they must necessarily present a unity and no disparity, since it is presupposed that they have been revealed by *a single Being who knows*. However, they present evident differences that have not failed to be noticed even by Shankara himself and especially by Ramanuja. He settles the matter by maintaining that what opposes his theory of Brahman without a second is a resource used by authors to reach readers with less understanding, he divides the different interpretations but accepts them all.

In my opinion, the matter is resolved in a more humane or natural way. I have no doubt that the authors of the *Upanishads* have had a transcendental experience and have perceived Brahman itself, that is, they agree on the essentials of the matter, but then they have had to interpret this experience with their speculative faculties and their sentiments. If they are of an intellectual type and with a greater capacity for abstraction, like Shankara, they will stay with the Absolute itself, if they are more sentimental they will tend to represent an object of devotion and establish a dualism, although it will depend on the degree of identification of the subject with Unity.

According to my experience, there is a universal Consciousness in itself, which emanates energies or virtues necessary for life and which reside in all beings and in everything created, which are expressed in everything that lives, in each cell, in each bacterium, and that are manifested in the human being in his body and in his mind, and become evident when he reaches a certain level of consciousness. But matter, at the moment it begins to be such, that is, when it ceases to be pure spirit, although always impregnated with it, to live as matter, as an animal, seeks its own expression, it needs it to survive; in other words, it requires *relative independence*. This will never be absolute, because this would be an excess, a going beyond oneself, which would be equivalent to a mental imbalance, madness, and if the excess is bodily it would be a disease.

This said, the correct way to live is in accordance with the *primary manifestations*, with the original energies that the universal Consciousness emanates. Living beings, although they use these energies, generally ignore them, but in higher mammals they can already be appreciated for their expressions of goodness, need for order, beauty, etc. The same thing happens in humans, with the difference that they can make them conscious through the progressive perception of them. This is the work of the unitive faculties, moral, aesthetic, religious and philosophical, which, well directed, following the current of these spiritual energies, can go back to the Sources of Life.

From what has been said, in my conception there would be a certain duality of spirit and matter, since, as I said, the latter, due to its condition, needs a certain independence, but this must be relative and always maintain an essential dependence. Now, to the extent that the spirit distances itself and becomes independent, its mind darkens and becomes alienated, since its intelligence feeds on the light of universal Intelligence, and inversely, the closer it gets to its Origin, through the harmonious integration of its faculties, dependent on the unitive faculties, and approaches its Unity, which by its nature is perfect, it is perfected and spiritualised. When one manages to become independent of matter and discovers the pure Spirit, one becomes independent and frees oneself. We can verify this, at least, in those who are wiser, those who, due to their proximity to universal Consciousness, are directly nourished by its manifestations, which, as we said, are the virtues themselves.

I think that what has been said does not contradict what Hindus and Buddhists understand by liberation, there is only a difference in nuances when interpreting the relationship of Brahman with matter and one that we must recognise if we want to be faithful to reality and not adapt it to ideals. Brahman is in everything but he is not the same as everything. This resume the idealistic pantheism.

To recapitulate the relationship of my conception with Vedanta: already the *Aitareya Up*. had found the Unity between the Vedic gods and Nature: "This One is Brahman, it is Indra, it is Prajapati, it is all the gods." In the same Unity will converge the Trimurti or Trinity of Hinduism. Thus we read in the *Kaivalya Upanishad*, "He is Brahman, He is Shiva, He is Vishnu, He is All." And in the *Brhadaranyaka Upanishad*, "Offer sacrifices to this god or to that other, each of the gods is a manifestation of Him, for He is all the gods." Therefore, we can conclude that all the *Upanishads* agree on the unity of the gods, that is, that polytheism becomes monotheism in the form of henotheism, that is, by inclusion and not by exclusion of the gods; with which I fully agree.

Then there is the relationship of man with Brahman; the *Upanishads* also agree on this: "He who knows all this remains firmly established in Brahman." (*Kena IV,9*), "Anyone who knows Brahman becomes Brahman." (*Mund. III,ii,9*) Shankara will insist on the same. With this, monism is ratified, with which I also agree.

The relationship of Brahman with Nature would remain. We have already pointed out that despite the nuances, the *Upanishads* tend to unify them. The *Gita* has, to my mind, the definitive answer: "When one sees the multiplicity of beings residing in the One *and the plurality proceeding from the One*, he becomes Brahman." (*XIII, 30*) In which I agree without hesitation, since I consider the knowledge of the First Reality essential to all subsequent knowledge. The *Kena Upanishad* had already expressed it: "He is the Mind of the mind, the Life of life." And even more clearly in the *Mundaka Upanishad*, "The knowledge of Brahman is the basis of all knowledge."

The problem, as we have seen, is Shankara. This is my conclusion: what Shankara did not fully understand is that *things also Are when they are One with Brahman*. He seems to see it in a moment, as the disciple testifies at the end of the *Vivekacudamani*, but then the world ultimately vanishes in the cloud of Maya. The opposite seems to happen to Aurobindo, when he incorporates the world he loses the vision of Brahman in Himself; as if the Maya had fallen over Brahman. Once again we verify that the truth is in the golden mean. The solution was already announced, although not defined, in the *Aitareya Upanishad*: all creatures "have the Consciousness that grants them reality (...) and this Consciousness is Brahman." (*III,3*)

My experience dictates it to me like this: I would not define, to avoid all personality, the first and last reality (Brahman) as a Being, *but as pure Consciousness, which is what gives Being to all beings*, which is verified when individual consciousness disappears, precisely due to its own purification process, and only *pure Consciousness* remains, the *universal Consciousness* permeating the world and illuminating the infinite intelligences; this is the *Unity of the Universus*.

On the Observer

I affirm, incidentally, that there is a *universal Consciousness* that I can identify with Brahman, which the *Upanishads* call the Observer or *the Knower*, but it turns out that according to these texts it also knows what happens in our particular minds, which does not correspond to a universal Consciousness. The *Brhadaranyaka Upanishad* (*8.III,7,15*) tells us, "He who dwells in all beings and within all beings, whom no being knows", (with reason, I would add) "whose body is all beings" ... So far I have no objection, but, to continue, "and who controls all beings from within, He is your Self, the *internal Controller*, the immortal." If he controlled all beings from within, we would have to impute our faults to him or we would not exercise our vices with such impudence, and human relationships would be more beautiful and harmonious; so this addition, in principle, does not hold.

However, there is the intuition of a truth behind this statement. Indeed there is an observer, an internal controller in us that transcends our reason and knows our intentions, which we can call moral conscience in principle, that we all know, some more and others less. This moral conscience belongs to *unitive or altruistic consciousness*. I have usually referred only to the first because it is the consciousness that we must ultimately awaken, and because these two consciousnesses overlap at one point; but to be precise in this matter we should separate them. We can say that altruistic consciousness is potentially unitive. Altruistic consciousness is what distinguishes the noble man from the vulgar, the former hears and obeys it, the latter does not, however both are linked to the *individual perspective* that is usual in the human being. This altruistic consciousness is a means towards the transcendent and surely the most indicated to achieve it, because thanks to it intuitions are sharpened and elevated feelings are awakened, but it is a means, not an end.

Unitive consciousness obeys the *essential perspective*, it is the result of the unification of the mind, it is this unification that shapes this consciousness that is the true centre of human consciousness, since it lies between individual consciousness and universal Consciousness. Only then, when there is a permanent or unitive relationship between these two consciousnesses, is the human being able to act correctly, that is, without moral failure; although he may be mistaken in his application in the concrete acts. This is the *unitive man*, the one who is in permanent contact with universal Consciousness or Brahman. However, it is not this, he is not absorbed in the direct contemplation of Brahman itself constantly. If the spirit were in this state of absorption, which is transcendent, it would not be able to attend to particulars, for this it must move and enter space and time. From this it follows that Brahman cannot attend to particulars, he cannot enter the multiple and diverse world without said displacement, or *process of unitive individuation*. For action in this concrete reality there is *unitive consciousness*, which is between the human and the divine. The *unitive man* perceives that there is an Observer, but when it comes to acting it is he who is in control, not Brahman, of which he will be an expression or manifestation, but not Itself. The *Upanishads* themselves say so: "Brahman has no arms," etc. But here lies the error of the author of the *Brhadaranyaka*, the existence of the observer does not imply that there is a *Controller* of our actions.

The *Brhadaranyaka* itself expounds at length on death and on the destiny of the soul afterwards. But reincarnation in superior and inferior beings, including insects, is not limited to this world, there are, in this *Upanishad*, celestial worlds where the gods dwell, and in these worlds there are different planes, Brahmaloka being the highest, since Brahma dwells in it, which would be personalised Brahman. I do not have to dwell on this mythology, I am only interested in highlighting the fact that Shankara in his commentary does not deny the existence of these celestial worlds or the gods that inhabit it, for which reason his Absolute wobbles dangerously; albeit to get away with it, he incorporates all of these worlds into Samsara. Supposedly, then, the enlightened one would be beyond them and the Creator of the universe himself; but, although he finally orders the matter logically, it is difficult to accept it on the plane of philosophy. The reader will remember that for Prabhupada, surely inspired by the *Brhadaranyaka*, Krishnaloka is the ultimate desired paradise, which philosophically holds even less.

In short, although the *Upanishads* are an inexhaustible source of wisdom, because they effectively guide us from the ultimate Reality, this does not mean that we must accept without question everything they say or be obliged to justify what is doubtful or contradictory. The indisputable value of the *Upanishads* resides in the fact that they all converge on the ultimate Reality, thus leaving a paradigm to which all aspirants to the knowledge of the Transcendent must abide, who are thus compelled to transcend their individual perspective and reach an elevated level of consciousness and knowledge before philosophising and establishing a doctrine. This has not happened in the West where there is no reference to which thinkers must adjust, so each one thinks from the level of consciousness that has touched him by nature. The result is what Schelling rightly called *the scandal of philosophy*, since he saw that no agreement has ever been reached, which has resulted in the discrediting of this discipline.

Hindus and Buddhists start from the premise that they must evolve to reach the level of consciousness necessary to understand. My philosophy adheres entirely to this epistemological premise. The great philosophies are deduced from Brahman downwards, they imply prior knowledge of Brahman, hence the greatness of the *Upanishads*.

On the Atman

I have repeatedly said throughout this work, *I* think, in *my* experience, according to *my* perception, etc., because language has forced me to do so. I do not believe, in accord with Buddhism, that there is a subject, a self that remains the same in which perceptions, thoughts, beliefs and so on are based. I perceive like the Buddha, Heraclitus and Bergson (commented on in *The Evolution of the Spirit*), that everything flows and changes incessantly, particularly the mind that never stops, except in moments of absolute contemplation. According to my understanding this happens: the permanent flow is a non-transmissible experience, but in order to make intelligible the external and internal world in which he lives, the human being stops reality with concepts that are fixed. The first basic concept that he has created for this purpose is the self, to which he adds other concepts that he relates to it; this mechanism is what we call reason, which in order to relate needs the faculty of remembering. So that the self, reason and memory form the basic trilogy necessary to rational knowledge. But since all three are static, none corresponds to moving reality. In my conception this contraption has, like all reality, a metaphysical origin: there is an *immutable Reality* that is not perceptible by the senses or by reason. But this could not exist without an intuition of the *Immutable* of which man is not aware but which he uses because he needs a fixed reference, so that knowledge begins in the *Consciousness that is One with said Reality*.

In this way, the human being has endowed all the reality that he knows and is knowing with concepts and has created a world and a universe full of concepts that are like photos, so to speak, of reality, but not the film that it really is. No one will deny the usefulness of this knowledge, but it happens that this world of abstractions does not reveal Reality as It Is, which is transcendent to the self, reason and memory. From which it follows that in order to perceive that Reality it is necessary to transcend this trilogy, which is the basic mechanism on which the habitual way of knowing depends.

This brings us to the initial topic, since the spoken and written language has been configured according to the resource or assumption that there is a self, a stable subject that serves as a reference to the multitude of objects of knowledge. That is to say that to transmit my knowledge I have been obliged to use a language that does not correspond to the Reality that I wanted to expose, for the simple reason that there is no other, except art (see *The Roots of Art*) but that is not the language used by philosophy. When I say, then, I think, I perceive, etc., it is not exactly so, because as I said, everything flows and changes ceaselessly. The self and the concepts generated by reason are like scaffolding that we constantly superimpose onto each other, which respond to reality but do not correspond to Reality as It Is. Now, since this Reality is the object of philosophy, and the object of my work, the reader will have to be condescending and understanding and see behind or beyond the language.

It will be said to me, rightly, that there is a subject in which knowledge converges, but let us not forget that the knowledge of which one is thinking is the one derived from reason, which is *cumulative* and static. I certainly do not deny in an absolute way that there is a vertex in which all knowledge converges; although the matter is too risky and delicate to admit it without further ado, since there is the constant danger of falling into the self. To specify the nature of this vertex I will use an illustration: it is like an electric current that flows constantly and that keeps us alive, thinking and feeling. But the matter does not end there, rather it begins there, the philosophical search begins there, with the inevitable question, where does this current come from? I have already said it in another context: it comes from *Élan vital* and Intelligence-instinct, which have a transcendent origin. The danger here lies in turning that experience into a concept, because then we stop the current and confuse it with the socket.

I believe that with this abbreviated explanation and this simple illustration, the disparity that exists between Buddhism and Hinduism on this point, undoubtedly very complex, is settled, since it deals with the existence or non-existence of the soul, which the first tends to deny and the second to state emphatically. In my opinion, what Buddhism (which is pragmatic on the spiritual plane) fears is that it will fall into the aforementioned error; it is for this purpose that it denies the *atman*, so that it does not fall into the static concept of a subject that remains the same. In order to understand Buddhism and my conception of reality, including the mind, it is essential not to forget, not for a minute, which in constant movement there is constant transformation. The one that was a minute ago is no longer in the present, the river in which we bathed a few seconds ago is no longer the same as it is now; Heraclitus' experience is identical to the one we are exposing and to that of the Buddha and that we illustrated as electricity, trying to express the *Élan vital* and Intelligence-instinct on which all living beings depend, and when they cease to receive them they perish. This is the conclusion: Only the core of the *Universus* is immutable; and for that is the essential reference.

The difference between Buddhism and Hinduism is minimal, since the latter maintains that there is a substance as subtle as one can imagine that is permanent, the former, the same substance that changes in its flow. The theory of the transmission of karma, which both hold, makes necessary the existence of something that underlies, remains and is transmitted from one existence to another, although the permanent transformation that Buddhism maintains means that it is not exactly the same at the moment of birth and one minute later. The subtlety of this conception prevents it from accepting that the *atman* measures an inch and that it is housed in the heart as one *Upanishad* maintains, but if we do not take this as *revealed*, we will see that the doctrinal distances are minimal and insubstantial.

Hinduism, in fact, constantly strives to lead to the experience that the atman is actually the universal *Atman*, strictly speaking it can be said that this is the raison d'être of this doctrine. We have already seen that the *Upanishads* and the *Gita* insist on this purpose, Shankara's systematic attack on the ego is intended to make it clear that this reference is an illusion and has nothing to do with the *atman*. Fundamentally, the common aspiration, which includes my philosophy, is to overcome what I understand by *individual perspective*, to reach the *essential perspective*, which is that of *universal Consciousness* itself, which is the equivalent of the universal Atman whose main attribute is knowledge.

On Revelation

I have not stopped expressing that in my philosophy the concept of revelation is unnecessary and contradictory because it implies or suggests the intervention of a personal God, which does not agree with the Absolute. Although I cannot stop observing the effectiveness that it has had in India when applied to the *Upanishads*, it refers to the highest authority that endorses these texts of undoubted wisdom.

It is not a question here of being for or against the dogma of revelation, but of expressing the truths as they are shown in their essence and in accordance with reason. For the rest, if "he who knows Brahman becomes Brahman" then not only the Rishis of the past are the ones who hold knowledge. Nor is it legitimate, in the name of an arbitrary orthodoxy, to torture the texts to adapt them to a particular vision, as Shankara and Ramanuja do; and I am quoting the most orthodox commentators. The most notable and recurring contradictions of both thinkers are specifically due to their attempt to adjust to the texts considered as revealed; which goes against the same texts and discredits their philosophies. To this we must add that there are very few, about a dozen, *Upanishads* that have been selected from more than one hundred, and that have been recognised and incorporated as *revealed*. My proposal, then, is to freely interpret these texts, select from them the parts in which we can agree, the really inspired, true, reasonable and coincidental ones; the *Isha*, in this case, would remain intact and could serve as a reference.

The arbitrariness of this faith in revelation in Hinduism becomes clear when we see that *Srutis* are considered intermediate texts between the Indus culture and the end of the *Upanishads*, with Shaivism having been incorporated to occupy a predominant position, albeit having nothing to do with orthodoxy. Something similar happened with Krishna, a god born from folklore and disclosed by the epic, in particular by the author who interpolated the *Gita*, and later by the *Bhagavata Purana*. We need not recall the influence that the entire epic has exerted on the Hindu tradition, but we do need to recall that not all these texts are considered to be revealed. What then is the need to preserve the dogma of revelation? Moreover, it presents these philosophical problems of difficult resolution. For example, if Brahman is Shankara's Absolute, it would not concern itself at all with granting some men *the grace* to reveal to them the scriptures which would later be accepted as *Srutis* by the Brahmans; the same ones that have finally incorporated Shiva and Krishna.

Although in my conception there is no place for the *revelation* granted by the grace of a heteronomous Being, I must admit that the experience of the Sacred is expressed as revelation, precisely because it is not one (the self) that has it, but decidedly another, but the *belief* in the revelation consists in a return of the spirit to the habitual self that takes the "other" as such and the Transcendent as separate, for which reason the self-rationalises and personalises it; it is this that leads to religious dualism.

The obstacle that I see in understanding the convergence of Hinduism, Buddhism and the Hellenic tradition is precisely *the dogma of revelation* that has closed so many doors when it comes to accepting the wisdom of other doctrines in the history of religions, in particular, as we know, in the case of Christianity and Islam, given their intolerance and arrogance that has led them to the aberration of wars in the name of supposedly revealed religious doctrines; although it is obvious that they obeyed political and economic interests. This is not the case with Hinduism, but faith in the dogma of revelation, although with more attenuated effects, has contributed to separation and exclusivity, which contradicts its inclusive tradition.

This is what interests me to highlight: *where experimental knowledge ends, that is, philosophy, belief begins, which is usually the domain of religion*. I think it is the duty of the philosopher to establish the limits of knowledge, in the phenomenal world, what have been done by Kant, and in the noumenal or transcendental world, in which I am trying my best to express. I maintain that the rule that must be followed to discriminate correctly is that of putting experience before doctrine. All religions, to a varying degree, have a content of beliefs, what does not in agreement is to give them prominence by applying the dogma of being *revealed*.

On Spiritual Techniques

It is not my intention to present a "new" yoga, which would undoubtedly be more attractive to today's man who searches for novelties with uncontrollable anxiety, because, unfortunately, the consumer mentality has also affected the spiritual field. I have a particular aversion to novelties and a natural inclination for the classic. I strictly believe that everything has already been said in the spiritual realm, so what is presented as "new" implies an ignorance of what has been said and what is being said, that is, of oneself, of the internal selfish mechanisms that lead to seek success in the approval of third parties, since success ends with self-knowledge. This in turn leads to the disappearance of the self, while in the search for the recognition of others ignorance begins. The correct thing is to reach the Source itself and from there pour those waters into the world, even if the same thing is said, because the important thing is to ratify the eternal truths. My intention is to insist on the necessity of spiritual practices whose purpose is to raise the level of consciousness of the aspirant.

I have already spoken sufficiently in previous works about the *planes of understanding* and the *levels of consciousness* within which the spirit, which is our true self, moves. Well, what these practices specifically do is bring the spirit out of its habitual way of seeing, thinking and feeling, elevating it towards higher planes from which all reality, the *Universus*, appears to it in a different way.

The faculties used for this purpose are the *unitive* ones, that is to say, the philosophical, religious, moral and aesthetic ones. I have dedicated a specific treatise to each of these faculties and the disciplines that result from them, to which I refer the interested reader, aware that every human being has natural tendencies that incline him towards one or another of these disciplines. And it is there, precisely, where we notice the wisdom of yoga, which has not stopped noticing, discovering and methodically developing different ways of knowing for different individuals, characters or personalities.

The reader will note that I have not followed the traditional yoga's, but will also confirm that the means I propose overlap with the traditional methods; that I only propose to direct the spirit towards the same objective, emphasising my particular vision of the psyche, and of the faculties that I consider specific for spiritual tasks, the unitive ones, which I have separated and independent, although not opposed, to the external faculties that generate *cumulative knowledge*.

As I have already advanced my vision of the psyche and exposed it in other works (the reader can find an outline of it in my *Psychosophy*), I will limit myself here to the following summary: I have distinguished five planes of understanding, since each one understands external and internal reality its own way. An external plane, discernment; an internal plane, the subconscious; two intermediate planes, that of the intellect or intuitions; that of feelings; and a central, vital or direct perception plane. Exterior to all of them would be the senses that are channels of reception without understanding. Traditional psychology has paid attention to these faculties, but not to the central plane, which is precisely the vital one for the spirit, and tends to confuse discernment with the intellect of those who are unaware of their transcendent capacity. My theory of the displacements of the spirit is also unknown to them. In the act of knowing, the spirit moves through all the planes, not only between them horizontally but in each of them vertically, although in this direction it will be limited by the level of consciousness it has reached. It is here where the vital plane plays its preponderant role, since it is the royal path to elevate the level of consciousness; hence the need to *centre* the spirit on it.

In this centralisation, meditation, understood as the control of the movements of the spirit in the manner of Patanjali, is essential. So is contemplation, understood as the *direct perception* of external reality, and *morality*, understood as control of the displacements of the spirit caused by the countless intentions of the self, that is, of its desires, fears and passions in general.

The reader will observe that I have dispensed with *prana-yama*, one of the basic yoga's, because it responds to a particular worldview of the Hindu, despite considering it very useful, I have given priority to aesthetic vision and contemplation, which is not explicitly found among the traditional yoga's.

We can visualise the core or background of the *central or vital plane* as the mirror of Consciousness. It *directly* reflects external and internal stimuli. Thus, for example, if we contemplate a beautiful object, we will know that it is beautiful because it has affected the mirror of Consciousness that knows and contains the Beautiful itself; this is basically the aesthetic phenomenon. Born artists have access to this awareness that in their case we can call aesthetic consciousness. But in general they do not reach all the way to the very vertex of Consciousness; much less the common man, who quickly diverts the spirit with thoughts, sentiments, relationships, memories, etc. The artist has the ability to retain his vision without being distracted, so that he can later express what he has perceived; whether he does it well or badly will depend on his technique. If the object is a beautiful person, by the same means we will perceive its beauty, but, as we know, this triggers other mechanisms that obey our animal nature; control of these mechanisms depends on the vigilance of our moral conscience. In the same way, a diamond or gold can be beautiful, but it is usual that they trigger the mechanisms of desire that prevent us from seeing their beauty itself. Strictly speaking, although the Beautiful itself and the Good itself are clearly perceived by artists or moral men; intuitions or experiences of a religious and particularly philosophical order are necessary.

The couple of examples that we have given speak of present events, so they are easily understandable, but the matter becomes enormously complex when we incorporate the past that we have accumulated in our memory from the external plane, from our sentiments and from our internal plane. Our usual selves are entirely dependent on these memories; oneself, per se, does not exist except as the set of these memories that one accumulates and accommodates as scaffolding, with the reasons for each one present, reasons to which one usually adapts the weak calls of the aesthetic, moral, religious and philosophical consciousness to justify their selfish acts.

If we return to our mirror image of our Consciousness, where the consciousnesses mentioned converge, we will find it covered with the stains left by all our deviations, reasons and sentiments that we have been leaving in the memories on the different planes, and on the consciousnesses themselves. It is enough to think of the countless unresolved situations that we have accumulated in our internal or subconscious level as a result of neglect of our moral conscience.

Thus, in the cleaning of said mirror lies the knowledge of ourselves, since what we really are is said Consciousness. We are certainly not what we think we are; although this is what we do every day, and that is why we never reach an end in this resolve, because each thought that originates from the self is another stain that we apply on the mirror. As can be seen, the task is cleaning, not construction; it consists in clarifying our vision of the soul.

From what has been said, the basic moral task is not to do this or that, as is generally believed, but to clean the mirror so that our moral conscience is clearly reflected and illuminates our actions, and for this it is necessary to review all the immoral acts, however small they may be, that we have done. This, we must admit, is practically impossible in today's world. When I speak of contemplation as a spiritual technique, I imply a primarily contemplative life, because only in this way can we do our accounts correctly and clear up our moral debts and thus carry out the proper cleaning.

It will be understood that everything that has been said are theories born from practice; we do not get anywhere by theory alone, especially on the plane of beliefs, which, although it is the one most used in the field of religion, leaves us stuck halfway in the belief that we already know the matter. Something similar can happen to us in the psychological field: it is not enough to be clear about these mechanisms, if one does not have the certainty of having transcended the self, reason and memory, and of having entered the realm of the Sacred, which is the nucleus of religion, and the Absolute, which is the core of philosophy, there is still a long way to go.

The cleanliness in its entirety depends on the penetration and vigilance of the moral conscience; its importance will be understood. It is not that we should be good, but that we are good to the extent that we know each other and bad to the extent that we ignore each other. There is no possible ascent outside of moral conscience. Said cleaning process, however, is not everything, the vision of the Transcendent depends on intuitions and experiences. Intellectual intuitions can penetrate and transcend visible reality and show us the Transcendent, something like the clouds parting for a moment and letting light in, only to close again immediately afterwards. Almost all Western philosophers have used these intuitions, but the fleeting vision of light does not allow the self to change perspective. It is through *unitive experiences* that include sentiments, and the totality of the faculties, that the spirit, as if dragging the entire mind, manages to reach and remain in the Transcendent. It is this experience that allows the spirit to definitively change perspective and abandon the individual perspective and settle in the *essential perspective*, where there is neither ego nor the duality that it generates. This is the Liberation that produces Happiness and leaves only Unity.

Perhaps the most notable difference between my philosophy and Hinduism, and we could say with religious doctrines in general, is that I emphasise the *positive aspects* of the material and spiritual reality of life, since the *primary manifestations of the Essence* themselves are positive, just as morality is not seen as a list of prohibitions but as an ascending and transcendent path, more as what must be done than what we should not do. In this I follow the example of *the ancient Greeks, whose moral paradigms were positive*. If we look at the virtues in this way, we will see that they all tend to detachment and disengagement, that is, to the transcendence of the spirit.

This, fundamental in my ethics, should be clear: all virtues tend to transcend the self, as is clear in courage, generosity, magnificence, and the rest of the virtues exposed with unsurpassed clarity in Aristotle's ethics. Morality, then, does not tend to restrain the spirit, but exalts it and encourages it to transcend itself. It is understandable why I present my philosophy as a *vital spiritualism* (In *The Roots of Morality* the reader will find the explanations necessary for this synthesis).

In any case, I regard spiritual techniques or yoga's as the most conducive way to prepare the aspirant for the knowledge of the Transcendent, and all of them dispense with reason. This is not understood by Western thinkers in general. For more than a century, from Husserl to this side, they have been determined to discover the most innovative epistemology, which has not gone beyond intellectual entertainment. They do not understand that it is not possible to theorise about knowledge whose object is unknown; this if it is intended to reach the first principles, which our epistemologists seem to have already forgotten. In India this direction is inverted: first knowledge is achieved and then the paths to achieve it are expressed. Otherwise it is like drawing a map towards an unknown destination, assuring that it *must be there*, and not that it *is* here.

It will be understood that what is exposed in this chapter is a bird's eye view that only intends to give an idea of my way of seeing these matters of the spirit that have already been exposed in eight books that precede the current one. Apparently this vision has little to do with Hindus and Buddhists, but if we superimpose it on these doctrines we will see that the means are similar and at no time are they opposed, and the objective, which is decisive, is the same. And, I must insist on this point, my search has been personal, and if I have followed a trajectory, it has been that of idealism in the West, whose roots, trunk and branches are Greek. But they converge on the same objective, on the same conclusion, on the ultimate reality of the Indic doctrines. That is to say that in the most essential the Hellenic tradition and the Indic tradition (*dharma*) converge in the same vertex, in the same universal Consciousness.

On the Mind and the Yoga's

My proposal, which obeys my experience, does not contradict Indian yoga. It does not contradict it, but there are some assumptions in which it differs that need to be exposed. Probably due to the influence of Samkhya, yoga, particularly that of Patanjali, maintains too clear or radical a difference between the knowledge of material and spiritual reality and, because of this, between the faculties that deal with the one and the other. The difference that is established is such that it identifies the mind with the senses, to the point that it considers it to be one more sense. Hence, I infer, the emphasis placed on denying the mind, on stopping its movements or modifications (*vrtti*). Patanjali himself begins his work by defining yoga as the suppression of said modifications (*vrtti*) of the mind. This leads to conceiving the mind as a negative, irrelevant apparatus, which must be detached and overcome to reach other higher and spiritual states of consciousness.

In my conception, Everything that comprehends the Cosmos is in the Mind, and it is this reality that I have called *Universus*. The Cosmos, as an Order, is so because it is impregnated with a Spirit whose forces determine it. They do not determine it to be this or that, to acquire one form or another, since universal Consciousness does not show that it has a Will, and if it had in an immeasurable amount, there is no way for the human being to know it, because for him infinity is absolutely transcendent. Everything seems to show that the Spirit is independent of matter but this it depends on It. It is like the sun that does not want birds, fish, trees, flowers, microbes and humans to be in a certain way; the sun does nothing more than illuminate and heat, which is essential for life, but living creatures has to figure out how to come to be and exist. The practically infinite forms of life that we contemplate on this planet that have touched us (leaving aside the multiple expressions of life feasible in the universe) are sufficient proof that nature as *natura-naturata* depends on *Natura-naturans* (allow me to use the well-known distinction that Spinosa makes), of the Spirit, of the universal Soul to become, but then it is left to its luck and its intelligence-instinct to survive and grow. I believe that the stars are the primary material expressions that generate the necessary light for life, but their origin is found in the *primary manifestations of the Essence*.

This circumlocution is necessary to understand my conception of the universal Mind or Consciousness of which our particular mind forms part or participates in, as well as all living beings that possess an intelligence-instinct, although to different degrees and however rudimentary they may be. In the same way, they possess and participate in the *primary manifestations of the Essence* that underlie all existence, which the human being has the capacity to make fully conscious in his mind and to appreciate them in other beings. But, for certain, it does not make it conscious with the external faculties that current psychology calls conscious, but with its *unitive* or spiritual *faculties*.

I would then agree with Hinduism that one has to overcome the external faculties, but not the *whole* mind. The Élan-vital, the Intelligence-instinct, Love, the Beautiful and the Good are perceived by all human beings in some way, although only the most evolved make them fully conscious. The normal man does not perceive them in himself, but he feels and knows them in some way. Thus, for example, Order, another *primary manifestation*, although it is not perceived in itself, organises our thoughts and actions and there would be no industries without it, no sciences nor any society, but rather chaos would reign. But as I said, beings are free when interpreting these manifestations; thus we see, for example, that there are different forms of government but they all tend to order society. I believe that there has been and is a confusion between discernment and the intellect, for this reason I have separated them, the former attends to external affairs, the latter can attend to them if it is at the service of the self, but it *has transcendent functions* if it is in contact with the unitive faculties and illuminated by universal Consciousness. It is this function of the intellect that makes idealistic philosophies possible, as this book that the reader has been following, and *gnana yoga*.

We see then that these *primary manifestations* are always current and active in the mind. The problem resides in the fact that we do not perceive them in their Essence and we interpret them according to our particular interests, that is, selfishly, with our utilitarian faculties, so that they are entirely distorted. That is to say that although these *manifestations* exist, although the human mind receives these instances and possesses those potentialities, it obeys its animal instinct more because it has not overcome its *state of survival*.

Although these premises are different from yoga and Hinduism, we come to find the same objective, which is to overcome the current mind. But, as has been said, not the whole mind, because the goodness that we feel, the beauty that we perceive, the order that we need, and the love that we enjoy, as long as we take advantage of them properly, *are means of transcendental knowledge*. One only has to give them another use, higher, more spiritual, that allows us to get out of the animal state. Neither is this,, pure restriction, sacrifice and asceticism, as religions in general tend towards, since the objective is Happiness, although certainly, we must not confuse it with animal pleasure, with the taste for the jungle from which we must definitely leave. In other words, the ego must be left behind, and in this fundamental design my philosophy coincides entirely with the yoga's of the Indic doctrines.

I would like to highlight another way of seeing and dealing with spiritual techniques: my philosophy has Unity as its objective and means, while Patanjali (following Samkhya) seeks to break away from nature, Prakrti and the mind that he considers all linked to it, for ascetic means and, very particularly, for the concentration of the mind. My philosophy uses Unity as a means and has it as an end; I believe that there is no precedent for this psychological resource either in the East or the West. I refer to the *progressive unification of consciousness* until reaching a *mental Unity* that in unison generates the perception of the Unity of universal Consciousness. The harmonious integration of all the faculties consists of a progressive moral cleansing that leads to a fully purified consciousness, since it is in the moral conscience where our thoughts, and even before, our intentions are reflected as in a mirror. When the mirror is clean, the ego is entirely exposed to the light of consciousness, so it cannot progress and is neutralised; it is only then that spiritual knowledge and the path to the Transcendent begin. Plato and particularly Plotinus warn of the need for this purification to reach the One, although they see it as an ideal of numerical perfection in the manner of Pythagoras. I have exposed the difference between what I understand by Unity and the One of Plotinus in *The Search for Universal Consciousness*.

The *positive paradigms* that I propose may be foreign to Patanjali's yoga, but not to Hinduism. We find them in the Vedas and in the epic; the validity of the *Mahabharata* and the Ramayana is evident, the vast majority of Hindus keep it alive, and in the festivals, where all kinds of people converge by the million, the *sadhus* in particular, are notorious. The cult of the sun, the cow, the sacred trees, the moon, the conjunction of the stars, the countless places of pilgrimage where the spirit has manifested itself or manifests itself constantly, such as in rivers (we do not need to emphasise the importance of the Ganges, revered in its long history in hundreds of cities, and particularly in Benares, the sacred city par excellence), etc., *reveal the vital and positive aspect of Nature*.

Advaita Vedanta may deny Nature, but the Hindu in general, who is a pantheist at heart, does not. This must be established: Hinduism is not born from yoga, but *from the perception of the Spirit that underlies all beings and Nature in general*; it is this innate, characteristic and traditional capacity that has shaped the Dharma. And, as we have already anticipated, the Greeks shared this capacity.

On the Powers

About the powers of the spirit to which Patanjali and other authors refer (they naturally abound in the epic) I can say little because they exceed my experience. However, an argument could be made to justify their existence. The experience of the Transcendent implies the overcoming of time, space and the principle of causality. Thanks to it, the spirit finds itself in another dimension in which another Intelligence reigns, I can attest to this, in which past, present and future merge into an Absolute. This intelligence is presented as unlimited and infinite and we do not know (or I do not know) the use we can make of it. In my personal case I have limited myself to extracting all the philosophical consequences that derive from that Absolute that I experience as universal Consciousness, but it would not be surprising if it had other uses.

I have met very wise yogis and seen numerous ascetics in India, but I have not verified supernatural powers in them, despite having travelled a lot for some years in that immense country, perhaps I have not had enough time to judge these facts, which are strange by nature. Although I confess that I have been astonished to see a yogi sleeping peacefully on a mattress of hundreds of thorns of more than one inch each. Yes, I have verified in yogis numerous times a particular ability to bare the soul of their interlocutors just by looking into their eyes for a long time; they do not look at the clothes he is wearing or the vehicle he is arriving in, as a Westerner would, but behind the eyes and with astonishing insight. Now, I do not believe that these yogis can literally read the thoughts of other people as Patanjali affirms, because this would imply entering into particulars that correspond to the speculative faculties, but I do believe that they can see what underlies those thoughts, the intentions, the motivation that stimulates them, it is this perception that corresponds to the *unitive faculties*, which see the essential and global aspects of situations. Any sensitive person can discover in a glance the evil intention of an aggressor, just as the desire that she reads in the man's gaze is immediately revealed to a woman; in these cases they do not read their thoughts but what underlies them.

From what I have been able to see and experience, human beings have the ability to foresee, that is, to anticipate the future; they can feel that something is going to happen or is happening in another place, usually to a being to which they are connected to, this is, I think, an experience that we all have had at one time or another. For my part I have been able to experience the following: Walking along a narrow path bordered on both sides by ancient cypress trees, I saw a man appear at the other end about 80m away. He approached with his head down but when he raised his head and looked at me, I saw myself in his eyes, as if my spirit had moved into his mind. I had that experience again, but no longer with a person but with the exposed roots of an old tree that I was contemplating; from them I saw myself. This happened to me, naturally, in a period in which I led an extreme contemplative life. I have lived with a woman who had the ability to predict events that would occur years later and to intuit events that were also remote in the past. She was very contemplative, she practiced some yoga's and sympathised with Zen. It is not difficult to conjecture that yogis can increase these faculties to the maximum. But all this happens on a mental and spiritual plane. It does not enter into my conception that they can move with the body as if it were of a spiritual nature; matter has its limitations and it is precisely these limitations that yoga tries to overcome.

I believe that from these same faculties and intuitions latent in man arises his need to create devices that fulfil these functions, such as the telephone. I have nothing against these inventions, only that, as happens with remedies that have their harmful effects, these devices numb said faculties and stimulate the external ones that alienate us from what is essential.

This topic leads us to wonder about the scope of these transcendental faculties. The examples that I can give are only humble, but real, samples of our potential compared to the powers that the yoga's speak of, but all of them are linked to my theory of the displacements of the spirit, which I summarise as follows: *The spirit,* as I call it, as I have advanced, is the nucleus of intelligence that is dynamic and constantly moves through all the faculties of the mind, including the transcendental ones, that is, transcends the individual faculties that revolve around the self. *Universal Consciousness*, experience tells us, has no limits. From it emanates all intelligence and feeling (which is a form of knowledge), from it emanate the unitive faculties and from these are derived the external faculties that obey an *individual perspective*. However, these faculties know differently. If the spirit centred in the *unitive faculties* intends to know the particulars, *it is alienated* from its universal nature and falls into discernment, that is, into the individual perspective. From this perspective, that of the self, an inversion of perspective occurs, for this reason the subject *believes* that it is he who generates that intelligence, which he has actually appropriated and has put into his service.

The problem, then, of *the powers* (*siddhis*) resides in transforming unitive or spiritual knowledge into material. Well, as I said, these faculties know in a different way; the *unitives*, despite knowing the essentials of the matter and in a global way, do not know (in my experience) about individuals. In any case, there is no doubt that the spirit, in addition to moving towards its transcendent faculties, moves in time and space; although I do not know how far it can go. On the origin of this mechanism that must have occurred when man became aware of his individuality and separated and alienated from his universality, I have expanded in *Origin and Destiny of Man*.

I believe that *the powers* of the Sibyls or diviners in ancient Greece obeyed these mechanisms. Focused on their unitive faculties, they knew the essential and global nature of the matter, but for this reason they did not give concrete answers as required by reason. But this does not mean that they were "irrational", but that they expressed another plane of understanding that obeyed other faculties, the unitive ones, which although they are not "precise" like the cumulative ones, are higher and more spiritual. They perceived order or disorder having as a reference the *Order of the Universus* (although I do not know if all of them were in direct contact with the Absolute, surely they had intuitions of it); hence the sacredness of their work. The high flight of Greek tragedy is explained because it takes place at that level, from that elevated perspective the ephemeral events of mortals were observed. (I refer the reader to *The Tragedy* in *The Roots of Art*.)

Focused on his Absolute, Shankara does not clarify for us the powers that the liberated one acquires in life, although sometimes he suggests them and there are some *Upanishads* that affirm them. For this reason I consider Ramanuja's clarification necessary and fair: "The glory of the liberated selves (souls) is absolutely devoid of cosmic activities." (*Brahma-Sutras 4,4,21*) That is, as is evident, they cannot alter the universal order; in this they are not the same as the Creator.

The *Gita* affirms the absolute unity with Brahman. "He who has attained the consciousness of Brahman acquires the infinite powers of perception." (*XIII,14*) But not only that, as "He is One with everything", "from him comes destruction and creation." (*XIII,16*) On this point, I agree, in part, with Ramanuja, these powers cannot be possessed by the human being. Merge into the One, I concur, see from the One too, but these powers are beyond the human condition. The spirit is unified with the Spirit, but only in spirit, the powers over matter belong to another order. Strictly speaking, no one possesses that power, not even Brahman, unless we believe that this is a personal God who decides the fate of the universe according to his will, which is philosophically untenable. The emanation of the Essence generates matter and living beings, but it does not create them directly or destroy them when it wants to, since this would imply rational intentions improper of the Divinity. Matter and beings depend on the Essence but they are free to their nature and they also depend on Nature. The Union is a fact of conscience, the unity is with the universal Consciousness, not with a personal God, it belongs to the order of knowledge, not to the material order; in a word there are no such powers either in Divinity or in men. The *Gita*, to my understanding, confuses these orders and the nature of Brahman. The *Gita* is part philosophy and part literature, I am dealing only with the philosophical side; miracles have no place in this field.

To my knowledge, the concept of miracle is of Judeo-Christian origin. In Greece, as in India, there is talk of powers possessed by certain exceptional men or granted by the gods. Thus, for example, Cassandra and Tiresias have divinatory powers because Apollo has granted them to them. In India the powers are acquired by yoga; the Hindu firmly believes in the efficacy of these spiritual techniques. Even the gods, if they do possess these powers, it is because they have been practising yoga for millennia; hence their superiority over humans who have very limited time for these practices.

Hinduism, as we have seen, maintains the existence of a universal energy that affects both matter and mind called Prana. What the yogi proposes with Pranayama is, according to Vivekananda, to master that energy, because if he succeeds he can master practically everything, that is, achieve supernatural powers. We are here very far from Pranayama as rhythmic breathing to calm the mind and avoid its movements (*vrttis*). In my view, although there is an uninterrupted relationship between spiritual and material energies, there is no direct or mechanical relationship, there are different steps with their nuances, not easy to distinguish, both for the spiritualist and for the scientist.

India has produced many enlightened people and none of them have thought of creating or destroying even part of the world. Only in the imagination of epic literature do we find these wonders. In any case, what is certain is that no one has had enough power to put an end to man's vices; which is the greatest service that could be offered to humanity.

On Reincarnation and Karma

Hinduism, Buddhism and the Far East in general are known to accept the theory of reincarnation without objection. We also find it in Greece among the pre-Socratics, in Plato, and even in Rome as is clearly exposed by Virgil from the mouth of Anchises in the dialogue he has with Aeneas in Hades itself. Incidentally, it should be remembered that the Aeneid was officially presented by Augustus Caesar as the work that expressed the most genuine Roman tradition.

I do not hesitate to adhere to this theory because it seems to me the most acceptable of those that man has produced in relation to our future after death. However, I have not included it in my philosophy because it insistently appeals to experience and, as is only natural, I believe that nobody has in life the experience of what happens beyond it.

The immense respect I have for the *Upanishads* (and for the Buddhist *Sutras*) is that they are based on the experience of the Transcendent, which can be had while alive; all my work, which now has set out to confirm the essential truths of the *Upanishads*, testifies to this. However, not only do they accept the theory of reincarnation and karma, but they speak of them expressly. The *Brhadaranyaca Upanishad* speaks of "a subtle body directed by intelligent itself (self) that when separated from the members of the physical body, rushes to find a new abode." For when the physical body dies, the self, which resides in the heart, remains conscious and remembers the past acts so that it is the vehicle of karma: "Man becomes according to his acts. The man of good acts becomes good, the man of bad acts becomes bad." And, very much in keeping with a basic Buddhist principle, "he who has desires remains subject to rebirths." "But the one who has stopped his desires does not undergo rebirth." And immediately afterwards it affirms, like other *Upanishads*, that "Whoever realises Brahman, becomes Brahman" (*IV, 1-7*)

We see that the theory of reincarnation and the law of karma are intimately linked to the realisation of the Absolute or Brahman. Now then, experience is one thing and belief is another and, in my opinion, these do not exceed their own plane, while the knowledge of Brahman is an experience. The matter is complex, since it is possible to perceive the existence of a *universal moral Order* by which one knows that one must do good and avoid evil, and know that our particular behaviour is part of a universal moral mechanism. However, there is no experience of the functioning of the mechanism of punishment or reward, that is, of karma. Proof of this is that the *seers* or Buddhist sages, whom it would be too arbitrary to judge as ignorant, have a different idea of this mechanism, since they do not believe in an individual soul that changes its body without changing its spiritual nature. Tibetan Buddhists, for their part, not only believe in the individual soul but also claim to recognise in whom that soul reincarnates. Moreover, in some texts, both Hindu and Buddhist, there is talk of a Paradise; there, for example, the heroes of the Mahabharata end their journey. If it were an *experience*, I infer, there would not be so many differences.

Since Hindus accept the *Upanishads* as revealed works (*sruti*), their commentators do not establish the difference that I have just pointed out, rather, belief and knowledge are interrelated to such an extent that it would be forcing the point to separate them. In any case, let it be clear that it is not my intention to look for a weakness in these sublime doctrines, but only to be strict from the point of view of the theory of knowledge as required by my philosophy, which, I insist, seeks to corroborate the experience of existence of universal Consciousness or Brahman, which is decisive.

I do not reject the theory of Karma because, although I cannot attest to it, it somehow works or should work. As I see it, it works like this: the human being is essentially consciousness. This consciousness is full of concrete ideas, it is loaded with them, too full, too heavy for a pure Consciousness. That is why he cannot identify with It. If he tries to, he is reflected and falls as if by its own weight on the concrete world. Although I do not want to say that it happens literally in this way. I could also say that the human soul is driven by an inertia that it needs to survive, very useful for this life but not for the Eternal. As pure Consciousness implies Peace, with said inertia it does not achieve it, so it returns, or continues, on its earthly path. But, what is that reincarnate? The most essential of us, the most intimate aspirations, what we have decanted in life, the energy that we have created.

On the Internal Plane

Elsewhere I have explained the relationship between the plane of direct perception and the internal plane. I have called it the internal plane and not the subconscious because, as we will see, it is a plane of understanding that we can make conscious in a particular way. In *The Evolution of the Spirit* I have spoken of a displacement of the spirit of *homo sapiens* from its internal faculties towards external faculties: the intellect and discernment. It is this displacement that has caused the change from the mythical to the rational mentality. However, this evolution has not meant an absolute improvement in all orders, but simply another way of processing what is perceived. Naturally, the rational interpretation is clearer to the modern mind, but it does not imply a better original perception of the object. The decisive thing is to see with the greatest possible clarity what is captured by the plane of direct or vital perception, which is reflected both in the external and internal planes, which process it in their own way.

Regarding the perception of spiritual reality, I would say that the *Sacred* would be the reflection of said plane of direct perception on the plane of feelings, while the Transcendent would be said reflection on the plane of the intellect, which knows that reason has been transcended; both are transcendent to visible reality; this reflexion also occurs on the internal plane. From which it follows that archaic man may have had a closer and clearer vision of the spiritual object than a modern philosopher. To this we must add that archaic man was surely more *integrated into the world* than current man. I have already explained this as due to the process of alienation with respect to his Essence and the exteriorisation of the spirit that has settled in discernment, an *external faculty* of reason, which only knows things and nothing of spiritual reality.

Regarding the internal plane, I would like to clarify what happens in a state of an elevated level of consciousness. Several *Upanishads*, in particular the *Chandogya*, speak of three states of mind: the waking state, the sleeping state in which we dream, and the state of sleep in which we do not dream (deep sleep, *susupti*). They assign particular importance to the latter because they think that in it the Self is more in contact with itself, because there is a cessation of the flow of the mind (*vrttis*) that is a basic principle of yoga. “When man is thus asleep”, (in deep sleep) “he is united with Sat”, (Self, Brahman) “he merges into his own Self.” (*Chand. 6,8,1*) The idea, as maintained by the *Brhadaranyaka Upanishad*, is that man in a state of deep sleep is absorbed by the Self. This theory assumes that the very breath of life is housed in the most intimate part of our being “in the lotus of our heart.” I do not deny that it can be so, only that since there is no awareness of this state, it can only be sustained by inference.

Despite the fact that the *Mandukya* had finished this matter by adding another higher state of consciousness, Shankara once again insists on the state of deep sleep, since his obsession is to end with the external world: “When the external world remains closed, the soul is happy, and this joy of the soul brings the vision of Paramatman” (the Great Soul). “Then the closure of the external world is the springboard for liberation.” (*Viveka. 335*) Thus he maintains that in the state of deep sleep “the Atman shines in its glory.” (*Viveka. 107*) If we consider nothing more than this, deep sleep would be enough, but it is not. On the contrary, Ramanuja says that in this state there is no knowledge because there is no object of knowledge, which is relatively correct, but his usual dualistic way of observing is not applicable to this matter of order transcendent to the subject.

Having been dealt with in various texts, it is not surprising that the *Brahma-Sutras* (*3,2,7-9*) again deal with *susupti*. In his commentary on these texts, Ramanuja correctly tells us, “The sleeping soul is still in the sphere of samsara” (ignorance). “So deep sleep is not liberation.” (*3,2,9*) His position is consistent: while the soul is in the body, it is subject to karma and the imperfections that it entails (*3,2,10*). However, “The creation of dreams comes from the Lord, and is only his Maya.” (*3,2,3*) It is interesting to point out that Maya for him reaches only dreams, while for Shankara it extends to the waking state and to everything we see in this state, therefore everything is like a dream. In my opinion, in the state of deep sleep, since there is no consciousness, there is no knowledge, there is no contented soul or joy, there is no ignorance or knowledge, there is no one, except nothing; although it may be inferred that the Self underlies this state.

Fortunately, the *Mandukya Upanishad* ultimately settles the issue by clarifying that the highest state is not that of deep sleep, but of a fourth state of consciousness, which it calls *Turiya*, where pure intuition dominates, where there is neither subject nor object, which is transcendent and therefore unthinkable, where peace and happiness reign, which is Atman. This coincides entirely with *unified or universal Consciousness*. I would like to remind the reader that we have already found the connection of the *Sattva*, in its highest state, with the Purusha in Patanjali; in the Turiya of the Madukya, and in Shankara’s pure *Sattva*, an *announcement of a transcendent consciousness in the human mind*, a recognition, albeit in a latent state, of what I understand by *unitive consciousness*, a bridge to a supra-consciousness.

I would like to express my experience of the internal plane in the state of sleep. The cleaning of the mirror of our consciousness, to which I have already referred, leads, after a long process, to the disappearance of the memory of the internal (subconscious) plane, so it is as if it were left without content. In this case, the internal plane will be able to generate new images, but they will be very much in accordance with the high level of consciousness and will not in any way be undesirable interferences produced by the stains generated by the repressions or deviations of the external plane, something that does not take place in a clean and vigilant mind. In other words, dreams disappear because the content of the inner plane remains empty. This plane is also a faculty of understanding, but, like discernment, it is of indirect perception, although it understands and builds in its non-rational way, since it dispenses with time and space, *what is perceived on the central or vital plane*. So if from now on images are reproduced that reflect this central plane, which directly perceives the essence of the circumstances, in the sleeping state they will be luminous, beautiful, soft, pleasant and, above all, revealing and creative. These images can be controlled so that the spirit, not the self, can exchange them for other images if it wishes or wander through them as a spectator.

About this state, which I have referred to as *The Control of Dreams*, in my *Psychosophy* there is no reference in the *Upanishads*. I speak of a state of contemplation, without a subject, of the dream world. It is the same consciousness that *observes* the individual or self-consciousness, the *unitive consciousness when it sleeps*. That is to say that although asleep, the spirit participates in the state of supra-consciousness. Even though, this is only possible in a prolonged contemplative life and after paying all the debts to the moral consciousness.

The internal plane, like the external plane or discernment, indirectly receives the direct perception of the vital plane, so when it reaches an elevated level of consciousness, it receives those luminous and creative images to which I attribute the most inspired sources of art, in particular of mythical-religious art. That is to say that the mythical creation has a scope that reason does not discern, when the *internal plane makes a particular interpretation of the transcendental intuitions of the vital plane*.

On Maya

Shankara maintains not only the existence of Maya, but that "it is as powerful as God, without beginning and that it has created the universe". (*Viveka. 108*) This flagrantly contradicts the *Upanishads*: In the *Taitiriya Upanishad* we read, "Salutation to That (Brahman) (...) from whom the whole universe was born", and "Brahman is omnipresent because it is the material cause of space", (which encompasses the universe). (*Tait. I,XI,4*) In the *Mundaka Upanishad*, "All this is Brahman." (*II,ii,11*) And in the *Chandogya Upanishad*, "All this is but the Self." (*VII,25,2*). These examples are enough. Since Maya, for Shankara, has the three qualities of *Sattva*, *Rajas* and *Tamas*, (*Viveka. 108*) I infer that he is speaking of Prakrti, which would be like the creative substance of the universe, the generator of said energies or qualities of the same, which moreover determine the way of being and acting of the beings that compose it. With all the evidence Shankara inherits that clear division of the Samkhya between the world and the Transcendent that he calls Atman or Brahman. While he admits that he is connected to his soul, he lacks any connection to his mind; it is this disconnection, in my opinion, that does not allow him to unite the two realities. His illumination must have been instantaneous, surprising, unexpected, without previous intuitions that announced immaterial reality to him. In an abysmal leap he must have found himself facing Brahman, and there he remained in the conviction that it was the only reality.

The concept of *Maya*, which has several meanings or nuances that bring the material world closer to or further away from reality, reaches its extreme in Shankara's capital work, the *Vivekacudamani*. Indeed, the concept of *Maya*, which he so often introduces in his comments to the *Upanishads*, is taken to its extreme: "Brahman is real, the universe is unreal", which, as I have already commented, is entirely untenable and contrary to my philosophy and that of Aurobindo, and not very faithful to the *Upanishads* themselves.

Like Samkhya philosophy, Shankara divides and separates the spiritual (Purusha) from the material (Prakrti) reality, but with one difference, Samkhya fully accepts the existence of Nature, Shankara does not. Actually this is the point that has raised the most controversy, since the World and the life it implies are presented by Shankara as Maya, generally translated as Illusion.

Schopenhauer's conception of the Will, who had read the *Upanishads*, is similar to Shankara's Maya: it is a universal force that, although it grants life, keeps us imprisoned in it, does not allow us to escape; we only manage to overcome it in moments of contemplation and aesthetic rapture, for one, and by illumination for the other; but in both cases it is escaping from this world. For Shankara everything in it is darkness, it is the shadow of the veil of Maya that covers not only the world but the Atman. (*Viveka.107*) Shankara also identifies Maya with ignorance (*Viveka.108*), but, as has been said, he does not see ignorance as an undeveloped stage of the mind, but as a closed world where Maya reigns. And this is what leads him to divide the two absolutes absolutely: Brahman and Maya, the former as existent, the latter, as non-existent (*Viveka.20*), other times as neither real nor unreal (*Viveka.109*), but never as existent; our life, in all cases, is diffuse, gloomy, miserable and even despicable. (*Viveka.87*)

Decidedly, Shankara does not occupy himself with the relationship of the Noumenal with the phenomenal, of Spirit with Nature, of the Immutable with the Becoming. His philosophy seems impeccable to me and very conducive to getting us to the First Principle, but he definitely sins by omission, although not by default. He fails to provide the second step. His theory of *Maya* leaves us in a limbo that ultimately does not satisfy us, since we all experience that life has at least some reality.

There have been no shortage of philosophers who have reproached him for this omission, but their solutions have not seemed correct to me. In general, the error of these critics consists, rather than in filling the space that Shankara has left unfinished, doubtful or insufficient, in questioning the first principle, the absolute Brahman of the great thinker, which, in my conception, I emphasise, does not need modification. These critics do not notice that when thinking about Brahman, they assign rational attributes to it, that is, they fall within the categories of time, space and causality, and finish by personalising it in some way. This happens to Ramanuja and Aurobindo who, in order to explain Nature, assimilate it to Brahman, which inevitably leads them to denature it, since the nature of Brahman is absolutely spiritual. They do not notice that if Brahman *wants*, *desires* or *grants* (like *the grace* necessary for enlightenment in Aurobindo), it is already within the field of reason, it assimilates to the human mind and remains personalised. Brahman does not speculate, so it does not need the speculative faculties. Brahman does not think, it emanates.

An objection has been raised (Radhakrishnan) to Shankara that in a nature reduced to *Maya* there is no room for morality. I believe that the objection is not valid, because for those who have achieved *this Knowledge*, the last problem that arises is moral, since with it they are endowed with a solid and impeccable moral conscience, because they have reached their Roots and understand them. It is, then, on the other hand that I see the lack in Shankara, and it is that he offers us only the fruits of morality, but he tells us nothing about *The Roots of Morality* (I refer the reader to this work). Well, it is precisely in these *Roots* where we find the much sought-after relationship between Spirit and Nature, between Brahman and man.

This should be well understood: we must discard the idea or belief that *Maya* means non-existent; this would mean that Shankara himself would be denying his own existence as well as that of his writings that would be addressed to no one, nor would anyone aspire to enlightenment. This, in my philosophy, does not offer a great difficulty: between a naive realism, which accepts this material reality as it is represented to the subject's senses, and the denial of reality, there is a middle term that is adequate, and that is how the concept of *Maya* should be or suits being interpreted; Buddhism comes to the same conclusion.

I believe that Shankara's Vedanta has created a *duality between Brahman and the universe*, and his followers do not end up breaking with it, although none of them go to the extreme of interpreting *Maya* as an absolute illusion. Rather, we see that reality is taking shape and concretion over time. Vivekananda, for example, despite not daring to break with Shankara in a categorical way, is far from denying Nature. In a more rational and true way, by *Maya* he understands the relativity of this world, due to its instability and contradictions. Shankara also sporadically alludes to this world as relative, which is then more comprehensive but contradictory to his Absolute without a second. For Vivekananda, inversely, the Absolute vanishes when we apply space, time and causality to it, which is absolutely true and fully agrees with my vision. And in this is the key to the matter, because if we look with reason we see this world from the perspective that it generates, and if we look with our unitive faculties in its pure state we perceive the universal Consciousness or Brahman.

Shankara's strength lies in his perception and knowledge of Brahman, not in his *Maya*. Shankara is the greatest representative of absolute monism, without a doubt, but he leaves us without solving the problem of the existence of the universe with all its living beings, which possibly has billions of beings that we do not know about on other planets, which is not a small thing, and, let us not forget, with the existence of Shankara himself, which is too contradictory to reason, and which, after all, helps us to solve the things of this world.

That is why his concept of Maya is diluted with time. A century after Vivekananda, Aurobindo openly declared himself against

Shankara's illusion and in favour of the existence of this world. Becoming, as Aurobindo correctly proposes, must be accepted, but the solution he presents is not ultimately satisfactory, since Brahman acts as an independent being with its own will, which makes it similar to a Person and generates a duality, although not in the Christian way, which, as we have seen, is the theory that Aurobindo most emphatically rejects. The idea of an involution of the spirit to become matter in Aurobindo's conception seems unnecessary to me and, much more, the idea of a *fall* of man, a very ancient myth also incorporated in Judeo-Christian Genesis. This myth is surely the product of an intuition of Divinity as perfect and of the evidence that matter and human life are not, but the interpretation is very elementary. *Universal Consciousness* does not need to involute to produce the World, nor for that reason to become a Person.

However, *the duality of Brahman and the universe* that Advaita proposes continues in Hinduism. The duality is that of Spirit and Nature, but not as one existing and the other non-existent, but as Absolute and relative, as permanent and impermanent. Furthermore, the Spirit does not remain isolated or alone, but penetrates and permeates Nature. This is perceptible by means of the *Samadhi of the Void*, of which the Mahayana speaks, to which we have already referred, which shows itself in the World. Besides the Spirit, the Consciousness of the World is also perceptible in our individual conscience; *the Spirit in the Universus is a fact, a verifiable reality.*

In Shankara the individual spirit merges with the Spirit but from the Spirit it turns its gaze towards the world and contemplates it from It; and from this *perspective*, naturally, the world appears as in a dream, with something of the unreal, like *Maya*. However, Shankara comes to admit that the Maya cannot strictly be defined as existent or non-existent. This conception and language, typically Mahayana, will be used later by Vivekananda; although neither, as good Brahmans, admit said authorship. What Advaita does not want to accept, and rightly so, is that Brahman undergoes some *transformation*, because this effectively betrays the transcendental experience. However, somehow it generates the material reality that, impregnated with spirit and that even receiving the primary manifestations that underlie life, also obeys the forces and needs of matter; and this is Nature: Spirit and matter. The Spirit remains the same, matter undergoes permanent transformation, as the Buddha and Heraclitus maintained. And since we perceive the Spirit in our consciousness, we tend to overcome the imperfection of matter and become pure Spirit; and it is this perception, latent in the majority of living beings, that generates philosophy and religion.

In the West, whose philosophical tradition is Greek, this world can be seen as a dream, but never as unreal or non-existent; this is absurd to the vital Greco-Roman spirit, and, to my knowledge, no thinker has thought of raising it. Seen as a dream, between the material and the nothing, yes, because this is the perception of the real, the *unitive vision*, which has not gone unnoticed by Plato and the poets. The vision of and from the Transcendent also leads Plato to see phenomenal reality with a hint of unreality, that is, of *Maya*; as it invariably corresponds to *the perspective* that the spirit acquires when it observes from the Absolute. This unreality makes Plato think that this material world is an image or copy of the transcendent Reality. *Maya is not, then, an invention of the East, it is the result of an experience of the Transcendent and of the vision of the world that it generates.*

The intuition of the Transcendent is not, moreover, the exclusive patrimony of the mystic-philosophers. The case of born artists can be explained if we consider that they were born with their spirit displaced towards their unitive faculties. The (true) artist is because he intuits that there is *something* that transcends the beautiful object that he contemplates, and since from this perception he looks at his life and at the World, these are represented to him as a dream. In *The Roots of Art* I have given numerous examples of artists who declare this way of seeing in their poems or literary works. It is enough to quote here *La Vida es Sueño* by Calderón de la Barca, who is quoted with admiration by Schopenhauer who shared this vision. We verify then that the idea of *Maya* is not born with Hinduism, although this has given it a particular and variable form according to the authors, but that it is the product of the unitive faculties and the perspective that they generate when the spirit intuits the Transcendent; intuition which is, in turn, a consequence of the Primary Manifestations of Universal Consciousness. One of them (I clarify that I only separate them to make them intelligible, since in their Essence they are a Unit) is the Beautiful; which is what artists perceive in things endowed with beauty. In other words, what happens in the artist is a relative perception of the Transcendent, although, in most cases, he is not fully aware of it.

In the *Ramacharitamanasa*, the *Ramayana* of Tulsidas, the demon Ravana possesses the divine power of *Maya*, thanks to which he creates countless Ravanas to terrify the enemy, but Rama manages to dispel this illusion. However, reality remains an illusion, for in the words of Rama's brother: "Friends and enemies are an illusion. Birth and death, prosperity and adversity, destiny, time, all the phenomena of the world; everything that is seen, heard or thought with the mind is born of ignorance, and in reality none of that exist;" although he admits that "on this night of existence only yogis remain awake." At the end of this epic, Shiva himself confirm: "The formidable army of *Maya* extends throughout the universe." *Maya* himself has made a puppet of the world." "*Maya* is the handiwork of Sri Rama, one cannot free oneself from its clutches, except by the grace of Rama;" although he adds that *Maya* is unreal when understood." That is to say, understand this once and for all, that the unreal is not the world, but *Maya*; for the men of knowledge (Vidya). Although fantastic, Hindu literature, points in the same direction as philosophy.

In any case, this must be established: neither *Maya* nor the Void can be interpreted as nihilism. What leads to this interpretation is the objective knowledge of the material, but let us not forget that they manifests as a philosophical or religious experience, not a scientific one, *they are a result granted by the vision from the Transcendent or essential perspective*. The *Maya* cannot be interpreted as an ontological reality (or unreality), since this vision leads to the absurd, but rather as a psychological and epistemological reality.

Maya, if it is understood as an *absolute illusion* of the universe intentionally generated by Brahman, as Shankara goes so far as to say, is absurd. The non-existence of Nature, of ourselves who contemplate it and who, furthermore, perceive Brahman and experience our own existence, is unsustainable. On the other hand, why would Brahman want to generate a cloud that prevents us from seeing Him in the World if the ultimate purpose of our existence is that same vision? In the same way, *Maya* understood as an action heteronomous to man is a primitive conception and a burden that must be overcome. The Immutable is what gives Being to the mutable; without that Being this world, this life is, effectively, *Maya*; I think Shankara would agree on this.

In my conception it is a philosophical-psychological problem, since it is the erroneous location of the nucleus of consciousness in the external faculties that prevents us from seeing the transcendent reality or Brahman. The *Gita*, fortunately, does not go so far as to deny this material reality, but influenced by an *Upanishad*, it tells us that He (Krishna) is the author of *Maya*, which is contradictory because of what has been said, because if He wants our liberation, He does not have to generate obstacles on the way, which also contradicts the natural impulse to transcend ourselves that Patanjali speaks of; an impulse that we can verify without effort in our consciousness.

Patanjali's proposal of Ishvara, despite not reaching the fullness of Brahman, has a specific meaning as a clear object for our devotion. In Shankara Ishvara completely loses his raison d'être, since he is covered by the cloud of *Maya* generated by our ignorance; a being declared illusory beforehand can hardly be inspiring and predispose us to worship him.

Buddhism, for its part, has insistently sought to clarify the concept of *Maya*. For this doctrine, when reality is seen as a dream the mind is in its correct state; which coincides with *my vision of the perspectives*. The concept of illusion had already been used by the primordial *Prajnaparamita* Mahayana text. There we read "Those who wish to discipline themselves in *Prajnaparamita* should do so as if they were disciplined in *Maya*" (illusion). "All beings are like *Maya* and like a dream." "Supreme enlightenment itself is like *Maya* and like a dream." "*Nirvana* is, in truth, like *Maya* and like a dream, how much more the rest of the things!" We see that far from presenting us with this vision and state in which "everything is seen as a dream" is negative, he elevates it to the highest level, calling it Samadhi Mayopama (like *Maya*). This is how the *Surangama Sutra, IV* expresses it: "The Samadhi of seeing all things as an illusion." The *Lankavatara*, another basic text of Mahayana, insists on this Samadhi, which would be at the beginning of a series of spiritual realisations that lead to the ultimate stage, that of the condition of Tathagata. The nuance highlighted by the *Lankavatara* seems precise and enlightening to me: "Things seen from their nature itself are like *Maya*, (which here means) like a dream, because in one way they are perceived as real, and in another, they are not perceived as such;

all things are perceived in two ways, according to the ignorance or knowledge (of the subject)." (*LXX*) Here the *set of perspectives* on which my philosophy insists is clearly exposed.

This doctrine of the middle path does not deny material reality, though it does not fully accept it. The Buddha himself warned about extremes: "Everything is, that is one extreme, everything is not, is the other extreme; the truth is in the middle." (*Samyutta Nikaya*). And the Mahayana will clarify: "No-birth and no annihilation is what I call Nirvana." (*Lankavatara Sutra, LXXVII*). It is in that middle term that the Void is found, which in no case should be translated as nothing. "Everything is unborn, but this does not mean that there are no objects." (*Op. cit.*) The Mahayana had finally overcome this duality by declaring: "Nirvana is Samsara and Samsara is Nirvana."

Shankara has the same vision and even uses the same language as the Mahayana. In his most representative work, the *Vivekacudamani* he asserts: "From the Consciousness of Brahman the World is seen as a dream." (*Viv. 425*) And when he contemplates the two realities: one is neither real nor unreal, and the other is Nirvana. But he categorically concludes, "This entire universe is identical with Brahman." (*Viv. 406*), and the enlightened one "sees the many in the One." (*525*) All these overlaps lead us to wonder if the most orthodox of Hindus is not the most Buddhist of all. Aurobindo had his reasons for identifying Advaita with Buddhism. But they are expressing the same experience.

Shankara must have felt these forces that impelled him to do good, to preach, to contribute to the enlightenment and liberation of human beings, but it did not occur to him to think of the Roots of morality, but, as I said, of the fruits. And that is why he did not see the fundamental relationship between Brahman and Nature. He remained as if dazzled by the light of Brahman and enclosed in it and, naturally, beyond that splendour, everything seemed impermanent, instable, vertiginous and alien to that fundamental immutable Reality, that is, like *Maya*. Indeed, this is what happens from that *essential perspective*. "The dust dance in the light while the empty space does not move. What is left is Emptiness, what it moves is the dust". (*Surangama Sutra*)

I agree that "the shutting out of the external world is the stepping-stone to liberation" (*Viv. 335*) but after correspond to open to it. If the spirit moves then beyond and enters time and space, Nature appears in all its splendour and Life in its fullness. And it is this experience that closes the cycle of life. Universal Consciousness must be reached and experienced, but then it is up to us to return spiritualised, enlightened about life. This is what I have called the *unitive individualisation process*. Thanks to it, the unitive man has present and a priori his moral conscience, for which he has *the pleasure of doing good* (the Aristotelian moral ideal), and the desire to integrate as much as possible all beings in the *primordial Unity*. Which he does not forget at any time because he keeps the Observer present (who is not a heteronomous Controller) who resides in his *unitive consciousness*, now fully embodied. And, incidentally, he does not forget his Origin nor his ascending state and function; therefore he expands his knowledge, so that everyone, as far as possible, reaches it, which is the same function of *universal Consciousness*.

On the Limits of Transcendental Knowledge

This problem can only be solved if we start by clearly seeing the mechanisms of the mind, which is what I have done since the beginning of my work (See my *Psychosophy*). To put it succinctly: we count on an indisputable rational proof that demonstrates that the Noumenal is transcendent to reason (E. Kant), and on countless verifications of it by all those who, having reached the Noumenal, maintain that not only can this knowledge be reached by other means but cannot even be expressed with reason

The sciences deal with the phenomenal, which is understood thanks to the forms of time, space and causality, while philosophy deals with the Noumenal or Transcendent. I am speaking of philosophy itself, we can leave aside the materialist theories that deal with matter; although they are very far from expressing scientific knowledge, that is, they are neither philosophy nor science. The attempts of the sciences to try to explain the Noumenal seem valid to me, but, from what has been said, I am very much afraid that they will always be sterile, for this reason I do not assign philosophical importance to them.

Amazed by Newton's discoveries and rational proofs, Western thinkers have ever since sought to present philosophies as "scientific," which has vainly misdirected and delayed the true goal of philosophy. And the matter has been aggravated by the position of the professors of this discipline, who, naturally, have not had a transcendental experience, otherwise they would be philosophers, who have assigned much more importance to said rationalist and pseudoscientific thinkers than to idealists, and much less to the mystics. That is to say that in Western universities for centuries students have been diverted from the true objective of philosophy and from the means to achieve it, with the most far-fetched and elaborate theories of knowledge whose results are necessarily sterile.

Thus, in the West, with the invention of pseudo-scientific philosophies, that is, with the displacement of the spirit to the speculative faculties, which inevitably lead to dividing reality between subject and object within the determining categories of time and space, the spirit and philosophy have been lost from the *First Reality*. There have been some exceptions that I have detailed in *The Quest for Universal Consciousness*, which I will not repeat here. However, the reader might benefit from reading this work, because my intention in it, apart from to exhibit my philosophy, is to demonstrate the existence of a universal Idealism, in which both East and West participate.

By establishing the limits of reason, Kant changed the course of the history of thought in the West, at least for those who think, and think well; who are a minority that, unfortunately, do not change the history of man, made up of numerous factors that have little to do with reason. Even knowing this, I would like to make my contribution by establishing *the limits of transcendental knowledge*, something that Kant did not and could not do, given the schemes that he had imposed on himself. It is not my purpose to refute thoughts that do not conform to these limits, but to leave a reference that could be useful to both philosophers and the religious, so that they know when and how much they are straying from Reality.

When speaking of the limits of transcendental knowledge, I do not want to make the mistake, so usual in philosophers, of ordering the Universe according to personal experience. Thus, for example, Kant himself denied the possibility of having intellectual intuitions that would reveal Noumenal reality, the Transcendent, for the simple fact that he had not had them, just as Ramanuja, who had not had them either, believed that Brahman was unknowable.

Some preliminary clarifications are necessary: My philosophy does not start from a particular perspective, but from an essential perspective that would not be such if beyond it there were other ways of seeing; it speaks of a unified Consciousness in which there are no elements within it and elements outside of it would be inconceivable. Nevertheless, I can ask myself: Is there not something that transcends this vision? The Buddha is said to have remembered his past lives, that is, he knew about his reincarnations and his karma; we already addressed with this when speaking of powers. The Buddha, who was as pragmatic as he could be in the spiritual field, warns of the uselessness of these powers for knowledge.

The immortality of the soul is a subject that worries Plato from his first writings to his last works where he finally fully accepts it. In the *Apology* and even in the *Phaedo* the immortality of the soul is not taken as a certain thing but as a hope. Socrates expresses like this: "if I were to claim that I am wiser than anyone in anything, it would be in this, knowing that I have no adequate knowledge of things in the underworld, I recognise that I don´t know them." (*Apol. 29b*) But at the end of his *Republic* in an extensive myth he details the fate of souls, that is, karma. Plato, quite rightly, placed *belief* in third place in the order of knowledge (*Rep. VII 534a*), although he does not clarify where beliefs begin in his doctrine; this happens when he enters the field of religion, although he has the discretion to present them as myths.

Plato says using a language very similar to that of the *Upanishads*, "the soul is most similar to the divine, is immortal, intelligible, uniform, indissoluble and identic to itself". (*Phaedo 80b*). From these premises Plato infers the fate of souls in the afterlife. But, when speaking of the *destiny* of souls, that is, of *karma*, we see that *Plato jumps to the plane of religion* and adopts, as he confesses, the Orphic mystery tradition: "Been in such a condition, (the soul) it goes away into that which is like itself, into the invisible, divine, immortal, and wise, and when it arrives there it is happy, freed from error and folly and fear and fierce loves and all the other human ills, and as the initiated say, lives in truth through all after time with the gods". The souls, he assures us, "go, each in accordance with its own habits" (*Phaedo 82a*) For this reason (he says entirely in accordance with Buddhism and Hinduism), "philosophy sees that the most dreadful thing about the imprisonment is the fact that it is caused by the lusts of the flesh", philosophers "refrain from all bodily desires", because "no one who has not been a philosopher and who is not wholly pure when he departs, is allowed to enter into the communion of the gods" (*Phaedo 82 c,e*) The initiates in the Orphic mysteries, we have already seen, exclaimed: "I am of the same lineage as the gods." And so we see that the limits of philosophy with religion are imprecise and, when we want to agree, we go from one to the other, as well as from Greece to India, since the *Upanishads* declare the same thing.

It will already be clear to the reader that my philosophy prefers to dispense with the concepts of God and gods. However, it leaves the doors open to them in the conviction that they have their reason for being and that, far from being the product of ignorance, *the gods are the product of relatively latent intuitions of the Transcendent*. To ignore them would be ignorance, since one is then alienated from the unitive or spiritual faculties. The *divinities are Ideas* that the human being needs as paradigms, as references that project him towards the Transcendent, which is nothing but his Destiny. Therefore, all the paths that bring you closer, that open your mind towards that goal, are valid and even necessary.

That the divinities are paradigmatic ideas is a verifiable fact, since they express the virtues that emanate from the Essence of the *Universus* (which I do not call God to avoid any personal nuance), and that are essential for the knowledge of it. That it is light, represented by the sun, like Vishnu and Apollo (to which we could add Egyptian, Mayan, Inca, etc. gods), we have already seen. That it expresses Love, all religions say so, and Plato had Love as a goddess who tended to unite living beings. That it generates Life and establishes Order, as we see in Zeus, and in Brahman. Good has always been a manifestation of divinity, and in Plato and Plotinus they become One. And the Beautiful, which could not be absent in the Greek spirit, is the Idea that follows in dignity.

We see then that the gods or their attributes express what I have called the *primary manifestations* of said Light or Essence, that is, that there is in the believer a certain perception of the Transcendent; thus Aphrodite is Love and Beauty, Apollo Intelligence and Beauty, Zeus Order, etc. All divinities open consciousness in some way, so to pretend that there is a true God or gods and that the others are false, shows ignorance of these psychic and spiritual needs, it is fundamentalism intent on establishing dominance over people. In addition, those who have other Ideas could do the same and the one who would prevail would not be the one with the best ideas, but rather the best soldiers; and in fact that is what has happened. But let us leave this aside, since it is already politics and not philosophy or religion.

There is a point that I would like to try to clarify because it is at the very core of Vedanta. We have repeatedly seen that the Upanishads identify the one who knows Brahman with Brahman. Ramanuja does not accept this because he understands that the human being does not have the powers of God to create and destroy. It is somewhat right, because it is one thing to become One with Brahman, and another to encompass it, to be a drop of the ocean is to be an not to be ocean, since one enters into something that was already there, it is not to be Poseidon, the Lord of the ocean. To merge into the Light is to be filled with light, but it is not to generate it, it is not to emanate the primary manifestations in the *Universus*, even if one participates in them.

To identify with God can imply the danger of an inflation of the ego on a cosmic scale. While submission to God tends to eliminate the ego; this devotional aspect is very positive, because with the ego on our backs, as we have already seen, it is not possible to reach the peak of knowledge; albeit this is one way of looking at it, because in reality such a danger does not exist. The liberated, in effect, is freed from his ego and lives in Unity with Brahman. Whoever identifies with God and believes that he can dispose of reality as he pleases, is not settled in knowledge, but on a belief that leads him to a psychopathic delusion. In the experience of Brahman the ego is diluted and what remains as an individual is so small that it generates moderation.

I admit that there is a generating Energy *in*, not behind the Universe, inseparable from it, although it does not seem to depend on it. Although there is no way of knowing if there is a Will or a Being behind it, I leave the possibility of a Person aside because philosophically this theory does not hold up. This Energy or élan vital, as Bergson thought, is life-generating, but it is accompanied by other manifestations that act as moderating forces in matter and living beings that prevent them from falling into chaos; they only have this dependency. The same happens with the mind of living beings, who have these latent energies and evolve to the extent that they make them come true. They are free to go towards Order or to choose chaos, that is, to choose between wisdom and madness.

Another subject that I am interested in dealing with is that of the prayers that are directed to the divinities and the favours that are granted when they are heard. This necessarily implies one or some personal divinities that in my opinion do not exist objectively, although I cannot deny that they have a *unitive force*. This is what I want to say: when praying, the devotee tunes in with the spiritual energies, integrates into the spiritual order and thus creates the propitious circumstances for his prayer to come true, and harmonising with said spiritual circumstances is decidedly positive and uplifting.

Let us take as an example the grace of illumination that, as we have seen, for Aurobindo is granted by the Lord. I do not believe so for the aforementioned reasons, but it is evident that to reach such a state one must go through various stages of consciousness and, according to Patanjali, through a rigorous training of the mind. That enlightenment occurs after having created these *propitious circumstances* should not surprise us. La Fontaine's fable *The Cart Driver who got Stuck in the Mud* is very relevant, where the cart driver begs the Titan Atlas to give him a hand to get his cart out of the mud, but he does not help him with his strength, he only tells him what to do, it is the cart driver who puts his hands to work following his instructions, and in this way he can get the cart out and continue on his way. The fable ends with the adage: "God helps those who help themselves"

To my knowledge, which is based on experience, death marks the limit of what is knowable; beyond it beliefs begin. Philosophy and religion separate at the border established by death, where the kingdom of the afterlife begins, which can only be filled with beliefs. My philosophy does not deny the reality of the afterlife, rather it opens the doors to it, but it cannot guarantee that it will be one way or another. What it cannot admit in any way is that after death it will be possible to obtain what has not been acquired in life; this is a gratuitous belief that is not supported by any experience that can support it. I do not want to say that the entire field of religion is belief, I only want to highlight some aspects that transcend life and experience. Death is the absolute unknowable, but, paradoxically, it is the mirror in which what is most essential to life is reflected. In front of death, frivolity, greed, arrogance and other vanities vanish like clouds in the wind; it calls us to Reality, it makes us think in the transcendental.

The problem with God as a Person is that he refers us to our accumulative faculties, which are not suitable for experiencing the universal Spirit and which generate a distance that keeps us away from the Transcendent. That is why God has ended up in heaven and is unattainable, whereas the Sacred is here, living in us and we are living in Him. I consider that this experience is sufficient and I do not believe it is essential that for there to be religion there must be a God-person, as Radhakrishnan believes. We live in the Temple of Nature and God is not on an altar but in our consciousness, therefore our intelligence and feelings participate in universal Consciousness. This experience is the fullness of religion, philosophy and our existence.

A God-person, it is seen, does not guarantee the good in this world, because we can believe or not that he observes us, but if we are constantly observing our self, egoism disappears. That is why I do not agree to renounce this world to find a God beyond it. The point is to spiritualise this world, not deny it, and this is spiritualism at its best. By exploiting Nature we are smashing the icons of this Temple. The sciences, let it be said in passing, are for understanding the world, not for knowing how to destroy it. You can, then, call it God if you want, for my part I prefer to call it Consciousness because it is Consciousness in the world and of the world and it is the very core of our consciousness; we only have to delve deep into ourselves to acquire the totality of Consciousness.

It is my *belief* that the spirit that has reached the Light has to unite with it, strictly speaking, it has already become One with it in life, it knows this, and it is logical for it to believe that it will continue to be so. As for those who have not merged into the Light, which is the Intelligence of the *Universus*, it is reasonable to believe that they will return to matter. In any case, I do not glimpse, in this case, any opposition or contradiction between experience and belief, since light (this is a philosophical experience or one of the spirit and scientific experience or one of matter) generates life. Everything, then, is an eternal cycle that is Life, and it is to the experience of it that my philosophy points.

If I stick to my experience I cannot conceive of a divine Person behind what I perceive. I perceive, yes, a Light, entirely spiritual, in the absolute Transcendent, which is unlimited, which encloses the absolute Knowledge or Intelligence and generates an inexpressible happiness; in this, I think, I agree with the stricter *Upanishads*. I perceive that from it emanate the virtues that are poured out over the world and into the minds of beings: Life, Order, Love, Intelligence-instinct, the Good and the Beautiful, without which the universe could not exist or be sustained. Without which there would be no fundamental incentives that move living beings, there would be no love that tends to unite, share, help and reproduce, there would be no morality, without which no society would be possible, there would be no aesthetic sense, no contemplation, no art, without which we would not be sentient beings. I perceive these virtuous emanations not only emanating from the primordial Light, but also in the Void present between beings and things, and these impregnated with them. I also perceive them in the core of my consciousness and therefore they impel me to emanate that content; that is why I write, there is no other reason.

I do not perceive a Will or desire behind that Absolute, we all know that these are expressions or passions too human to be divine. Thus, with much knowledge, the *Upanishads* and the *Gita* tell us that we must act without them and without the expectation of reward in this and the other world. And this is because we must act in the likeness of divinity, which lacks ego. That is why postulating a universal Self seems to me to be a cosmic mistake.

I perceive that this spiritual Light, which is Pure consciousness, emanates Intelligence, but I do not perceive that behind it there is a Lord whose knowledge allows him to see what happens in particular consciousness's; moreover, when thinking this, my spirit moves and *falls* into my external faculties and the universal Consciousness ipso facto ceases to be such. Nor can I know that he made this universe for his entertainment (Lila), as some *Upanishads* and Aurobindo affirm, or *for* whatever, since only the ego and reason have desires; it simply Is and attracts beings to its Being.

In short, in my conception, although there is a transcendent primordial Light, it is projected onto Nature (*Prakrti*), so that this and the Spirit (Purusha) come to be one single thing. This is what

I have called *idealistic or monistic pantheism*, which should not be confused with naive pantheism, which assimilates the Spirit to Nature and not vice versa, although there is in it a (latent) intuition of the Transcendent; the one looks from an *essential perspective*, the other from an *individual perspective*. Then, we must not forget that the Transcendent is only to reason and not to the totality of the Mind or Consciousness, and that beyond it there is a One Consciousness that encompasses everything, and that from it the Transcendent ceases to be such, for it implies a duality; if I have used this concept, it has been as a paradigm or incentive to overcome individual consciousness.

What gives the correct perspective to the spirit is the Unity of Consciousness, the unified Consciousness, which is projected onto Nature. The mistake that I see repeated over and over again, paradoxically in knowledgeable people, is that of attaching too much importance to reality seen from external or speculative faculties, as if what is beyond them were another reality, but if we look at the whole from the *essential perspective*, we verify that reality is One.

Vital Idealism

I have called my philosophy *vital idealism*, because although it is projected towards the transcendent Idea-Reality of Unity, which is the Unity of consciousness, once it is reached, it is poured out upon life which it includes in its Unity. It will be understood that it is not a personal ideology because it neither induces nor supposes nor creates anything, but merely observes and expresses said Idea-Reality; universal Consciousness pours itself into life and constantly creates existences. Even at the risk of repeating myself, I would like to make clear what I understand by this overturning of life, for I would rather fall into repetition than be misunderstood.

In my conception, man's destiny is the awakening of universal Consciousness, this is the end of the road, after which there is no further but there is here, it is a return where even the fullness reached by that knowledge is put at risk, because the human world is full of vices that the common man is bent on exercising. Fullness is not here, but there in the Transcendent. Life in the concrete world is a derivative, it is what overflows from Life. It is this experience of Life in its universality that is the goal, which, however, only happens from the perspective of the Transcendent, from universal Consciousness.

Universal Consciousness contemplates Itself and constitutes, as Parmenides expressed it, a closed circle, an absolute and transcendent Unity and Totality. Parmenides, Shankara and, in the line of this thinker, various Hindu mystics, maintain that this Reality is the only one, and they remain, to the extent that they can, in that state of absorption, as universal Consciousness itself, contemplating themselves. But their spirit and nature do not allow them to remain in that state, and so, when they return, they perceive the material world as illusory. Most of these privileged few return directly to this concrete world, which inevitably leads them to establish a duality.

There is, however, an *intermediate Reality*, which is Plato's great discovery, ratified by Plotinus and the author of these lines, which they called the intelligible world or the world of Ideas. I have already explained in previous works the differences I have with them, so I will briefly present my vision of this intermediate Reality. When the spirit returns and stops on the way, it can contemplate the emanations of universal Consciousness, which are the *primary manifestations* to which I have already referred, which are poured into Nature, a priori, before applying to it the forms of time and space. Well, these emanations are the same Life, *Life itself* in which Nature is in Order, is Good and is Beautiful. I believe that the human idea of Paradise comes from the latent or unconscious intuition of said Reality.

Later, on its return, the spirit encounters time and space, and then the material and multiple world. When I speak then of a *return to Life*, I am not referring to everyday life, but to that intermediate Reality, which is the *state of consciousness that I have called unitive*, and, I will say it once more, this is the correct state of the human spirit, of *unitive man*, who can look upwards, as it were, to universal Consciousness and integrate into it, which is the state of *unified Consciousness*, or downwards, to the human world and his personal circumstances. This intermediate state allows him to integrate the two realities.

It will be clear, then, that what I understand by *vital philosophy* is not the return to everyday life, but the return to Life in its fullness, of which the former is an extension or prolongation. To be precise, my philosophy tends to overcome definitively the animal stage of survival, generator of all human miseries.

Conclusion

Obviously, these discussions about the limits of metaphysical reality only make sense for those who have been venturing into this field for some time, and do not make sense for those who have not transcended the physical world. To these I reiterate that the human being is a species in the process of developing both physically and spiritually, that it is in a state of transition, that it has not yet come to be, that it still has a long way to go and to evolve. So much so that he has only become aware of his individuality but not of his universality, that is, that he still has a whole universe to go through and a whole Consciousness to discover. Discovering, showing and facilitating access to that metaphysical reality, thanks to which the human being ends his path and reaches its fullness, is the mission of philosophy, as I understand it. Hence my interest in showing the universal confluence of the mightiest rivers that flow into the Ocean of Universal Consciousness.

Those of us who propose a knowledge of the Transcendent must admit, by simple statistics, that those who have achieved or can achieve this knowledge are very few and even exceptional. Morcover, so far is the human being from this goal, that most simply do not believe or bother to achieve it. For this reason I consider that, from the social point of view, it is not very edifying to generate the conviction that this life is disposable material, nor is it the division of men between the wise and the ignorant; which although it entails a truth, is an extreme, because although the All is in the Absolute, not everything is absolute. It is easy to see that there are countless nuances, there are those who, without having reached the greatest knowledge, transcend themselves in some way due to their talent, kindness, altruism or other virtues, and who are exemplary in their measure. It is in these nuances that the key to the matter lies.

We have already verified that universal Consciousness (Brahman) is in our individual consciousness, which explains the nuances that result from the degree of proximity or distance that we take with the core of our consciousness. From this derives a verifiable fact that, to my knowledge, has not been highlighted in the following terms: the more we integrate and unify our mind, the closer we get to Unity, the wiser, more good and human we are, and, conversely, the more we move away and disperse, the more bestial we are, to the point that when we disintegrate we become alienated; and this alienation can be individual or collective, since it is contagious, which generates periods of perigee or decline in peoples.

This *simple truth* is available to everyone and is valid for everyone, so it should be known to everyone. Perhaps it is not necessary to warn the Hindus of this, because, from what I have been able to verify, that high paradigm is in force in that people that in this fundamental aspect shows itself as an example for humanity. Moreover, their recognised spirituality is the consequence of the latent or conscious intuition of said simple truth, and by the conviction, maintained by the tradition, the Dharma, in charge of the Brahmans, that the great Truth, the knowledge of Brahman and the liberation that entails, is the ultimate goal of life.

The reader will have noticed my constant interest in avoiding all kinds of dogmatism, that I do not try to establish incontrovertible truths, but to show those that I consider more feasible and difficult to be questioned. It will have been noticed that although I have avoided incorporating beliefs because they are very fragile in the field of philosophy, I do not reject them, I limit myself to pointing them out as uncertain paths that can be conducive or in-conducive. There are no promises here, no sins, no condemnations or punishments, only proposals that I take to be the correct ones.

I have to emphasise, once again, that my intention has not been, at any time, to demonstrate the weaknesses of Hinduism, since there are none, far from it, its strength lies precisely in the structure of the Dharma that includes the aforementioned convergences. My purpose is to show, as the *Upanishads* once did, the firm and certain references that derive from a strict philosophy. That is to say, that there is a real and solid foundation that, strictly speaking, is valid for both the Dharma and the Buddhist Dhamma. My stated intention is to show the convergence of Hinduism and Buddhism, showing their common roots, as well as Western Idealism; in short, the triumph of universal Idealism.

My conclusion on Hinduism is this: in India what we could call natural syncretism or amalgamation expressed in the *Gita* has triumphed. Syncretism between experience and belief; between two ways of conceiving the religious phenomenon; between monism and dualism; between Brahmans and popular beliefs, between philosophy and literature; between science and mythology. In short, the Dharma, which is Hinduism, has triumphed.

Later I had referred to the death of a little dog that had accompanied me for many years in my retired life. That death affected me in such a way that it made my heart sick, which until then had functioned like a young man's. Because of this, this book, which should be complemented by my previous works, will be the last one I write. The reader will wonder how that fact could have affected me so much. The answer is intimately linked to the most essential content of this book. The pain that it caused me did not come only from that being, all the pain of this World was concentrated in it, from which I had been somewhat distracted with my writing, so that all that sorrow, all that immeasurable weight fell on my chest and oppressed my heart. The Buddhist, who knows how Karuna works, will understand this event. On the tombstone of the little dog, whose name was Shanti, I felt the need to engrave with a hot iron: Shantih – Shantih – Shantih; the Hindu will know how to understand this.

Epilogue

I have given numerous examples of the parallel between the Indic and Hellenic civilisations, but the most revealing similarity is that the raison d'être of philosophy, as understood by the Greeks, to attain Wisdom, is still valid in Hinduism and Buddhism. In other words, the Indian civilisation has remained faithful to this fundamental principle of the Hellenic civilisation and has managed to preserve it much better than in the West. In addition, from this Wisdom (Cit) Happiness (Ananda) is derived, essential principles common to said civilisations, which are those that determine the guideline of history, the essentials of thought and real human evolution. The Greeks called their gods the happy and the immortal, and their great aspiration was to be like the gods. To these ends, the Indian civilisation has known how to prioritise spirit over matter and in this way has kept the torch burning with whose light I am trying to illuminate the gloom that reigns in the West and that is spreading in the East. From what has been said, there follows the current (and eternal) paradigm of humanity: to be wiser, happier and to aspire to immortality.

End of my Enneads